T0254217

Manufacturing Performance Management using SAP OEE

Implementing and Configuring Overall Equipment Effectiveness

Dipankar Saha
Mahalakshmi Syamsunder
Sumanta Chakraborty

Apress®

Manufacturing Performance Management using SAP OEE: Implementing and Configuring Overall Equipment Effectiveness

Dipankar Saha
Kolkota, West Bengal
India

Mahalakshmi Syamsunder
Bangalore, Karnataka
India

Sumanta Chakraborty
Bangalore, Karnataka
India

ISBN-13 (pbk): 978-1-4842-1151-9
ISBN-13 (electronic): 978-1-4842-1150-2
DOI 10.1007/978-1-4842-1150-2

Library of Congress Control Number: 2016940067

Distributed to the book trade worldwide by Springer Science+Business Media New York, 233 Spring Street, 6th Floor, New York, NY 10013. Phone 1-800-SPRINGER, fax (201) 348-4505, e-mail `orders-ny@springer-sbm.com`, or visit `www.springer.com`. Apress Media, LLC is a California LLC and the sole member (owner) is Springer Science + Business Media Finance Inc (SSBM Finance Inc). SSBM Finance Inc is a Delaware corporation.

For information on translations, please e-mail `rights@apress.com`, or visit `www.apress.com`.

Apress and friends of ED books may be purchased in bulk for academic, corporate, or promotional use. eBook versions and licenses are also available for most titles. For more information, reference our Special Bulk Sales–eBook Licensing web page at `www.apress.com/bulk-sales`.

Any source code or other supplementary materials referenced by the author in this text is available to readers at `www.apress.com`. For detailed information about how to locate your book's source code, go to `www.apress.com/source-code/`.

Printed on acid-free paper

Contents at a Glance

Contents

Foreword

As Robin S. Sharma once said, "What gets measured gets improved." In the industrial space, the process of continuous improvement is founded on this concept. There are always new and challenging ways to drive improvements in processes and workflows, but understanding their priority, cost, and impact on the rest of the system isn't always easy. It comes down to tracking the resources–people and machines–that are performing the work and then managing any variations that arise from the standard process. People are needed at the operations level to deal with variations, and there's no shortage of machine tools to provide technical feedback on how well a process is running. In fact, these tools have been refined so much that one can easily apply the concepts of manufacturing-process improvement to improving things in one's own daily life.

Take the example of commuting to work in the morning rush and trying to avoid traffic. I might start the process by planning out a route via a GPS or an online maps website and noting the expected duration of the trip. Then after taking the route, I can compare the actual time to the planned time, and also the quality of my experience during the commute. From there, I may try alternate routes depending on the given time of day or things like weather, construction, annoying intersections, and so forth. This is essentially what the Overall Equipment Effectiveness (OEE) metric is measuring, but it is applied specifically to manufacturing processes. While OEE isn't a singularly perfect metric and can't be looked at in a vacuum, it does cover many scenarios, and it can be a tool that provides guidance to an overarching continuous-improvement strategy like Short Interval Control. It can be a tool with which your organization can determine where the industrial engineering budget is spent.

For those of you who have been part of the SAP MII community from the start, you know that we are continually innovating as a collective group, building off of the success of one, or many, customers and using these stories as a mechanism by which to grow new and innovative solutions. Without this kind of ecosystem and sharing of stories we would be much further behind than we are today. We owe a great deal of our success in this space to key experts in the MII field, a few of whom have authored this book–Dipankar Saha, Mahalakshmi Syamsunder, and Sumanta Chakraborty. Dipankar has a long and rich history with the MII product, having co-authored a previous book on MII, and is very active in the SAP Community Network (SCN) for MII, writing many notable and forward-looking blogs and documents on MII. Mahalakshmi is a leading expert on the SAP Manufacturing Suite and has many online documented resources and successes in the automation and performance-management arena. Last, but certainly not least, is Sumanta, whom I have had the pleasure of working with at SAP for many years now, where he is the lead Product Owner for the development of the SAP OEE solution. His cool and personable manner of working through problems behind the scenes and in front of customers has proven how valuable a resource he is to our organization, as people have been asking for an OEE solution for many years and his work has made that a reality for them.

The efforts of those mentioned, along with the efforts of the countless others who have contributed to knowledge sharing and innovation, are the lifeblood of what enables this community to thrive. I am very blessed to be part of it and am truly in awe of the work done all around the globe to further promote effective and organized manufacturing operations. I am looking forward to the next step in innovation. We have many ideas and many contributors, and this is a true testament to the power of our community and the creative thinkers who make it up.

—Salvatore (Sam) Castro
Director, LoB Manufacturing, SAP Labs, LLC
Dresher, PA, USA
February 2016

About the Authors

Dipankar Saha works for IBM India as IT Architect & Service Delivery Lead for SAP Manufacturing. He has co-authored several books on SAP MII & ME and regularly participates in different public forums, events, and seminars presenting papers on topics related to SAP manufacturing. He has worked on several SAP MII, OEE, and ME implementation projects, globally defining solution architecture and managing solution deliveries. Previously he worked for SAP Labs India and was involved in the design and development of SAP MII. Dipankar is a SAP Certified Associate Enterprise Architect. He has over fourteen years of experience in the IT industry and has a bachelor's of technology degree in chemical engineering.

Mahalakshmi Syamsunder is a manufacturing solution consultant currently working for IBM India. She has contributed to solution consulting for various manufacturing and utility clients. She also carries a deep expertise in shop-floor automation and was involved in design, development, training, and implementation of projects on SAP MII, ME, OEE, and plant automation. Mahalakshmi has a bachelor's degree in electronics and communication engineering, and a master's degree in technology management. She has five years of experience in the automation space and over seven years of experience in SAP manufacturing.

Sumanta Chakraborty is an experienced professional with over eighteen years of cross-industry experience in various roles. As a mechanical engineering graduate from NIT, Durgapur, India, he started his career in automobile manufacturing and gradually moved into the development of enterprise software products centered on manufacturing, ERP, and supply-chain management. For the past twelve-plus years Sumanta has been with SAP Labs India Bangalore, and is currently in the role of SAP OEE Product Owner, with end-to-end product-management responsibility at the global level. He works with SAP customers and partners across the globe with a team that is spread across continents. Sumanta is very well known in the SAP manufacturing ecosystem.

Acknowledgments

While I have been engrossed with the workings of manufacturing performance management using SAP OEE, I did not think it possible I would one day pen a book on the subject. The idea of writing this book for the gainful academic and pragmatic benefit of IT professionals and aspiring students of this amazing and expanding body of knowledge germinated around February 2015.

Even as the premonition of penning this book struck and convinced my imaginations, I could not have possibly conceived the book as you read it without support and inspiration from many quarters. Firstly, to my parents who from earthly origins and indefatigable zeal raised me and bestowed upon me enviable qualities of scientific inquiry and humane values. My father, P. Subramanian, and mother, S. Rajakumari, have been invaluably supportive and encouraging in their love and affection for me. I offer my infinite salutations at their lotus feet with a prayer of continuance of their infinite blessings and inexhaustible love and affection for me.

Secondly, my husband, Syamsunder, whom I exclusively adore as his abiding wife. I cannot imagine the toil of my effort bearing fruition without his unstinting support, feedback, and help on several drafts of this volume. Late nights, mornings with me not having the rise of the splendid sun for the better part of the year, and totalitarian reclusiveness from societal obligations are some among many occasions when he assumed the additional charge of our family and household. Many thanks for your understanding and encouragement through this exciting journey from the germination of an idea to a paginated book hopefully worthy of readership. Vedesh Sheetal, the apple of my eye, my son, only six years of age, broke all known conventions of hyperactivity associated with him to knowingly or otherwise offer his approval of support for this endeavor. I shall more than make up lost time and motherly affection on him after sharing this body of knowledge with you.

Lastly, I dedicate this book, my humble offering of gratitude, to my gurus in education and the industry, and to my current manager, Dipankar Saha, who had the trust in making me an author. I do wish you will benefit from the book, and I look forward to your patronage in future editions and books I plan to pen on information technology.

—Mahalakshmi Syamsunder

Product development around manufacturing and the supply chain has always been my area of expertise. But writing a book to articulate my knowledge and expertise was always a challenge and additional hard work. While taking up such a challenge, I cannot forget the two most affectionate people of my life, my parents, who have brought me up and taught me that there is no substitute for hard work. My dad, Bimal Chakraborty, and my mom, Anurupa Chakraborty, along with my brother, Subhro Chakraborty, have been the people who have made me the person who I am today. There are also three beautiful lives at home, my loving wife, Sampa, and two little daughters, Soumi and Ishani, who are always waiting for me to be with them when I'm at home. Needless to say, writing a book is always an additional effort and it takes up personal time that is usually reserved for them. I'm really grateful for their tremendous support and encouragement to finish my work on time. Last but not least, building a successful SAP OEE product that helps our customers manage manufacturing performance would have never been possible without an excellent SAP OEE development team that SAP Labs India has provided me. Finally, I'd like to thank the SAP manufacturing community of customers, consultants, and practitioners who have continuously collaborated with us to build the product and will ideally take this product forward.

—Sumanta Chakraborty

For my family and friends who have inspired me to write this book

And for the SAP community who may find this book useful

—Dipankar Saha

Writing a book is not an easy task, and behind the scenes there are always many who contribute selflessly to make the book a success. We'd like to take this opportunity to thank all those without whose help this book would not have seen the light of the day.

First of all we would like to thank Rita Fernando, Celestin Suresh, John and Matthew Moodie, our editors for this book. Rather than being just editors, they acted as our guide and mentors and immensely helped to make the content perfect, so that you, our readers, get a product of high quality.

We'd like to thank our families, without whose help and constant support this endeavor would have been just a dream. They tolerated us and provided constant support when we burned much midnight oil writing the book.

We are grateful to the SAP OEE product development team at SAP Labs India, namely Anil Kumar Tota, M Saurabh Sharma, Prayas Das, Pruthvi Kumar. L, Sandip Jha, Sulaksh Gupta, and Tarun Rawal, who helped us all through reviewing the book content despite their busy schedules and providing help and support whenever required. We'd also like to thank Nalini B A, Rajesh Kamath, Sailaja Vadlamudi, Sandhya Srinivas, Shalini Kohli, Shilpa Maniyar, Sriram Kannan, and Yamini Priya Bhavirishetty from SAP Labs and Suman Mukherjee, who have provided their support in reviewing the content at different points in time.

We'd like to thank Kalpati Srinivas, Sudipta Mukherjee, Chandan Jash, Swapna Mukherjee, Moumita De, Pallavi Shah, Sudipta Chakraborty, and Laboni Bhowmik of IBM, who have enriched the content at every step. Despite being our friends and colleagues, they did not for a moment hesitate to constructively criticize the content when required and also helped us with facts, figures, and other technical suggestions that ensure a much more fulfilling experience for you, the reader.

We'd also like to thank G Venkatraghavan, Somnath Dey, Subhabrata Ganguly, Anup K Ghosh, Sauti Sen, and Asidhara Lahiri of the IBM leadership team and Juergen Weiner, Veronika Schmid-Lutz, Dharmendra Kumar, Rajeev Kansal and Chethak T K from SAP leadership team, without whose encouragement and support the process of writing this book would not have been as smooth as it was.

Last but not least, we'd like to thank the SAP Community Network, without which we would not been able to collaborate and learn so much, and where we always find help whenever required from the community of developers, users, and experts. We owe you.

Dipankar Saha
Mahalakshmi Syamsunder
Sumanta Chakraborty
Kolkata & Bangalore, India
February 2016

Introduction

SAP Overall Equipment Effectiveness (OEE) is a manufacturing performance-management solution from SAP used for managing and measuring execution and performance in manufacturing industries. This book is intended to provide a thorough guide for using and customizing SAP OEE. It is the product of many months of effort, and we bring together our knowledge and expertise in this topic with the lessons we have learned through several SAP OEE implementations. We sincerely hope that, as the first book on the topic, this will be a useful resource for all those who intend to use and implement SAP OEE.

Target Audience

This book is intended for consultants, developers, and users implementing and using SAP OEE.

Structure of this Book

This book is organized into nine chapters as follows:

Chapter 1 explains manufacturing performance management and how different KPIs are used to measure it. It also explains the OEE standard and its calculation, as well as the importance of enterprise to manufacturing execution systems' integration for data collection and analysis.

Chapter 2 explains the OEE solution as delivered on the SAP MII platform along with its architecture and different components of the solution. In addition it covers the overall usage and benefits of the solution.

Chapter 3 explains the add-on component for SAP OEE available in SAP ERP and how to configure the master data, configuration data, and transactional data required for SAP OEE. It also reviews the configurations required in SAP ERP to transfer the data to SAP MII for setting up OEE.

Chapter 4 explains the OEEINT component available in SAP MII to transfer OEE messages bi-directionally, how to do the basic configurations in MII for OEE, and how to transfer the different messages from SAP ERP to MII for OEE and then how to monitor them in MII.

Chapter 5 explains the configurations required in SAP MII for OEE along with the user roles, configuration wizards for OEE, and different worker UI configurations in MII for setting up OEE dashboard and OEE configurations transport.

Chapter 6 explains how to configure, set up, and use OEE dashboards or worker UI. It explains the different types of standard dashboards available in SAP OEE and how to report downtimes and various other operational data required for OEE calculations. It also explains the standard data flows in SAP OEE, with the database tables involved in the transactions. It also covers the OEE KPI calculation logic and the mechanism by which to trigger the order confirmations and goods movement from SAP OEE to ERP and replicate the data to SAP HANA for analytics.

Chapter 7 explains the different customization and enhancement options available in SAP OEE along with the OEE data model, customizing OEEINT workflows, and OEE analytics on SAP MII. It also explains different scenarios for enhancements on SAP OEE and different industry-specific use case scenarios.

Chapter 8 explains the new features available in SAP MII 15.1, such as the Goods Movement application, Plant Maintenance notification creation, alerts in OEE dashboard, data collection at machine level, upload reason code, and downtime data; it also explains the goods-movement reporting process in SAP OEE.

Chapter 9 explains the different analytics options available in SAP OEE and how to use them. It explains the local plant-level analytics development, consuming local SAP MII data through SAP Lumira, as well as global consolidated reporting at the corporate level using SAP HANA by replicating the data from SAP MII. It explains the different standard reports available in SAP HANA for OEE.

The appendix explains in detail the different configurations and their purpose specific to each worker UI in OEE.

The glossary details the different technical terms and their description as used in all the chapters.

CHAPTER 1

Manufacturing Performance Management: An Overview

This chapter will explain manufacturing performance management and how it is used to measure and monitor the performance of assets and processes involved in manufacturing execution. It will also look at how industry would be affected without the measuring process in place. In addition, it will explain how to optimize manufacturing performance by defining and measuring the metrics.

Manufacturing companies, like any other business in today's world, face tremendous pressure to optimize operational costs, increase resource utilization, and improve product quality. With competitive markets and globalization, common factors for almost every industry, optimizing and improving processes and costs is the only way to survive. To enable optimization and improvement of quality, the first step is to measure the operational parameters so that suitable actions can be taken to quickly improve them.

Manufacturing performance management is the method by which the operational performance of manufacturing execution–such as resource utilization and availability, rate of production, and first-pass quality of the produced product–can be measured and analyzed to understand the gaps and scope of improvements. Without having a manufacturing performance-management practice in place it is almost impossible for a manufacturing business to survive, as the planners and decision makers cannot understand the scope of needed improvements and opportunities for optimization.

Measuring performance needs to ensure the collection of operational and planning data from different heterogeneous sources and then must analyze them to understand the impact. First of all, it requires a solution via which the data from various sources can be accumulated in a single place by integrating with different types of systems and applications that generate the data at various granularity levels. The planning data are typically available in the ERP system at the corporate domain, whereas most of the operational data are available at the plant sites in manufacturing execution systems, with the plant historian, in legacy databases and applications, or manually collected on paper. Once the data are accumulated from different data sources, it needs to be aggregated and analyzed to generate meaningful metrics from it.

Therefore, to implement manufacturing performance management, a solution is required that can enable the collection, aggregation, and analysis of manufacturing planning and operational data as well as provide meaningful insight so as to optimize manufacturing operations.

Need for KPIs to Optimize Manufacturing Performance

This section will explain the need for key performance indicators (KPIs) to measure, monitor, and analyze manufacturing and production performance, along with how to benchmark the process performance using KPIs. We will also look at how OEE and other KPIs help in capturing production losses and achieving optimal production performance.

D. Saha et al., *Manufacturing Performance Management using SAP OEE*,
DOI 10.1007/978-1-4842-1150-2_1

Any growing or established business needs to be closely and carefully managed to ensure the success of new investment decisions and expansion plans, and to sustain their success and their competitive advantage. KPIs are at the heart of any system of performance measurement and target setting. When properly used, they are one of the most powerful management tools available to a business. KPIs provide a definitive measure for production and resources performance.

Let's take an example of a consumer products manufacturing company where food products are manufactured and packaged in semi-automated production lines. There are machines in the production line, such as a filler or a palletizer, that are bottleneck machines–i.e., they are critical and mandatory work centers in the processing flow path. They have a limited capacity, which affects the capacity of the overall production line. The downtimes for the bottleneck machines cause production delays. The planners and other stakeholders want to know the availability of the machines compared to their planned availability. The availability of the machines varies over time due to different factors, such as mechanical faults, unavailability of raw materials, human errors, and breaks, which need to be captured with corresponding reason codes.

Also, there are other metrics that the plant management and planner need to monitor–such as the material yield for orders, shifts and production lines, quality (acceptable/good quality yield versus planned yield), and rate of production–that help in understanding the bottlenecks and scope of optimization and improvements. KPIs are measurable quantities on the time scale, as well as on other dimensions. For example, the machine availability KPI can be based on the time when the machine is available, calculated for each hour, each eight hours (a shift), or each day, factoring in its downtime and planned availability. The KPI can also be measured for each product being produced on it or each operator who operates it. In this example, apart from the time dimensions, other dimensions for the availability KPI are product and operator, as KPI may vary for different products and operators for various reasons. In addition, each KPI has a target value, which is the threshold limit for the measure of the specific KPI. The KPIs can be positive, negative, or bi-directional depending on whether the KPI measure value tends to exceed the target (positive) or to come in below the target (negative). When it is bi-directional it can exceed or be below the target value depending on certain conditions. For example, power consumption can be bi-directional KPI, whereas the availability and efficiency of a machine are positive KPI; machine downtime and safety incidents are examples of negative KPI.

To measure the performance of manufacturing process and resources it is necessary to define the KPIs and measure them continuously to ensure the process is stable and optimized. KPIs are defined as quantifiable factors that are clearly linked to the drivers of business success. For any manufacturing company, certain KPIs are defined with specific targets that need to be achieved or exceeded (or to not be exceeded) based on their type. The KPIs used in manufacturing industries vary depending on the industry type and manufacturing process.

Some of the common KPIs used by manufacturers, broken down by business goals, are as follows:

- Improve Quality

  Yield Count (Good or Bad) relates to the measure of the total number of units of product produced in a production line for a production run, shift, or day. It provides a basic indicator of the production personnel and/or the machine efficiency, as well as whether the organization targets for production efficiency are being met.

  Rejection Ratio measures the scrap quantity versus the total quantity of units produced in a production line for a certain timeframe. It indicates the quality of the production process; a lower value is better for maximizing profit.

  Production Rate provides the speed at which the product is produced, i.e., total quantity produced in a given timeframe. The speed of machines varies, and it is important to maintain the optimized rate, as a too-high rate may affect quality and a too-slow rate may affect profitability.

- Reduce Inventory

  WIP Inventory/Turns is a commonly used ratio calculation to measure the efficient use of inventory materials. It is calculated by dividing the cost of goods sold by the average inventory used to produce those goods.

- Reduce Machine Downtime

  Machine Downtime refers to the time during which a machine or production line is not available for operation. It can be either the result of a breakdown or simply a machine changeover, and is considered one of the most important KPI metrics to track in manufacturing industries. Machine unavailability or non-operation time affects the productivity and profitability of the organization. Tracking downtime typically requires assigning a "reason code" to the event, so that the most pertinent ones can be tracked.

- Improve Efficiency

  Overall Equipment Effectiveness (OEE) is a multi-dimensional metric that provides an overall measure of the effectiveness and utilization of a machine or production line; this is determined by multiplying availability by performance and quality. This is one of the most important KPIs for any manufacturing company. Production managers always want OEE values to increase, because this indicates more efficient utilization of available personnel and machinery.

  Takt Time measures the amount of time, or cycle time, for the completion of a specific task. This could be the time it takes to produce a product, but it more likely relates to the cycle time of specific operations. This helps to determine where the constraints or bottlenecks are within a process.

  Time to Make Changeovers measures the speed or time it takes to switch a manufacturing line from making one product over to making a different product.

There are many other KPIs being used by different industries based on their manufacturing processes. Also, most KPI targets or desired ranges are benchmarked for specific industries and processes, which the manufacturers tend to follow. As there are multiple factors to be managed in the manufacturing process, it is essential to measure them as KPIs to ensure the performance is always on track.

Benchmarking and Target Setting

Benchmarking is a valuable way of improving and understanding business performance and potential. Benchmarking can be done by making comparisons with other businesses or internally within the business. A key driver of any business is the focus area of benchmarking.

For example, a manufacturing company can set its KPI targets (Quality, Customer Satisfaction, and so on) as a benchmark based on its counterpart running a similar successful business.

Comparing absenteeism rates or operator efficiency between similar departments may enable the business to spread good working practices from the best performing areas of your business to lower performing areas.

Target setting involves setting performance targets in the key areas that drive the business performance. Performance targets are a powerful management tool that can help deliver the kind of strategic changes that many growing businesses need to make. The top-level objectives of a strategic plan can be implemented through departmental goals, and setting targets based on KPIs is an ideal way of doing this.

KPI Targets should be specific, measurable, achievable, realistic, and time-bound.

KPIs provide a measure of productivity as well as of the losses, depending on their definition. It is critical for manufacturing businesses to keep track of losses such as time loss, material loss, productivity loss, and so forth, which provides important information on how to optimize the production process.

To summarize, it is important to define KPIs, set targets based on the manufacturing process, and continuously measure and track them so as to understand bottlenecks and how to increase efficiency, which in turn helps in increasing the profitability of the business.

OEE Standard and Its Calculations

This section will explain the definition of OEE, different types of losses, methods of loss capture, calculation of factors associated with OEE calculation that are followed as a standard approach, and benefits of OEE.

Any manufacturing process involves throughput from machines, and different types of losses are encountered in the production process. The losses are due to the unreliability of the machines and the operators as well as to other external factors, such as material or operational issues. To determine the production process' efficiency, it is important to understand and track the losses occurring. The losses in can be of broadly three types:

- Availability loss
    - Time loss for availability of resources or machines due to breakdowns or scheduled and unscheduled breaks
    - Loss due to setup, changeover process, material and labor shortages, etc.
- Speed loss
    - Loss in production due to reduced speed or increased cycle time due to machine, material, or human issues
    - Loss due to idling and minor stops that are not part of regular maintenance
- Quality loss
    - Material loss due to quality issues like rejects during startup, improper setup, etc.

To measure and track these, a KPI is required through which all the possible losses can be measured. Overall Equipment Effectiveness (OEE) is one such KPI that can be used to measure and track performance efficiency by capturing the losses. OEE is an essential metric and basic methodology for manufacturers pursuing a "lean" manufacturing strategy–that is "zero waste" in their "value streams."

For many manufacturing companies OEE is becoming a very important and mandatory KPI with which to measure and track. OEE is defined as the effectiveness of a machine or production line that is used for the manufacturing process; it uses the following formula: `Availability x Performance x Quality`

Where:

- Availability (of machine) = net operating time/total planned operating time
    - Net operating time = total operating time - downtimes
    - Total operating time is the shift duration based on the factory calendar
- Performance = actual rate of production/planned rate of production
    - Actual rate of production = cycle time = total quantity produced/total time taken
    - Planned rate of production = Nominal or Rated speed of production. E.g., 100kg/min or 1000 pieces/hr.

- Quality = units of good quality produced/total units produced
    - Units of good quality = total units of produced - total units of rejected

As is evident from the above formulas, OEE targets three distinct points of loss that can be potential areas of improvement for the manufacturing process. To measure and calculate OEE KPI, you must capture certain information from the production process. This information can be collected directly from the manufacturing automation system, if available, or can be manually collected as well. The typical data that needs to be collected are as follows:

- Downtimes for the resource/production line, with reason code; i.e., start and end time of the machine downtimes, from which the downtime duration can be calculated
- Total yield of the machine/production line in a specific time window; e.g., shift or hour
- Total yield quantity not conforming to first-pass quality. This includes scrap and waste as well as reworked material quantity that does not pass the quality tests the first time

The preceding parameters need to be captured continuously, and with that information the OEE KPI can be calculated periodically for specific time periods, which provides an indication of the losses and the effectiveness of the manufacturing process. Typically, for most of the manufacturing industries, 85 percent OEE is considered a benchmark for a minimum target.

Once the OEE KPIs are calculated and analyzed, they can be drilled down to find out the root cause of a low OEE value and to understand the actual points where the losses are occurring, which can then possibly be optimized. OEE is measured for resource or machines used in the manufacturing execution process, usually the bottleneck ones that control the throughput of the process. Typically in a filling and packing line, the filler machine is considered the bottleneck in some cases, and so it may be the most critical resource for that production line.

To measure and calculate the OEE, it is necessary to continuously collect the downtimes, material loss, and rate of production for that resource. The data can be collected automatically, if it is an automated production line with a Plant Historian system or Manufacturing Execution system capturing the pertinent information. This is done via sensors connected to the machines. Otherwise, the production operator must capture the operational data manually for each production run or shift–for example, how long the machine was idle or down, quantity of material produced, and scrapped or reworked material, as well as the rate of production–based on which the OEE KPI can be calculated.

The machine downtimes measured in OEE are of various types, as shown in Figure 1-1. The plant operating time is based on the factory calendar, which is the total time the factory operations are running. This calendar accounts for planned downtime for scheduled maintenance, scheduled breaks, and idle time due to lack of production plan. The rest of the time is considered as the planned production time based on the production plan. The planned production time versus the planned downtime and idle time measures the utilization of the machine, i.e., how much the resource is used for production.

Regarding the planned production time, the major loss happens due to unplanned breakdowns and downtimes of the machines, which when deducted from the planned production time provides the machine's productive time, or total operating time. This measures the availability of the resource.

There may be some delays or an inconsistent speed of production due to machine or human factors, which result in speed loss and a reduction in the machine's productive time; this gives a measure of the performance of the resource.

Finally, out of the net operating time, some of the yield may be scrap, waste, or rework, and the time used for producing good quality product is considered to be the fully productive time. This provides the measure of the quality KPI of the resource.

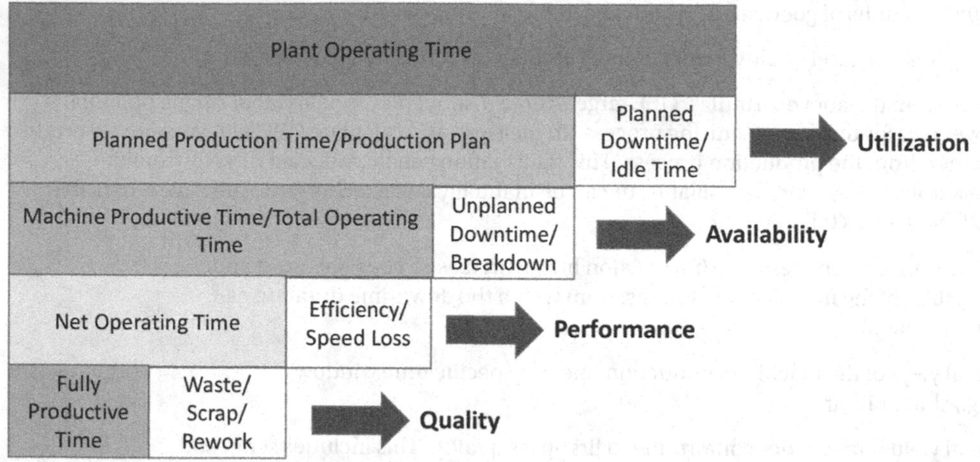

***Figure 1-1.** Production losses and KPIs for OEE*

Losses that are otherwise not easily visible and accountable can be highlighted by measuring OEE. Figure 1-2 explains a sample OEE calculation for a resource based on the production data in a shift.

Production Data						
Shift Length	8	Hours =	480	Minutes		
Short Breaks	2	Breaks @	15	Minutes Each =	30	Minutes Total
Meal Break	1	Breaks @	30	Minutes Each =	30	Minutes Total
Down Time	47	Minutes				
Ideal Run Rate	60	PPM (Pieces Per Minute)				
Total Pieces	19,271	Pieces				
Reject Pieces	423	Pieces				

Support Variable	Calculation	Result	
Planned Production Time	Shift Length - Breaks	420	Minutes
Operating Time	Planned Production Time - Down Time	373	Minutes
Good Pieces	Total Pieces - Reject Pieces	18,848	Pieces

OEE Factor	Calculation	My OEE%
Availability	Operating Time / Planned Production Time	**88.81%**
Performance	(Total Pieces / Operation Time) / Ideal Run Rate	**86.11%**
Quality	Good Pieces / Total Pieces	**97.80%**
Overall OEE	Availability x Performance x Quality	**74.79%**

OEE Factor	World Class	My OEE%
Availability	90.00%	**88.81%**
Performance	95.00%	**86.11%**
Quality	99.90%	**97.80%**
Overall OEE	85.00%	**74.79%**

***Figure 1-2.** Sample OEE calculation based on production data*

By analyzing the OEE KPI, the following benefits can be achieved in the production process:

Efficient and effective usage of existing equipment and facilities by

- reducing planned downtimes due to scheduled maintenance, breaks, material shortages, and so on, thus increasing the machine utilization; and by
- minimizing machine breakdowns and unplanned downtimes to increase availability.

Real-time visibility on the shop floor production, which aids in

- eliminating the factors for speed or production-rate loss– i.e., minor stops and misfeeds–that do not require maintenance, thus increasing performance;
- understanding the factors for quality loss so as to minimize the scrap, waste, and rework quantities;
- quantifying plant/line/machine performance; and
- analyzing recurring production losses and their sources, and coming up with ways to improve.

OEE acts as a stepping stone for the manufacturer to achieve world class production. It enables the manufacturer to realize financial benefits in terms of reduced downtime costs, repair costs, and quality costs and increased labor efficiency and productivity, which ultimately leads to increased production capability.

To summarize, OEE KPI provides a clear and useful measure of the performance and effectiveness of the manufacturing process and resources and provides a mechanism by which the process can be optimized. It does this by helping the manufacturer understand the main points of loss so they can take action to reduce them.

The Need for an Effective Operator Interface for Data Collection

This section will explain how important it is to have an effective operator interface in place before introducing a performance-management system on the manufacturing shop floor. It will explain the different aspects of an effective shop floor operator interface.

Any shop floor performance-improvement program needs some amount of data to be collected via manual interaction. Hence it is important to involve the shop floor operators and provide them with a user interface that they can use effectively. The basic purpose of an operator on the shop floor is to produce, to make. His primary duty is to operate the machines and to take care of them so that they do not break down. If a breakdown happens, his job is to get it running again or to initiate maintenance to repair it. Any other documentation task or data entry on a computer is seen as a secondary activity for him. Hence, an operator interface that needs to be used by the shop floor as part of the manufacturing performance-management solution needs to have features such as the following:

- The operator interface should add value, not another burden, to the operator in his daily work schedule. This should be the highest priority of the new user interface. His job should become easier than what it was in the absence of the new operator interface. Otherwise, it will be looked upon as another burden he needs to fulfil before the end of every shift. The user interface should reduce his workload, reduce complexities, and improve his efficiencies.

- The user interface should be designed for the operator. In the IT industry, while developing a user interface, we often miss the exact personas (the person who will be the actual user) and deliver something that is for a mix of personas. Drawing clear boundaries between what is an operator's interface and what is a supervisor's or manager's interface will greatly improve the acceptance of the user interface. Too much or too little information on the screen or too many clicks to navigate will be viewed as negative factors.
- A smart design of the operator interface will give him a seamless experience, much like his smart devices at home. In today's world, the probability is very high that the operator uses a smart device at home. Nowadays, like most of us, a significant part of an operator's daily life is centered around personal smart devices. This is changing our expectation and interaction pattern with any user interface today. Hence, a user interface should have an interaction pattern that is simple and intuitive, and should provide an experience as smooth and obvious as the operator is used to with his smart devices. This will increase the acceptance of the system to a great extent.

Shop-Floor to Top-Floor Integration

This section will explain the need for shop-floor to top-floor integration for manufacturing performance management. It will also provide an introduction to SAP MII and how MII as a framework ensures the shop-floor to top-floor integration.

To calculate and measure the OEE KPI, data must be collected about the various losses, such as machine downtimes, material wastage and scrap, production speed loss, and so on; this must be done continuously during the production runs. The data required for OEE calculations are available from different sources and measuring points, which can be either automatically available in some systems, or collected manually. The systems from which the manufacturing operational data can be collected are Plant Historian, SCADA or DCS, MES, or legacy database; these systems capture the process parameter data from various equipments and data-collection points in the production lines. Most of operational systems mentioned store the process data as time-series data–i.e., data-point value with the corresponding timestamp–and may provide OPC (OLE for Process Control) or other proprietary connectors through which the process parameter data need to be queried and aggregated in order to calculate the KPIs. The operational systems at the shop floor provide the real-time process data, but the planning data against which the actuals need to be compared reside in the enterprise planning and logistics systems, such as ERP.

It is also required to provide the transactional user interfaces through which the shop-floor users can manually capture data such as machine downtime, yield, scrap, and so on, as well as assign reason codes when the data are collected automatically.

Once the data are collected and the KPIs are calculated, one needs a dashboard with reports and analytics through which the OEE and other KPIs can be monitored and analyzed.

It is a common problem for the manufacturers who have multiple real-time and planning systems to aggregate and analyze the data centrally in near real-time mode. Without a system that can do that, the manufacturing shop-floor users lack the visibility and understanding of the actual situation on the shop floor and don't know how to optimize the process by minimizing the losses.

To address these challenges, a platform is required that can easily integrate with different types of operational systems on the manufacturing shop floor, as well as with the planning system at the enterprise level, and that can aggregate the data by user-defined logic to derive meaningful KPIs and then provide a visualization platform through which the KPIs and the information can be monitored and analyzed.

SAP Manufacturing Integration & Intelligence (SAP MII) is such a platform and is provided by SAP as part of its SAP Manufacturing portfolio of products, which aim to address the previously mentioned challenges. It is a stand-alone, web-based solution that runs on SAP NetWeaver Java WebAS. As its name makes clear, SAP MII provides two basic functionalities:

- Integration with different applications in enterprise and manufacturing plants
- Intelligence on process information via reports, analytics, KPIs, alerts, and so on

For the integration functionality, SAP MII provides different types of connectors and interfacing mechanisms to exchange messages bi-directionally from SAP ERP, MES, Plant Historian, SCADA, and other legacy applications using different technical protocols as required. It provides Message Services to receive messages from any external system–such as ERP and MES–and SAP JCo and JRA interfaces to execute RFC (Remote Functional Call) and BAPI (Business API) in the SAP ERP system. Using SAP Plant Connectivity (PCo), which is an add-on component with SAP MII, SAP MII provides near real-time connectivity to almost all types of shop-floor automation control systems via various protocols, such as OPC (OLE for Process Control), ODBC (Open Database Connectivity), and OLEDB (OLE Database Connectivity), as well as proprietary protocols for specific SCADA and Plant Historian systems, such as Citect, OSISoft PI, iHistorian, and so on. It also provides Web Service-, JDBC-, FTP-, and HTTP-based integration capabilities with external systems through its business-logic services.

The intelligence is provided via custom reports, analytics, and dashboards, which are developed using the visualization service and the business-logic engine, where custom business logic for data processing can be developed as required based on the data collected from different systems.

Additionally, SAP MII provides a framework to map process data points as tags, which are available in the Plant Historian and SCADA systems using the Plant Catalog Services (PIC), to persist data as required using manufacturing data objects (MDO), and to define KPIs and alerts using KPI and Alert frameworks. It provides Business Logic Services (BLS), using which any type of custom business logic can be developed by graphical modelling. SAP MII also provides a component as an adaptor framework called SAP Plant Connectivity (PCo), which is used to connect to SCADA, Plant Data Historian, and other real-time systems via OPC and various other protocols, both by ad-hoc query and real-time notifications of a change of values in the source system.

Being a custom development and composition platform, any type of integration, analytics or monitoring, and transactional application can be developed on SAP MII. It can be used to collect the data from the manufacturing operations systems in near real-time, as well as provide transaction user interfaces with which to collect the data manually and develop business logic to aggregate and process the data so as to derive certain KPIs.

A SAP MII solution overview is shown in Figure 1-3.

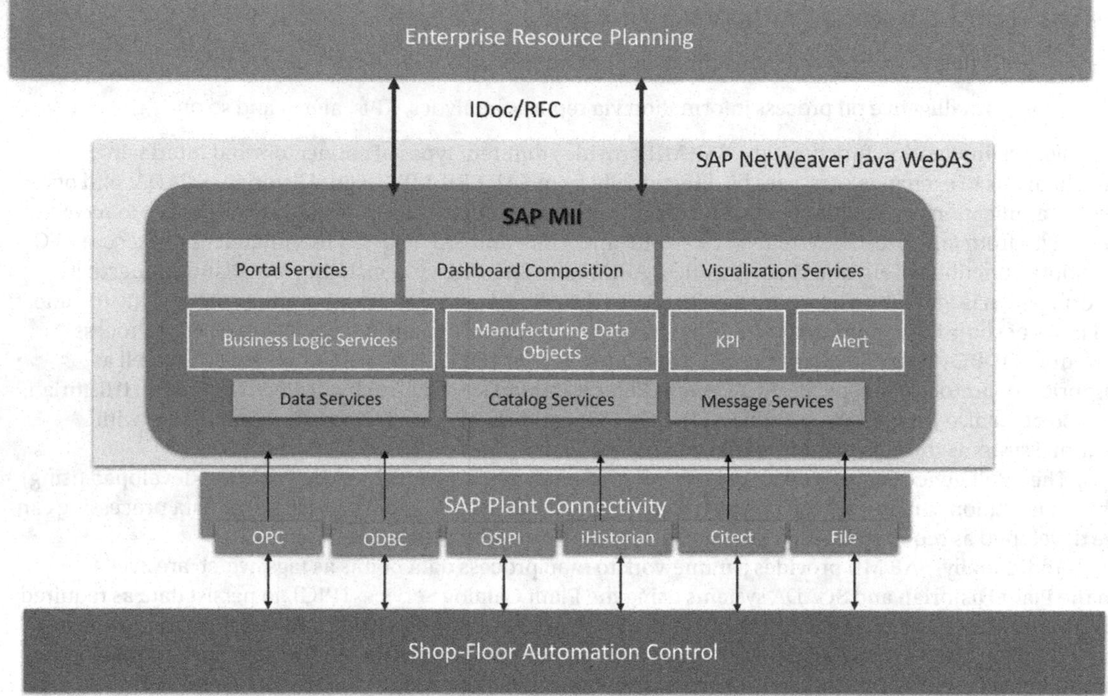

Figure 1-3. *SAP MII overview*

Thus, SAP MII provides a powerful platform on which to develop manufacturing KPI management solutions by collecting data from various sources, persisting and aggregating them by specific business logic, and providing analytics with which to monitor and analyze the KPIs and data in real-time.

Summary

In this chapter, you have learned why measuring and monitoring KPIs is critical to the success of any manufacturing company, and how SAP MII can be used as a platform to develop KPI management solutions for manufacturing operations.

In the next chapter, you will learn about the SAP OEE solution on MII and how it can help in manufacturing performance management.

CHAPTER 2

SAP OEE: A New Product for Manufacturing Performance Management

This chapter will explain how SAP OEE is developed on the MII platform and how MII is used as an integration component (OEEINT) between ECC and OEE. It will also describes various features and components of SAP OEE.

As we learned in the previous chapter, Overall Equipment Effectiveness (OEE) is an important KPI that is critical for any manufacturing business to measure so as to understand the losses and points of optimization. With this information, they can make their products more cost effective and increase profitability. Three types of KPIs need to be measured in order to measure OEE:

- performance or speed of the process
- availability of the machines
- quality of the product

To measure these elements, the data for operational parameters such as yield quantity, scrap quantity, cycle time, machine downtimes, and so on need to be collected in real-time. Once collected, it needs to be stored and aggregated, at which point the OEE KPI can be calculated and analyzed.

SAP OEE on MII platform

SAP OEE is a solution developed by SAP to address these requirements and is to be used on the manufacturing shop floor to view and collect data during manufacturing execution, and ultimately it will analyze the OEE and different production KPIs related to OEE. The solution is based on three different platforms or products–SAP ERP, SAP MII, and SAP HANA.

- SAP ERP is used to define the master and planning data, such as the material master, work center master, plant hierarchy, reason codes for deviations, data-collection elements, and production or process orders.
- SAP MII is used to provide the plant-operator dashboards through which the production operators can view and record operational details.
- Finally, SAP HANA, which is SAP's in-memory database and platform for high-volume data analysis, is used to calculate and analyze the OEE and related KPIs.

D. Saha et al., *Manufacturing Performance Management using SAP OEE*,
DOI 10.1007/978-1-4842-1150-2_2

Figure 2-1 explains the overall model for the SAP OEE solution.

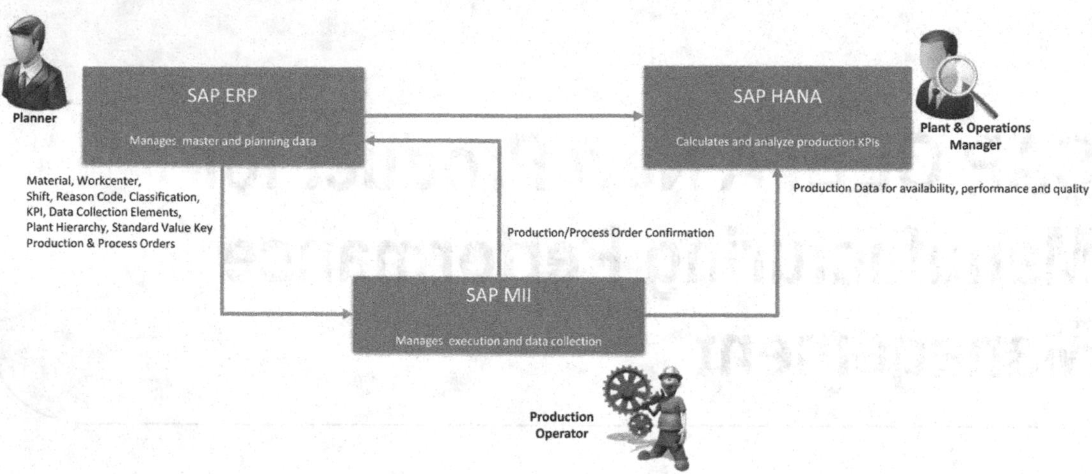

Figure 2-1. *Overview of SAP OEE*

SAP MII is typically deployed at each manufacturing plant site, and it gets the relevant data from SAP ERP and provides the operator dashboards. In this way, SAP MII provides the front-end application for the SAP OEE solution. Since MII is the platform with which to integrate shop-floor systems, it can also integrate with the manufacturing automation systems, if available, to get the real-time information about production execution; otherwise, it gets the information from manual data recording in the production operator dashboards, which are also called PODs or Worker UIs. Typically the Worker UIs are used to record the start and stop of order operations or phases, yield, scrap, rework and waste quantities, and machine downtimes with reason codes. All this information is captured and persisted in the MII database, and is then transferred to SAP HANA. In the SAP HANA component of OEE, the availability, performance, and quality KPIs, along with the OEE KPI, are calculated for all plants. SAP HANA provides a set of pre-defined analytics content for OEE and offers the flexibility to do the analysis from different dimensions as per user need.

Solution Architecture of SAP OEE

This section will explain the application architecture of SAP OEE.

As explained in the previous section, the SAP OEE solution is based on three major components: SAP ERP, SAP MII, and SAP HANA. The minimum version of SAP ERP required by SAP OEE is SAP ERP 6.0 (EhP0 and above). For the SAP OEE features, the ERP add-on component required to be installed is called SAP Overall Equipment Effectiveness Add-On for SAP ERP (OEE_ERP). This provides the data model and the master and transactional data replication framework with OEE on MII.

Similarly, a component needs to be installed on SAP MII called OEE_MII. The OEE_MII component 15.0 (in SAP MII 15.0) works on SAP NetWeaver Java 7.31 and NW 7.40. But the OEE_MII component 15.1 (in SAP MII 15.1) works on SAP NetWeaver Java 7.50.

For SAP HANA, HCO_HBA_OEE 1.0 (SP06 or above) and HCO_HBA_APPS_OEE 1.0 (SP06 or above) components need to be installed that have SAP HANA 1.0 SP08 revision 82 or higher and SAP HANA Analytics Foundation 1.0 SP02 as the minimum support stack.

Additionally, SAP MII may use SAP Plant Connectivity (PCo), which is an add-on component with SAP MII. It must be installed as a Windows service, which provides the connectivity to shop-floor automation systems with SAP MII if it is used to fetch the data for OEE.

It is also possible to install and use SAP OEE without having SAP HANA or the HANA components. In that case, the standard analytics for SAP OEE, which is delivered by SAP for global corporate-level analytics, will not be available. But local plant-based reporting needs can be met by using SAP Lumira with a local SAP MII. Additionally, custom analytics can be developed on SAP MII itself by querying the data from the OEE database, which is hosted along with the NetWeaver database in the SAP MII server.

The data are synchronized between SAP ERP and MII through IDoc and RFC interfaces, which are used for sending the messages to MII and updating in SAP ERP, respectively. A framework for the message replication with SAP ERP is available as part of the OEE add-on on MII called the OEEINT (OEE Integration) framework. It provides a framework to manage the workflows of messages inbound and outbound to and from MII for OEE. SAP delivers a set of workflows required for OEE data exchange with SAP ERP, along with the corresponding mappings.

Once the data is received in OEE from SAP ERP by IDoc messages, it is stored in the OEE database, which is hosted in the same database of the SAP NetWeaver WebAS.

In OEE, the plant hierarchy (and relevant master and configuration data), reason code, and UoM are replicated, and the production-line view is made available. Once the production or process orders are received from SAP ERP, those are displayed in the operator dashboards for execution.

The operator dashboard is provided as a framework, with a set of dashboards delivered by SAP that can be enhanced by simple configurations and developments. The operators can view the order operations and record the production and loss data with reason codes, as well as view the order confirmations, through the operator dashboard in MII.

If shop-floor automation systems are available, and are using SAP Plant Connectivity (PCo), the interfaces for the same can be developed to get the machine downtimes, order start and stop events, as well as view yield and scrap quantities.

Enhancement of the interfaces and logic can be developed using Business Logic Services in MII by creating custom transactions. The user can view the shift reports and the KPIs, which are dynamically calculated in real-time, through the operator dashboard in MII itself.

If SAP HANA is used for analytics, the master and configuration data from SAP ERP and the transactional data from SAP MII (OEE) are replicated in HANA through the System Landscape Transformation (SLT) server provided with HANA. It directly replicates the data from the tables in the underlying databases of SAP ERP and OEE. You can analyze the downtime losses, performance losses, quality losses, and the KPI reports in SAP HANA, as they are delivered by SAP as pre-configured reports. The SAP HANA analytics of OEE consolidates the data from multiple plants (multiple MII systems) and provides the capability to view the reports for any of the plants/production lines/machines from a single HANA server. Additionally, SAP HANA reports provides options to drill down through the loss reasons up to ten levels to find the exact root cause. As the SAP HANA server has data from multiple plants, it also provides options to compare manufacturing performance between different plants/production lines/machines.

Figure 2-2 shows the architecture of SAP OEE solution.

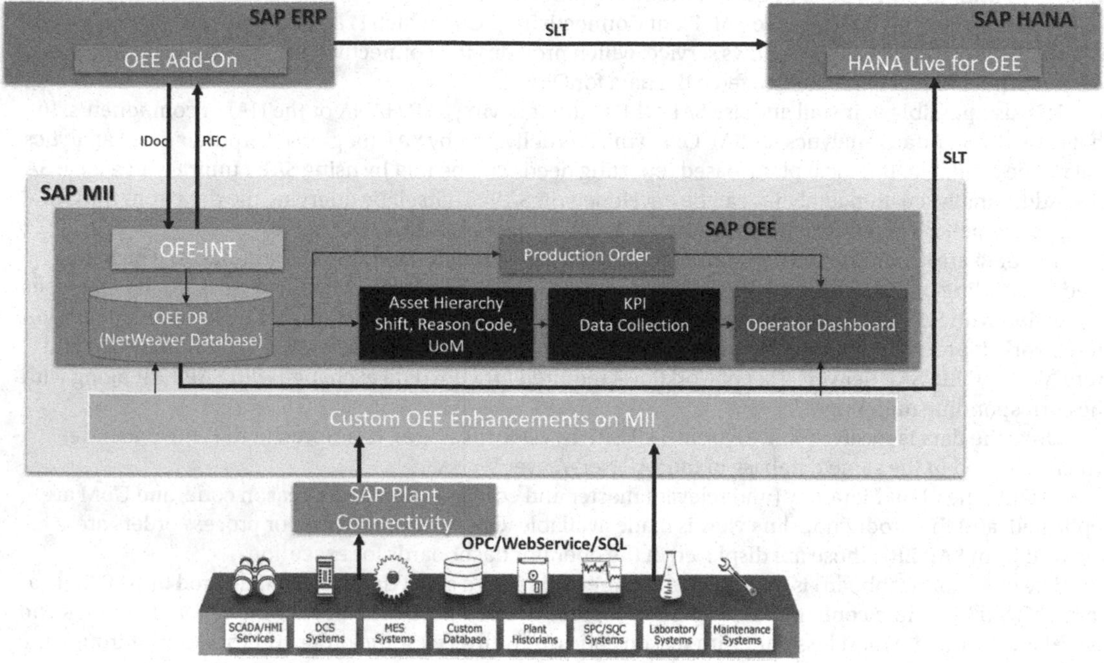

Figure 2-2. *SAP OEE architecture overview*

The SAP MII component, along with SAP Pco, is typically deployed at each manufacturing plant site, with SAP ERP and SAP HANA centrally deployed at the corporate data center, as shown in Figure 2-3.

This is useful when integration with shop-floor automation control systems at manufacturing plant sites is required, as well as when supporting a large number of users at each plant site. It also helps to provide site survivability in case the network connection between the plant and the corporate network is not available at certain points in time.

Having all the data in the OEE component pre-synched from SAP ERP allows the users on the shop floor to carry on with their regular activities of order execution and corresponding data collection. Data updates to SAP ERP are buffered and retried through the OEEINT framework, so that updates occur when the network connectivity is available again. It is also easier to provide site-specific customizations in OEE for the operator dashboard, custom analytics, and shop-floor automation integration by deploying SAP MII at each site.

Also, plants with state of the art automation systems can use automated data collection from shop floor to OEE by using SAP PCo to a great extent. If required, though, SAP MII can also be deployed centrally for multiple plants when the integration needs for each plant and the number of users at each plant are minimal.

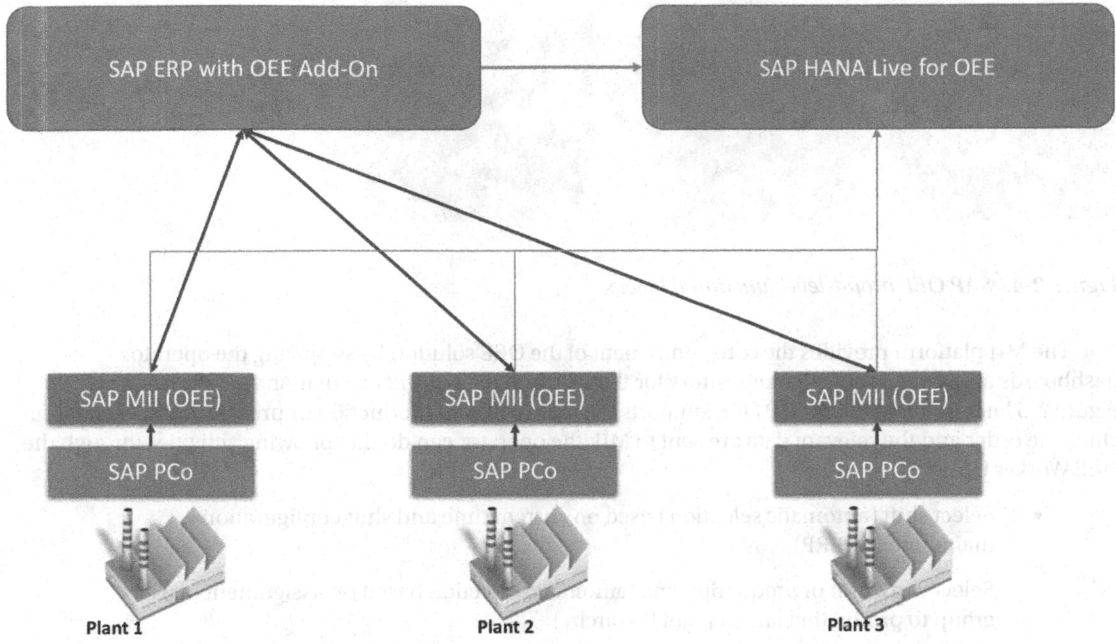

Figure 2-3. *SAP OEE deployment architecture*

SAP OEE: Product Overview

As you now understand the major components and systems of the SAP OEE solution, let us now explore the individual components and features of the solution.

SAP OEE Functional Model

SAP OEE provides a solution for capturing all kinds of data from the shop floor required for performance management. This includes the collection of data required for OEE calculations and analysis for a production process. The master data–such as material master, classification, material group, work center, plant hierarchy, shift, and reason code–are set up in SAP ERP as it is the leading system for handling master data for the enterprise. Production or process orders are also generated as transactional data in SAP ERP, as it is the planning system for manufacturing. Similarly, all the configuration data–such as KPI, production activities, data-collection element, data element, and so on–are also configured in SAP ERP, as it is the repository the OEE–related configuration data. These data are then sent to MII for order execution and data collection, which is done via the OEE dashboards by the production operators; confirmation of these tasks is sent back to SAP ERP. Finally, the analysis for the production KPIs is done in SAP HANA by replicating the data from SAP ERP and MII. Figure 2-4 shows the functional blocks of SAP OEE at a broad level.

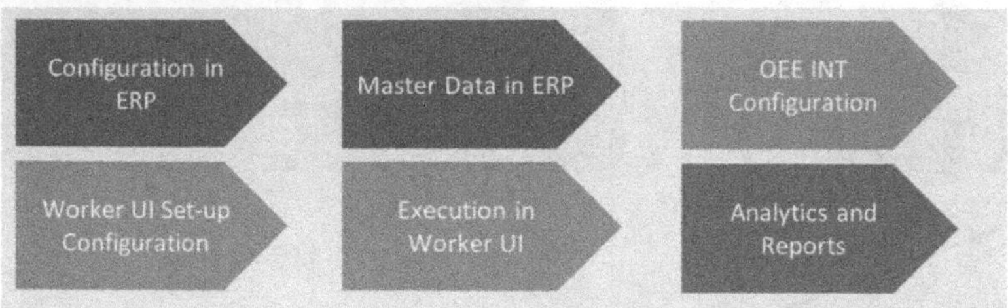

Figure 2-4. *SAP OEE broad-level functional blocks*

The MII platform provides the core component of the OEE solution by supplying the operator dashboards and a data-collection repository for the OEE and related KPI calculations. As shown in Figure 2-5 later in this section, SAP OEE supports the typical flow of production or process-order execution. Once the order and the relevant data are sent to MII, the operator can do the following activities through the OEE Worker UI:

- Select shift (automatic selection based on current time and shift configurations maintained in ERP)
- Select work unit or production line (automatic selection based on assignment of user group to production line in plant hierarchy)
- View production or process orders for the selected line and shift
- Select and start order
- Select/report/edit/delete the following data-collection elements:
    - Report machine stoppage and uptime (machine downtime with reason code)
    - Report utility data (machine, setup, labor, energy)
    - Report speed loss
    - Report yield, scrap, quality, and defects
    - Report any other custom data collection element
    - Report material consumption (goods issue) and declare production (goods receipt)

All the preceding activities are performed through the OEE Worker UI, and the data are stored in the MII database for OEE as well as updated in SAP ERP as an order confirmation (with yield, activity, and goods receipt) wherever applicable. Certain data such as machine downtimes, speed loss, and utility data are not updated in SAP ERP and are stored in MII only. The data are replicated to HANA through the SLT server if configured.

The dashboards are configurable and can be enhanced to add new functionality. A framework called the worker user interface is provided for the same purpose in MII to configure the dashboards as required. The dashboard provides the data-collection framework for production as well as real-time visibility of the production process and machine availability. It shows the downtimes of the machines, order status, and the real-time OEE of the shift while executing an order.

Let us take an example of a food-manufacturing process. The production process may consist of one or more production lines with weighing and kitting machines, oven or mixer machines, and filling and packaging machines. There may be multiple oven or mixing machines for preparing the semi-finished product, which is transferred to the single filling and packing machines for final packing and declaring of the goods receipt to the warehouse. For the filling and packing line, typically the filler or the palletizer can be considered as the bottleneck, as any stoppage of those machines may affect the production process.

A functional overview of the SAP OEE solution is shown in Figure 2-5.

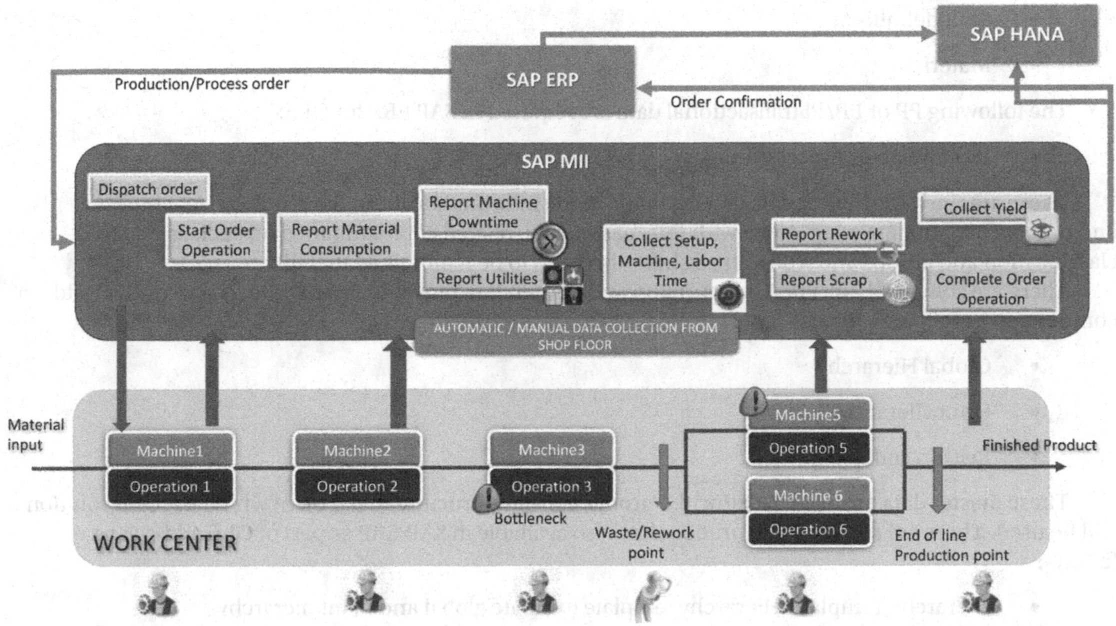

Figure 2-5. *SAP OEE functional overview*

The production supervisor may want to record the production data and order confirmations of the production lines as well as understand the losses that may be occurring due to machine stoppages, material losses, or human errors during production. The SAP OEE solution is used in production lines by the operators so as to understand which order is to be executed at which time and with which material. They will start and execute order operations through the OEE Worker UI and record any machine stoppages, using reason codes to specify the downtime. In this way the order confirmation will get updated in SAP ERP almost in real-time. The OEE and other relevant KPIs for the current shift are calculated and displayed on the dashboard in MII. The planners and supervisors can analyze the production KPIs and compare them for each production line and plant from the OEE application, which helps them to understand the frequency and root cause of any downtimes and losses that are affecting profitability so that they can take some action.

Thus SAP OEE provides an end-to-end solution for manufacturing execution and data collection along with a framework to calculate KPIs and analyze them so as to monitor and minimize losses.

SAP OEE Add-on Component in ECC

This section will explain how the OEE add-on component is utilized to create and maintain the OEE-related master and configuration data.

The SAP ERP system acts as the leading system for master and planning data maintenance in the SAP OEE solution. It is used to manage all the master data in the production-planning module that are relevant for OEE as well as some master and configuration data required specifically for OEE.

The following PP or PP/PI master data are required in SAP ERP for OEE:

- Plant
- Work center
- Shift definitions
- Material

The following PP or PP/PI transactional data are required in SAP ERP for OEE:

- Production or Process Order

These are the basic master data objects that provide information about the products, machine, and process of manufacturing. Along with this master data, related configuration data such as material classification and groups and work center shifts also need to be maintained for OEE.

There are some OEE-specific configuration and master data provided in SAP ERP as part of OEE add-on component, as follows:

- Global Hierarchy
- Plant Hierarchy
- Reason codes

These master data are used to define the production-line structure in the plant where the OEE solution will be used. There are certain configuration data also available in SAP ERP as part of OEE add-on, as follows:

- Hierarchy Template: Hierarchy template to create global and plant hierarchy
- Hierarchy Node Classification: Classification of the nodes of the hierarchy
- Machine Groups: Groups to logically aggregate similar machines in the plant hierarchy. *Machine* is a new type of object available as part of OEE.
- Production Activity: Activity types performed in the work center during production that are mapped to Work center standard values
- Data Element Types: Groups of data elements that categorize the individual data elements; SAP delivers a standard set of data element types.
- Data Elements: These elements form the basis of KPI calculation by categorizing the data being collected (e.g scheduled downtime has data elements listed as "SCHD_DWN")
- Data Collection Context: This gives context to the data collection element.
- Data Collection Elements: This is a combination of data elements and data collection context that defines the fields in which data should get collected on the data collection screen of the OEE Worker UI.
- KPIs: KPI definition for OEE. Custom KPIs can be defined as well, along with four standard KPIs that are available by default. The targets of these KPIs can be maintained in the plant hierarchy definition.
- Reason Codes: These are loss reason codes used to tag machine downtime, scrap, waste, and rework during production reporting.

Along with the master and configuration data, the planning data also need to be set up in SAP ERP. SAP OEE supports both production and process orders for discrete manufacturing and process manufacturing, respectively. By having the master and configuration data along with the planning data, such as production orders, defined and maintained in ERP, OEE solution simplifies the data-maintenance process and helps to avoid data duplicity.

Once all the preceding data are set up in SAP ERP, they need to be transferred to MII for execution and reporting in the OEE Worker UI, which will be explained in the next section.

SAP OEEINT for Integration of ECC and OEE

SAP MII needs to integrate with SAP ERP to receive the master, configuration, and transactional data as well as to update the order confirmations while executing a production or process order. SAP OEE provides a framework called OEEINT on SAP MII to integrate with SAP ERP. With this framework you can define and manage message workflows so as to process and transfer the messages between ERP and MII. Typically, SAP ERP sends IDoc messages for the master, configuration, and transactional data, which are received in MII and saved in the OEE database. SAP MII sends the order confirmation messages, which are used to execute BAPI interfaces in ERP to update the same against the corresponding order.

OEEINT provides a configurable workflow framework where you can specify the business logic with which to do validation and enrichment of the messages, as well as XSLT (XML Style Language Transformation) to transform the messages from ERP to OEE structure and vice versa. SAP provides a set of workflow configurations for the messages that are required in order for OEE to transfer from ERP to MII and vice versa with the required validation and enrichment logic, interface mapping, dispatching, and error-handing logic. As it is an extensible framework, you can also enhance the standard message workflows for OEE that are provided by SAP by adding additional validation logic or mapping. Because OEEINT is based on the SAP MII platform, you can easily create the validation logic and mapping using a BLS transaction in MII, which is the graphical logic development engine. You can also create XSLT mappings for message transformation. An example is when you are adding additional details for material in a master or production order while sending it to MII. Instead of enhancing the interface in ERP, you can develop the additional logic in an MII BLS transaction and include in the corresponding message workflow to query the information and add it to the IDoc message after receiving it in MII.

Though SAP provides all the required message workflows for OEE, you can add additional workflows, if required, for any custom enhancements. For example, if you want to develop a plant maintenance order transfer scenario in OEE, which is not available by default, you can define a new message workflow to send PM work orders from SAP ERP for any equipment maintenance. You can also create different types of workflows, such as standard workflows to transform and dispatch the message from MII to either ERP or OEE database, split workflows to split a message based on message content, and correlation workflows to merge multiple messages based on message content. SAP-provided workflows use only standard workflow types.

OEEINT also provides a queue monitor with which you can monitor the messages processed by OEEINT workflows. You can monitor the type of message along with its identifier, such as plant, order number, and so on, as well as the current status of the message processing. You can also specify the retry limit of the message, where in the case of errors while executing the target interface, the workflow framework retries sending the message multiple times as defined by the retry limit specified. Also, the MII workbench is enhanced with additional OEE-specific custom action blocks that perform the automated data collection from the shop floor. The BLS transactions developed using these custom actions can be hooked to the OEE standard execution flow to fulfill the custom requirements.

SAP OEE Operator Dashboard (Worker UI)

This section will briefly explain one of OEE's standard capabilities, the operator interface, via OEE dashboard (Worker UI).

Once messages are received in MII from ERP, containing data such as the plant hierarchy, material master, work centers, shifts, production orders, and so on, the orders need to be executed so as to capture the transactional data for operation confirmation–yield, scrap, rework quantities, material consumption and utility, machine downtimes, and additional parametric data. The operation confirmation with this data is sent to SAP ERP as the order confirmation, while some information, such as machine downtimes and additional parametric data, is stored in the OEE database in MII only to then transfer to SAP HANA for further analysis. Also, OEE and other related KPIs defined in OEE configurations are calculated in real-time and displayed in OEE dashboards for the plant users.

SAP provides a set of standard dashboards for OEE, but the dashboards can be customized or new dashboards can be created using the OEE dashboard framework provided in MII. All the dashboards are developed using SAP UI5 as the user-interface technology and Java for the backend logic. You can define different activities for screen elements using SAP UI5 as well as logic components to be used in the dashboard using MII BLS transactions or in Java, and then use them in the dashboard configuration.

Because they are developed on SAP UI5, all OEE dashboards are mobile-browser compatible as well as desktop browser compatible, and can be accessed from various devices. This is useful for shop-floor users who will be accessing the application with specialized touch-screen devices while working on the production line.

You can assign dashboards for different production lines and for different user groups, so that a user, when logged in to MII, will get the dashboards assigned to his/her user group based on the selected production line. If multiple dashboards are assigned to the user group, then the user can select any of the dashboard at a time. You can also select a shift and view the orders available for execution during that shift, then begin executing the order, such as starting or stopping an operation, and recording the yield, scrap, data collection, machine downtime, and so on. You can have different types of dashboards customized for different user groups, such as an operator dashboard for data collection and operation execution, a production supervisor dashboard for shift review and line KPI monitoring, and so forth. Refer to Figure 2-6 for a sample OEE dashboard.

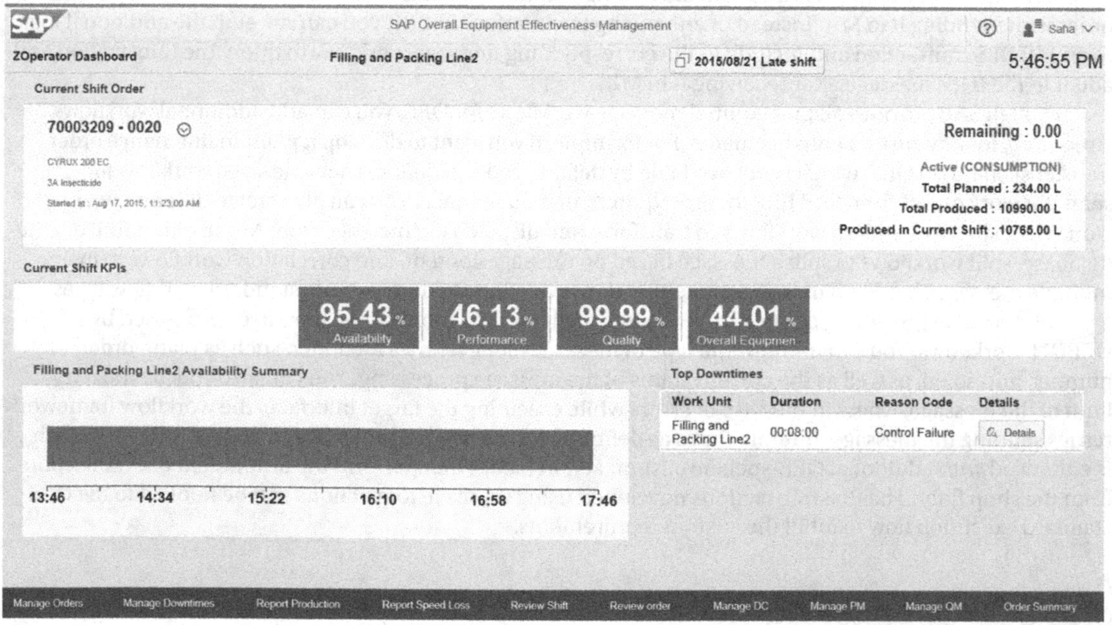

***Figure 2-6.** SAP OEE dashboard*

To enhance the dashboard functionality, you can also define an extension configuration for each production line to trigger certain functions on specific events, such as start order operation, stop order, complete order, report data, report uptime, close shift, and so on. You can develop an extension as logic within MII BLS transactions and create an activity for it, then link it with the events for the production line, which will be triggered when the event occurs; for example, checking if there is any machine downtime already there for the production line when the operator starts an order operation from the OEE dashboard.

Thus the dashboards in OEE provide a single-window system for all the execution activities and data recordings for the manufacturing plant users, as well as provide a real-time view of the OEE KPIs for the plant users.

SAP OEE Reporting and Analytics

This section will explain about the different options SAP OEE provides for reporting and analytics.

SAP OEE provides options to analyze the data collected from the shop floor both at local plant level and at the global corporation level. The plant-level analytics are enabled by consuming the data collected on the local MII server through SAP Lumira. As the data comes from a single MII box, these kinds of reports are limited to the production lines configured on that MII system. For such local plant-level analytics, SAP OEE delivers a plug-in that can be used in SAP Lumira to consume the MII data through CSV files. More about this will be covered in chapter 9.

For consolidated global-level analytics, SAP OEE delivers standard HANA content. In this case, a centralized HANA server should be connected to all the plant-level MII boxes. Data is copied to this central box through System Landscape Transformation (SLT) replication. The SAP OEE HANA content delivers a set of standard views that help in analyzing the data either through standard visualization tools like SAP Lumira or through the SAP OEE HANA web application. As SAP HANA is an in-memory database solution and application platform, it provides the capability to analyze a huge amount of data easily via different types of analysis. SAP HANA provides an in-memory database where the OEE data models are maintained and the data are replicated from ERP and MII. This is done using SLT, which is a standard replication mechanism available in the HANA platform, along with other SAP systems. The analytics logic and queries are also maintained in OEE HANA content, as different types of views and analytics reports on SAP UI5 are also provided on the HANA platform. SAP provides the standard data model for OEE, along with the analytics queries and reports on HANA, as a HANA Live component, an add-on to the OEE solution. Though it is a technically optional component, by using the HANA add-on for OEE you can get the analytics and reports for OEE without any custom development. The SAP-provided reports on HANA for OEE are as follows:

- Loss Analysis Report: Provides the reports for different types of losses, such as speed loss, quality loss, downtimes loss, and so forth, based on reason codes. A daily/monthly/weekly trend analysis is also provided. The reason codes can be drilled down level by level for root-cause analysis.
- KPI Analysis Reports: By using these reports you can analyze the different OEE KPIs based on those defined in the OEE add-on in ERP with respect to the plant hierarchy. You can also view the trend analysis for the OEE KPIs over a period of time and see an asset utilization analysis.
- Data Collection Report: You can view the different reports for data collection in OEE based on the data elements or data collection elements and analyze the trends and measures.

For most of the analytics, you can drill down across the plant hierarchy to analyze the KPIs that are rolled-up; for example, you can analyze performance of the dependent assets or KPIs, which helps you to understand how the granular KPIs and losses are affecting the overall performance.

You can also customize and modify the standard reports provided on HANA according to specific requirements by modifying the views, queries, and web reports on SAP UI5. Without using HANA there are no standard reports for OEE delivered in MII or ERP, and you may need to develop custom reports on MII by developing the logic and user interface on the MII platform.

SAP HANA is installed centrally as a global instance, whereas SAP MII instances for OEE may be plant specific, one for each plant or for a group of plants. By having reporting on the HANA platform, it is easier to collate the data from multiple plants from different MII instances that are deployed at each plant site and then analyze cross-plant KPIs; for example, comparing the OEE or asset utilization KPIs for similar production lines across different plants to compare the performance and losses between different plants. You can configure to move the data from MII to HANA at certain periodic intervals or upon any data change in the OEE database in MII, which may provide near-real-time analytics on the HANA platform.

SAP OEE: Benefits

This section will explain about benefits of SAP OEE.

As you have learned the different components and features of OEE, you can now understand how the SAP OEE solution helps in the manufacturing-execution data collection for calculating the KPIs and losses that may occur during production. SAP ERP is the planning and logistics execution system, while MII provides the real-time platform for execution and data collection. The HANA platform is used for cross-plant KPI analysis and reporting for OEE. SAP OEE complements the existing ERP implementation and provides an end-to-end solution connecting the planning, execution, and analysis for measuring losses and production KPIs, which helps to optimize the production process and minimize losses.

SAP OEE can be used for various manufacturing industries, mostly for process industries where you need a solution to capture the production information continuously and measure the OEE and production losses for multiple machines by either manual or automated data-collection methods.

Overall, SAP OEE provides the following benefits:

- Provides a rapidly scalable means for manufacturing performance management on the shop floor. It would take several months to develop and implement such a performance-management solution on MII, which the customers get as a standard solution with SAP OEE.
- Enables the production operators to view the schedule and order details through a simplified user interface and to collect and record the data for the manufacturing process
- Simplifies bi-directional integration with SAP ERP and manufacturing shop-floor systems for real-time data collection and production confirmations
- Provides near-real-time analysis at local plant level and global corporation level for determining the hidden root causes for several production losses and optimizes the process on a continuous basis

Summary

In this chapter you have learned about the features and components of SAP OEE and its overall solution architecture. You have learned the functionality and features of SAP ERP, SAP MII, and SAP HANA as components of the OEE solution and how data collection and analysis for OEE and related KPIs are achieved by SAP OEE.

In the next chapter you will learn more about the OEE add-on for SAP ERP and how to configure the different master and configuration data required for OEE.

CHAPTER 3

The SAP OEE Add-on Component of ERP

This chapter will explain how the SAP OEE add-on component installed in SAP ERP helps in the configuration and maintenance of OEE-specific master data and configuration data. It will also detail the required ALE settings to be configured for the transfer of OEE master and configuration data as IDocs. SAP OEE provides seamless integration of the master data and transactional data in SAP ERP with the plant-level SAP MII system for production and other related data collection and reporting.

The SAP OEE application uses production-related master data from SAP ERP along with the real-time data captured in MII to calculate OEE KPIs and provide data for analyzing plant performance.

It is essential to set up these master data as a single source of reliable data by leveraging the OEE master-data setup features of ERP, which are created and maintained in SAP ERP using the OEE add-on component OEE_ERP.

Once the master and configuration data are defined in ERP, the data required for shop-floor execution are transferred to the shop floor SAP MII systems through IDoc interfaces. The master data required for the analytics are transferred to SAP HANA system using SAP Landscape Transformation (SLT) from SAP ERP.

OEE Master Data in ERP

This section will explain OEE-related master data, its purpose, and the steps required to configure and maintain it, as well as how the master data facilitates the execution of OEE and KPI functionality using the OEE add-on component of ERP.

OEE uses the following master data:

- Existing master data in ERP
    - Material master data
    - Work center and associated capacities, shift definitions, and UOM
    - Factory Calendar
- OEE- specific master data (available in OEE add-on)
    - Global hierarchy
    - Plant hierarchy
    - Plant reason codes

D. Saha et al., *Manufacturing Performance Management using SAP OEE*,
DOI 10.1007/978-1-4842-1150-2_3

You can configure this master data in SAP ERP from the SAP Easy Access menu: *Logistics* ➤ *Production* ➤ *Overall Equipment Effectiveness* ➤ *Master Data*. Refer to Figure 3-1.

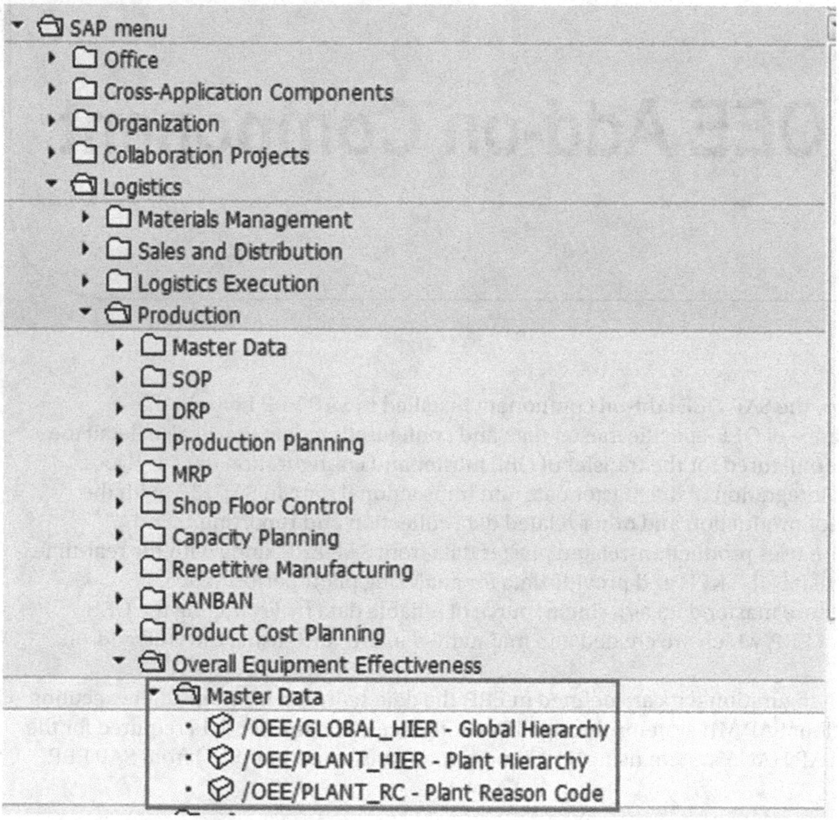

SAP menu
Office
Cross-Application Components
Organization
Collaboration Projects
Logistics
Materials Management
Sales and Distribution
Logistics Execution
Production
Master Data
SOP
DRP
Production Planning
MRP
Shop Floor Control
Capacity Planning
Repetitive Manufacturing
KANBAN
Product Cost Planning
Overall Equipment Effectiveness
Master Data
/OEE/GLOBAL_HIER - Global Hierarchy
/OEE/PLANT_HIER - Plant Hierarchy
/OEE/PLANT_RC - Plant Reason Code

Figure 3-1. *SAP Easy Access menu with OEE*

Before we get into the details of OEE-specific data setup, let us have a look at shift configurations for a work center. OEE uses the work center–integrated shift definitions for collecting the production and loss information on the shop floor.

Shift Configurations

Usually the manufacturing execution process on the shop floor works in shifts. A shift is a type of work schedule in which group of workers rotate through set periods throughout the day, typically performing the same kind of work. Shift work is common in production environments where repetitive tasks are performed and production takes place around the clock.

SAP OEE requires the shift definitions, the collection of shift-specific production data and losses, and the calculation of shift-specific KPIs. This helps in analyzing the shift's performance specific to equipment, line, plant, and so on. These shift details are used in the work center, or resource shift definitions in ERP are defined for production planning.

Production planning in ERP is done based on the work center's capacity level. Each work center is assigned a shift definition and is associated with the plant hierarchy used in OEE, which we will explore in a later section. Upon the transfer of these work centers, shift definitions, and plant hierarchy from ERP to MII, OEE gets the plant- and work center–specific shift details and the laborers' working patterns.

Ideally, a work center or resource in ERP will have the shift configuration maintained. You can either maintain the existing set or create a new set of shift configurations.

Configure Shift Grouping

Shift grouping is the shift header under which you can define the shift definitions, shift sequence, and work break schedules.

1. Use transaction code OP4A or use SAP Easy Access Menu in SAP ERP:

   Logistics ➤ Production ➤ Capacity Planning ➤ Available Capacity ➤ Shift Sequence

2. Select the pen icon to add new or maintain existing shift grouping.

3. Enter shift grouping name and its description.

4. Select the created grouping name and select the "Work break schedules" option in the left-hand hierarchy.

5. Select the pen icon to add new or maintain existing break schedules for the shift group. (Refer to Figure 3-2.)

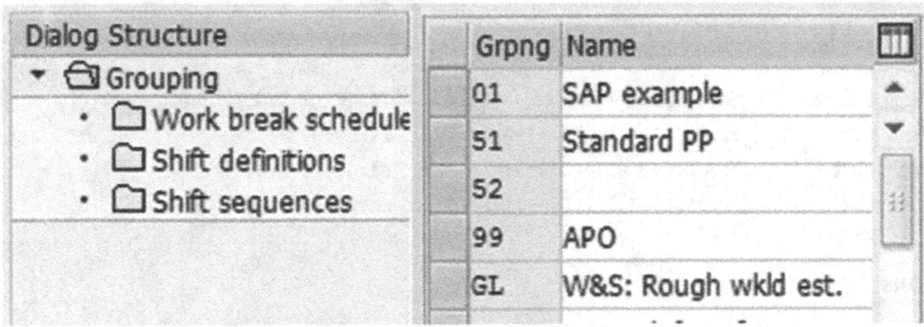

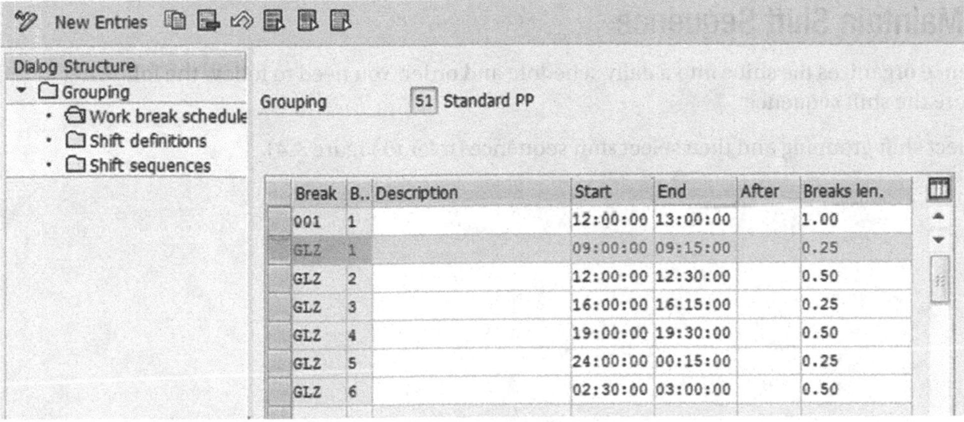

Figure 3-2. *Configure shift grouping*

■ **Note** Shift breaks are entered with start and end times and a break code. When "Use shift breaks" is checked in the plant hierarchy node (master data of OEE), these shift breaks will be automatically considered when calculating the OEE KPI. Shift breaks are defined by a start time and an end time.

Configure/Maintain Shift Definitions

You configure the shift definitions to define the number of shifts and their duration as per your factory calendar and production requirements:

1. Select the configured shift grouping from the preceding section and select the "Shift definitions" option in the left-hand hierarchy.
2. Select the pen icon to add new or maintain existing shift definitions.
3. Define a unique shift ID, description, start date time, end date time, and break. (Refer to Figure 3-3.)

   These shift definitions will be downloaded to OEE and will be followed as the shift pattern in the plant once this shift is assigned to a work center.

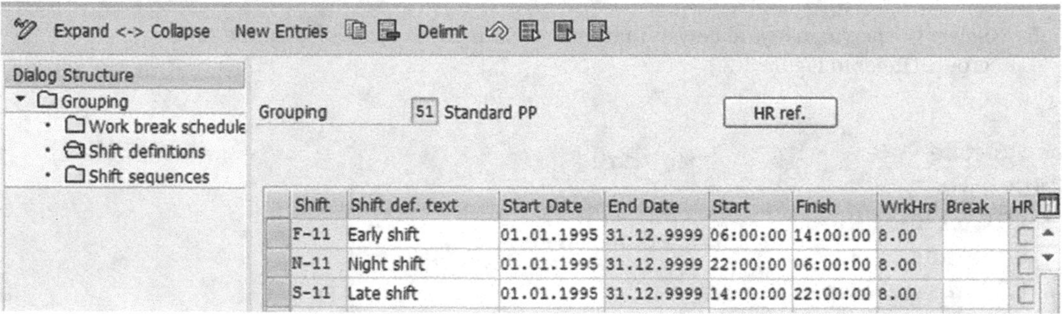

Figure 3-3. *Configure shift definitions*

Configure/Maintain Shift Sequence

The shift sequence organizes the shifts into a daily schedule and order. You need to follow the following steps to configure the shift sequence:

1. Select shift grouping and then select shift sequence (refer to Figure 3-4).

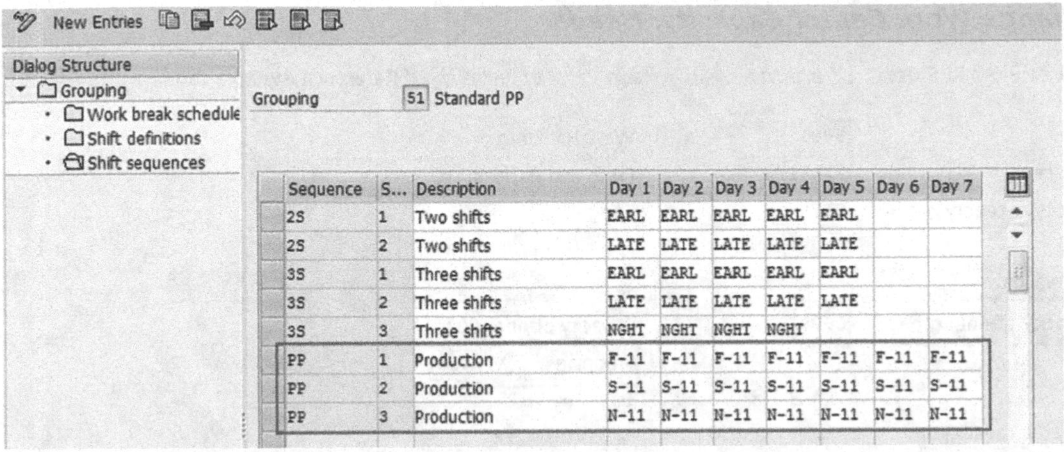

New Entries

Dialog Structure
- Grouping
  - Work break schedule
  - Shift definitions
  - Shift sequences

Grouping 51 Standard PP

Sequence	S...	Description	Day 1	Day 2	Day 3	Day 4	Day 5	Day 6	Day 7
2S	1	Two shifts	EARL	EARL	EARL	EARL	EARL		
2S	2	Two shifts	LATE	LATE	LATE	LATE	LATE		
3S	1	Three shifts	EARL	EARL	EARL	EARL	EARL		
3S	2	Three shifts	LATE	LATE	LATE	LATE	LATE		
3S	3	Three shifts	NGHT	NGHT	NGHT	NGHT			
PP	1	Production	F-11	F-11	F-11	F-11	F-11	F-11	F-11
PP	2	Production	S-11	S-11	S-11	S-11	S-11	S-11	S-11
PP	3	Production	N-11	N-11	N-11	N-11	N-11	N-11	N-11

Figure 3-4. *Configure shift sequence*

2. Enter the sequence name, sequence number (the order of shift), and description.
3. Define the preceding shift sequence from Day 1 to Day 7 based on your plant requirements and calendar.
4. For each day, enter the shift defined in the previous step in the required sequence.

   OEE displays the shifts in the operator dashboard as per this sequence only.
5. Save the entries.

Associate Shift with Work Center Capacity

You need to assign the shift definitions to a work center, as each work center may operate in a different shift pattern depending on production requirements. To assign the shift to a work center, you have to perform the following procedure.

1. Use transaction code CR02 or go to SAP Easy Access menu: Logistics ➤ Production ➤ Master data ➤ Work centers ➤ Change
2. Enter the plant name and work center name with which the shift needs to be associated.
3. Select the Capacities tab and select the Capacity button on the bottom.
4. Assign the capacity planner group, grouping, active version, factory calendar ID, and base UOM. (Refer to Figure 3-5.)

   The capacity planner group is required in order for a capacity planner to know the capacity he has to work with during the planning process. Grouping defines the shift sequences and shift definitions that are used to maintain the available capacity. Factory calendar ID is the calendar of your country maintained in ERP, while active version is the version number of the available capacity. Active version is used in scheduling and capacity planning and is a mandatory setting. The base unit of measure is the unit of measure of the capacity, e.g., Days.

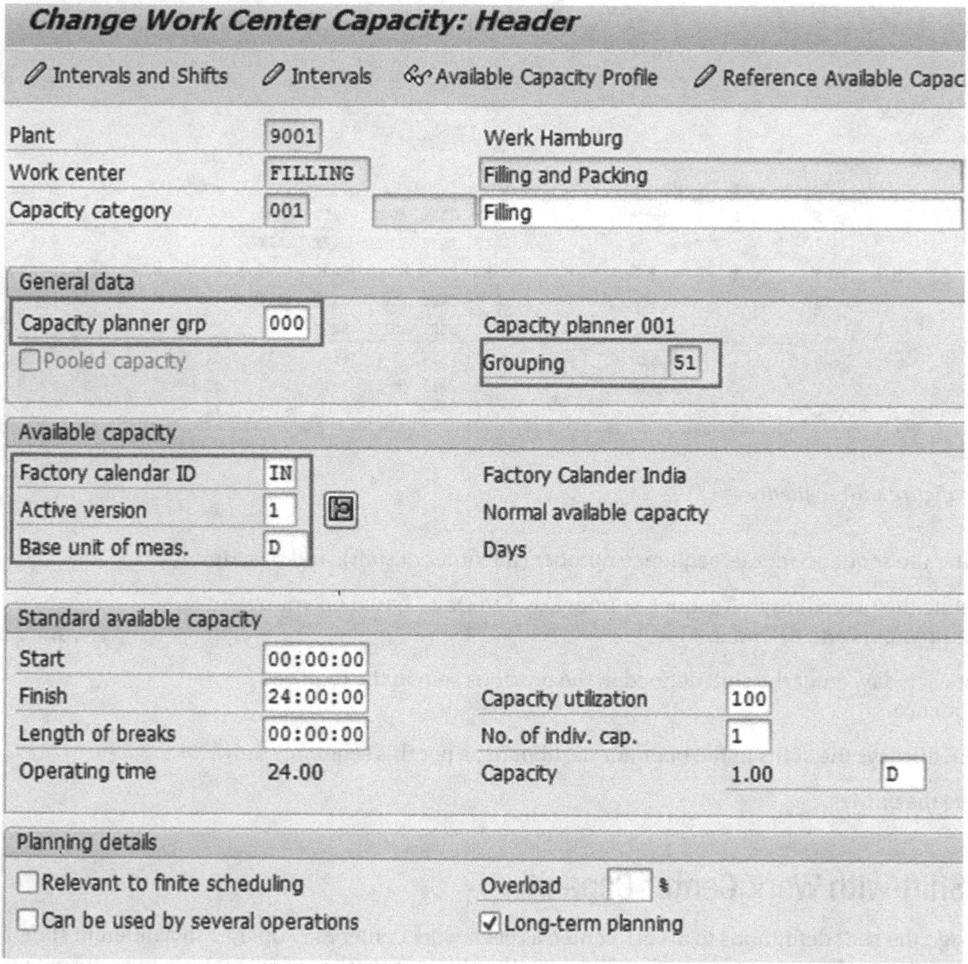

Figure 3-5. Assign shift to a work center

5. Select the Interval and Shifts button on top. (Refer to Figure 3-6.)

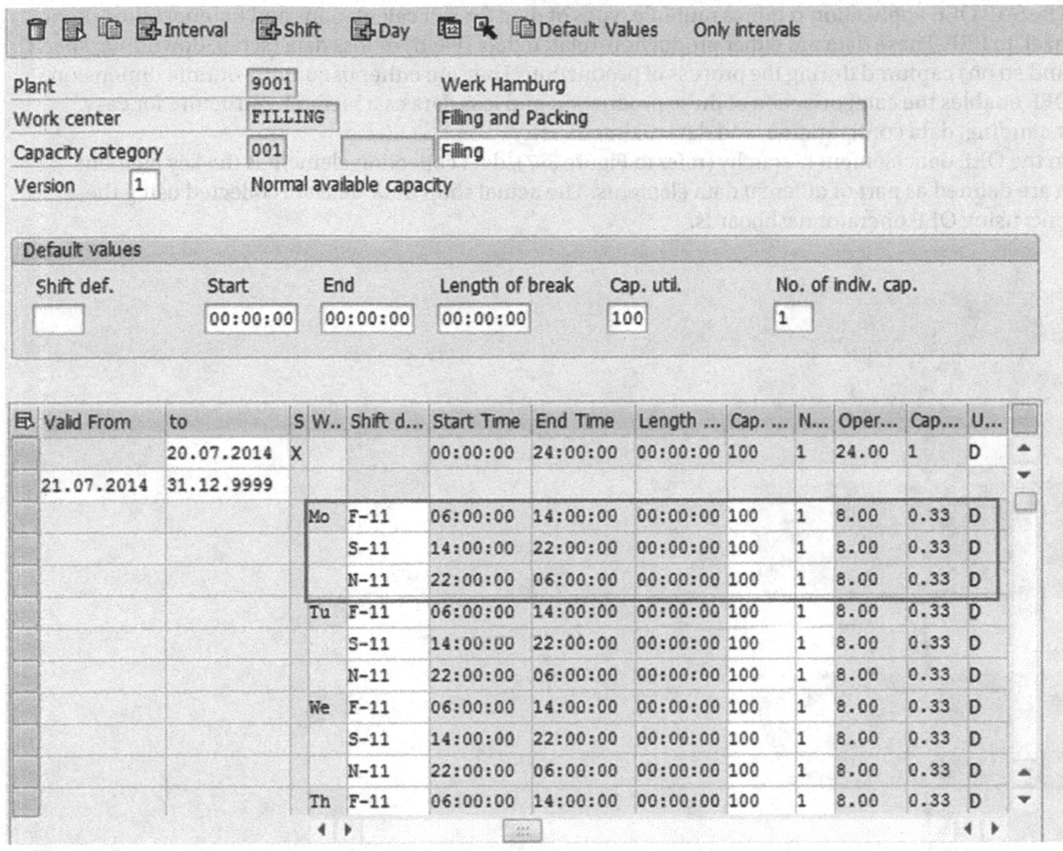

***Figure 3-6.** Configure daily shift intervals*

6. Select Interval and enter the validity period for the shift assignment.
7. Select Shift and enter in the previously created interval the shift name under the shift definition column. On selection of the shift name, the shift duration automatically appears along with other capacity details.
8. Follow step 8 to configure different shifts for the day.
9. Select Day to add more days for the week and follow steps 8 and 9 to configure the shifts for each day of the week.
10. Save the changes.

OEE Configuration Data in ERP

This section will explain the purpose of and steps by which to configure OEE-related configuration data, such as data collection elements, data elements, KPI definitions, machine groups, production modes, production activities, hierarchy-node classifications, UOM and dimensions, standard value key and formula parameters, and factory calendar.

The SAP OEE application requires multiple types of data for KPI calculations and to report shop-floor data back to ERP. These data are either production-related data (yield) or loss data (scrap, downtime, speed loss, and so on) captured during the process of production. They are either of quantity or time dimension. SAP OEE enables the categorization of these production and loss data as a hierarchy structure for easy understanding, data configuration, and data maintenance.

In the OEE data element hierarchy (refer to Figure 3-7), data collection element is the key element which are defined as part of different data elements. The actual shop floor data are collected using these elements using OEE operator dashboards.

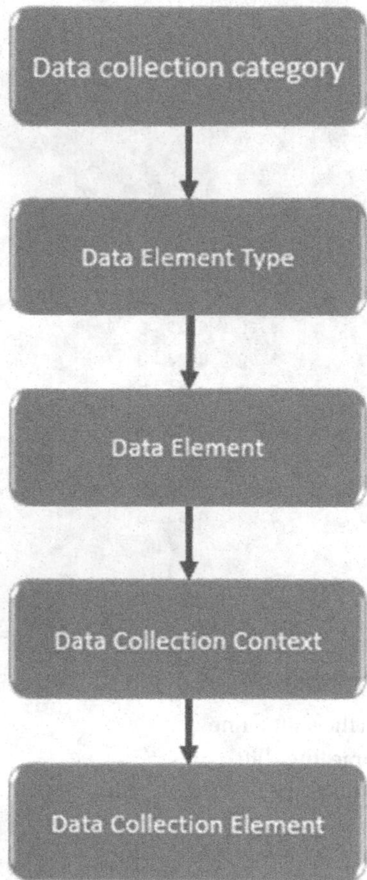

Figure 3-7. *OEE configuration data hierarchy*

The other hierarchy structures help the categorization of data elements and data collection elements.

Data Collection Category

Data collection category is the data type of the data being collected by OEE; e.g., production data and loss data.

All the sub-elements after this in the hierarchy fall under either of these data types. These two data types are preconfigured in the OEE add-on during the component installation.

Data Element Type

A data element type is used to categorize the OEE data elements. It is the hard-coded system element that defines the basic structure of how OEE is modelled and calculated in the solution.

By default, the OEE application delivers data element types for collecting and calculating OEE KPI. The system default data element types for capturing OEE data are the following:

- SCHED_DOWN (scheduled downtime)
  - Scheduled downtime is a planned maintenance time for a resource. Downtime for the purpose of maintenance is scheduled as a part of the manufacturing day and, in some cases, as an integral part of the manufacturing process. It also includes performing routine actions that keep the device in working order. The goal is to keep emergency and unscheduled maintenance to a minimum.
  - Scheduled downtimes can be defined at the plant level from the SAP MII main menu ➤ Worker UI Management ➤ Scheduled Downtime Maintenance or from the standard dashboard. Refer to chapter 6.
- UNSCD_DOWN (unscheduled downtime)
  - All the unplanned downtime reported from the shop floor.
- SPEED_LOSS (speed loss)
  - Reduction of production due to reduction of line speed.
  - Actual production duration - rated production duration
  - Speed loss is calculated based on reported production quantity and standard rate/nominal speed. Speed loss is reported and managed through the OEE dashboard.
- YIELD
  - Produced good quantity
- REWORK
  - Quality defects during production
- SCRAP
  - Waste produced during production
  - Yield, rework, and scrap can be reported manually through the dashboard or automatically from the shop floor using PCo (plant connectivity)
- NOT_APPL
  - Data element type for a non-OEE data element

SAP OEE identifies the preceding list of elements as reported elements; i.e., these data are collected by the operator in the UI either manually or automatically. This list can be enhanced with the creation of custom data element types as per the business requirements, which may or may not be OEE related. The custom data elements should fall under any of the preceding OEE-defined data element types. For non-OEE-related data elements, the data element type should be NOT_APPL.

The system default data element types for calculating OEE and its associated KPIs are the following:

- TOT_PRD_TM (total production time)
  - Total available time considering 24 hours in a day and all seven days as working
- LOADING_TM (loading time)
  - Calculated as order completion time - order start time
  - Excludes scheduled downtimes, order hold time, and shift breaks (is set to true in plant hierarchy for the line).
  - In OEE, loading time for a shift is an aggregation of the loading time of each order executed in that shift.
- NET_PRD_TM (net production time)
  - Calculated as loading time - unscheduled downtime
  - Availability KPI = NET_PRD_TM / LOADING_TM
- NET_OPR_TM (net operating time)
  - Calculated as NET_PRD_TM - speed loss
  - Performance KPI = NET_OPR_TM / NET_PRD_TM
- VAL_OPR_TM (value operating time)
  - Calculated as NET_OPR_TM - quality loss
  - Quality KPI = VAL_OPR_TM / NET_OPR_TM

SAP OEE identifies the preceding list of elements as calculated elements; i.e., these data are calculated by SAP OEE using the elements reported by the operator in the UI. This list is hard coded in the OEE add-on.

When the OEE application is implemented for multiple plants, each plant may have different data collection needs. All those data collection elements can be created under data element types and can be used across sites.

This process of creating and maintaining the configuration data at one place in ERP ensures a single source of standards and no data duplication.

Data Element Type Configuration: Reported Element

1. Use transaction code SPRO ➤ SAP Reference IMG ➤ Production ➤ Overall Equipment Effectiveness ➤ Define Data Element Types
2. Select New Entries (refer to Figure 3-8).

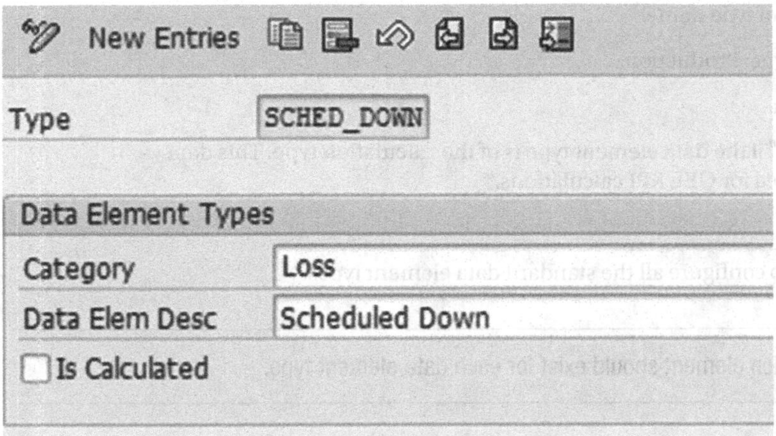

Figure 3-8. Configuration data element type: reported element

3. Enter the data element type name.
4. Select the category type: Loss.
5. Enter the description.
6. Do not check "Is Calculated" if the data element type is of the collection type.
7. Save the entries.

Data Element Type Configuration: Calculation Element

1. Use transaction code SPRO ➤ SAP Reference IMG ➤ Production ➤ Overall Equipment Effectiveness ➤ Define Data Element Types
2. Select New Entries (refer to Figure 3-9).

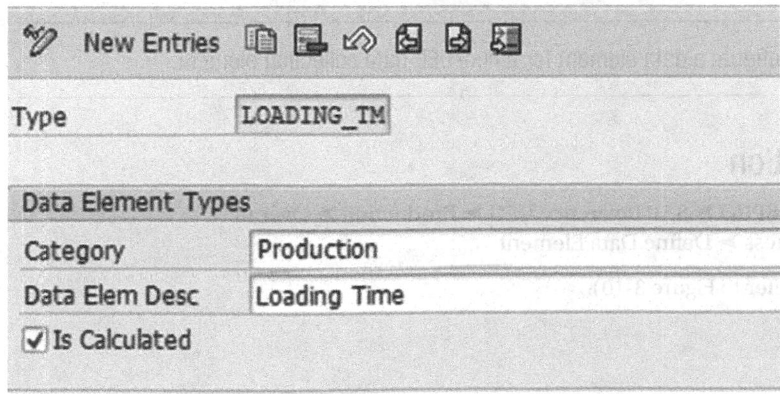

Figure 3-9. Configuration data element type: calculation element

3. Enter the data element type name.
4. Select the category type: Production.
5. Enter the description.
6. Check "Is Calculated" if the data element type is of the calculation type. This data element would be used for OEE KPI calculations.
7. Save the entries.

Follow the preceding steps to configure all the standard data element types.

■ **Note** At least one data collection element should exist for each data element type.

Data Element

Data elements are data components that store the OEE-specific shop-floor data reported through the operator dashboard and calculate the standard KPIs using the stored data.

OEE operator dashboards are predelivered user interfaces used to collect the shop-floor production information during production execution.

For example, good-quantity production and production losses, such as scrap, rework, speed loss, and downtimes, are collected and used in calculating the standard KPIs.

To capture the different data inputs required for KPI calculations, data collection elements are configured in the operator UI. In summary, data collection elements are data components that collect data from the operator through the UI, and data elements are the level of abstraction for the data collection elements.

Data collection elements can be used to capture OEE- and non-OEE-specific data. This ensures OEE is an application to leverage beyond KPI.

For example, data elements can be used for non-OEE data like material consumption, line set speed, and standard value parameters like machine time, labor time, and so on. SAP OEE does not restrict you to collect data which are just required for the calculation of four standard KPIs but it allows you to collect non-OEE KPI related data as well which could be part of other plant requirements. It is scalable and flexible.

■ **Note** It is not mandatory to configure a data element for a non-OEE data collection element.

Data Element Configuration

1. Use transaction code SPRO ➤ SAP Reference IMG ➤ Production ➤ Overall Equipment Effectiveness ➤ Define Data Element
2. Select New Entries (refer to Figure 3-10).

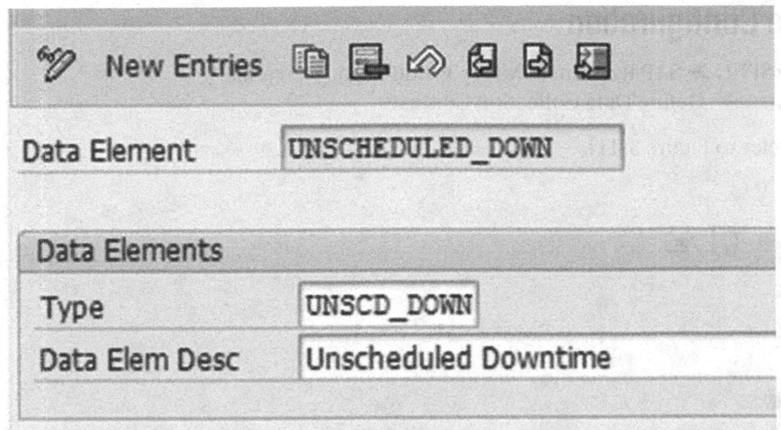

Figure 3-10. *Configuration data element*

3. Enter the data element name.
4. Select the type; associate the relevant data element type created in the previous section with this data element.
5. Enter the data element description. This description will be used and presented wherever this data element is utilized.
6. Save the entries.

Follow the preceding steps to configure all the data elements.

Data Collection Contexts

Data collection contexts help you to define the contexts of the data collection elements. Data collection elements are logically categorized based on the contexts for which they are being collected. This is similar to data collection category, which defines the data type of element being reported and calculated.

Data collection contexts are specific to the standard activities type (`RecTypeGrp`) defined for work centers or resources in PP and PP/PI. For example, if a data collection element is used to collect data for ERP transactions, the context is used to associate the data with the reporting types and activities defined in PP and PP/PI. Default contexts in OEE are finished materials, raw materials, utilities, setup, teardown, and so on. This facilitates the hassle-free integration of OEE with ERP for production confirmation and material consumption.

For example, the predefined data collection contexts specific to finished material and raw material are as follows:

- `FIN_MAT` context is related to yield, scrap, and rework data collection types to facilitate the yield confirmation, scrap confirmation, and rework transactions in PP.
- `RAW_MAT` context can be related to the yield and scrap data collection types to facilitate the material consumption and scrap consumption update transaction in PP.

Data Collection Contexts Configuration

1. Use transaction code SPRO ➤ SAP Reference IMG ➤ Production ➤ Overall Equipment Effectiveness ➤ Define Data Collection Contexts
2. Select New Entries (refer to Figure 3-11).

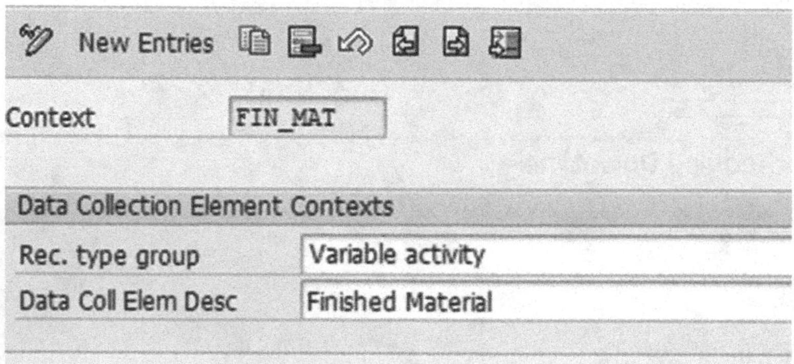

Figure 3-11. *Configuration of data collection contexts*

3. Enter the Context Name: `FIN_MAT`
4. Select `RecTypeGrp` and set to `Variable activity`. The `RecTypeGrp` defined in PP and PP/PI is associated with the context defined. Default values include `Variable activity`, `Processing`, `Setup`, and `Tear down`.
5. Enter the data collection element description.

Follow the preceding steps to configure custom data collection contexts.

Data Collection Element

Data collection elements are data components that are configured as data fields in the user interface to collect the shop-floor information. These collected data may or may not be OEE specific. Data collection elements specific to OEE are further used in KPI calculations.

Data Collection Elements Configuration

1. Use transaction code SPRO ➤ SAP Reference IMG ➤ Production ➤ Overall Equipment Effectiveness ➤ Define Data Collection Element
2. Select New Entries (refer to Figure 3-12).

New Entries

Data Collection Elem	GOOD_QUANTITY

Data Collection Element

Data Coll Elem Desc	Produced Good Quantity
Data Element	GOOD_QUANTITY
DC Elem Type	Quantity
Context	FIN_MAT
Dimension	
☐ Order Indep. Collect	
Plan UOM	
Data Elem Desc	Good Quantity Produced

Figure 3-12. *Configuration of data collection elements*

3. Enter a data collection element name.
4. Enter the description.
5. Associate the data collection element with the data element.
6. Select the data collection element type: Quantity/Time.
7. Associate the data collection context.
8. Select the right dimension.
9. Check "Order Indep. Collect" if this data collection element is an order-independent data collection. For example, set speed is the line speed, which is collected from the shop floor and is order independent; i.e., the set speed is not specific to a particular order but rather is specific to a particular line or work center. Data collection elements like yield, scrap, and so on are order dependent.
10. Enter the unit of measurement (UOM).
11. Save the entries.

Follow the same steps to enter all the standard and custom data collection elements.

Figure 3-13 is the hierarchical structure of the OEE-related configuration data for data collection category: production.

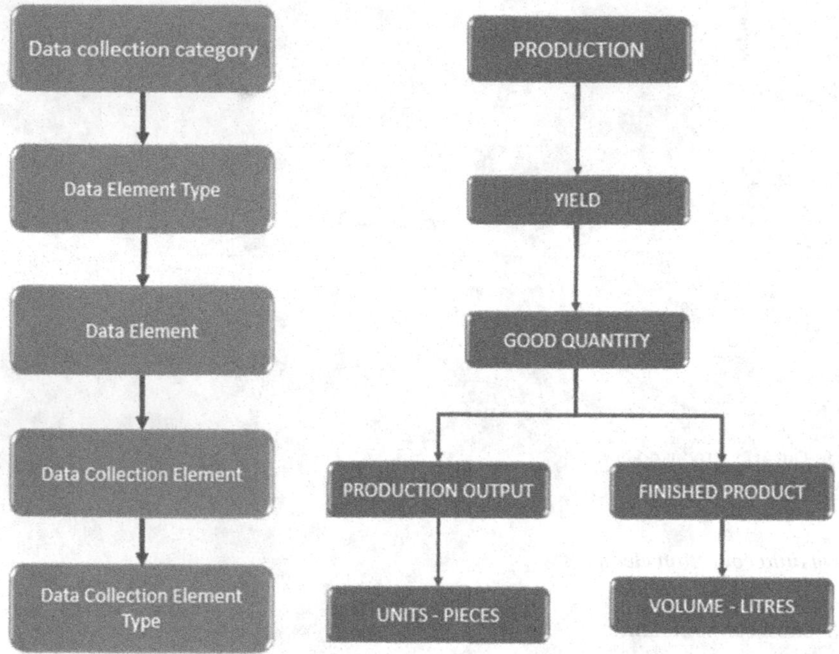

Figure 3-13. *OEE Configuration data hierarchy: production data category*

Figure 3-14 is the hierarchical structure of the OEE-related configuration data for data collection category: loss

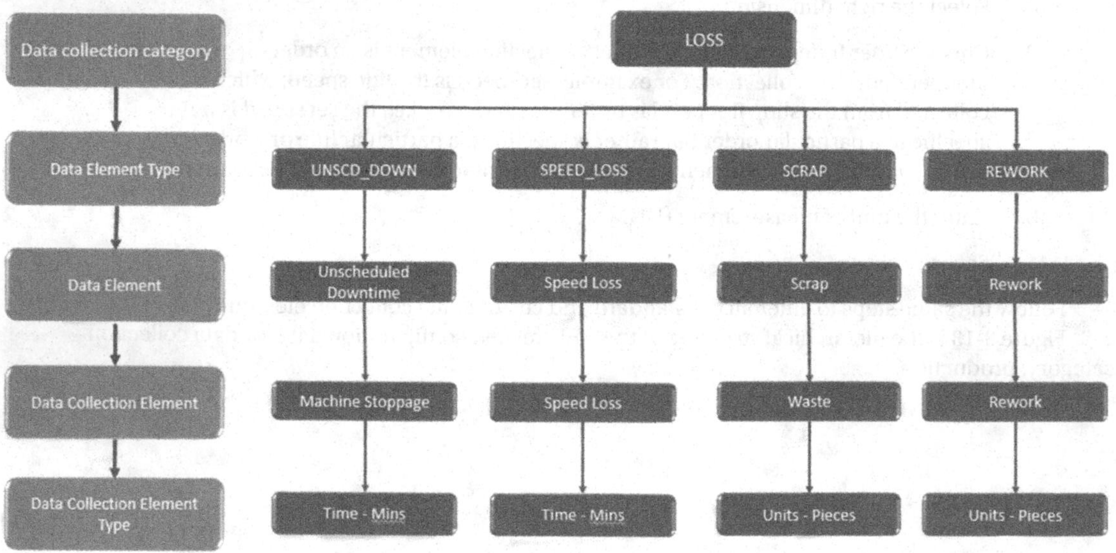

Figure 3-14. *OEE Configuration data hierarchy: loss data category*

Hierarchy Node Classification

Hierarchy Node classification allows you to define a category or a classification with which multiple nodes in a global or plant hierarchy can be associated (Refer to Hierarchy Model in OEE section later in this chapter). This helps in HANA analytics for comparing performance across comparable assets in the plant hierarchy or across plants based on the defined node classification.

You can assign a classification to a plant, work center, or machine node type. Grouping node types cannot be classified.

For example, a node classification can be created for a technology. In a plant, some lines or product ranges might be produced with a specific state of the art technology. Those work center nodes can be assigned to a technology classification, which helps HANA to analyze the performance of the line based on that technology.

A node classification can be created to specify a product line. All of the lines, work centers, or machines in the hierarchy can be assigned to a category to specify that they are utilized for that product line. When analyzing OEE performance, a report could be generated to compare the performance of the process for the particular product line.

Hierarchy Node Classification Configuration

1. Use transaction code SPRO ➤ SAP Reference IMG ➤ Production ➤ Overall Equipment Effectiveness ➤ Define Hierarchy Node Classification
2. Select New Entries (refer to Figure 3-15).

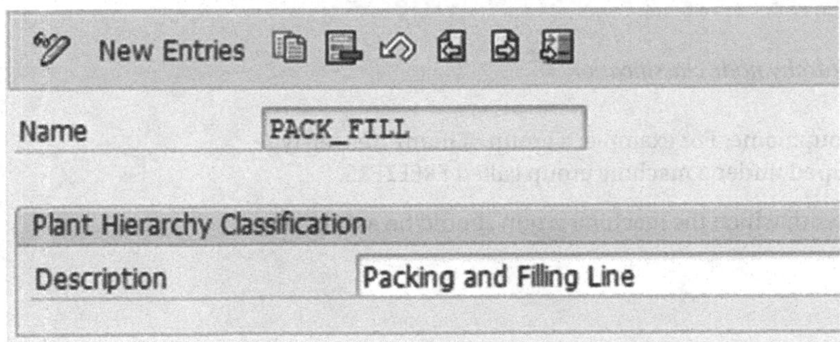

Figure 3-15. *Configuration of hierarchy node classification*

3. Enter the category name; e.g., a line name, vendor name, and so on.
4. Enter the category description.
5. Save entries.

Machine Groups

Machine groups are a way to group similar machines. This is used as an additional dimension in the analytics for comparing performance across comparable machines in the plant hierarchy or across plants.

For example, a machine group can be created to specify the vendor of the machine. All of the machines in the hierarchy can be assigned to this machine group to make it clear that the same vendor manufactures them all. When analyzing OEE performance, a report can be generated to compare the performance of the machines of the particular vendor.

Machines under different work centers, which perform similar functions, can be grouped under a machine group, which enables HANA to compare the performance of the machines across different work centers. This will enable one to identify the poor-performing machines for a particular line.

Machine Groups Configuration

1. Use transaction code SPRO ➤ SAP Reference IMG ➤ Production ➤ Overall Equipment Effectiveness ➤ Define Machine Groups
2. Select New Entries (refer to Figure 3-16).

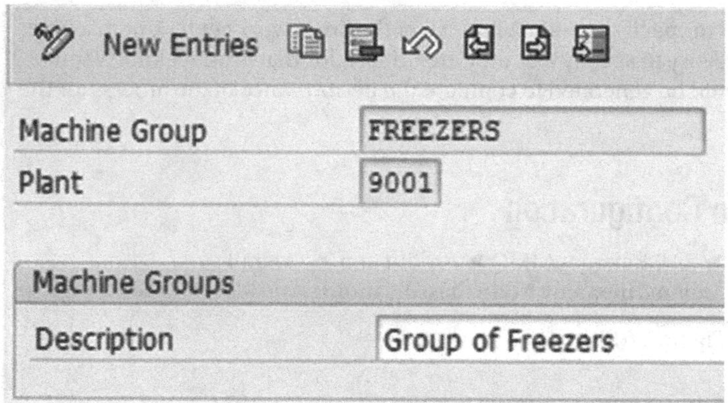

***Figure 3-16.** Configuration of hierarchy node classification*

3. Enter the machine group name. For example, a group of many freezer-type machines can be grouped under a machine group called FREEZERS.
4. Enter the plant name with which the machine group should be associated.
5. Enter the description.
6. Save the entries.

Follow the preceding steps to configure different machine groups. These machine groups can be associated with a plant hierarchy machine node.

Production Modes

Production modes in OEE are used to define a production process and associate it with the different order types maintained in PP and PP/PI.

■ **Note** An OEE production mode can be associated with multiple order types, but an order type can only be associated with one OEE production mode.

These production modes are downloaded to OEE in MII from ERP and used during order execution. OEE handles both production and process order scenarios and hence the production modes specific to each piece of data are stored in HANA. The production modes can also be used as one of the filter criteria during HANA analytics.

Production Modes Configuration

1. Use transaction code SPRO ➤ SAP Reference IMG ➤ Production ➤ Overall Equipment Effectiveness ➤ Define Production Mode
2. Select New Entries (refer to Figure 3-17).

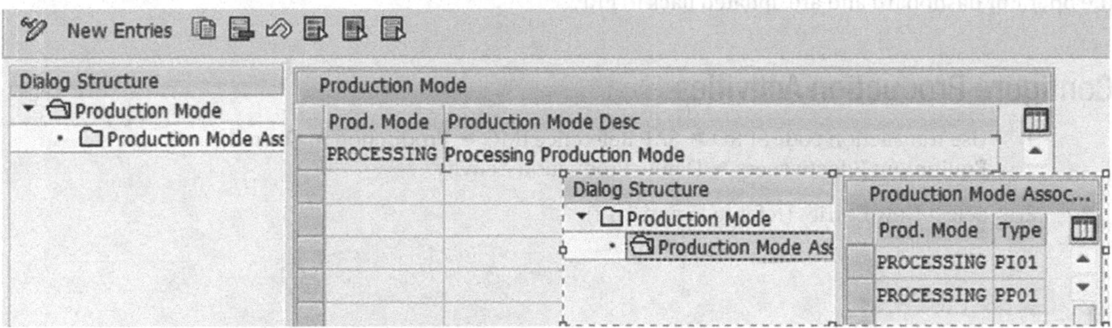

***Figure 3-17.** Configuration of production modes*

3. Enter the production mode name; e.g., Processing.
4. Enter the description for the production mode.
5. Select the created entry and select the "Production mode associated order type" option in the left-hand hierarchy.
6. Select New Entries.
7. Enter the production mode created in step 3.
8. Enter the production order type maintained in PP and PP/PI viz PI01 and PP01. PI01 is the order type for process order and PP01 is the order type for production order.
9. Save the entries.

Production Activities

Typically on a shop floor different types of production activities are carried out, namely processing, setup, changeover, consuming, and so on. This normally depends on the industry type. Hence, it is essential and good to have a solution that will allow for configuring different production activities during order execution. The operator should be able to visualize the current production activity, which will ensure all the different activities are captured with respect to duration. This will help in analyzing the line performance and efficiency within the shift.

Production activity in OEE allows the configuration of production into multiple process groups like line setup, consuming, producing, changeover, cleaning, and so forth as per your plant requirements. Configuring production activities in ERP and downloading to OEE enables the shop-floor operator to capture the actual duration of different production activities. Hence, manual errors are avoided as the system captures the actual shop-floor information with minimal manual inputs.

For example, for an order with configured production activities, the user is visually shown the sequential production phases and prompted to follow the sequential process. The operator has the flexibility to start the right production activity/phase as per the line's requirements, and this information is saved in the OEE database.

Production activity is totally independent of OEE calculations. It is again a filter or dimension used in HANA to analyze OEE KPIs.

Production activities can also be leveraged to record the standard values defined for a work center in PP and PP/PI, though this is not mandatory. The standard activities defined for the work center are captured via the operator dashboard and are updated back to ERP.

Configure Production Activities

1. Use transaction code SPRO ➤ SAP Reference IMG ➤ Production ➤ Overall Equipment Effectiveness ➤ Define Production Activity

2. Select New Entries (refer to Figure 3-18).

Production Activity

Prod. Activity	RecTypeGrp	Production Act Desc
PROCESSING	Variable activity	SHOP FLOOR ORDER PROCESSING
	Variable activity	
	Variable activity	

Figure 3-18. *Configuration of production activities*

3. Enter the production activity name and description.

4. Assign a RecTypeGrp to associate the OEE activity with the activities defined in PP and PP/PI for the work center under costing.

   RecTypeGrp, or Record type group, refers to how different production activities are collected during the order execution. For example, production activities can be setup time, machine time, labor time, or any other custom activities. These activities are grouped under specific record type groups like setup, teardown, variable activity, and so on depending on the purpose of each activity.

5. Save the production activity.

KPI Configuration

In chapter 1, we discussed the purpose and benefits of KPI, typically for a manufacturing industry.

In this section, we will look at how the OEE solution enables you to configure and use the KPIs.

SAP OEE allows you to configure any type of KPI. By default, it comes with the predefined design for the calculation of four KPIs, namely availability, performance, quality, and OEE.

The defined KPIs are associated with plant hierarchy nodes as per your plant requirements; A Plant hierarchy node which is marked for "Report Production" signifies that KPIs are calculated at this level. Hence, as per the plant requirement, the "Report Production" check box should be enabled. This node is ideally the work center node. Different KPIs can be configured for different plant hierarchy nodes.

Each KPI is to be defined with a target, which can vary for each node. These KPIs, which are integrated with plant hierarchy, are downloaded to OEE for real-time calculation and monitoring based on their target values. The KPIs are updated in real-time in the color combination based on the target range defined. Refer to Plant hierarchy configuration section Figure 3-44 in the current chapter to understand on the color combinations.

SAP OEE allows the definition of custom KPIs apart from the preceding four standard KPIs. A custom logic needs to be developed to calculate the custom KPI, and custom configurations must be done to display the custom KPI in the operator dashboard.

KPI Configuration

1. Use transaction code SPRO ➤ SAP Reference IMG ➤ Production ➤ Overall Equipment Effectiveness ➤ Define KPIs
2. By default, four standard KPIs will be available, and they should not be deleted.
3. Select New Entries to configure a custom KPI (refer to Figure 3-19).

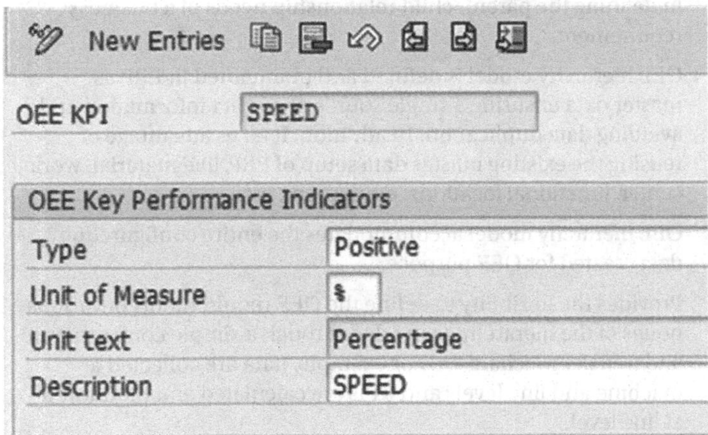

Figure 3-19. *Configuration of KPI*

4. Enter the KPI name.
5. Select the type. Type can be positive (high positive value close to target value is desirable), negative (low negative value close to target value is desirable), or bidirectional (value can be greater or lesser than the target value).
6. Select the UOM and description.
7. Save the entries.

Hierarchy Model in OEE

A hierarchy is a relational model composed of systems and sub-systems; it represents multiple levels of detail in describing the organization, plant, or production line. The model reflects how systems and sub-systems fit together, interrelate, and operate to provide the intended business function. As such, the hierarchy reflects both the structural and process flow characteristics of the plant or production line.

SAP OEE follows the hierarchy model in defining the structural model of a typical organization, right from an enterprise unit to machines on a shop floor of a plant.

The SAP OEE solution is capable of working with a multi-plant landscape to execute shop-floor orders, capture production and loss information, and calculate the KPIs and analytics reporting.

In this process, SAP OEE is expected to fulfill certain requirements and address the challenges from an execution-platform perspective. Table 3-1 lists the plant requirements and how SAP OEE addresses each requirement using the hierarchy model.

Table 3-1. *Requirements Versus Solution for OEE Hierarchy Model*

Requirement	Solution
Need to collate data from multiple plants for performance analysis	OEE hierarchy model enables data collection at machine and line nodes of hierarchy and aggregation at other nodes, ensuring better data modeling and analytics.
Corporate and plant-specific data should be configurable and flexible	OEE hierarchy model is completely configurable and flexible in defining the parent–child relationship needs of a business requirement.
Avoid data duplication and reuse capability	OEE hierarchy model is defined and maintained in ERP as master data ensuring a single source of correct information and avoiding data duplication. In addition, it takes advantage of reusing the existing master data setup of ERP, like material, work center, functional locations, equipment, etc.
Easy to use and configure	OEE hierarchy model accommodates the entire configuration data created for OEE purpose.
Flexible in terms of KPI calculations; i.e., system should be able to calculate KPI at plant/line/machine level as per the business requirements	Provides the flexibility to define the OEE requirements of various nodes of the hierarchy as needed through a simple configuration and transfer mechanism. For example, data are collected at machine and line levels and KPIs are calculated and monitored at line level.
Should follow a centralized approach in utilizing the data across multiple plants	OEE hierarchy configurations are centralized so the comprehensive list of elements can be defined, configured, and used in all plants, ensuring data consistency. However, plant-specific configurations are also facilitated.
Easy multi-plant performance reporting and analysis	Using HANA, OEE ensures easy analysis of performance reporting, as well as performance comparisons with a node classification for each node of the hierarchy model.

Global Hierarchy

Global hierarchy in OEE represents an organization or enterprise's hierarchy. There are four node types–corporate, region, country, and plant–which can be used in a global hierarchy, with plant as the lowest-level node.

The global hierarchy is used above the plant hierarchy for reporting and analyzing OEE across the plants. To configure both global and plant hierarchies, the hierarchy templates need to be defined.

Global Hierarchy Template Configurations

Hierarchy templates are required for configuring global and plant hierarchies. Typically, for an enterprise under a global hierarchy, different plant hierarchy templates (if the plant model is different) should be defined and used as the foundation when creating the plant hierarchy for each plant. These templates ensure hassle-free configuration of multiple and varied plant hierarchies. This section will detail how to configure the global hierarchy template.

1. Use transaction code SPRO and open SAP Reference IMG ➤ Production ➤ Overall Equipment Effectiveness ➤ Define Hierarchy Template

   Select New Entries and enter the new hierarchy template name–e.g., "GLOBALOEE." In the main window, check the "Global" checkbox. This is an indicator for a global hierarchy, as shown in Figure 3-20.

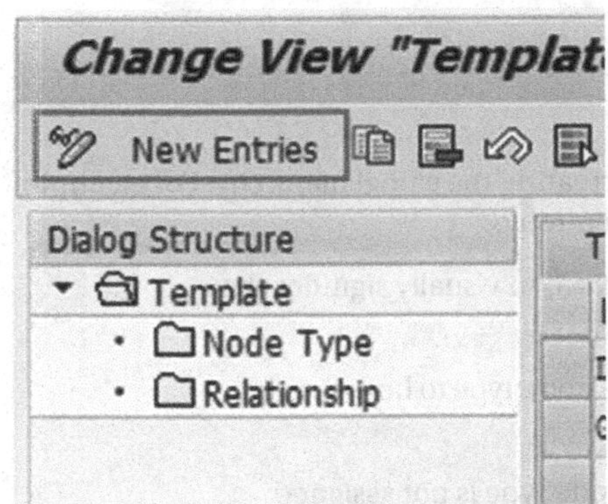

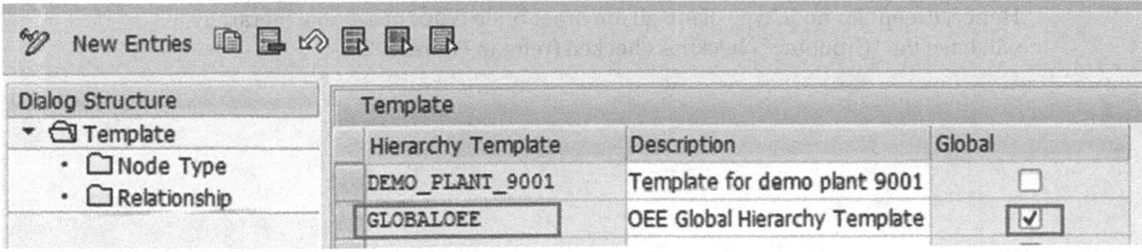

Figure 3-20. Configure global hierarchy template

2. Select the created template and then select Node Type on the left-hand pane as shown in Figure 3-21. Node-type configuration defines the different nodes required for a global hierarchy. The four nodes are enterprise, region, country, and plant, with the lowest node being plant. The other three nodes are flexible and can be defined as per the enterprise requirements. For example, the hierarchy nodes can be defined as region, country, site, and plant.

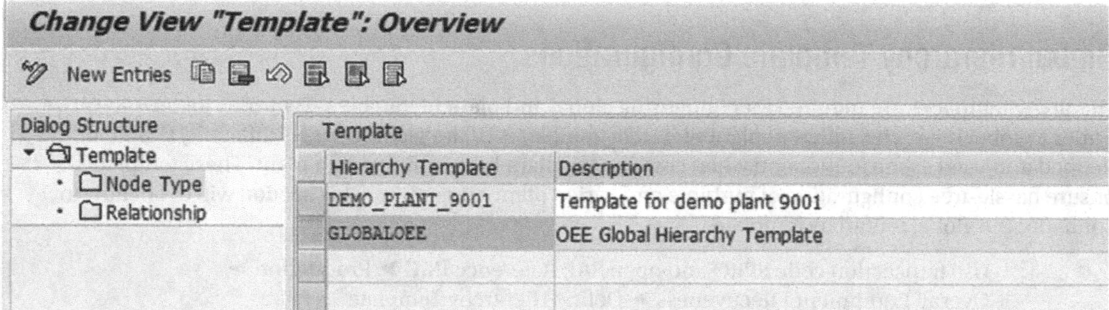

Figure 3-21. *Configure global hierarchy template: node type*

3. To define the node type, select New Entries and follow the steps in the following section for each node type (refer to Figure 3-21).

Defining Node Type

In this step, you will define the node type that will be used when creating the global hierarchy. For example, enterprise is a node type that forms the root node of the global hierarchy.

1. Display icon: Select the relevant icon from the list. This icon visually signifies the node type.

2. Node type description: Meaningful description of the node type to be created; e.g., enterprise.

3. Check "Grouping" checkbox. This signifies that the node type is not assigned to any work center, machine, or plant for planning or maintenance purposes. Hence, except for node type plant, all the other node types of a global hierarchy will have the "Grouping" checkbox checked (refer to Figure 3-22).

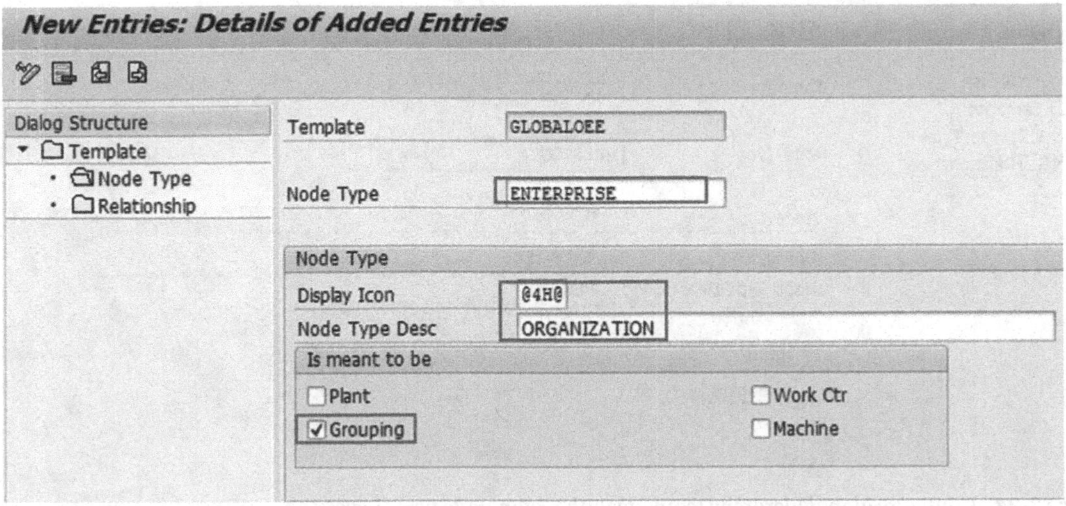

Figure 3-22. Configure global hierarchy template with node type Enterprise (Level 1)

4. Follow steps 1 to 3 to create other child node types like region, country, and plant (refer to Figures 3-23, 3-24, and 3-25).

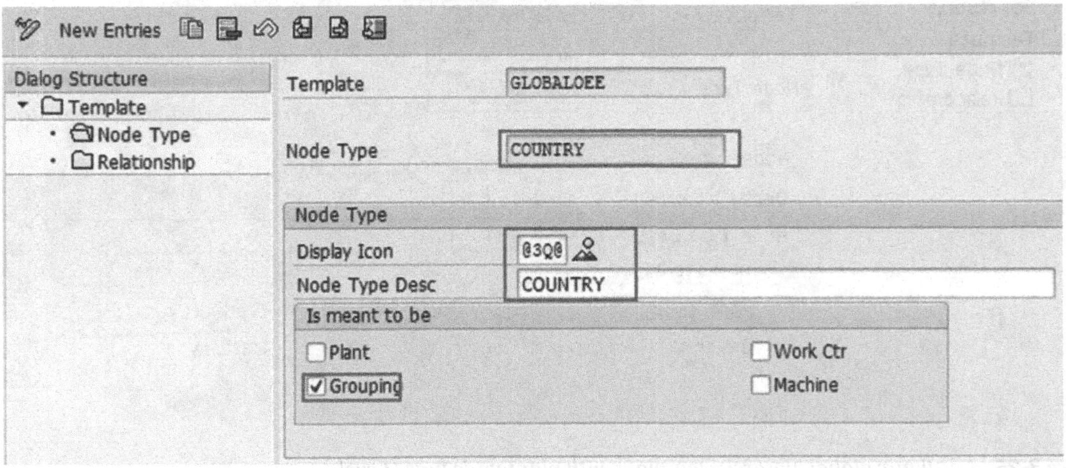

Figure 3-23. Configure global hierarchy template with country node type (Level 2)

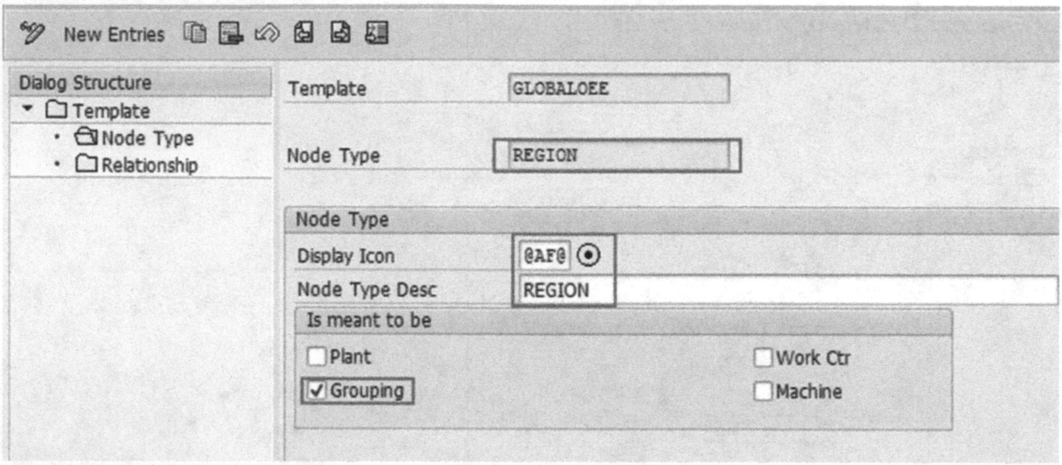

Figure 3-24. *Configure global hierarchy template with region node type (Level 3)*

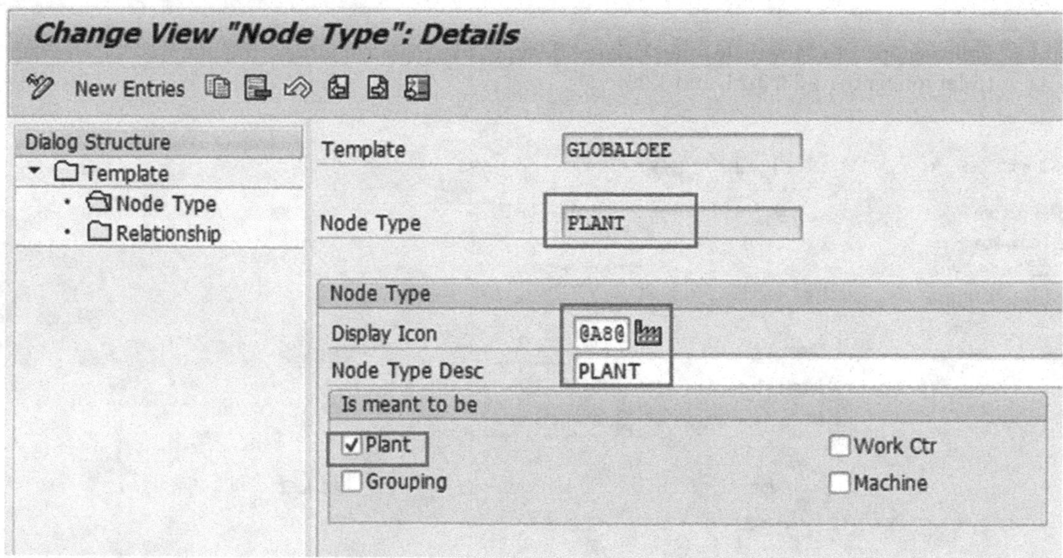

Figure 3-25. *Configure global hierarchy template with plant node type (Level 4)*

5. Go back to the main screen and select the Relationship option by selecting the global template and then New Entries (refer to Figure 3-26).

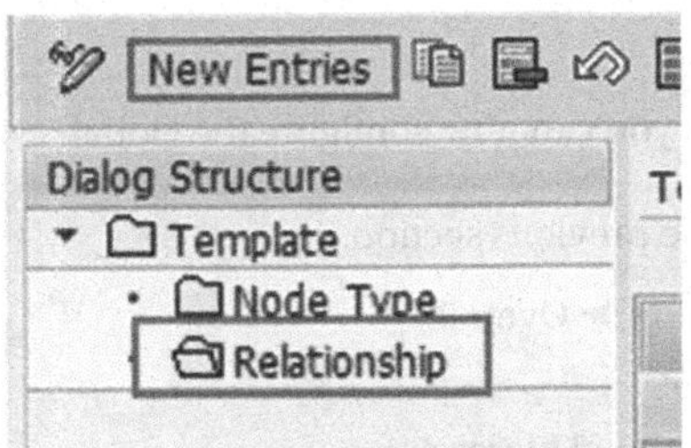

Figure 3-26. Configure global hierarchy template's node relationship

6. "Relationship" for a global hierarchy is a configuration to define the hierarchical relationship between the different node types created.

7. Enter the following parent-child relationships in a sequence as shown in Figure 3-27.

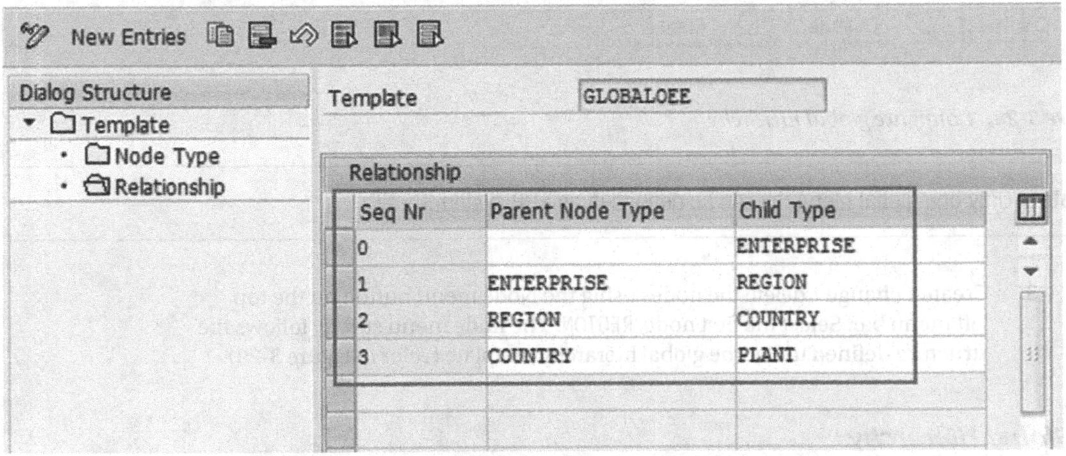

Figure 3-27. Configure global hierarchy template's node relationships

8. Sequence 0 at the top has the first node, enterprise, of the global hierarchy. Since there is no parent node for the first node, add it as a child type.

9. Sequence 1, region, is a child node with enterprise as its parent node .

10. Follow the previous steps to create all the nodes until the last node, plant.

11. Save the entries.

Global Hierarchy Configuration

You have configured the global hierarchy template. Using this template, you can now configure the global hierarchy.

Prerequisite: Create a global hierarchy template as described in the previous section.

1. On the SAP Easy Access menu, choose Logistics ➤ Production ➤ Overall Equipment Effectiveness ➤ Master Data ➤ Global Hierarchy
2. Enter a global hierarchy name and select Create. Select the global hierarchy template to be used (refer to Figure 3-28).

Figure 3-28. *Configure global hierarchy*

■ **Note** Only one global hierarchy can be defined in an ERP system.

3. Create / change / delete the nodes using the Node menu button on the top left menu bar. Select the first node, `REGION`. The node menu strictly follows the structure defined under the global hierarchy template (refer to Figure 3-29).

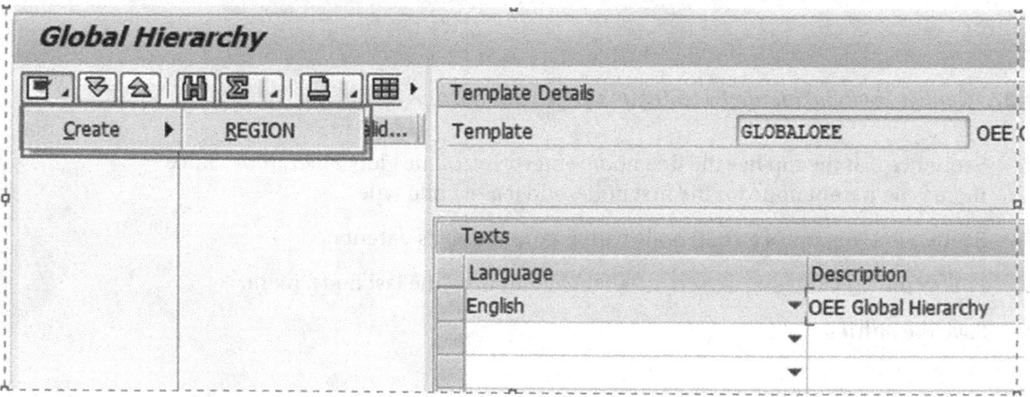

Figure 3-29. *Configure global hierarchy nodes*

4. Enter the region name (e.g., APAC) and click Enter.
5. Once the region is added, select the region and click the Node menu button to create the next node, country. Enter the country name and click Enter (refer to Figure 3-30).

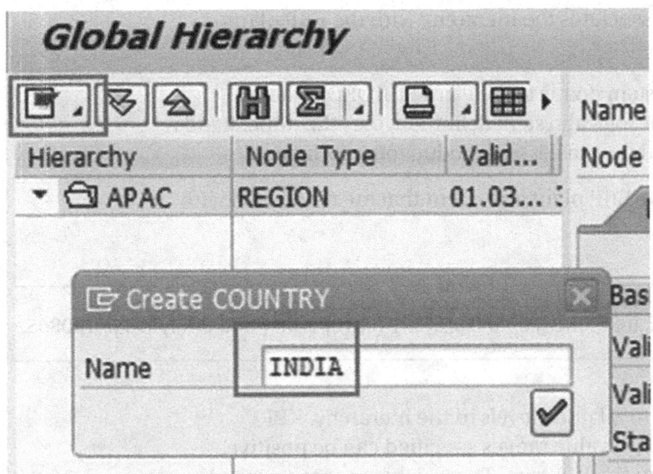

Figure 3-30. Configure global hierarchy nodes: Country

6. Follow the same steps until the last node, plant, is created.
7. For each node type, additional information (refer to Figure 3-31) can be provided to fill in the Details and KPI Targets tabs. For all the nodes other than plant, the Details tab has the validity periods and the status. The status of the hierarchy is displayed in the Status field, which is set to New for a newly configured global hierarchy.

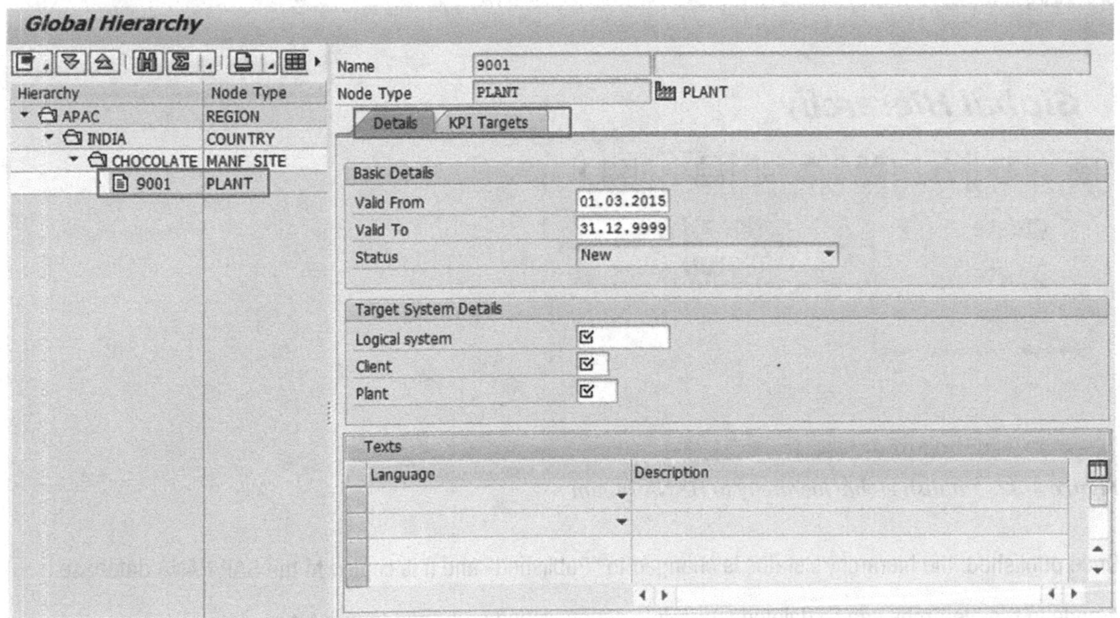

Figure 3-31. Configure global hierarchy: node information

8. For a plant node, the Details tab associates the hierarchy with the ERP plant, client, and logical system.

   a. Logical system: The logical system points to the Plant MII(OEE) system dedicated for plant(s). With the logical system definition, the OEE understands to which plant, it needs to send the master and production information.

   b. Plant and client: These are the ERP plant and client that are associated with the OEE master data.

■ **Note** A Plant node can be assigned to more than one global hierarchy for reporting and analytics purposes.

---

9. KPI Targets: KPIs can be assigned to all node levels in the hierarchy. KPI targets are material independent. KPI value ranges specified can be positive, negative, or bi-directional based on the KPI type. These value ranges are used while generating analytic reports. KPI targets for standard KPIs like availability, performance, quality, and OEE are defined here. Please refer to the KPI configuration section for more details.

■ **Note** Global hierarchy is transferred to the HANA system.

To publish a hierarchy to SAP HANA, select the "Publish" option available on the secondary click of the different nodes of the hierarchy (refer to Figure 3-32). If SLT is configured, the hierarchy information will be replicated to SAP HANA.

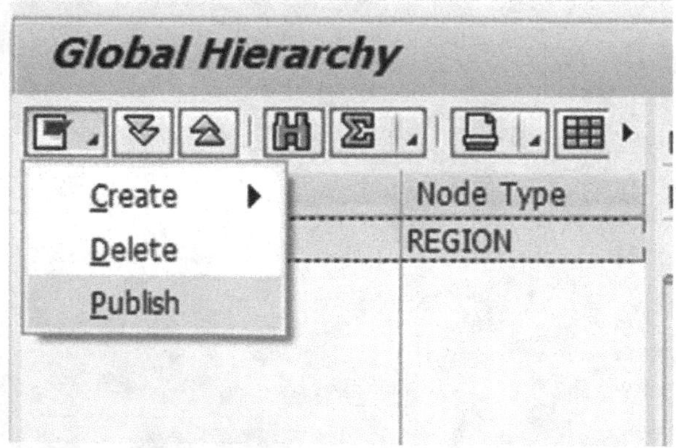

***Figure 3-32.** Publish global hierarchy to HANA system*

Once published, the hierarchy's status is changed to "Published" and it is copied to the SAP HANA database.

A node in the hierarchy can be deleted only if it is not published or is valid from a future date.

Benefits of Global Hierarchy

The following are the benefits of using the global hierarchy:

- Global hierarchy enables to define the structure of an organization distributed globally, and gives a single and simple view of their global and plant-level performance.
- Global hierarchy is utilized for reporting and analyzing OEE and production data and losses by aggregating the information at the plant level under a region or country level.

Plant Hierarchy

Plant hierarchy is defined for each plant under a global hierarchy. Similar to global hierarchy, plant hierarchy is configured by creating hierarchy templates for the plant node.

The plant hierarchy model in SAP OEE is a definition of the shop-floor model. The plant hierarchy template in SAP OEE is used to define the actual production-line hierarchy for a plant. The template has multiple levels so that variants can be created. Only one plant hierarchy template can be used to define the OEE hierarchy for a plant. Multiple node types can be configured for a plant hierarchy, the highest level of the plant hierarchy must be a plant, and the lowest node should be a machine node (if exist) else it can be any other node.

The plant hierarchy follows the parent–child node relationships shown in Figure 3-33.

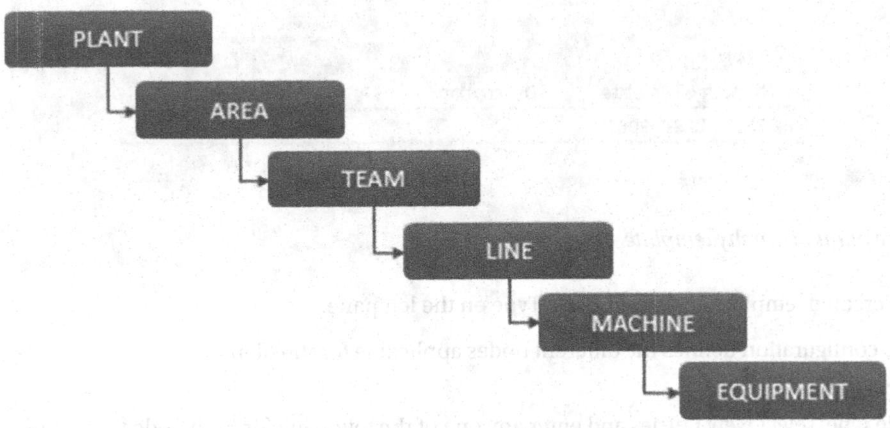

Figure 3-33. *Plant hierarchy parent–child node relationships*

Plant Hierarchy Template Configuration

The plant hierarchy template is similar to the global hierarchy template, with a variation in the number of nodes that can be configured.

1. To configure the plant hierarchy template use transaction code SPRO ➤ SAP Reference IMG ➤ Production ➤ Overall Equipment Effectiveness ➤ Define Hierarchy Template

2. Select New Entries and enter the new hierarchy template name; e.g., `DEMO_PLANT_9001`. In the main screen, do not check the "Global" checkbox, as it is a plant hierarchy and not a global hierarchy, as shown in Figure 3-34.

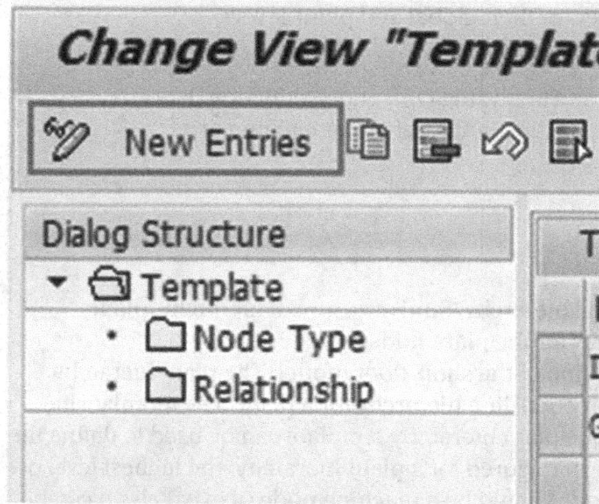

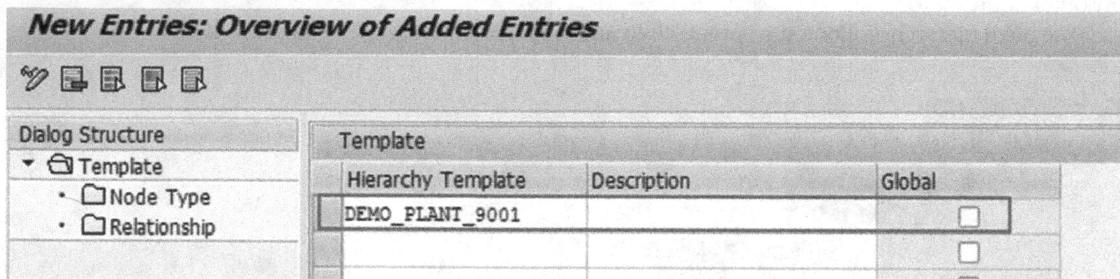

***Figure 3-34.** Configure plant hierarchy template*

3. Select the created template and select Node Type on the left pane.

4. Node type configuration defines the different nodes applicable for the plant hierarchy.

To define the node type, select New Entries and enter any one of the following for each node type, as in Figure 3-35:

- Node type as Plant
- Node type as Area
- Node type as Team
- Node type as Line
- Node type as Machine

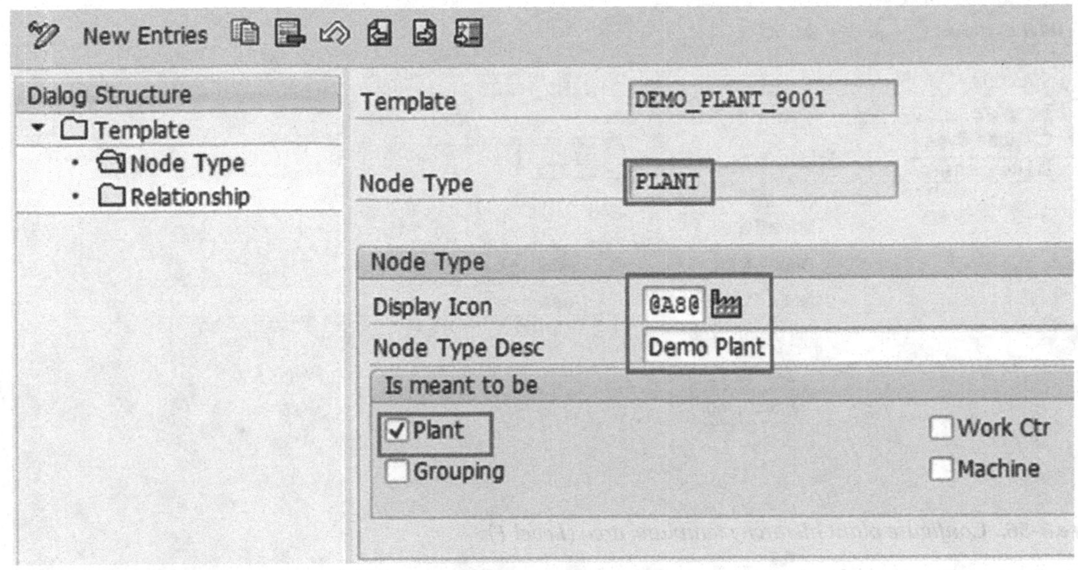

Figure 3-35. *Configure plant hierarchy template: plant (root node)*

Node Type as Plant

a. Node Type: `PLANT`. A plant is typically a site that is a physical location with facilities.

b. Display Icon: Select the relevant icon from the list.

c. Node Type Description: Meaningful description of the node type being created

d. Check "Plant" checkbox, as the node type is plant. Refer to Figure 3-35.

Node Type as Area

Areas are the physical zones in a factory where resources are consumed or stored, activities are undertaken, and inputs are transformed into outputs.

a. Node Type: `AREA` (refer to Figure 3-36)

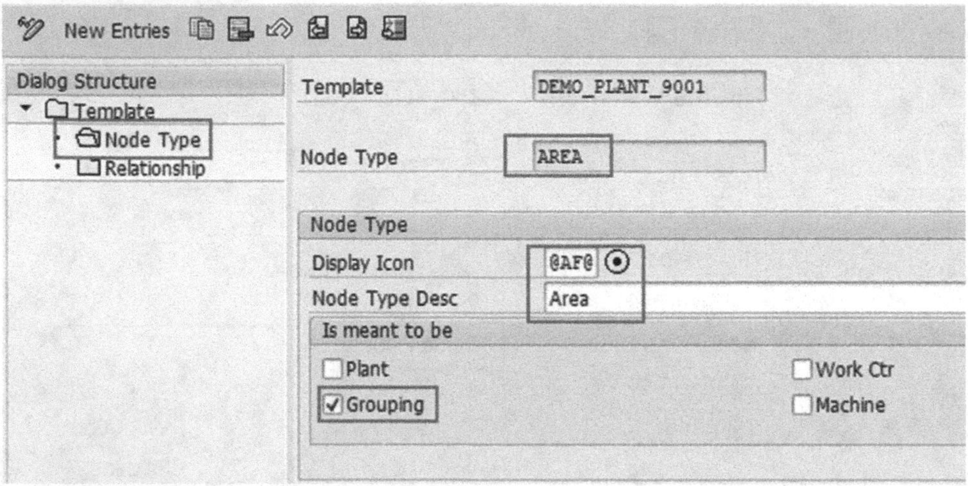

Figure 3-36. Configure plant hierarchy template: area (Level 1)

For example, in an ice cream manufacturing industry, the processing area has different subareas like mixing, filling, and packing.

b. Display Icon: Select the relevant icon from the list.

c. Node Type Description: Meaningful description of the node type being created

d. Check "Grouping" checkbox. This signifies that the node type is not assigned to any work center, machine, or plant for planning or maintenance purposes.

Node Type as Team

A typical processing area can have different teams, like production team, quality team, materials movement team, and so on. Different teams can be defined under the area node, and their production can be reported and KPI can be monitored and analyzed.

a. Node Type: TEAM (refer to Figure 3-37)

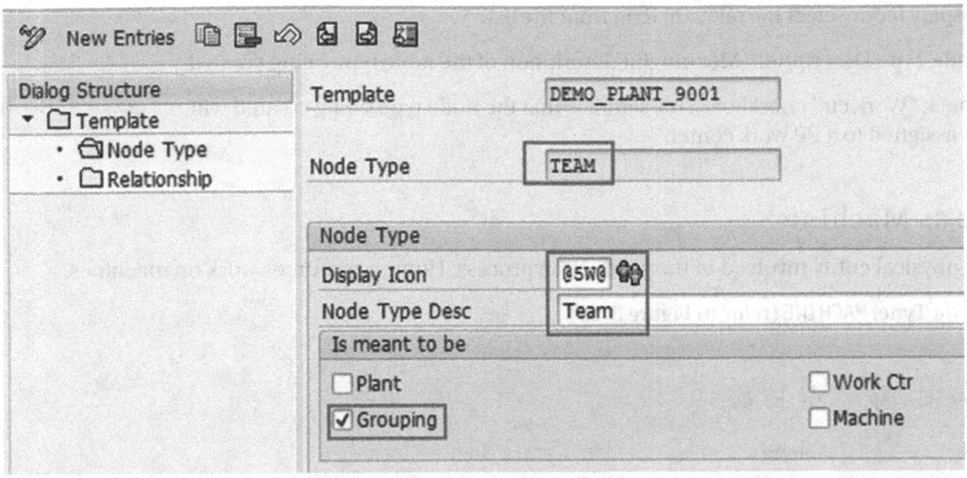

Figure 3-37. Configure plant hierarchy template: team (Level 2)

b. Display Icon: Select the relevant icon from the list.

c. Node Type Description: Meaningful description of the node type being created

d. Check "Grouping" checkbox. This signifies that the node type is not assigned to any work center, machine, or plant for planning or maintenance purposes.

Node Type as Line

A line or a work center consists of one or more machines, processes, tasks, or operations that together amount to a step within the work of that area. In OEE, a line is always associated with a PP work center for planning, production, and costing purposes.

a. Node Type: LINE (refer to Figure 3-38)

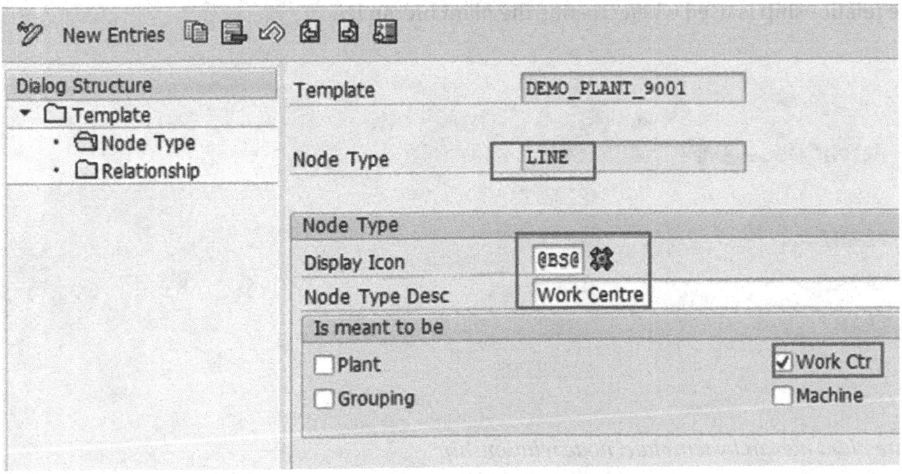

Figure 3-38. Configure plant hierarchy template: line (Level 3)

b. Display Icon: Select the relevant icon from the list.

c. Node Type Description: Meaningful description of the node type being created

d. Check "Work ctr" checkbox. This signifies that the node type being created will be assigned to a PP work center.

Node Type as Machine

A machine is a physical entity involved in the production process. Human resources work on machines.

1. Node Type: `MACHINE` (refer to Figure 3-39)

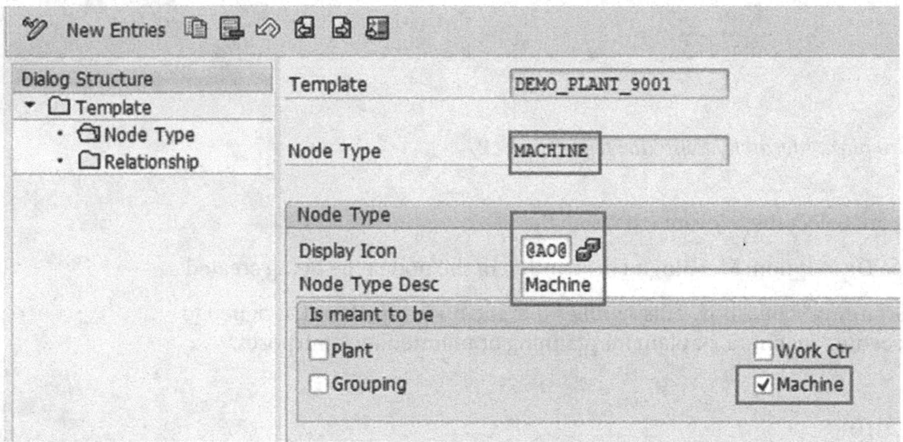

Figure 3-39. Configure plant hierarchy template: machine (Level 4)

Configure plant hierarchy template: node relationship (Refer to Fig 3-40). Once all the node types are configured and saved, the relationship button displays the configured nodes and their relationship as parent and child. The same relationship is used when creating the plant hierarchy.

Relationship

Seq Nr	Parent Node Type	Child Type
0		PLANT
1	PLANT	AREA
2	AREA	TEAM
3	TEAM	LINE
4	LINE	MACHINE

Figure 3-40. Configure plant hierarchy template: node relationship

2. Display Icon: Select the relevant icon from the list.
3. Node Type Description: Meaningful description of the node type being created
4. Check "Machine" checkbox. This signifies that the node type being created can be associated with the equipment and its functional location in plant maintenance.

■ **Note** You can define any node type for Global or Plant Hierarchy as per the business requirements and the above are just some examples. You can define multiple node types, but the last node of the plant hierarchy should be of type machine, if present. Otherwise it can be of type work center.

Plant Hierarchy Configuration

You have configured the plant hierarchy template. Using this template, you can now configure the plant hierarchy itself.

Prerequisite: Create a plant hierarchy template as described earlier.

1. On the SAP Easy Access menu, choose ➤ Logistics ➤ Production ➤ Overall Equipment Effectiveness ➤ Master Data ➤ Plant Hierarchy
2. Enter plant name "9001" and click Create. The created plant hierarchy can be viewed and changed using the "Display" and "Change" options.
3. Select the plant hierarchy template to be used; e.g., `DEMO_PLANT_9001` (refer to Figure 3-41).

***Figure 3-41.** Configure plant hierarchy*

4. Create / change / delete the nodes using the Node menu button on the top left menu bar. Select the first node, `PLANT`. The node menu strictly follows the structure defined under plant hierarchy template; e.g., plant, area, team, line, machine, and equipment.
5. Enter the plant name (e.g., 9001) and click Enter.
6. Once the plant is added, select the plant and click the Node menu button to create the next node, area. Enter the area name and click Enter.
7. Follow the same steps until the last node is created (refer to Figure 3-42).

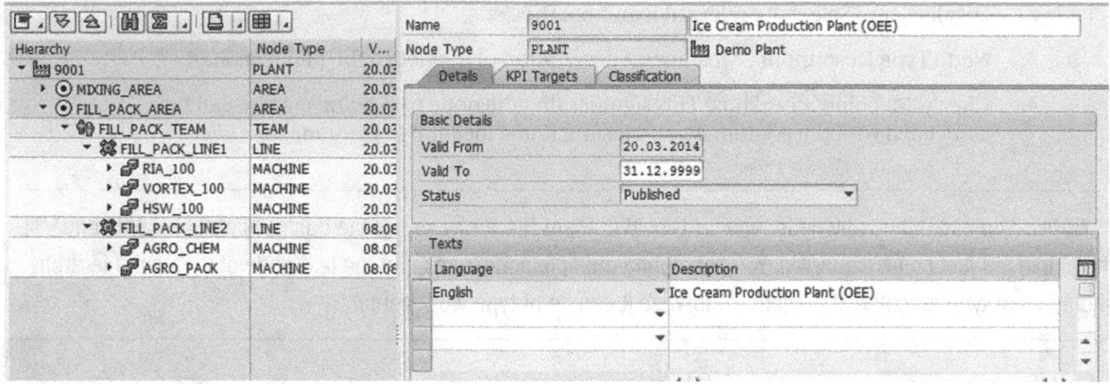

Figure 3-42. *Configure plant hierarchy nodes*

Now all the nodes of a plant hierarchy are created and ready for publishing to OEE. Let us review the additional information that you will need to configure for each node of the plant hierarchy.

Plant hierarchies have multiple configurations for each node. You can configure the specific options based on the business requirements.

For example, a plant may have a requirement to calculate and monitor OEE KPI at the line level and collect data at both machine and line levels. Also, for every line node, different KPIs may be applicable, as each node has a specific classification category for use in HANA analytics. All these requirements can be met in plant hierarchy node configurations.

■ **Note** Currently, OEE standard KPIs are calculated at work center level only.

Let us now see the details of each configuration option under the different tabs of the plant hierarchy.

Details Tab

This tab defines the basic details like the validity of the plant node, a description of the node in the configured language, and the status of the node, as shown in Figure 3-43.

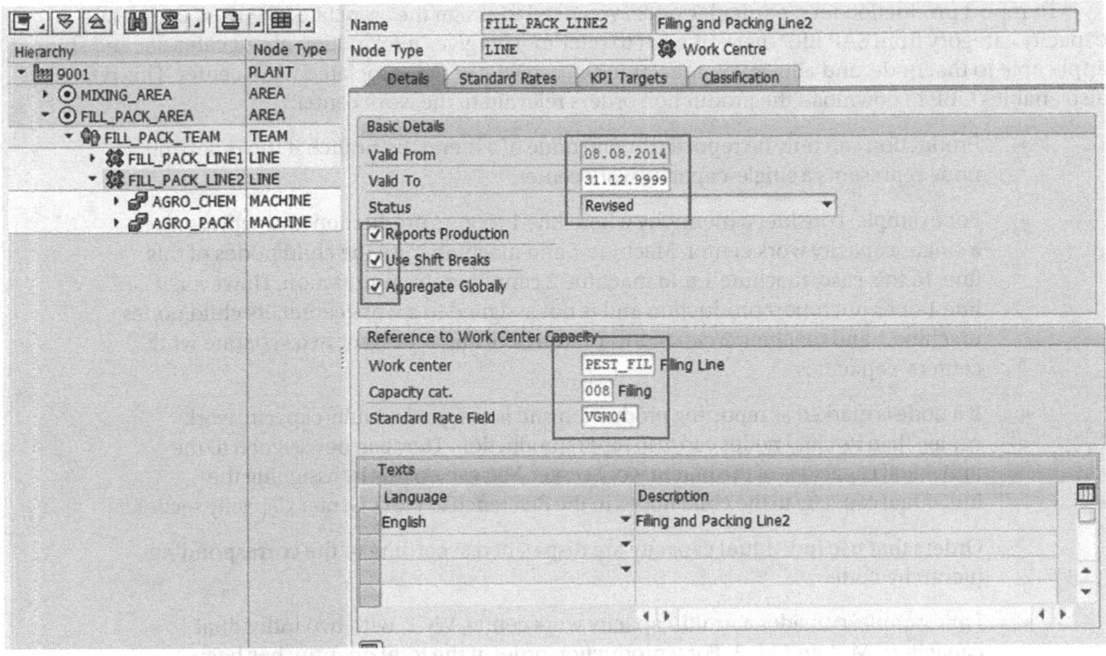

Figure 3-43. Configure plant hierarchy: details tab

Validity details:

The validity period of the plant hierarchy. Ideally, the Valid From date would be the date of hierarchy creation. However, you can define a specific validity period as shown in Figure 3-43.

Status:

The status of the plant hierarchy can be New, Published, Revised, or Deleted.

New ➤ Plant hierarchy node is created.

Revised ➤ Plant hierarchy node is modified.

Deleted ➤ Plant hierarchy node is marked deleted.

Published ➤ Plant hierarchy node is published to OEE. This status is a prerequisite to transfer the data from SAP ERP to SAP MII.

Texts:

You have to select the desired language and add a description for each node type. You can use this feature to maintain the description of the node type in different languages.

Reports Production:

You can report production at line and machine nodes in a plant hierarchy. For a line node, when "Reports Production" is enabled, production can be reported and the standard KPIs are calculated. For a machine node, when "Reports Production" is enabled, production can be reported, but no KPIs are calculated.

■ **Note** Report production is enabled for a machine node only if its work center's line behavior is configured to a "Multi-capacity single line" scenario. In this case, production can be collected and reported at every capacity level.

To report production for a particular node, you need to assign the associated PP work center and capacity category from SAP ERP that you want to refer to. This gives information about calendar and shifts applicable to that node, and allows you to refer to the capacity of the associated work center. This reference also enables OEE to download the production orders relevant to the work center.

- Production can only be reported at one node of a hierarchy branch if the reporting node represents a single-capacity work center.
- For example, consider a hierarchy where line 1 reports production and represents a single-capacity work center. Machine 1 and machine 2 are the child nodes of this line. In this case, machine 1 and machine 2 cannot report production. However, if line 1 does not report production and is not assigned to a work center, its child nodes machine 1 and machine 2 can report production, and represent two separate work centers' capacities.
- If a node is marked as reporting production and is assigned a multi-capacity work center, then its child nodes can also report production. They can be assigned to the individual capacities of the parent work center. You can do this by assigning the individual capacity to the child nodes in the Reference to Work Center Capacity section.

  Orders that use individual capacity are dispatched according to the corresponding hierarchy node.
- For example, consider a multi-capacity work center, WC1, with two individual capacities, M_1 and M_2. For a production order, if the total quantity has been split into individual capacities, then these split quantities are dispatched to the corresponding SAP OEE machine (capacity) nodes. These quantities are available at the machine nodes representing M_1 and M_2 on the OEE dashboard.

Reference to Work Center Capacity:

Work center: You need to assign the PP work center that is configured for planning, production, and costing purpose.

Capacity Cat.: Here, you need to assign the capacity category type of the work center being assigned.

Standard Rate Field: You can specify the standard rate of production using one of the standard value keys defined for the work center. Alternatively, you can also specify material-specific standard rates under the standard rate tab. When specified in both places, the standard rate field under the Details tab takes precedence.

Use Shift Breaks:

Every work center has the shift definitions in ERP. When the "Use Shift Breaks" option is checked, any shift breaks configured and existing in the shift definitions for the work center will be considered by OEE for OEE KPI calculations. Shift breaks will be accommodated as part of the loading time.

Aggregate Globally:

Select the "Aggregate Globally" option for a node if you want to include data reported at that node for KPI aggregation at the global level.

For example, production is reported only at the work center node, and hence KPIs will be calculated at this node. However, you want KPI calculated at the work center node to be aggregated at its parent node, team.

You can check this option for a child node only if its parent node is checked for this option. For example, the team node can be checked with this option only if the area node is checked with this option.

KPI Targets tab

The KPI Targets tab allows you to configure the standard and custom KPIs to be calculated and monitored for the selected node, and to define the KPI targets, KPI to be measured for a specific material (optional), KPI validity, type, and UOM.

KPI Targets:

Under this section, you can define the key performance indicators (KPIs) and their validity period for both standard and custom KPIs. The KPI definition can be material specific. If material is not specified, the KPI target is considered for all the materials (refer to Figure 3-44).

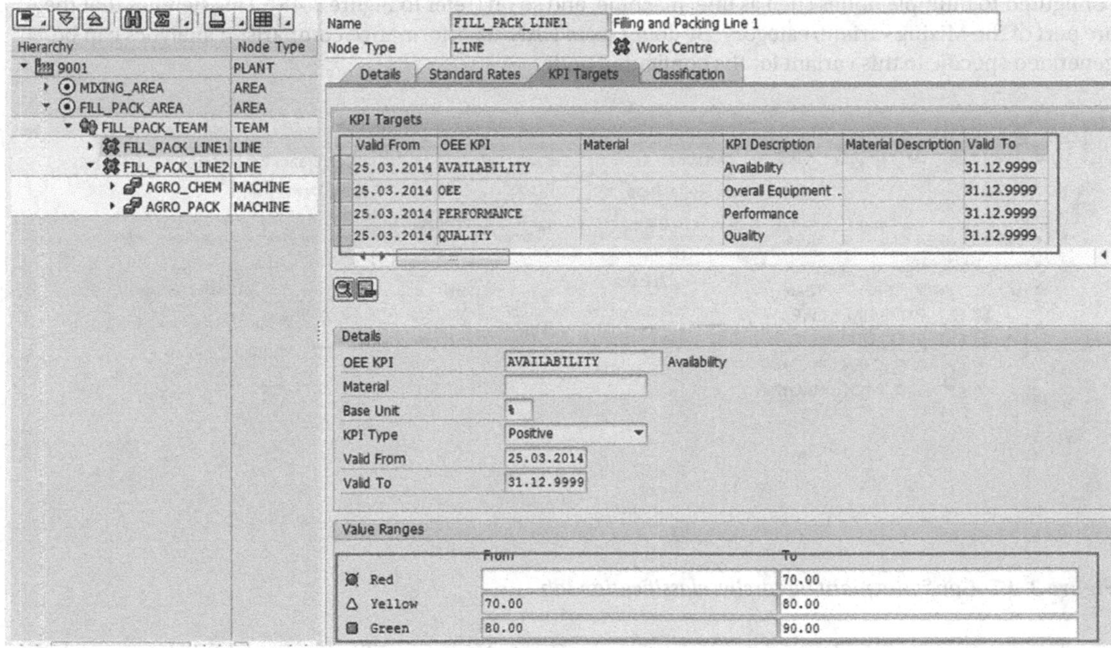

***Figure 3-44.** Configure plant hierarchy: KPI Targets tab*

You will need to create custom KPIs using KPI configuration to configure it here.

KPI Type, UOM, and Validity:

Under this section, you can define for a KPI its type, unit of measurement (UOM), and validity period. KPI can be positive, negative, or bi-directional based on the KPI being configured. These value ranges are used while generating analytic reports and on the real-time operator dashboard. You can define the unit of measurement for the KPI, along with its validity period (refer to Figure 3-44).

KPI Value Ranges:

Here, you can specify the target ranges of the KPI as per your plant requirements in the respective colors of red, yellow, and green, depending on the severity.

For example, you can set the OEE KPI targets as follows:

80 to 100 as green (higher/safe limit)

70 to 80 as Yellow (value limit before critical)

0 to 70 as red (critical value limit)

This target definition is reflected in the OEE KPI monitoring window of the OEE operator dashboard.

Classification Tab

Classification helps you to define the technical information about a node, which can be further used in analytics.

Hierarchy Node Classification:

This tab provides a mechanism for defining a category of classification with which multiple nodes in a hierarchy can be associated. This can be used as an additional dimension in the analytics for comparing performance across comparable assets in the plant hierarchy or across plants.

For example, if you want to compare the mixing process of two similar plants, say, that are producing ice cream, you can define the variant/category under classification as the Mixing work center, and this can be configured to multiple nodes such as line, machine, and so on (refer to Figure 3-45). This signifies that they are part of the Mixing variant/category. By doing so, in HANA, performance comparison analytics can be generated specific to this variant for the configured nodes.

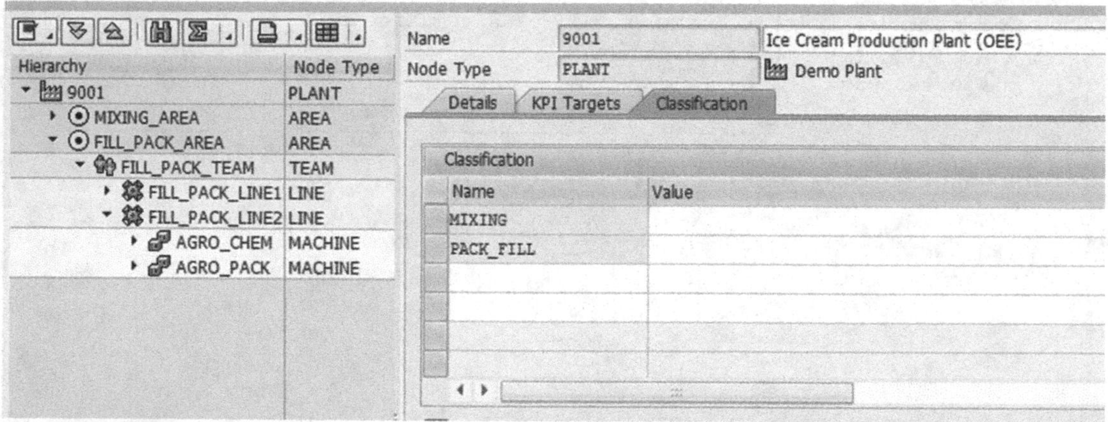

***Figure 3-45.** Configure plant hierarchy: classification tab*

The prerequisite is to define these variants under Create Node Classification, which will be covered in section: Hierarchy Node Classification below.

Standard Rates Tab

Production typically produces a product at the defined rate of speed or, in other words, at the "standard rate." This standard rate is material dependent. OEE KPI requires speed loss as one of the inputs to determine the standard "Performance" KPI. Speed loss is determined or calculated using the standard rate.

For a node at which you want to report production, you must define the standard rate (refer to Figure 3-46). Specify the time period for which the standard rate is valid. The standard rate is defined for a material. You can associate the relevant Task List Type, Routing/Recipe Group, and Operation/Activity. Define the nominal quantity that should be produced in a particular duration. To do this, in the Standard Rate section specify:

- Quantity and its UoM
- Duration and its UoM

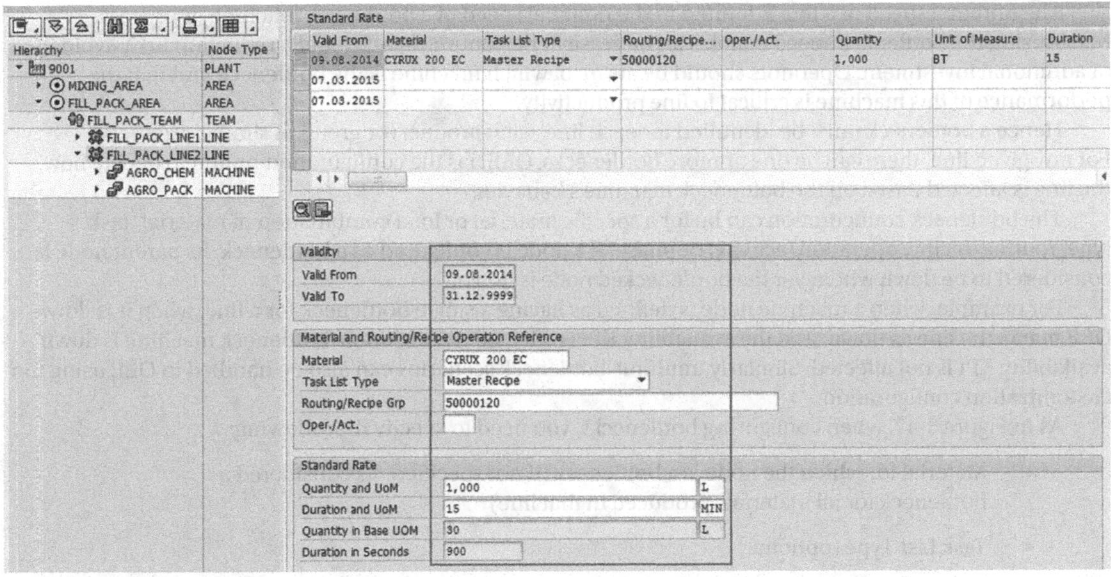

Figure 3-46. Configure plant hierarchy: Standard Rate tab

For example: 100 litres of quantity is produced in 15 minutes

---

■ **Note** If quantity and duration with the UoMs are not specified here, you cannot start the order operation from the OEE Dashboard.

The UoM you specify here must be same as the UoM, or one of the alternate UoMs, maintained in the material master data. If the UoMs are different, quantity entered through the OEE dashboard cannot be confirmed in ERP.

Alternatively, you can specify the standard rate on the Details tab (in Standard Rate Field). In that case, OEE obtains the standard rate from the production or process order.

Similarly, you can add standard rates for multiple materials.

Bottlenecks Tab

Typically, a bottleneck is the slowest machine/machines or process/processes that limits the production of a line, reducing its nominal speed.

You can optionally mark a machine node as a bottleneck. Ideally, the machines are defined as `bottlenecks`.

■ **Note** Definition of a machine being a bottleneck is a plant-specific requirement. OEE allows you to configure single, multiple, and multiple parallel bottleneck machines for a line.

The nominal speed of a line is limited to the nominal speed of a bottleneck machine or process. Maximizing the bottleneck speed enables an increase in maximum capacity and a reduction in or avoidance of additional investment. Operators should be aware of which machine is the bottleneck and that the performance of this machine is critical to line productivity.

Hence a bottleneck must be identified for each line, each product (or group of similar products). For any given line, there can be one or more bottlenecks. OEE has the configuration option to decide how the line is affected based on the bottleneck machine's behavior.

The bottleneck configuration can be for a specific material or for a combination of material, task type, routing/recipe, operation/activity, or phase. If a node is configured as a bottleneck, its parent node is considered to be down whenever the bottlenecked node is down.

For example, when a machine node is defined as having a single bottleneck for a line, when it is down OEE marks the line as down, and the availability KPI is affected. When a non-bottleneck machine is down, availability KPI is not affected. Similarly, multiple bottleneck scenarios can also be handled in OEE using the customization configuration.

As in Figure 3-47, when configuring bottlenecks, you need to specify the following:

- Material for which the node is a bottleneck (if not specified, its considered a bottleneck for all materials produced in that line)
- Task List Type (optional)
- Routing/Recipe (optional)
- Operation (optional)
- The data collection element through which this bottleneck node's downtime will be captured
- Validity period

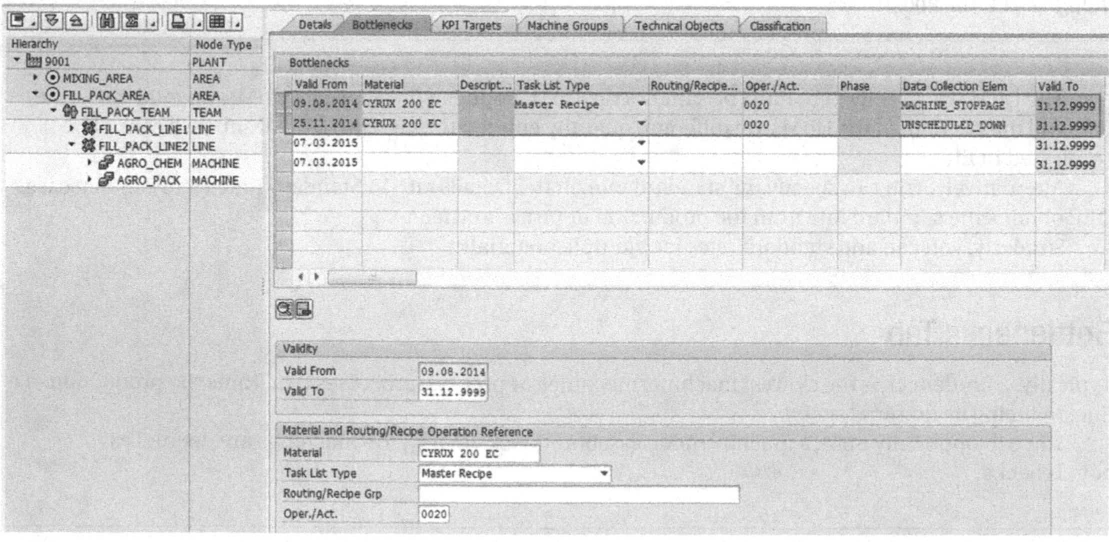

Figure 3-47. Configure plant hierarchy: Bottlenecks tab

Machine Groups Tab

The Machine Groups tab enables the logical grouping of the machines, similar to hierarchy nodes. The logical grouping acts as an additional dimension for comparing the performance of comparable machines in the plant hierarchy across multiple plants. Machine groups are applicable to the machine node only.

For example, a machine group could be created to specify the vendor of the machines, or machines with similar functionality supplied by different vendors, and so on, so that similar machines' performance can be compared, and different machines from a specific vendor can be compared for performance, acting as a source to identify the defects.

To configure a machine group, you need to create the machine group (please refer to Figure 3-48) using "Configure Machine groups" and add it under the Machine Groups tab for a machine node.

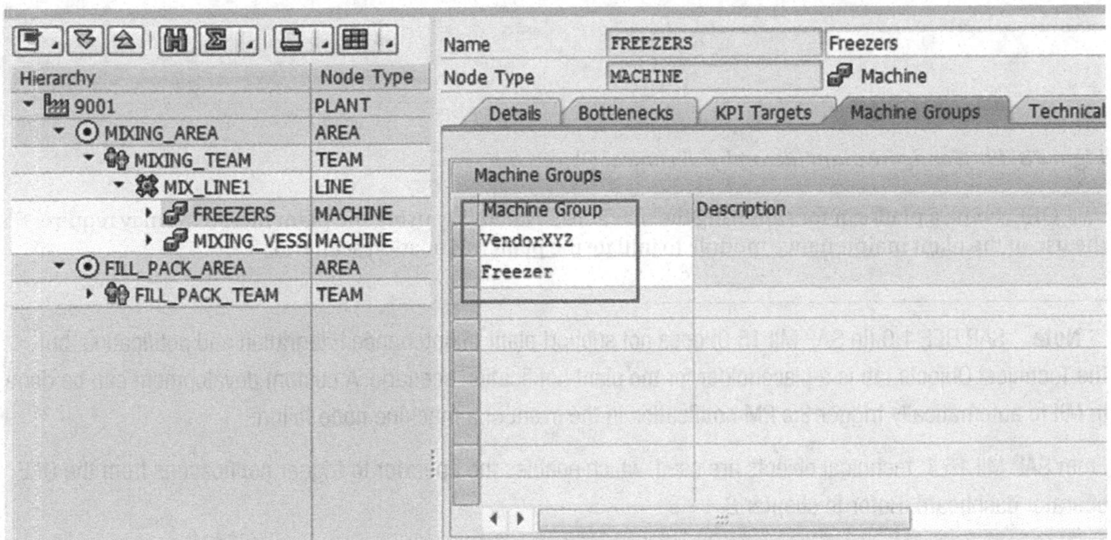

Figure 3-48. *Configure plant hierarchy: Machine Groups tab*

Technical Objects Tab

You can use the Technical Objects tab (refer to Figure 3-49) for a machine node to associate a machine with the existing functional location and the equipment of the plant maintenance module and thereby trigger PM notification upon machine failure.

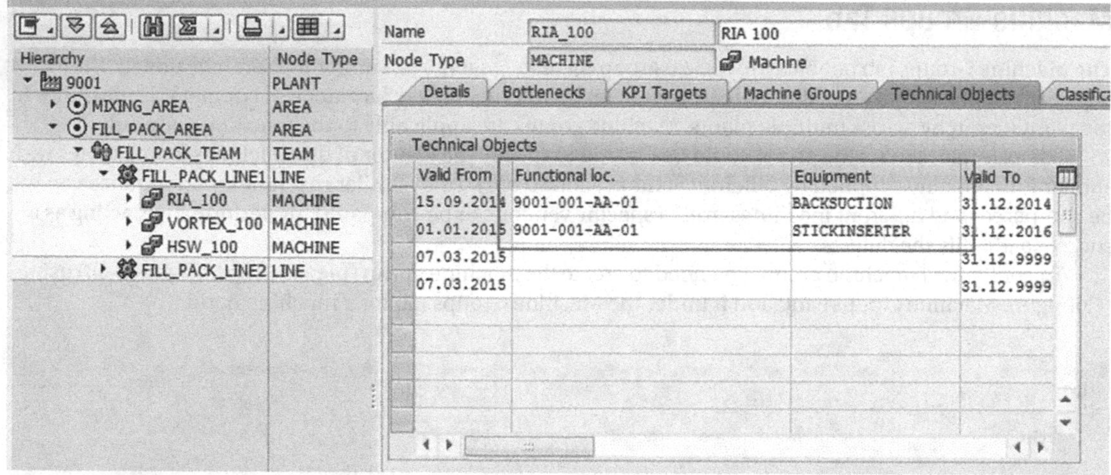

Figure 3-49. Configure plant hierarchy: Technical Objects tab

OEE, being a platform for capturing the machine's availability using the plant hierarchy, may require the use of the plant maintenance module to initiate the plant notification scenario.

■ **Note** SAP OEE 1.0 (in SAP MII 15.0) does not support plant maintenance integration and notification, but the Technical Objects tab is a placeholder for the plant notification scenario. A custom development can be done in MII to automatically trigger the PM notification in the event of a machine node failure.

From SAP MII 15.1, technical objects are used, which enables the operator to trigger notifications from the OEE operator dashboard. Refer to chapter 8.

Under the Technical Objects tab, add the functional location, the associated equipment, and the validity period. Ensure that the functional location and its equipment list are configured for the OEE plant.

Now the details of all the plant hierarchy configurations applicable for every node are completed.

Save and publish the plant hierarchy by selecting the plant node (refer to Figure 3-50) which will send the Plant Hierarchy to the SAP MII system configured as logical system.

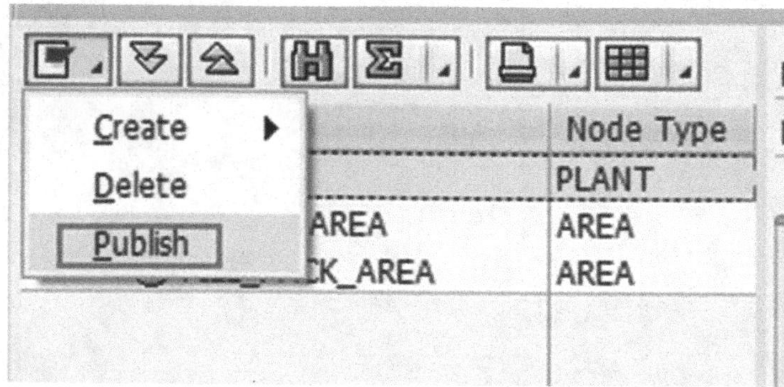

Figure 3-50. Configure plant hierarchy: Publish

Node Delete

You can delete a node only if:

- The node is not published or is valid from a future date. When you delete such a node, the node details no longer exist in the system, and events are not reported. The node is marked as deleted in the plant hierarchy.
- All downtimes reported either on the deleted node, or its parent or child nodes, are reported up. There are no orders running on the node or its parent or child nodes. This needs to be ensured manually before deleting the node.

Refer to Table 3-2 to understand the configurations applicable to each node.

***Table 3-2.** Plant Hierarchy Node Configuration Map*

Configurations Tab	Configuration Options	Plant	Area	Team	Line	Machine
Details	Validity	M	M	M	M	M
	Report Production	NA	U	U	M	U
	Use Shift Breaks	NA	U	U	O	U
	Aggregate Globally	NA	U	U	O	U
	Work Center Capacity, Capacity Cat, Standard Rate Field	NA	U	U	M	U
	Texts	M	M	M	M	M
KPI Targets	KPI Targets, UOM, Type, Validity and Ranges	U	U	U	U	U
Classification	Classification	O	NA	NA	O	O
Standard Rates	Standard Rate	NA	NA	NA	M	U
Bottlenecks	Basic Details	NA	NA	NA	NA	U
Machine Groups	Machine Groups	NA	NA	NA	NA	O
Technical Objects	Technical Objects	NA	NA	NA	O	U

Table Legend

M – Mandatory

O – Optional

U – User defined. Can be mandatory or optional based on business requirements.

NA – Not applicable

Reason Codes

A shop-floor machine can fail or go down for various reasons, like functional failure, material unavailability, operator unavailability, line failure, failure of another machine, and so on. Hence, capturing the right reason for the failure is essential.

Reason code is an identifier that uniquely identifies the reason why a machine is failed or down. Reason codes are the key piece information regarding the losses captured on the shop floor. They aid in performing a downtime analysis, a root-cause analysis, for every event.

Shop-floor machines are not intelligent enough to report the reason for their failure. Hence, it is a manual operator's decision to assign the right reason code at the right time for every machine or line failure.

Hence, OEE defines the reason code as master data, and it is represented in a hierarchical format along with the type of loss associated with the event. These reason codes are assigned to specific plant hierarchy nodes to avoid drilling down every time when assigning reason codes to losses.

Reason codes for specific time-element types will be displayed to the user. For example, any loss-of-time element types (UNSCD_DOWN and SCHED_DOWN) at the line node of the plant hierarchy are directly linked to the availability KPI. Therefore, the reason code specific to availability losses are linked to the line node and the machine affecting that line.

Similarly, for performance losses, the system calculates speed loss based on the standard rate maintained and production reported, and the user can manage and assign different reason codes.

The reason codes are downloaded to the OEE framework for the operator's use. The operator, using the dashboard, links the actual event with the right reason code and reports it to the OEE framework. Here are some guidelines:

- Reason codes are defined in ERP and are mapped to existing plants in ERP.
- Reason codes are configurable with ten tiers of parent-child relationships; i.e., up to ten levels.
- Reason codes specific to global hierarchy are defined at the first three levels.
- Reason codes specific to plant hierarchy are defined from levels four through ten.
- A set of reason codes is defined for each type of loss (time and material losses) applicable as per the shop floor. Every loss is defined as a data element type in ERP. For example, UNSCD_DOWN is a standard time element type, but one can create custom ones too. Based on the plant and the data collection element, reason code hierarchy is displayed. For example (refer to Figure 3-51), a line can be down for multiple reasons. A line down ultimately affects the line's availability, which further affects production.

To capture this, UNSCD_DOWN (downtime loss) is defined as a data element type, and a set of hierarchical reason codes is assigned to this data element type. Therefore, when a line is down, OEE understands it as an availability loss, and it accordingly affects the availability KPI value.

KPI is calculated based on the time element type. Reason codes are maintained with time element type. Based on context, corresponding reason code hierarchy is made available for assignment.

The same data element type can be associated with multiple nodes, with a different set of reason codes applicable to each node.

As in Figure 3-51, you can understand how the data element type UNSCD_DOWN is used for different nodes with different reason code assignments. In OEE, the reason codes can be defined specific to each node under General configuration/Reason code configuration. In the absence of this configuration, the complete reason code hierarchy is displayed for the operator to choose and assign the right reason code.

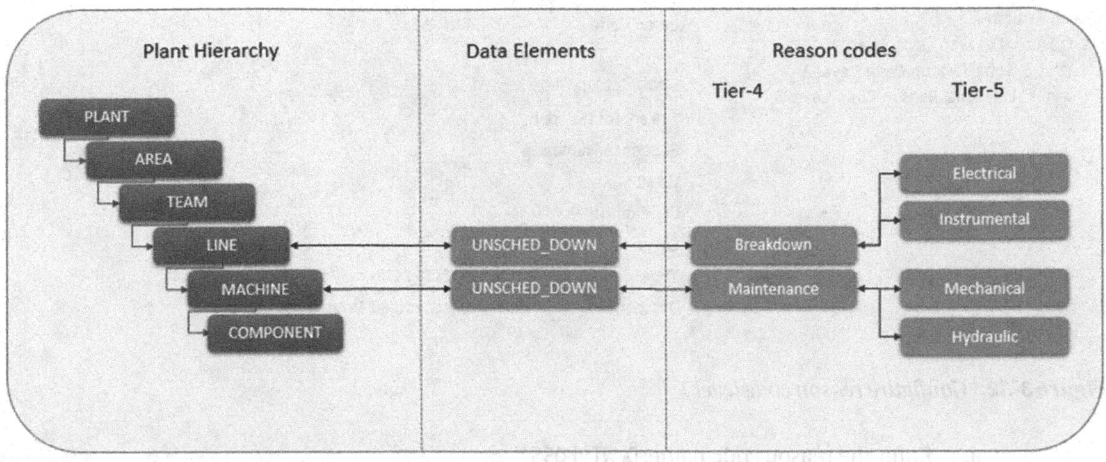

Figure 3-51. *Reason code categorization*

Reason codes can be maintained specific to plant and client and are integrated from ERP down to their respective plants. At the plant level, different plant hierarchies and their nodes can have different reason codes than their counterparts (other plants).

Global Reason Codes

This section will detail how to configure the reason codes.

1. Use transaction code SPRO and open SAP Reference IMG ➤ Production ➤ Overall Equipment Effectiveness ➤ Define Global Reason Codes
2. The global reason codes are the first three tiers of the reason code hierarchy and define the enterprise level of reason codes across plants.
3. Select New Entries to enter a reason code.

4. Enter the reason code name. Typically, you can define reason codes specific to the data element of type time loss.

■ **Note** Data element types belonging to loss-type categories should be configured before creating the global and plant reason codes.

---

5. In this example, let us create the reason codes for availability loss; i.e., unscheduled downtime (refer to Figure 3-52).

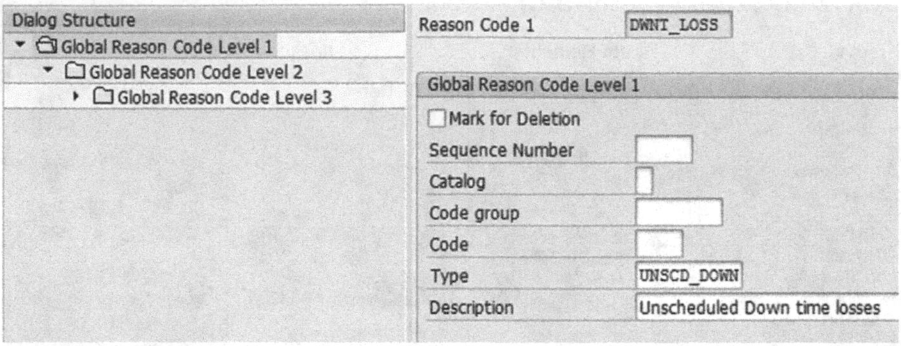

Figure 3-52. *Configure reason code level 1*

a. Enter the reason code name: `DWNT_LOSS`

b. Catalog, Code group, and Code should be used when you want to link the OEE reason codes with the existing Quality Management reason codes.

   a. From 15.1, there are two new parameters added namely *Mark for Deletion* and *Sequence Number. Mark for Deletion* is checked when you want to delete the created reason code. The same will be updated in OEE when sent from ERP. *Sequence Number* is the number that indicates the order of sequence for the reason codes to be displayed under a level.

c. Assign the data element of unscheduled downtime to Type. `UNSCD_DOWN` is the standard data element type.

d. Enter a description.

■ **Note** For availability/performance/quality loss, the data element type assigned should be the same throughout the reason code hierarchy; i.e., `UNSCD_DOWN` data element type should only be used across the reason codes for machine or line downtime.

---

6. Now the reason code for level 1 is complete. Select the created Reason Code 1 and select the Global Reason Code Level 2 in the left-hand hierarchy, then select New Entries. This will take you to the sub-dialog to create the reason code for level 2, which is associated with level 1 (refer to Figure 3-53).

Dialog Structure
Global Reason Code Level 1
Global Reason Code Level 2
Global Reason Code Level 3
Reason Code 1 DWNT_LOSS
Reason Code 2 DWNT_LOSS
Global Reason Code Level 2
Mark for Deletion
Sequence Number
Catalog
Code group
Code
Type UNSCD_DOWN
Description Unscheduled Downtime losses

***Figure 3-53.** Configure reason code level 2*

7. Follow step 5 to define the reason code level 2. You can maintain the same reason code name or choose a new one as per your plant requirements. You can also create multiple reason codes at each level to accommodate varied reason code requirements.
8. Follow step 5 to define the reason code for level 3 (refer to Figure 3-52).
9. Save the reason codes.
10. Refer to Figure 3-54 for a view of global reason codes configured from tier 1 to tier 3.

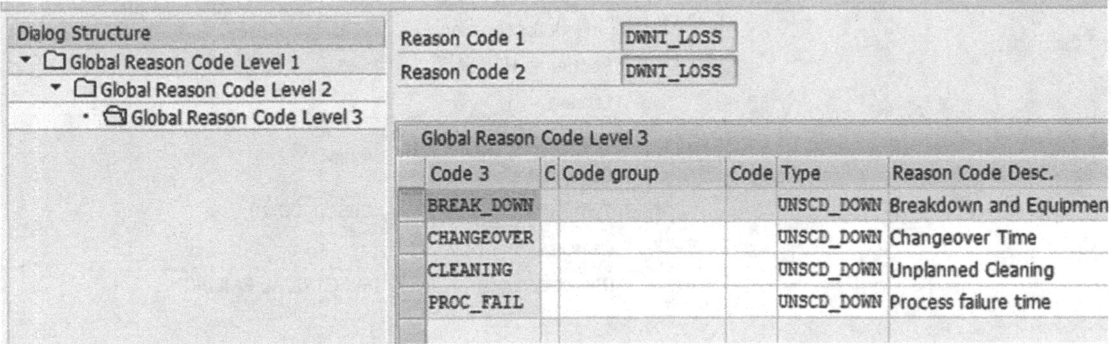

Code 3	C	Code group	Code	Type	Reason Code Desc.
BREAK_DOWN				UNSCD_DOWN	Breakdown and Equipmen
CHANGEOVER				UNSCD_DOWN	Changeover Time
CLEANING				UNSCD_DOWN	Unplanned Cleaning
PROC_FAIL				UNSCD_DOWN	Process failure time

***Figure 3-54.** Configure reason code level 3*

Plant Reason Code Configuration

This section will detail how to configure the reason codes for a plant hierarchy.

1. Go to the SAP Easy Access menu and choose Logistics ➤ Production ➤ Overall Equipment Effectiveness ➤ Master Data ➤ Plant Reason Code.
2. You can see the reason code hierarchy structure from level 1 to level 10. The first three levels are configured with global reason codes, as discussed in the previous section. In this section, we need to configure plant reason codes for levels 4 to 10.
3. Go to Global Reason Code Level 3 and select Reason Code 3, for which you want to configure the plant reason codes. Select Plant Reason Code Level 4 from the hierarchy, then select New Entries.
4. Enter the plant name (refer to Figure 3-55). The same reason code can be assigned to different plants using this plant assignment.

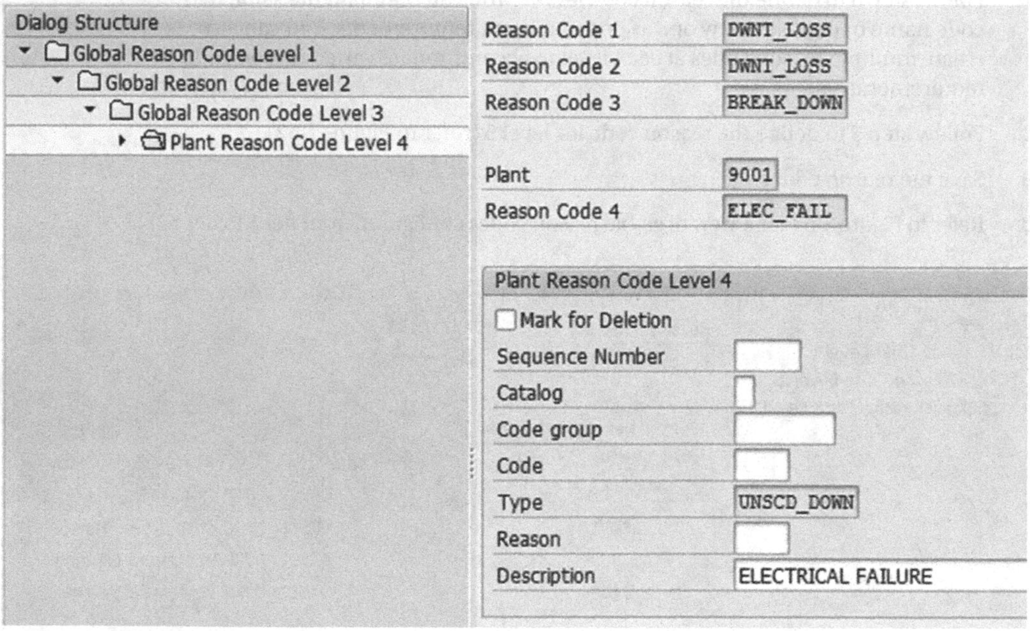

***Figure 3-55.** Configure reason code level 4*

5. Enter the Reason Code Level 4 Type and Description values as we did for global reason codes.
6. Follow the same steps to configure each level of reason codes as per the plant requirements.
7. Save the plant reason codes.
8. Refer to Figure 3-56 for reason codes configured up to level 5.

New Entries

Dialog Structure
Global Reason Code Level 1
Global Reason Code Level 2
Global Reason Code Level 3
Plant Reason Code Level 4
Plant Reason Code Level 5
Plant Reason Code Level 6
Plant Reason Code Level 7
Plant Reason Code Level 8
Plant Reason Code Level 9
Plant Reason Code Level 10

Plant 9001
Reason Code 1 DWNT_LOSS
Reason Code 2 DWNT_LOSS
Reason Code 3 BREAK_DOWN
Reason Code 4 MIXING
Reason Code 5 CONT_FAIL

Plant Reason Code Level 6

Code 6	C	Code group	Code

Figure 3-56. *Configure reason code for all levels*

For a machine or line down in the mixing line whose data element type is UNSCD_DOWN, an operator will be shown the reason codes configured for Reason Code Level 5.

Follow the preceding steps to configure up to level 10 as per the plant requirements.

Upload Plant Reason codes

In the previous section, you learned how to manually configure reason codes. OEE also allows a mechanism to upload the reason codes via an Excel spreadsheet with a predefined XML format.

1. From the main OEE menu, select Upload Reason Codes (refer to Figure 3-57).

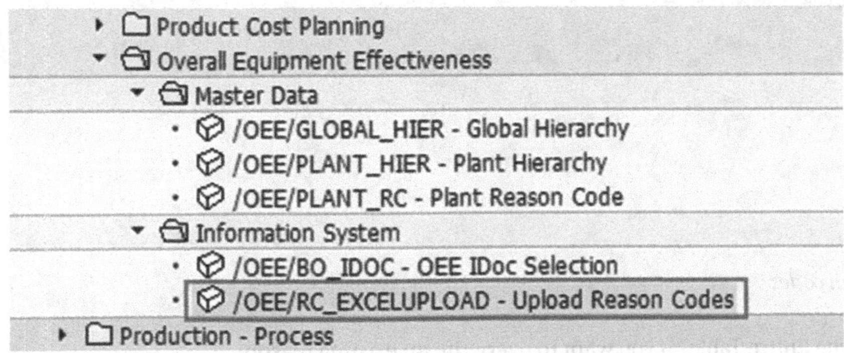

Figure 3-57. *Configure reason code from Excel*

2. Click the Upload button and upload the Excel file, which should be in a predefined XML format. You can get the standard XML format from the information page for Reason Codes Upload in OEE add-on. Also, you can use the following Excel file with columns as specified.

3. The columns are `Client`, `Plant`, `Reason_Code1` to `Reason_Code10`, `Description`, `QM_Catalog`, `QM_Catalog_Grp`, `QM_Catalog_Code`, `Type`, and `GRUND`.

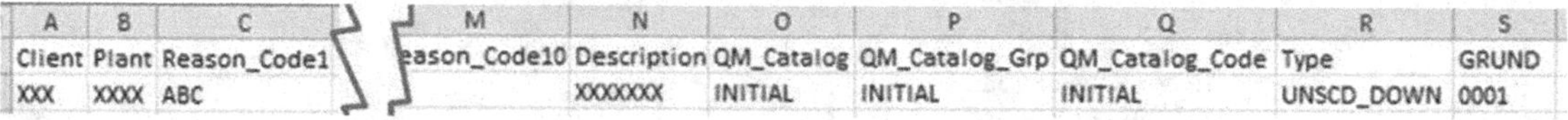

A	B	C	M	N	O	P	Q	R	S
Client	Plant	Reason_Code1	eason_Code10	Description	QM_Catalog	QM_Catalog_Grp	QM_Catalog_Code	Type	GRUND
XXX	XXXX	ABC		XXXXXXX	INITIAL	INITIAL	INITIAL	UNSCD_DOWN	0001

4. The preceding picture is the standard format that needs to be followed for the reason codes. You can refer to the previously entered sample data to add all the reason codes as per your plant requirements for all the reason code levels.

5. Leave the field empty under the reason code levels where the entries should be empty.

   For example, in the preceding picture, the `REASON_CODE1` column has a value and all the other reason code level columns are left empty. OEE understands this row to be the configuration for reason code 1 and that all the other reason code levels should be empty. Similarly, enter all the reason codes in the Excel file where appropriate.

6. Save the file in XML spreadsheet (*.xml) format. Once saved, the file can be opened both in XML and in .xls format.

7. Select the "Merge Entries Into Table" option for the first-time upload (refer to Figure 3-58).

Figure 3-58. *Upload reason codes*

8. Select "Overwrite Entire Table" if you want to overwrite an existing reason codes table.

9. Click the Execute button.

10. Notice the successful execution message.

11. Go to the plant reason codes under the SAP menu to check whether all the uploaded reason codes are available.

Refer to Figure 3-59 for an overview of the reason code hierarchy accommodating both global and plant reason codes. Level 1 to level 3 are the global reason codes, and from level 4 to level 10 are the plant reason codes.

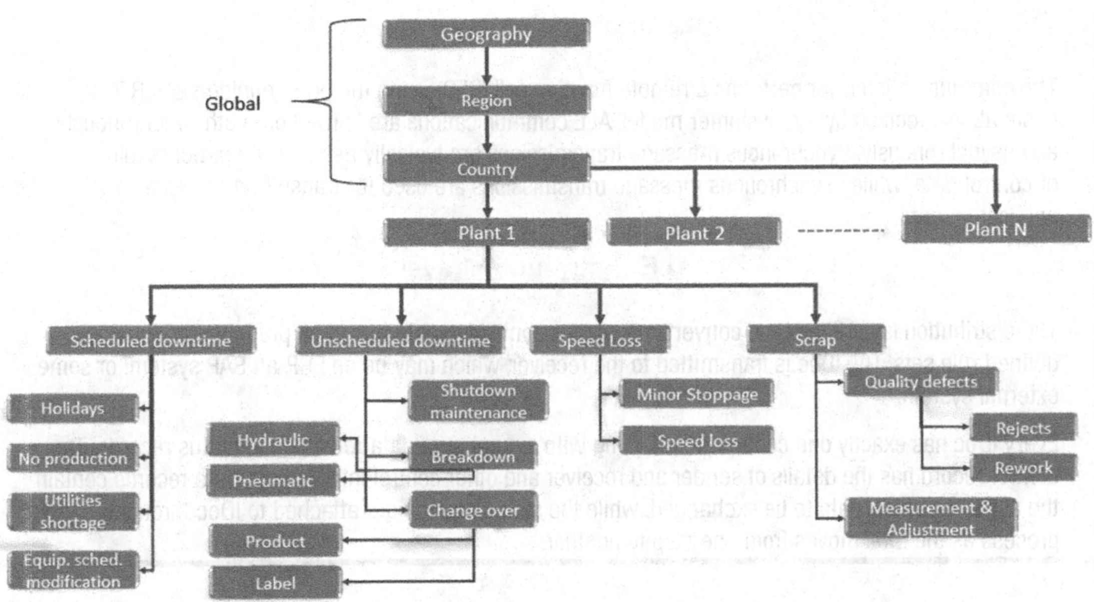

Figure 3-59. Reason code hierarchical structure

ALE Customizing Settings in ERP for Integration with OEE

This section will explain the steps required to set up the configuration in ERP to transfer OEE-related data from ERP to OEE.

The previous sections explained the OEE-relevant master data and configuration data that is required by the SAP OEE application for collecting shop-floor data and calculating OEE and its associated KPIs.

These data sets need to be transferred to SAP OEE through IDocs using MII message services. This is achieved through ALE customizing settings in ERP.

ALE (Application Link Enabling) is a methodology in SAP by which SAP systems can communicate with each other. ALE achieves this communication using a message-based architecture. In this architecture, the application layer creates an interface between the systems, the communication layer makes the remote call to the logical functions, and finally the distribution layer distributes the data from the sender system to the receiver system using filter functions.

ALE ensures guaranteed delivery between the sender and receiver systems. ALE can be used for the migration, maintenance, and exchange of master data, configuration data, and transactional data.

NOTE

ALE Application Layer

This layer provides ALE with an interface to ERP so as to originate or receive messages containing data to or from external (or other ERP) systems. The medium of interface for this data transfer is called an IDoc (intermediate document), which is a container for the application data to be transmitted. After a user performs an SAP transaction, one or more IDocs are generated in the sending database and passed to the ALE communication layer.

ALE Communication Layer

The communication layer performs a remote function call (RFC) using the port definition and RFC destination specified by the customer model. ALE communications are carried out both synchronously and asynchronously. Synchronous message transmissions are typically used for the direct reading of control data, while asynchronous message transmissions are used for transmitting or receiving application data.

ALE Distribution Layer

The distribution layer filters and converts messages containing data based on predefined or custom-defined rule sets. The IDoc is transmitted to the receiver, which may be an ERP, an SAP system, or some external system.

Every IDoc has exactly one control record along with a number of data records and status records. The control record has the details of sender and receiver and other control information. Data records contain the actual business data to be exchanged, while the status records are attached to IDoc throughout the process as the IDoc moves from one step to another.

ALE scenarios fall into three categories: master data, transactional data, and control data distribution. Although the underlying principles are the same for the different categories, there are differences in their functions and configurations.

ALE Customizing Settings in ERP for Communication with MII

The list of activities you need to do in ERP for ALE customizing settings are as follows:

- Define RFC destination
- Maintain a logical system
- Define a logical port
- Maintain a partner profile
- Maintain a customer distribution model

Define RFC destination

ERP needs an RFC destination in order to communicate with a target system; in this case it is SAP OEE.

1. In Customizing for Logistics - General, choose Supply Chain Planning Interfaces (SCPI) ➤ Production Optimization Interface (POI) ➤ ALE settings for POI ➤ Define RFC Destination or Use tcode SM59. Refer to Figure 3-60.

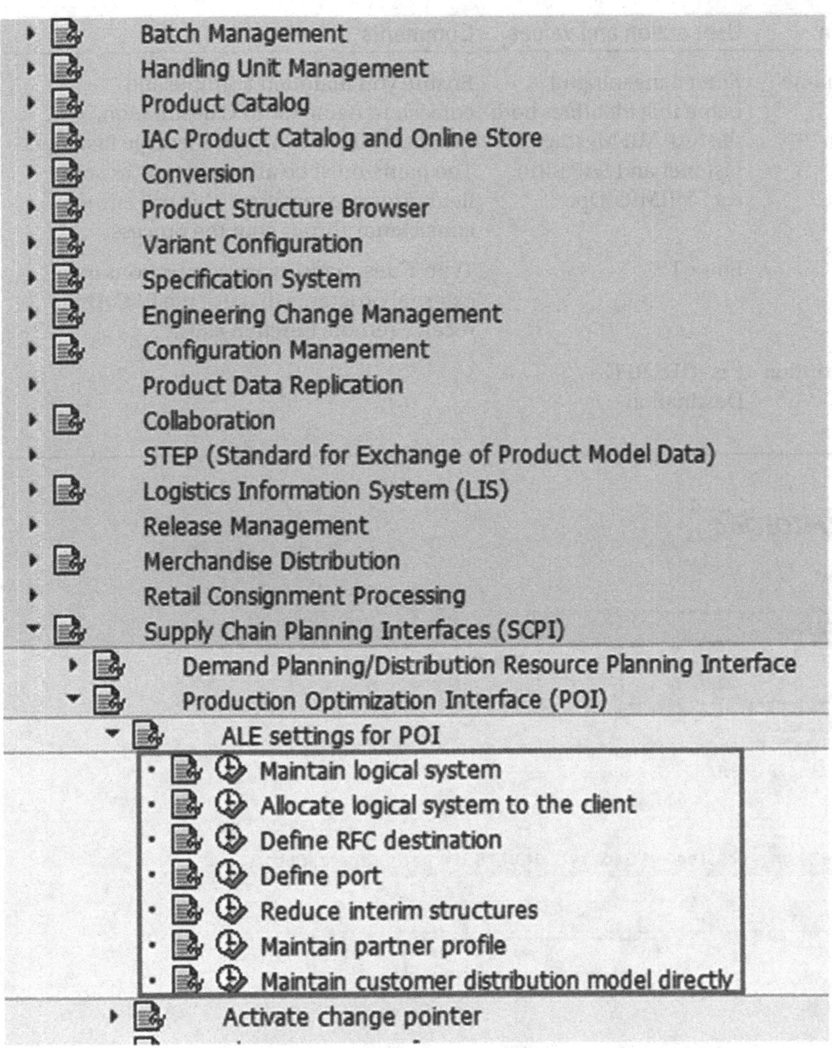

Figure 3-60. *ALE settings menu*

2. On the Configuration of RFC Connections screen, select the TCP/IP connections node and choose the Create icon.

3. On the RFC Destination screen, enter the following data (refer to Figure 3-61).

Field	Description	User action and values	Comments
RFC Destination	Standard name of an RFC destination	Enter a meaningful name that identifies both the SAP MII Message Listener and SAP ERP; e.g., MIIMIOIDoc	Ensure you maintain a simple and consistent name for RFC destination, Program ID, and SAP MII Message Listener. The name must be all uppercase, as some fields are case sensitive. This will ensure consistency throughout the process.
Connection Type	Type of RFC connection	Enter T	Type T destinations are connections to external programs that use the RFC API to receive remote function calls.
Description 1	Short description of the RFC destination	e.g., OEE RFC Destination	

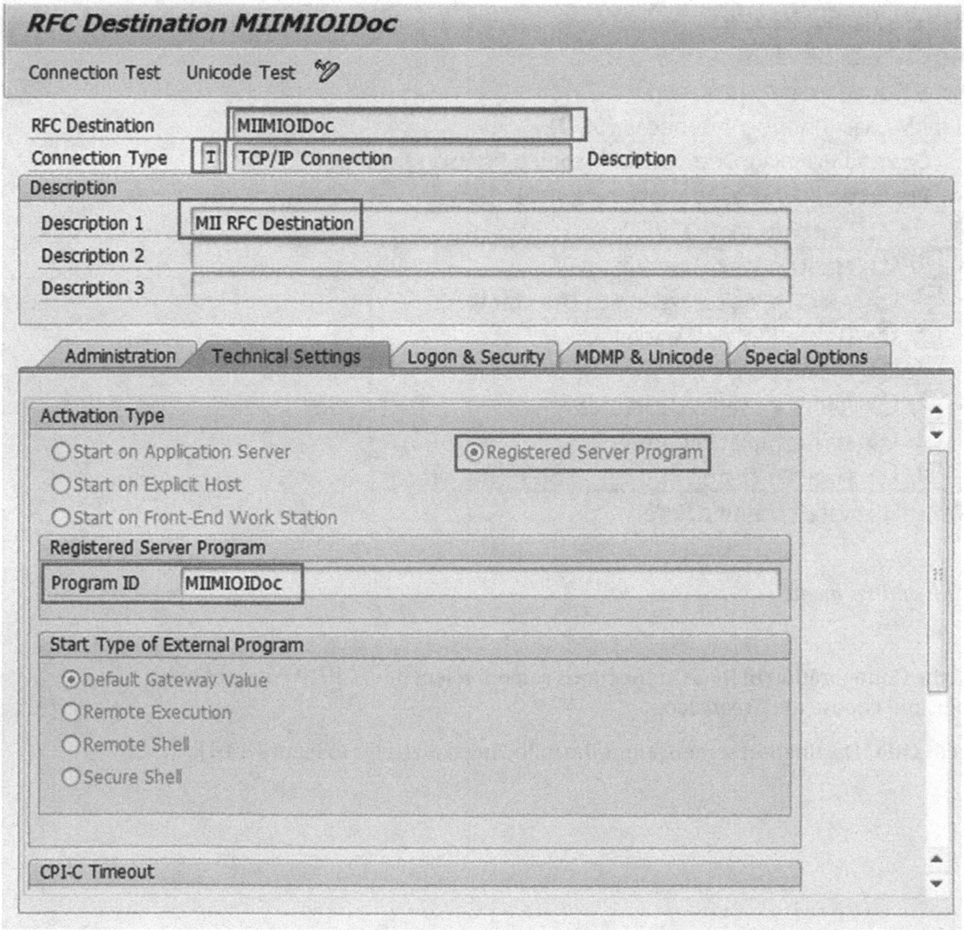

Figure 3-61. *Create RFC destination*

4. Press Enter.
5. On the Technical Settings tab of the RFC Destination screen, enter the following data (refer to Figure 3-62).

Field	Description	User action and values	Comments
Activation Type	Radio buttons	Choose "Registered Server Program"	Using the registration feature of the SAP gateway, RFC server programs can be started before; register at this SAP gateway and then wait for RFC call requests
Registered Server Program	Identification of a registered RFC server program	Enter the same name as the RFC Destination; e.g., MIIMIOIdoc	It is recommended you use same name for RFC destination and Program ID. The Program ID here corresponds to the Message Listener in SAP MII and must therefore have the same name.
Gateway Options Gateway Host	Gateway host name	Enter the SAP system application server	You can obtain the name of the gateway service by logging onto the application server and starting the transaction SMGW. The name of the gateway server can be looked up in the menu Goto ➤ Parameters ➤ Display ➤➤ (refer to Figure 3-63)
Gateway Service	Gateway service	Enter sapgw<SAP system number>	You can obtain the name of the gateway service by logging onto the application server and starting the transaction SMGW. The name of the gateway server can be looked up in the menu Goto ➤ Parameters ➤ Display ➤➤

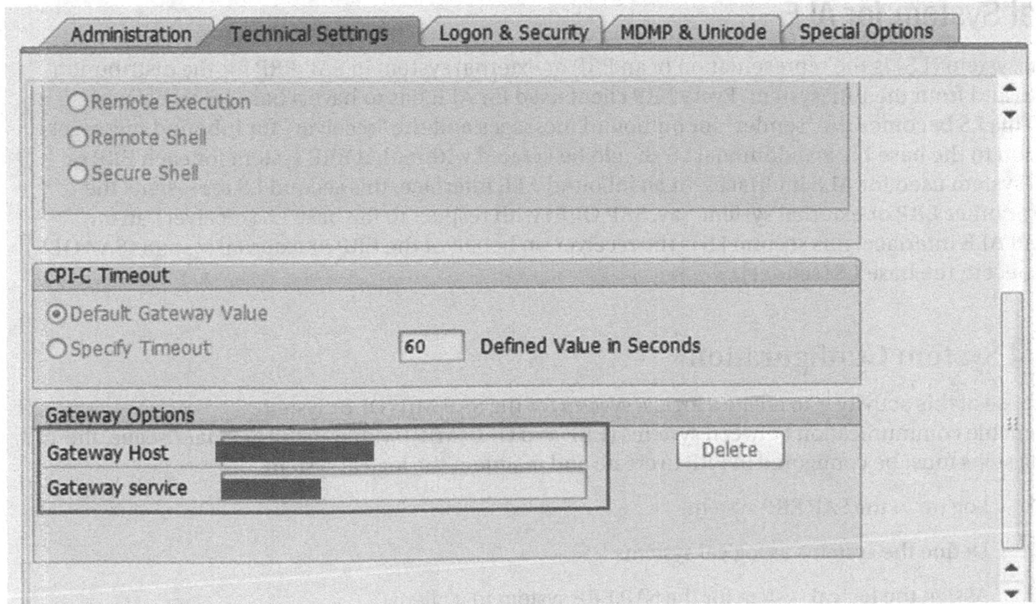

Figure 3-62. Create RFC destination: technical settings

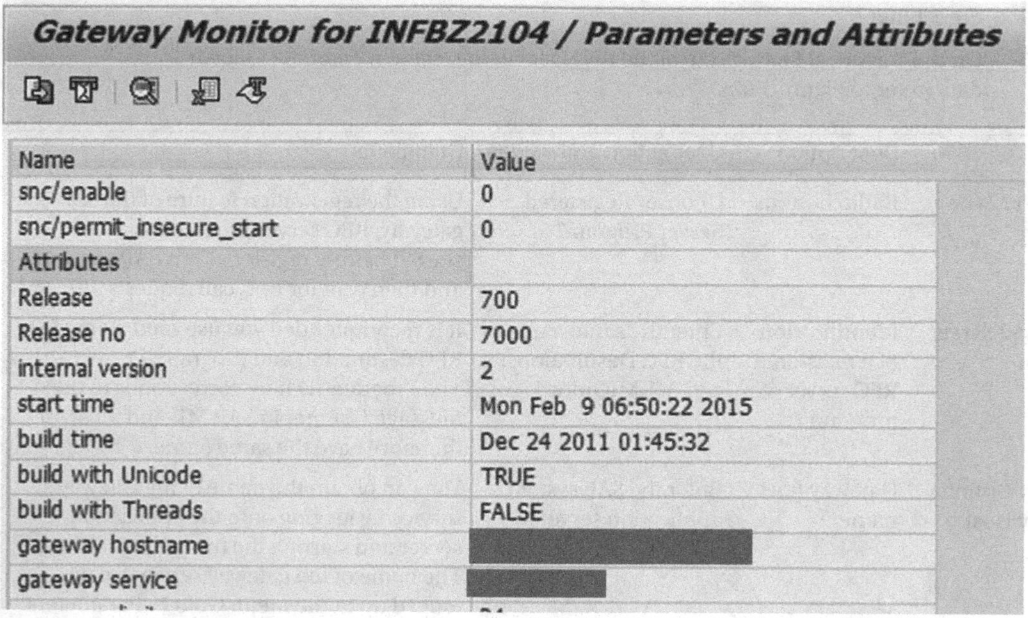

Gateway Monitor for INFBZ2104 / Parameters and Attributes

Name	Value
snc/enable	0
snc/permit_insecure_start	0
Attributes	
Release	700
Release no	7000
internal version	2
start time	Mon Feb 9 06:50:22 2015
build time	Dec 24 2011 01:45:32
build with Unicode	TRUE
build with Threads	FALSE
gateway hostname	
gateway service	

Figure 3-63. *Create RFC destination: gateway options*

6. Save the entries.
7. Configure the SAP MII IDoc Listener by executing CTC wizard (explained in chapter 4) and then test the RFC connection.

Logical System for ALE

A logical system (LS) is the representation of an ERP or external system in SAP ERP for the distribution of data to and from the ERP system. Every ERP client used for ALE has to have a base LS associated with it. This LS becomes the "sender" for outbound messages and the "receiver" for inbound messages. In addition to the base LS, an additional LS should be created within that ERP system for each ERP or external system used for ALE interfaces. In an inbound ALE interface, this second LS represents the sender (another ERP or external system, say, SAP OEE) with respect to the base LS (receiver). In an outbound ALE interface, this second LS is the receiver on behalf of the ERP or external system (SAP OEE) with respect to the base LS (sender).

Logical System Configuration

The purpose of this activity is to create a logical system for the SAP MII (OEE) system.

To enable communication between systems (ERP and OEE [MII]) within the system landscape, the following steps must be configured in ERP to create and maintain the logical system.

1. Log on to the SAP ERP system.
2. Define the systems as logical systems.
3. Assign the logical system for the SAP ERP system to a client.

This enables the systems to recognize the target system as an RFC destination. If the logical system has already been created, this activity can be skipped. Logical systems are defined cross-client.

1. Use transaction code SPRO ➤ SAP Reference IMG ➤ Logistics - General, choose Supply Chain Planning Interfaces (SCPI) ➤ Production Optimization Interface (POI) ➤ ALE settings for POI ➤ Maintain logical system.
2. On the Change View "Logical Systems": Overview screen, choose New Entries.
3. Enter the following data (refer to Figure 3-64).

Field	Description	User action and values	Comments
Log. System	System in which applications run integrated on a shared-data basis	Enter the name of the RFC destination previously created	Limit name to CHAR 10 to facilitate naming conventions of related objects
Name	Short, meaningful description of the logical system	Enter a short, meaningful description	

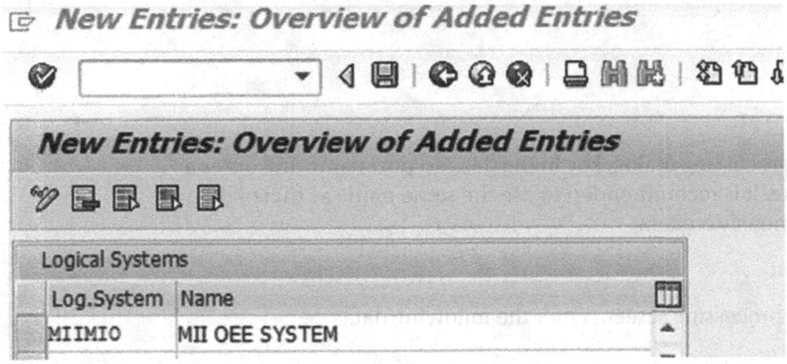

Figure 3-64. Create logical system

4. Save the entries.

Partner Port

A port is a logical representation of a communication channel in SAP, with the data communicated being IDocs. The types of ports that can be defined in ERP are tRFC, File, CPI-C, ABAP-PI, and HTTP. ALE can use all port types to distribute IDocs. tRFC and File ports can link to RFC destinations connected to ERP-to-ERP or TCP/IP.

1. Use transaction code SPRO ➤ SAP Reference IMG ➤ Logistics - General, choose Supply Chain Planning Interfaces (SCPI) ➤ Production Optimization Interface (POI) ➤ ALE settings for POI ➤ Define port
2. On the Ports in IDoc processing screen, select the Transactional RFC node and choose the Create icon (refer to Figure 3-65).

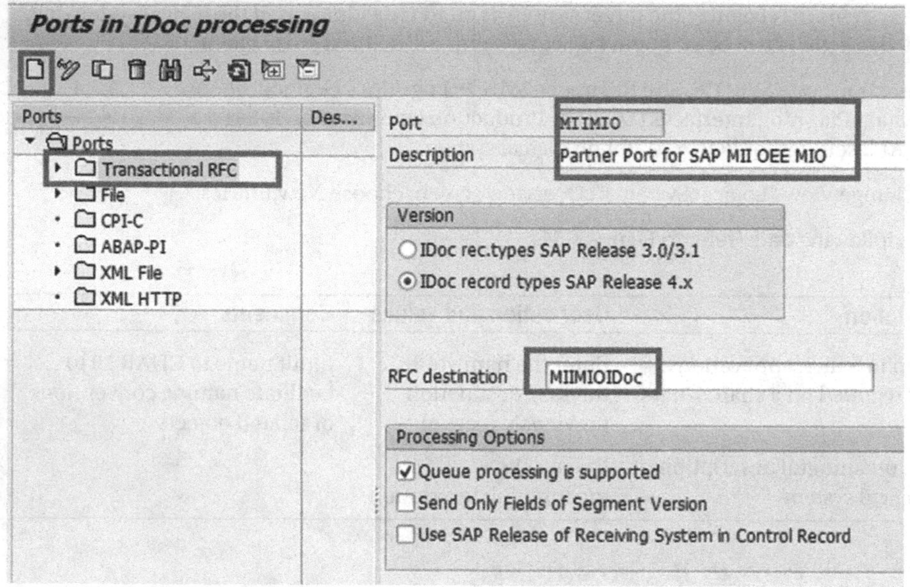

Figure 3-65. *Create logical port*

3. In the Ports in IDoc processing dialog, key in the desired port name and enter a descriptive port name. It is recommended to use the same name as that of the RFC connection previously created.
4. Choose the Enter icon.
5. On the Ports in IDoc processing screen, enter the following data:

Field	Description	User action and values
Description	Short description of the port	Enter a short, meaningful description
Version	Enables system to select appropriate control record	Select IDoc record types SAP Release 4.x
RFC destination	Standard name of an RFC destination	Enter the name of the RFC destination previously created

Partner Profile Configuration

A partner profile is an identifier for a system used for communicating messages. The type LS (logical system) is used for ALE communications. Every partner profile used for ALE must be based on an existing LS.

A partner profile brings together several ALE elements to define the parameters of communication between two or more systems. Inbound parameters, outbound parameters, and message control need to be configured for every IDoc message that needs to be handled. The main parameters are message types, IDoc types, process codes, partner functions, application identifiers, message functions, output types, and ports. Other parameters also determine the mode of processing and error handling.

A partner profile plays a major role and can be viewed as a gateway for ALE communications. It routes the specified messages through defined IDoc types to a given port after invoking the appropriate function modules for outbound processing. It receives IDocs of a specific type, and it identifies modules with which to post data to the application databases in the case of inbound interfaces.

1. Use transaction code WE20 or go to SPRO ➤ SAP Reference IMG ➤ Logistics - General, choose Supply Chain Planning Interfaces (SCPI) ➤ Production Optimization Interface (POI) ➤ ALE settings for POI ➤ Maintain partner profile
2. On the Partner profile screen, create a new profile for partner type LS (refer to Figure 3-66).
3. Enter the following data:

Field	Description	User Action and Values	Comments
Partner no.	Uniquely identifies a vendor, customer, or a logical system	Enter the logical system previously created; e.g., MIIMIO	
Ty.	Classifies the recipient of error notifications	Enter C (Job)	
Agent	Specifies the job (person or group of people) to be notified if processing errors occur	Use match code search to select the job number responsible for error handling	Job key is internally generated when creating agents

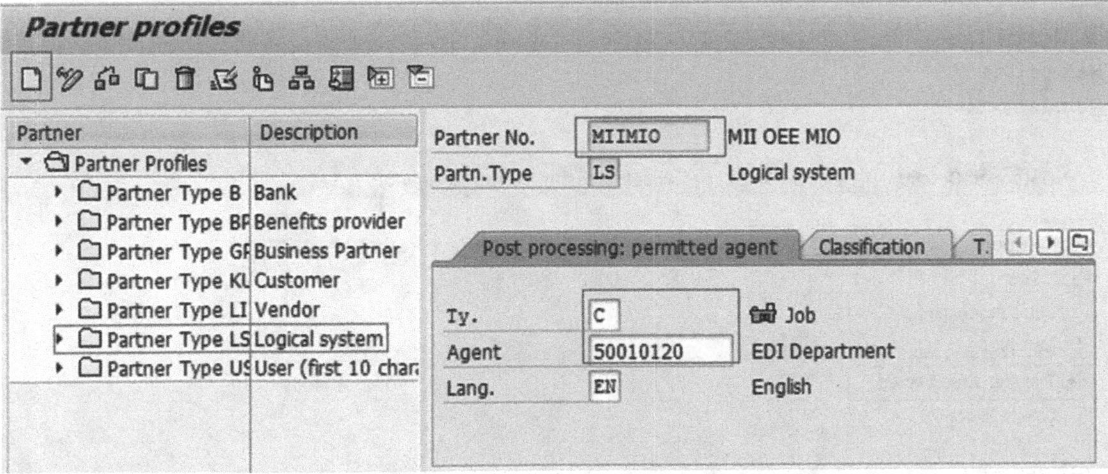

Figure 3-66. *Create partner profile*

4. Save your entries.
5. Under the Outbound Parameters table, choose the Create Outbound Parameter icon.

6. On the Partner profiles: Outbound parameters screen, enter the following data for each message type (refer to Figure 3-67).

Field	Description	User Action and Values	Comments
Receiver port	Specifies how the IDocs are transferred to the EDI subsystem	Enter the logical system previously created; e.g., MIIMIO	
Output Mode	Output is started immediately for each individual IDoc. The external subsystem is not started from SAP ERP. It must become active itself in order to fetch the data.	Select the radio button *Transfer IDoc Immed* and *Do not start subsy stem.*	
Cancel Processing After Syntax Error	If selected, the IDoc Interface terminates the processing in the event that a syntax error is found	Select the checkbox	

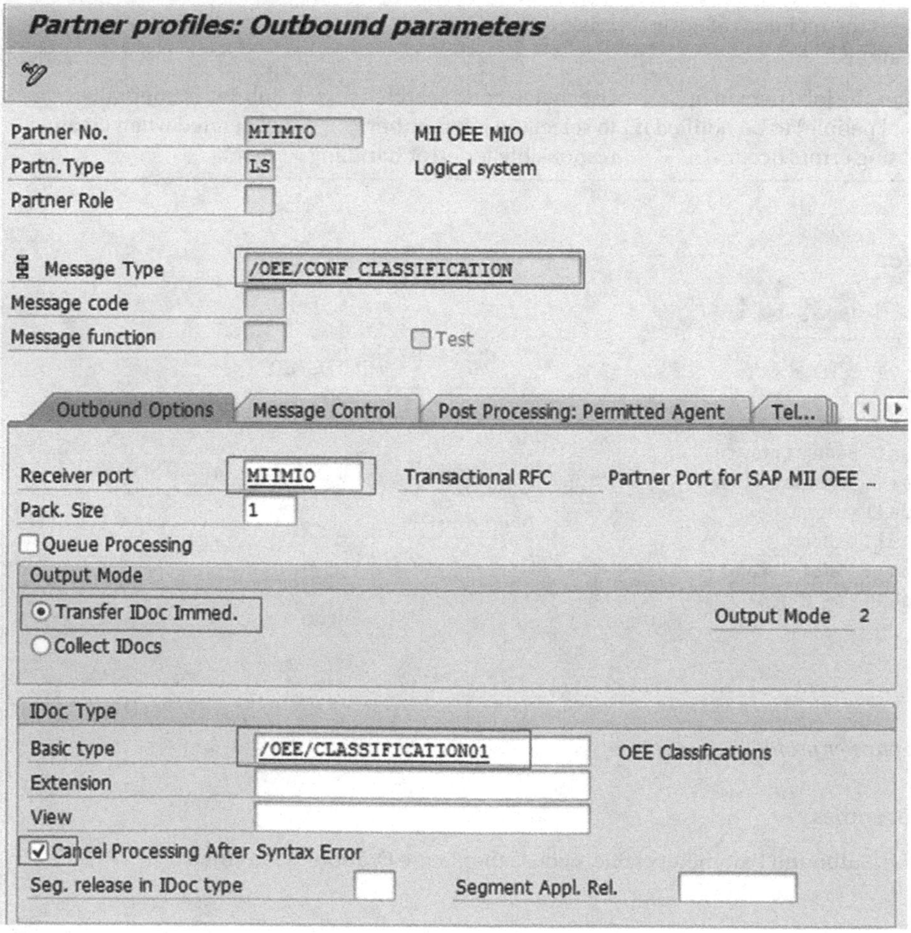

Figure 3-67. *Create partner profile port: outbound parameters*

Message Type

A message type represents the application message exchanged either between ERP systems or between ERP and an external system. A message type characterizes the data sent across systems and relates to the structure of the data, called an IDoc type. For example, MATMAS is a message type for Material Master, and LOIPRO is a message type for a Production order.

IDoc Type

An intermediate document (IDoc) type represents the structure of the data associated with a message type (MATMAS05 for message type MATMAS–Material Master, and LOIPRO01 for message type LOIPRO–Production order), while an IDoc itself is an object containing the data of a particular message type. IDocs are data containers with intelligence built in. Each IDoc contains one and only one business object.

For example, an IDoc of type LOIPRO01 and message type LOIPRO contains data only for one production order. Generally, the architecture of an IDoc is independent of the message type by virtue of ALE's ability to redefine it for any message type.

Table 3-3 shows the list of message types and associated IDoc types used by SAP OEE for master, configuration, and transaction data

Table 3-3. *OEE-Specific Message Type and IDoc Types*

Message Type	IDoc Type / Basic Type	Description
MATMAS	MATMAS05	Material Master
LOIPRO	LOIPRO01	Production Order
LOIWCS	LOIWCS03	Work center
OEE config data		
LOICAL	LOICAL01	Master Calendar
/OEE/CONF_CLASSIFICATION	/OEE/CLASSIFICATION01	Classification
/OEE/CONF_CLASSIFICATION_RECO	/OEE/CLASSIFICATION02	Classification reconcile
/OEE/CONF_DCELEM	/OEE/DCELEM01	Data collection element
/OEE/CONF_DCELEM_RECO	/OEE/DCELEM02	Data collection element reconciliation
/OEE/CONF_DCE_CTX	/OEE/DCECTX01	Data collection element context
/OEE/CONF_DCE_CTX_RECO	/OEE/DCECTX02	Data collection element context reconciliation
/OEE/CONF_KPI	/OEE/KPI01	KPI
/OEE/CONF_KPI_RECO	/OEE/KPI02	KPI reconciliation
/OEE/CONF_MCGRP	/OEE/MCGRP01	Machine Group
/OEE/CONF_MCGRP_RECO	/OEE/MCGRP02	Machine Group reconciliation
/OEE/CONF_PRDACT	/OEE/PRDACTIVITY01	Production Activity
/OEE/CONF_PRDACT_RECO	/OEE/PRDACTIVITY02	Production Activity reconciliation
/OEE/CONF_PRODMODE	/OEE/PRODMODE01	Production Mode

(*continued*)

Table 3-3. (*continued*)

Message Type	IDoc Type / Basic Type	Description
/OEE/CONF_PRODMODE_RECO	/OEE/PRODMODE02	Production mode reconciliation
/OEE/CONF_RC	/OEE/RC01	Reason codes
/OEE/CONF_RC_RECO	/OEE/RC02	Reason code reconciliation
/OEE/CONF_SHIFT	/OEE/SHIFT01	Shift definitions
/OEE/CONF_TIMEELEM	/OEE/TIMEELEM01	Time element
/OEE/CONF_TIMEELEM_RECO	/OEE/TIMEELEM02	Time element reconciliation
/OEE/CONF_TIMEEL_TP	/OEE/TIMEELTP01	Time element types
/OEE/CONF_TIMEEL_TP_RECO	/OEE/TIMEELTP02	Time element types reconciliation
/OEE/PLANT_HIERARCHY	/OEE/PLANT01	Plant Hierarchy
/OEE/PLANT_HIERARCHY_REC	/OEE/PLANT02	Plant Hierarchy reconciliation
/OEE/STDVALKEY_FORMULAPARAM	/OEE/STDVALKEY_ FORMULAPARAM01	Standard value formula parameters
/OEE/STDVALKEY_PARAM_RECO	/OEE/STDVALKEY_ FORMULAPARAM02	Standard value formula parameters reconciliation
SYNCH	SYNCHRON	Dummy IDoc for Synchronous communication
T006_A	T006_01	Units Of Measurement

7. Save the entries. Repeat the previous step to configure each message type-IDoc type combination shown in the outbound parameters table.

Customer Distribution Model

In an ERP system, the customer distribution model is a tool that stores information about the flow of messages across various systems. The customer distribution model uses an SAP-delivered distribution reference model as its basis (the customer distribution model can have distribution scenarios other than ones stored in the distribution reference model). The customer distribution model stores data that dictates the message (message types) flow to its logical systems. Many messages can flow to one logical system, and one message can flow to several systems. With the use of filter objects and listings, it is also possible to specify in a model the criteria for filtering information for a specific system. A customer distribution model can be created in an ERP system with that client's base logical system as the "sender" logical system.

Customer Distribution Model Configuration

1. Use transaction code BD64 or go to tcode: SPRO ➤ SAP Reference IMG ➤ Logistics - General, choose ➤ Supply Chain Planning Interfaces (SCPI) ➤ Production Optimization Interface (POI) ➤ ALE settings for POI ➤ Maintain customer distribution model directly
2. On the Change Distribution Model screen, choose Create model view

   Create model view .

3. On the Create Model View screen, enter the following data (refer to Figure 3-68).

Field	Description	User Action and Values	Comments
Short text	Short description of view of distribution model	Enter a short, meaningful description	
Technical name	View of ALE model	Enter a technical name	
Start date	Identifies the start of a validity period	Enter the start date of the validity period	
End Date	Identifies the end of the validity period	Enter the end date of the validity period	

Create Model View

Short text	MII OEE Distribution model
Technical name	MIIOEE
Start date	05.03.2014
End Date	31.12.9999

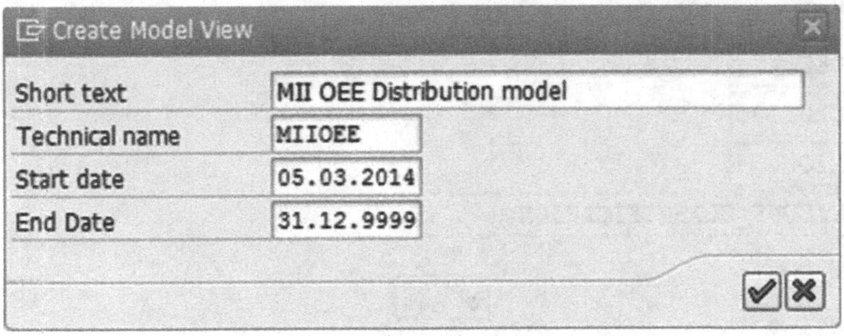

Figure 3-68. *Create customer distribution model: model view*

4. Choose the Enter icon.
5. On the Change Distribution Model screen, select the distribution model previously created and choose Add message type Add message type.
6. On the Add Message Type screen, enter the following data (refer to Figure 3-69).

Field	Description	User Action and Values	Comments
Model view	View of distribution model	Enter the name of the previously created distribution model	Refer to Figure 3-68.
Sender	Name of the logical source system for exchanging messages	Enter the name of the system sending the IDocs	This is usually the logical system name for the SAP client; the field gets automatically populated.
Receiver	Name of the logical target system for exchanging messages	Enter the name of the logical system previously created	

(*continued*)

Field	Description	User Action and Values	Comments
Message Type	Identifies different IDoc types	Enter the message type; e.g., /OEE/CONF_ CLASSIFICATION (refer to Table 3-3)	Enter the message type (refer table 3-3). Select Enter. The message type gets added. This step signifies that the selected message type will be transferred from the sender system to receiver system using this distribution model, which is further linked to the logical port and the partner profile defined.

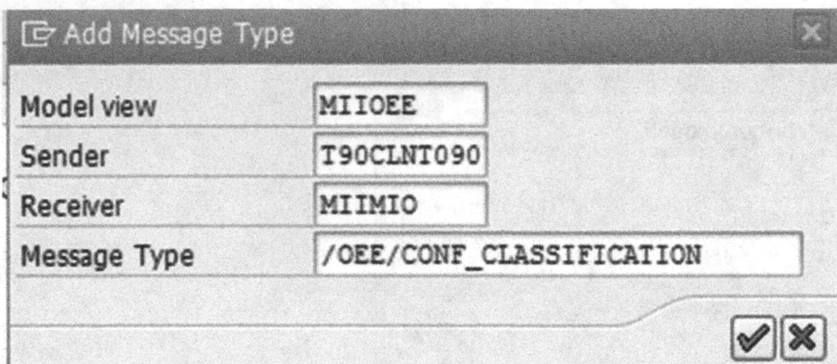

Figure 3-69. Create customer distribution model: add message type

7. Repeat the preceding steps for each message type that was created under the partner profile section as an outbound parameter (refer to Table 3-3).
8. Save the entries.

All the preceding ALE customizing settings are prerequisites for transferring the OEE-specific data from ERP to OEE.

Summary

In this chapter, you have learned about the purpose of OEE-relevant master data and configuration data and how OEE add-on helps in the creation and maintenance of these data, how master and configuration data are associated, and finally the ALE customization settings required for transferring the created master and configuration data to OEE.

In the next chapter, we will learn about SAP OEEINT, the integration component required for the integration of ERP and OEE.

CHAPTER 4

SAP OEEINT for Integration of ECC and OEE

SAP OEE consists of different components on SAP ERP, MII and HANA, and it is important to integrate them so that the information flows seamlessly, enabling an end-to-end solution. In this chapter you will learn how SAP ERP is integrated with SAP MII along with related configurations to be done in SAP MII.

As all the master, planning, and configuration data for SAP OEE are maintained in SAP ERP, which you learned about in the previous chapter, the integration of SAP ERP with SAP MII is important for getting the relevant data to SAP MII and sending the actuals back to ERP from MII after execution. As part of the SAP OEE solution, SAP provides a component on MII called SAPOEEINT (OEE Integration) that is used to synchronize the data between ERP and MII. As you have learned, SAP ERP sends the messages for master, configuration, and planning data via IDoc messages, while MII uses IDoc Message Listener, which is a standard feature, to receive the IDoc messages and process them, and to save them in the OEE database in MII. However, when MII sends the confirmation and goods-movement messages back to ERP, it uses the RFC and BAPI interfaces available in ERP, which are triggered from the MII Business Logic Services transactions through the OEEINT framework. All the messages flowing between ERP and MII can be monitored from the Queue Monitor, which is available in OEEINT on MII. The OEEINT architecture is shown in Figure 4-1.

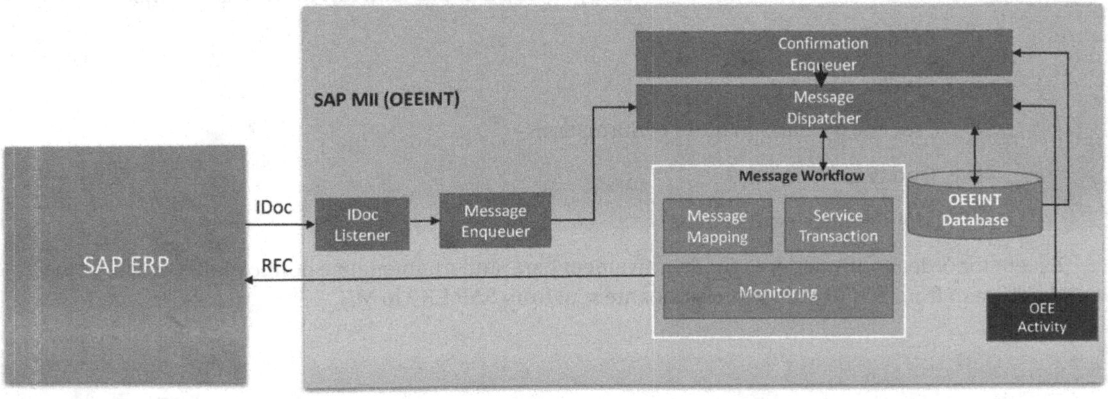

Figure 4-1. *SAP OEEINT architecture*

D. Saha et al., *Manufacturing Performance Management using SAP OEE*,
DOI 10.1007/978-1-4842-1150-2_4

There are three types of data transferred between ERP and MII for OEE through the OEEINT framework, as below. The individual data elements were explained in chapter 3:

- Configuration Data: Configuration data set up in ERP for OEE as follows:
    - Data collection elements contexts
    - Data collection elements
    - Data element types
    - Data elements
    - KPI definitions
    - Machine groups
    - Production modes
    - Production activity
    - Hierarchy node classifications
    - UoM and dimension
    - Shift definitions and break schedules
    - Standard value key and formula parameters
    - Factory calendar
- Master Data: Master data set up in SAP ERP for OEE as follows:
    - Plant hierarchy data
    - Reason codes (loss tree)
    - Work center and capacities
    - Material
- Transactional Data: Transactional data generated in ERP and MII for OEE as follows:
    - Production orders
    - Process orders
    - Process/production order confirmations
    - Goods movements
    - Maintenance notifications

Except for order confirmations, goods-movement data, and maintenance notifications–which, being actuals, are sent from MII to ERP–all messages are sent from SAP ERP to MII.

Configuration Templates for OEEINT

To integrate SAP MII with ERP for using OEE, you need to configure the connections and message routing between the two systems. Though it is possible to configure each object individually, it is much easier to configure the same automatically by executing a configuration template (CTC wizard), available in NetWeaver Administrator in MII server, that is delivered by SAP. After the MII server is installed with the OEE components, open the NetWeaver Administrator by the URL: `http://<host>:<port>/nwa`. Navigate to Configuration ➤ Scenarios ➤ Configuration Wizard and search for **OEE** in the filter expression. You can find four CTC templates available to set up OEE, as shown in Figure 4-2.

- The *SAP OEE NetWeaver Configuration* template creates the users and roles required for SAP OEE.
- *SAP OEE Integration Configuration* template creates the configurations for OEEINT; i.e., message workflows and related configurations.
- *SAP OEE Configuration* template creates the OEE dashboards, activities, and related configurations in MII.
- *SAP OEE Migration* template is only used to migrate an older version of OEE to a newer version after a service pack or release upgrade.

You need to execute the SAP OEE NetWeaver Configuration CTC first, followed by the SAP OEE Integration CTC and finally the SAP OEE Configuration CTC.

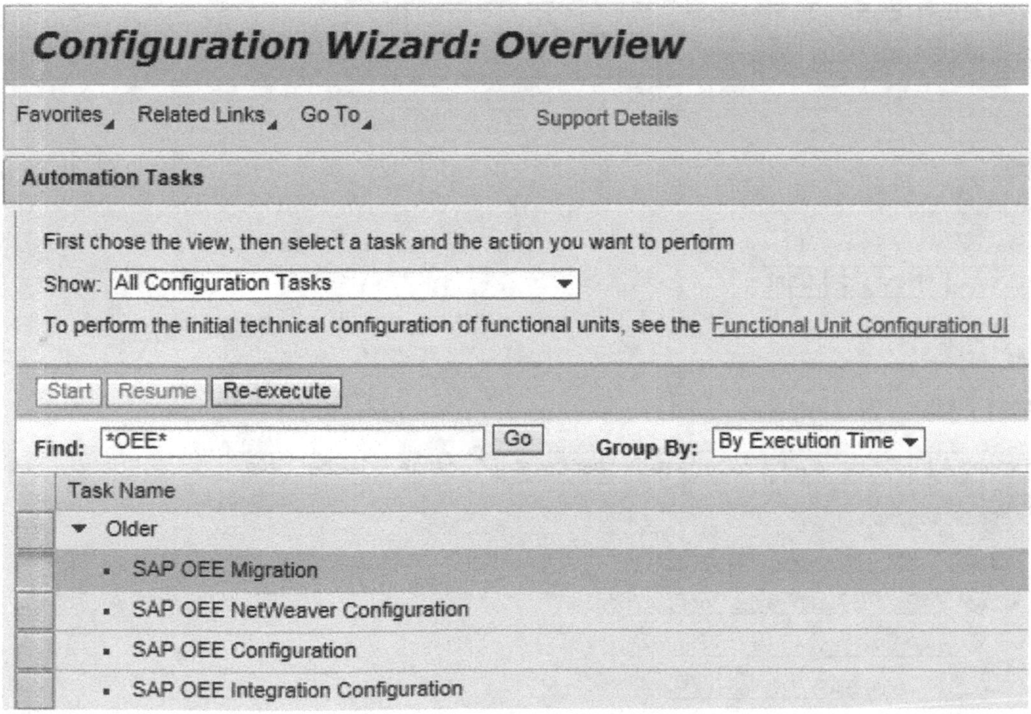

Figure 4-2. *SAP OEE CTC templates*

SAP OEE NetWeaver Configuration CTC

The SAP OEE NetWeaver Configuration CTC creates the relevant roles and users in NetWeaver User Management Engine (UME) required for OEE on MII. To start the configuration wizard, select it and click on Execute.

In the first step you need to specify the passwords for `OEE_ADMIN` and `OEE_INTEGRATOR` users, as shown in Figure 4-3, and click Next.

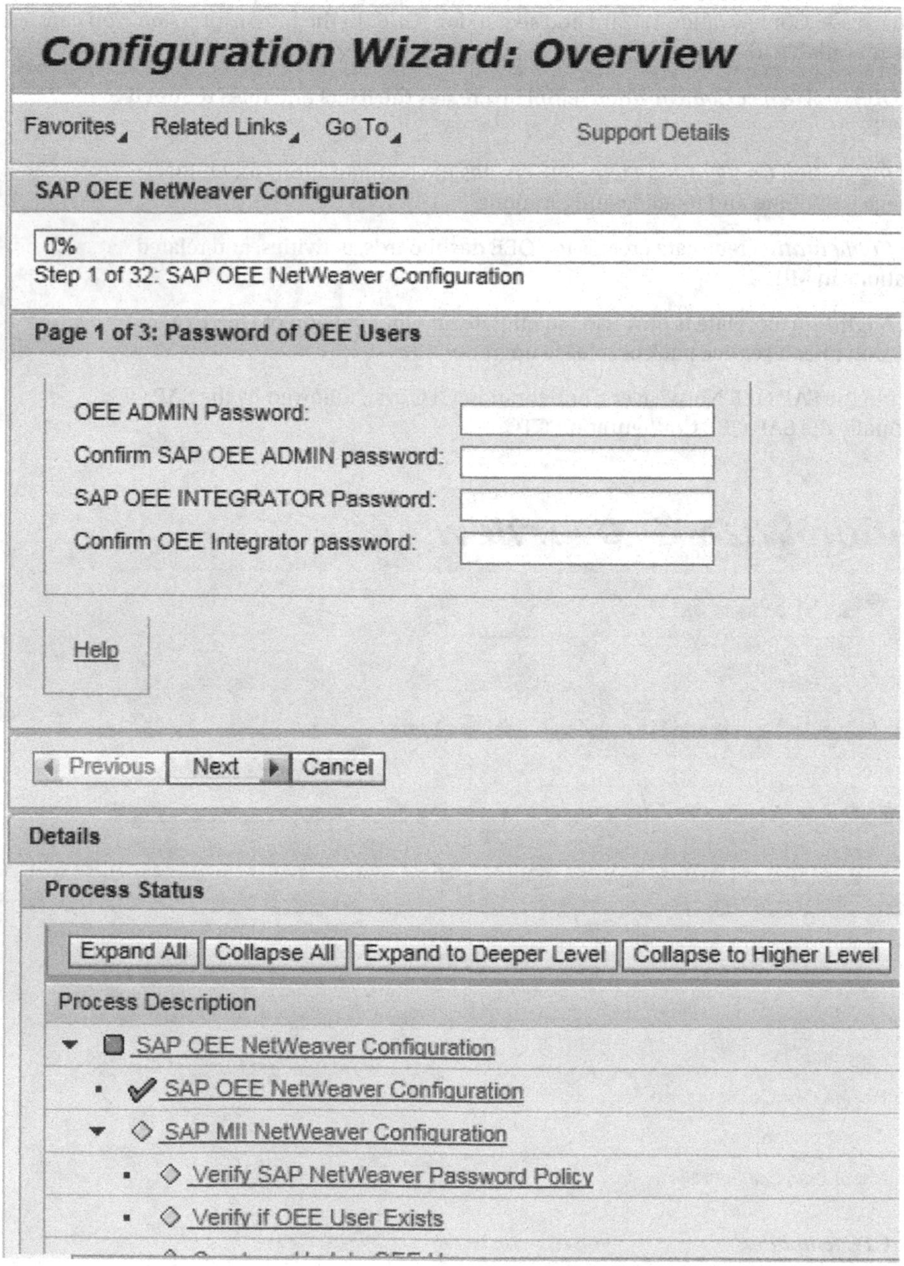

Figure 4-3. *SAP OEE NetWeaver configuration: step 1*

In the next step, you need to specify the host details of the OEE instance with the HTTP/HTTPS protocol as applicable, hostname, and port where MII is installed and click on Next, as shown in Figure 4-4.

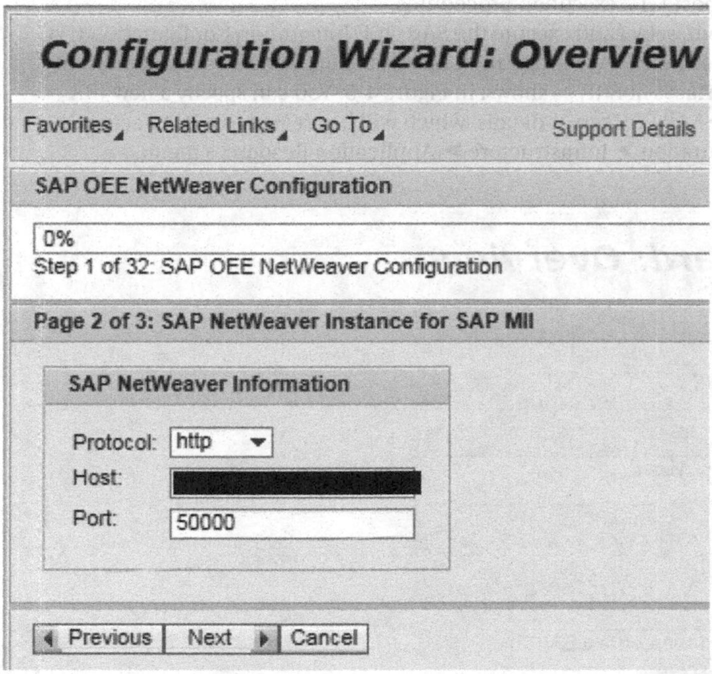

Figure 4-4. *SAP OEE NetWeaver configuration: step 2*

Finally, click the Finish button, which will create the necessary users and roles for SAP OEE in the NetWeaver UME of the MII server.

The following users are created in UME:

- `OEE_ADMIN`
- `OEE_INTEGRATOR`

Table 4-1 shows the UME roles created for OEE.

Table 4-1. *OEE User Roles*

Role	Description
OEE_ADMIN	Administrator role to manage all OEE configurations
OEE_INTEGRATOR	Configurer role to manage OEE workflows and OEEINT configurations
OEE_OPERATOR	Operator role to access OEE dashboards and report production and data collection
OEE_READ_ONLY	Auditor role to view all OEE configurations with read-only access
OEE_SUPERADMIN	Administrator role for system-wide configurations including user management
OEE_SUPERVISOR	Supervisor role to manage shift and orders

SAP OEE Integration Configuration CTC

This section will describe how this CTC configures SAP MII and integration-related SAP OEE elements for SAP OEE and SAP ERP integration and post-CTC execution procedures.

To configure the OEEINT component, select and execute the SAP OEE Integration Configuration CTC wizard. In the first step, you need to specify the JRA configuration details using the OEE component from MII that will execute the RFC/BAPI interfaces in ERP, as shown in Figure 4-5. You can specify a new JRA connection factory name along with the SAP ERP server details, which will be created as a JCA Factory in NetWeaver Administrator under Configuration ➤ Infrastructure ➤ Application Resources menu.

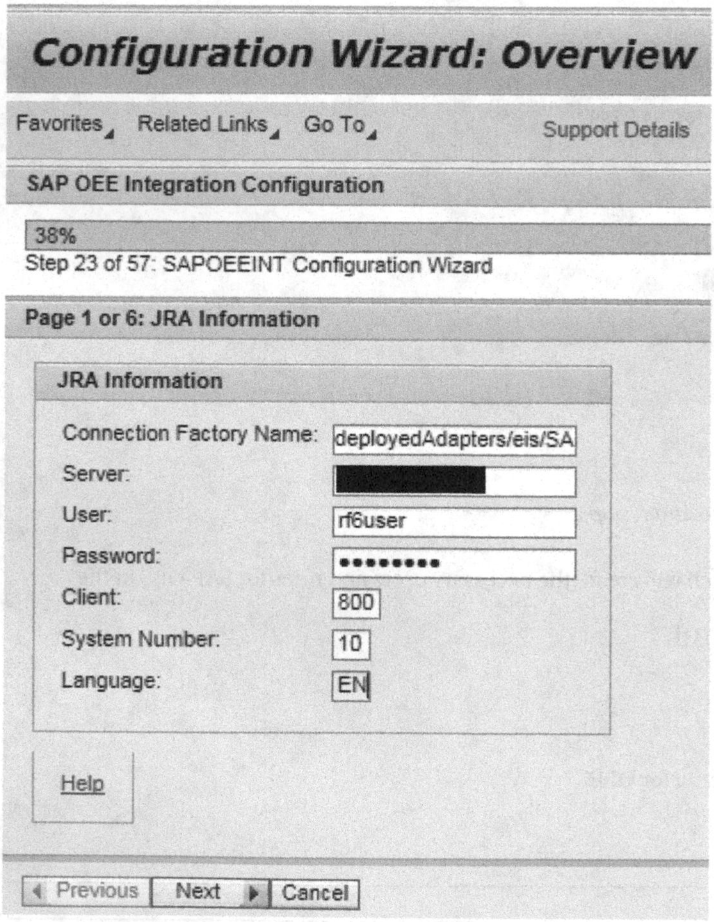

Figure 4-5. *JRA configuration for SAP OEEINT*

In the next step, you need to specify the plant code configured in SAP ERP, OEE_INTEGRATOR user password, the ERP client for the plant, and the JRA connector name, which will be created in NWA from the connection factory, as shown in Figure 4-6. You also need to specify the server time zone for the ERP and set the OEE Time Zone to be the time zone where the plant is located.

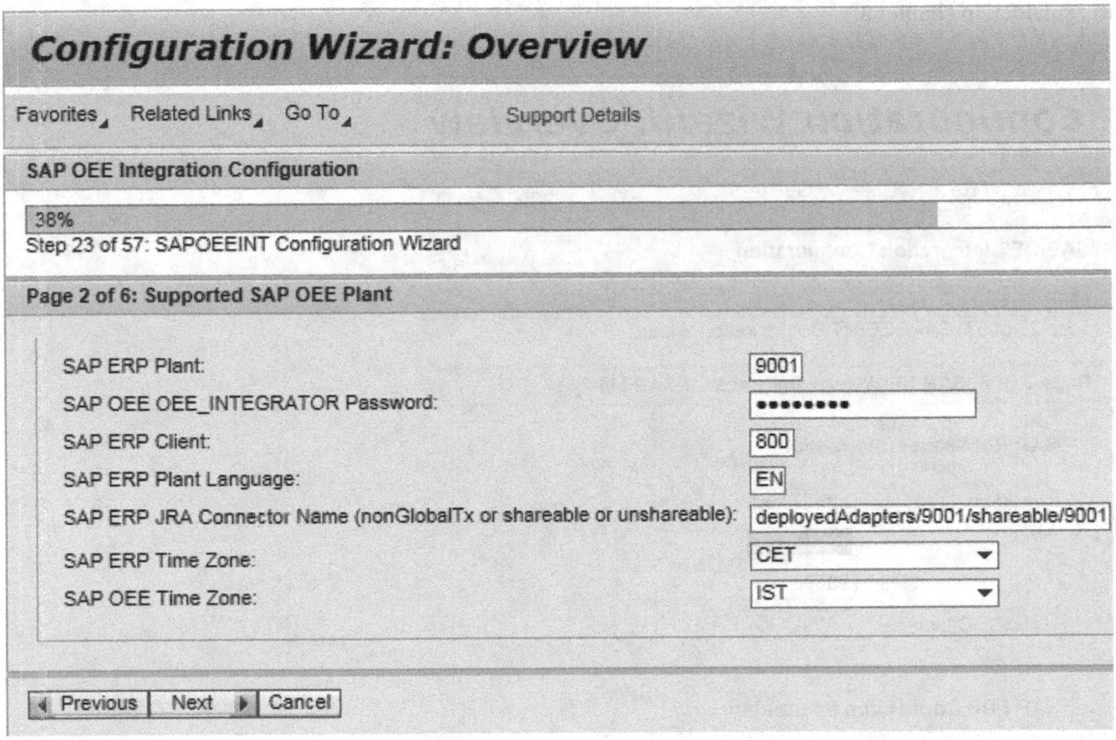

Configuration Wizard: Overview

Favorites Related Links Go To Support Details

SAP OEE Integration Configuration

38%

Step 23 of 57: SAPOEEINT Configuration Wizard

Page 2 of 6: Supported SAP OEE Plant

SAP ERP Plant: 9001

SAP OEE OEE_INTEGRATOR Password: ••••••••

SAP ERP Client: 800

SAP ERP Plant Language: EN

SAP ERP JRA Connector Name (nonGlobalTx or shareable or unshareable): deployedAdapters/9001/shareable/9001

SAP ERP Time Zone: CET

SAP OEE Time Zone: IST

Previous Next Cancel

Figure 4-6. *Supported OEE plant configuration*

In the next step you need to specify the IDoc listener details, which will be configured in MII to receive IDoc messages for the specified plant from ERP, as shown in Figure 4-7. In MII there are ten IDoc message listeners, provided as XMIIIDocxx (where xx stands for 01 to 10), one of which you need to select and then specify the MII server host name and port. You also need to specify the ERP server details and the RFC destination configuration in the ERP server, which is used by the ALE configuration to send the IDocs to MII, as explained in chapter 3.

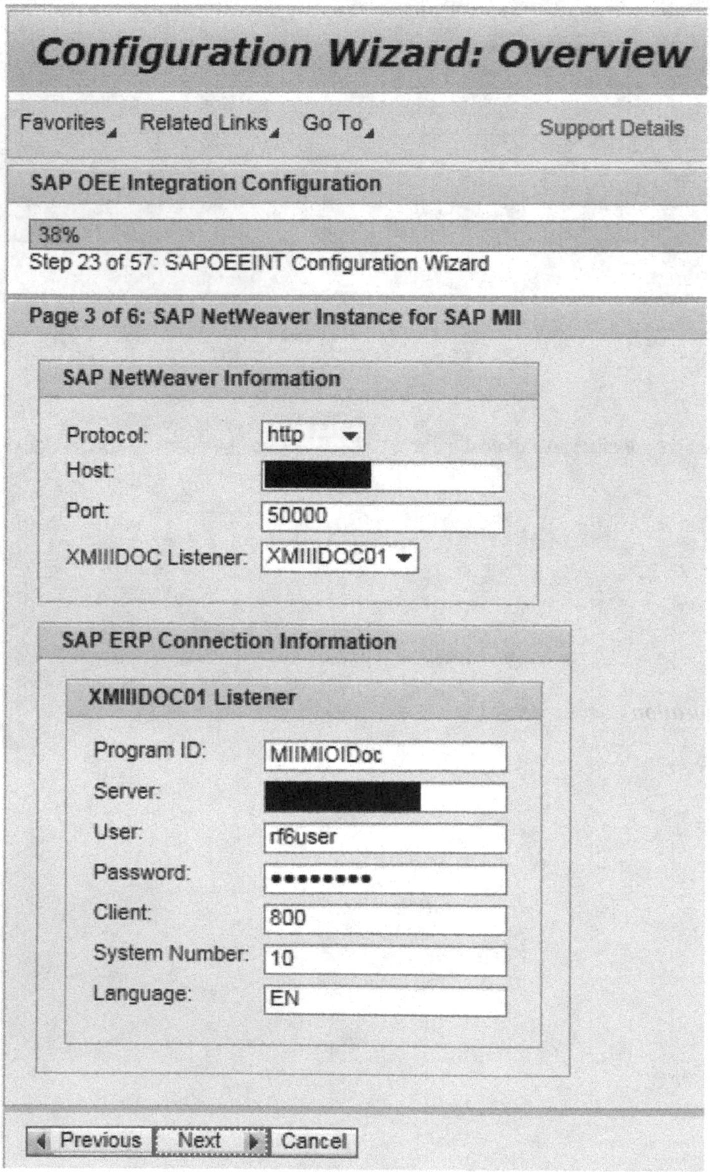

Configuration Wizard: Overview

Favorites Related Links Go To Support Details

SAP OEE Integration Configuration

38%

Step 23 of 57: SAPOEEINT Configuration Wizard

Page 3 of 6: SAP NetWeaver Instance for SAP MII

SAP NetWeaver Information

Protocol: http

Host:

Port: 50000

XMIIIDOC Listener: XMIIIDOC01

SAP ERP Connection Information

XMIIIDOC01 Listener

Program ID: MIIMIOIDoc

Server:

User: rf6user

Password: ••••••••

Client: 800

System Number: 10

Language: EN

Previous Next Cancel

Figure 4-7. *NetWeaver instance and IDoc listener configuration*

In the next step you need to specify the scheduler job configurations for OEE by specifying the number of messages and the time period of execution, as shown in Figure 4-8. By default the time period of the scheduled jobs is specified as 0 * * * * *, which signifies that the job will execute once every minute at the 0th second, which you can change if required. There are a total of four schedulers defined for OEE.

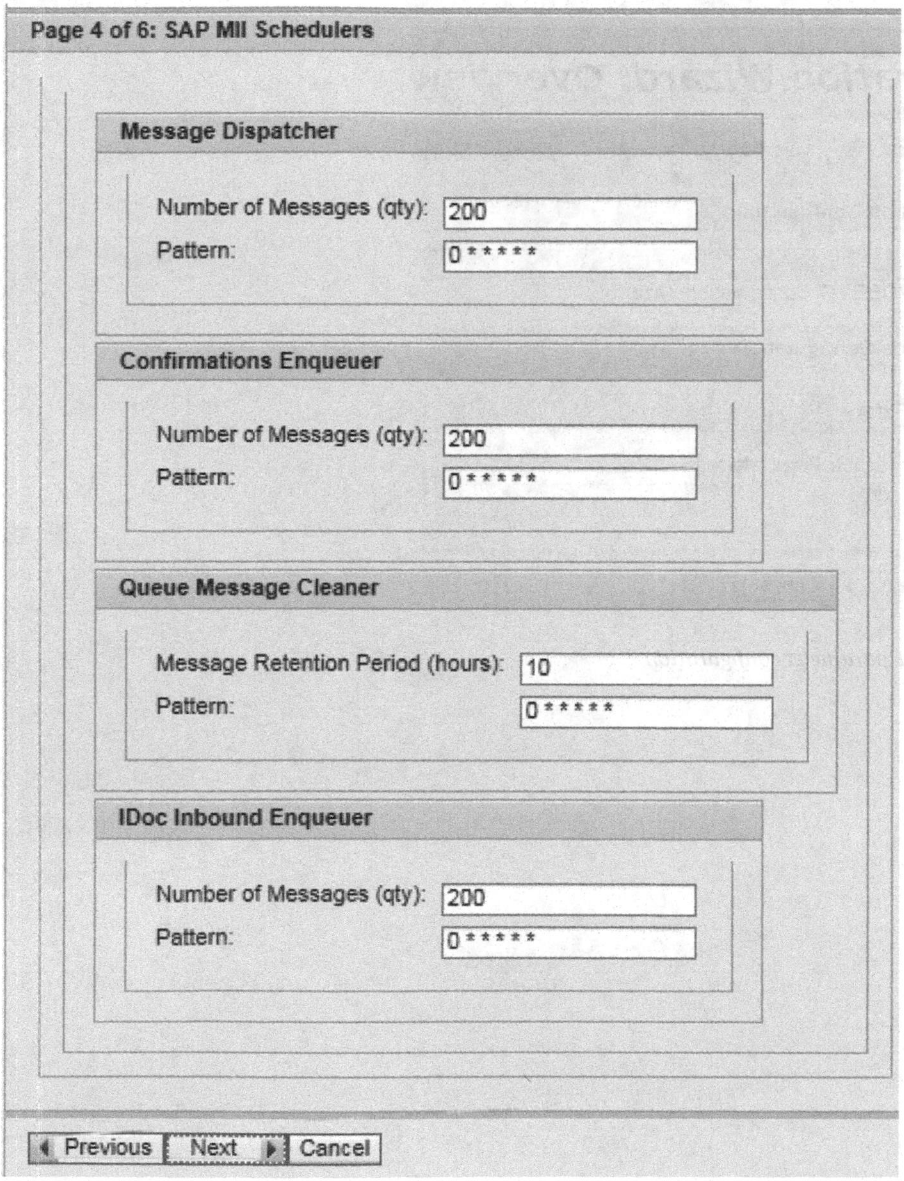

Page 4 of 6: SAP MII Schedulers

Message Dispatcher

Number of Messages (qty): 200

Pattern: 0 * * * * *

Confirmations Enqueuer

Number of Messages (qty): 200

Pattern: 0 * * * * *

Queue Message Cleaner

Message Retention Period (hours): 10

Pattern: 0 * * * * *

IDoc Inbound Enqueuer

Number of Messages (qty): 200

Pattern: 0 * * * * *

Previous | Next | Cancel

Figure 4-8. *OEE schedulers configuration in MII*

In the next configuration step, you can specify the control keys of operations in the production or process order that are relevant for OEE as pre-XSLT transaction parameters, if required. You can leave it blank if all operations in the order are relevant for OEE, as shown in Figure 4-9. If you specify the control keys, use a semicolon to separate multiple control keys e.g. ControlKey=ZR02;ZR03. You can also specify the same thing using the workflow configurations in OEEINT.

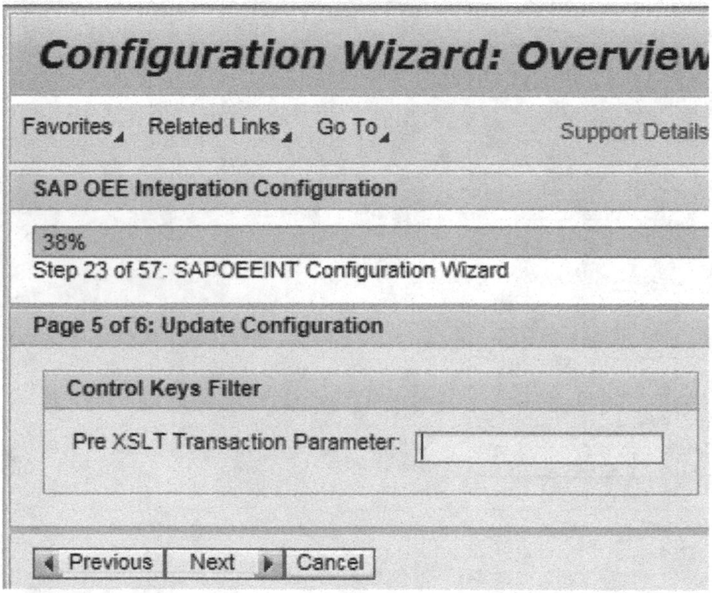

Figure 4-9. *Pre-XSLT parameter configuration*

In the next step, the user can check the "Select to Enter CSV Parameters" checkbox to enable the fields for entering the FTP location where CSV data files will be generated by OEEHANAAggregationService. The user can provide the FTP location and the frequency of execution of the scheduler, as shown in Figure 4-10.

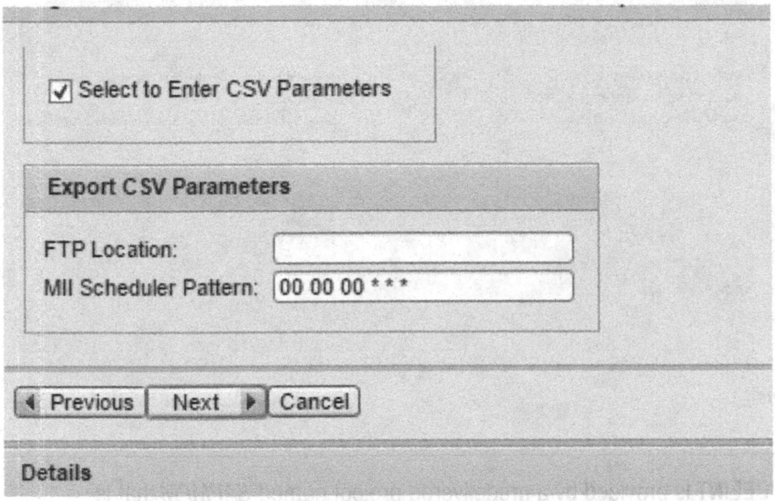

Figure 4-10. *CSV parameters for OEEHANAAggregation service*

That will bring you to the last step of this CTC configuration wizard; clicking on the Next button will complete the configurations for OEEINT.

Once the CTC wizard execution is complete, the JRA connections and IDoc listeners are configured in NetWeaver Administrator, and certain configurations for OEEINT are created in MII, which will be explained in the next section.

OEE Integration Configurations

This section will explain the configuration details of OEEINT in MII, which is required to process ERP's OEE-related data. Once you have executed the CTC wizards for OEE roles and OEEINT configurations, log in to SAP MII using the URL http://<host>:<port>/XMII/Menu.jsp. The OEE-specific menus are available under the ERP-Shop Integration for Worker UI and Worker UI Management menu categories.

Global Configurations

The global configuration provides certain configurations required globally in OEE, as shown in Figure 4-11. You can access it from the ERP-Shop Floor Integration ➤ Global Configurations menu. The global configuration properties are as follows:

- SAPOEEINT_RETRY_RETENTION_PERIOD - The time in minutes after which the system retries a failed message in OEEINT workflow.
- SAPMPM_UOM_CONVERSION_TXN - Deprecated not used anymore
- SAPMPM_ASYNCH_ENQUEUE_TXN - Deprecated not used anymore

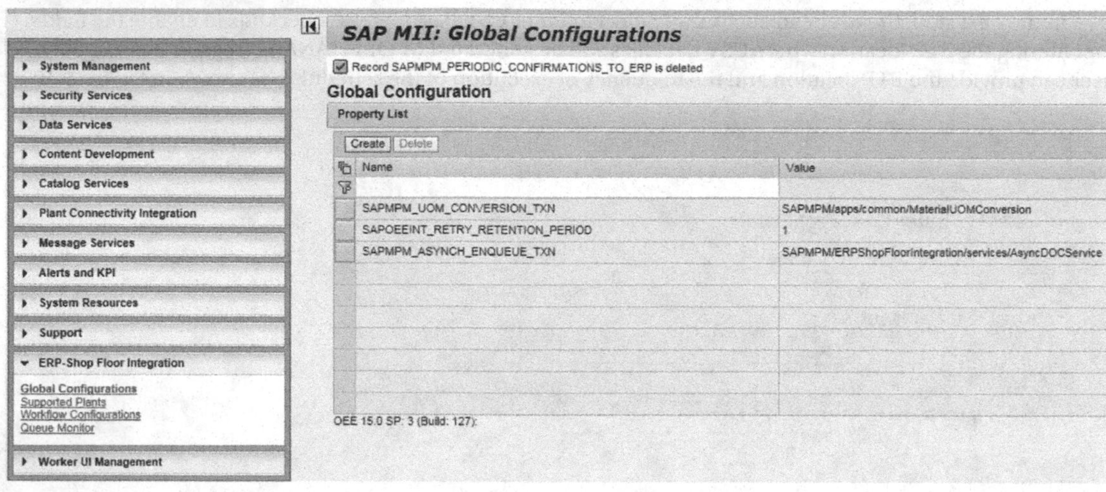

Figure 4-11. *Global configurations*

■ **Note** The SAP MII content for OEEINT is provided by a predelivered project named *SAPMPM* that is deployed during the OEE component installation. It contains all the data queries, business logic, and XSLT required for OEEINT. You can view the content of the project from the MII workbench.

Supported Plants Configurations

Supported plants configuration provides the configurations related to each plant for the OEEINT setup, as shown in Figure 4-12. You can access it from ERP-Shop Floor Integration ➤ Supported Plants menu. This configuration is mandatory in order to use an ERP plant in OEE, and it is created automatically when the OEE Integration CTC is executed for a plant. You can view and change the ERP client, language, JRA connector factory name, and the time zones of ERP and MII servers from this configuration.

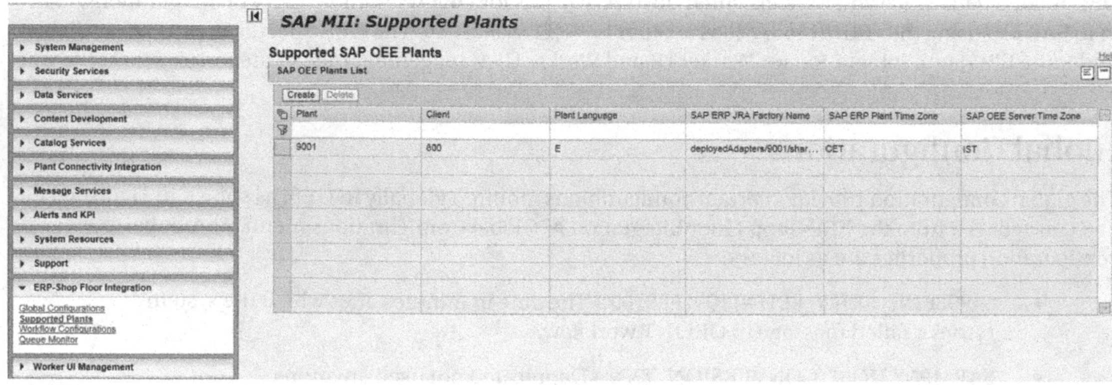

Figure 4-12. *Supported plant configurations*

IDoc Message Listener Configurations

Once you execute the OEE Integration CTC wizard, the IDoc listener gets configured in NetWeaver Administrator, along with the JRA connectors, to receive IDoc messages from ERP. The IDoc listener is a JRA resource adaptor that is configured in NetWeaver Administrator. You next need to update the IDoc message listener configuration in MII from the Message Services ➤ Message Listeners menu, as shown in Figure 4-13. You need to select the IDoc listener that was specified during the CTC execution and click on the Update button to update its configurations in the NetWeaver resource adaptor. Unless the IDoc listener configuration is updated in MII, it won't be able to receive any IDoc messages from ERP.

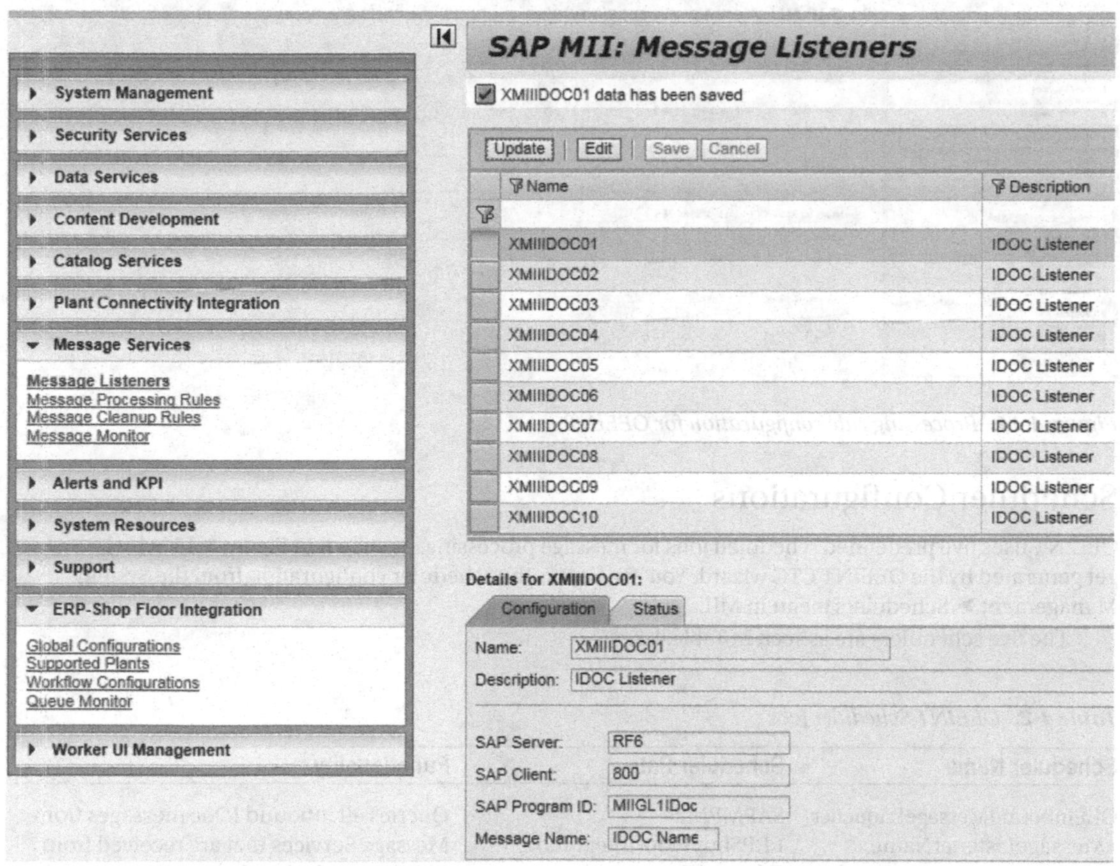

Figure 4-13. *IDoc message listener configuration*

Processing Rule Configurations

Processing rules are used in SAP MII to process incoming messages from external systems through the Message Services. A processing rule is created by the OEEINT CTC wizard named `XMIIIDOC01_ALL_MESSAGES`, as shown in Figure 4-14. It is used to categorize IDoc messages received from SAP ERP to be processed by the OEE schedulers. All the IDoc messages are tagged with the message category `SAPOEEINT_INBOUND_QUEUE`, a queue from which the OEE scheduler queries the messages and processes them using the corresponding OEEINT workflows. The processing rule is configured for the IDoc message listener specified in the OEEINT CTC wizard configuration and for all messages (specified by use of *).

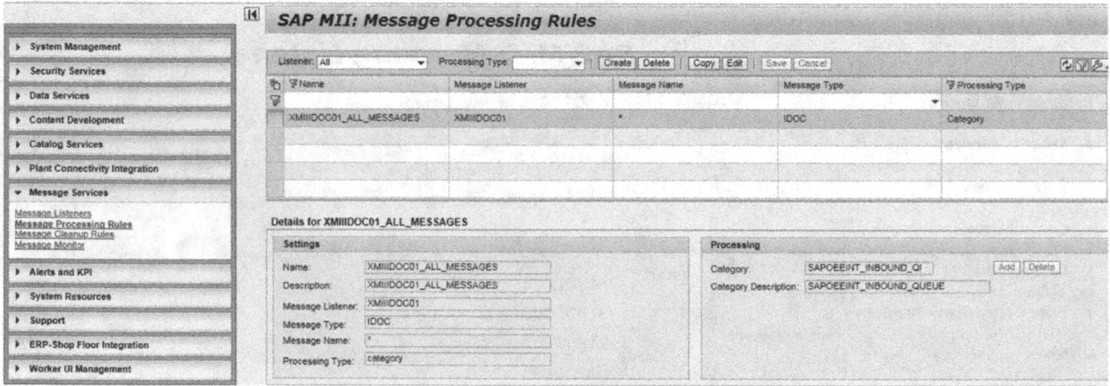

Figure 4-14. *Processing rule configuration for OEEINT*

Scheduler Configurations

OEEINT uses five predefined scheduled jobs for message processing, as shown in Figure 4-15, which get generated by the OEEINT CTC wizard. You can access the scheduler configuration from the System Management ➤ Schedulers menu in MII.

The five schedulers are as seen in Table 4-2.

Table 4-2. *OEEINT Scheduler Jobs*

Scheduler Name	Scheduler Path	Functionality
OEEInboundMessageEnqueuer_ <MessageListenerName>	SAPMPM/ ERPShopFloorIntegration/ InboundEnqueuer/ InboundEnqueuer	Queries all inbound IDoc messages from Message Services that are received from SAP ERP and adds them to the message processing queue database table in the OEEINT database. There are separate schedulers created for each message listener configured.
OEEMessageDispatcher	SAPMPM/ ERPShopFloorIntegration/ frame/dispatchers/ simpleDispatcher/ SimpleMessageDispatcher	Queries the messages from the OEEINT processing queue and executes the corresponding workflows to process them

(*continued*)

Table 4-2. *(continued)*

Scheduler Name	Scheduler Path	Functionality
OEEConfirmationEnqueuer_<Plant>_<Client>	SAPMPM/ ERPShopFloorIntegration/ Confirmations/ OrderConfirmationsEnqueuer	Queries the messages sent by OEE in MII; picks messages from OEE database for confirmations to be updated in ERP and adds them to the OEEINT processing queue. There are separate schedulers created for each plant-client combination
OEEQueueMessageCleaner	SAPMPM/ ERPShopFloorIntegration/ MessagePurging/ MessageCleaner	Deletes the messages from the OEEINT processing queue after the retention time specified in the schedule input has passed
OEEAutoCsvDownloadForReports	SAPMPM/apps/ ExportCsvForOeeReports/ ExportCsvForOeeReports	Creates CSV files for plant reports in SAP Lumira

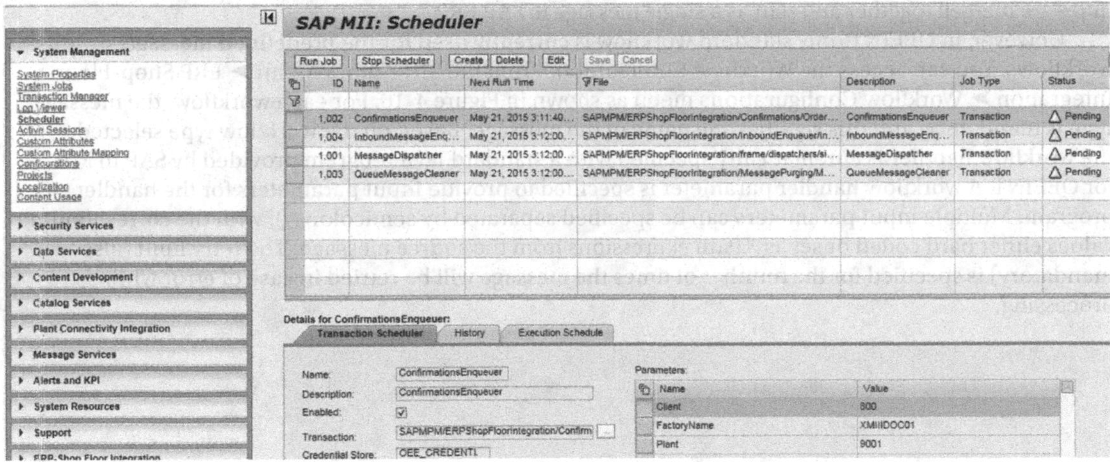

Figure 4-15. *Scheduler configurations for OEEINT*

■ **Note** The OEEINT content in SAP MII is provided by a predefined project called SAPMPM. It contains all the BLS transactions, data queries and XSLT files required for scheduler and OEEINT workflows.

Workflow Configurations

To transfer the messages that are exchanged between SAP ERP and MII, message workflows are provided in OEEINT, which manages the message processing, transformation, and updating in the OEE database. Message workflow is a framework developed as part of OEEINT where preconfigured message workflow configurations are provided for the standard ERP interfaces supported in OEE. You can also add new messages and enhance existing workflows. There are three types of workflows available in OEEINT:

- Standard Workflow
- Split Workflow
- Correlation Workflow

Standard workflow is used to process a message incoming to MII, and after transformation and validations as required it sends the message to the destination system; i.e., OEE database or SAP ERP.

Split workflow is used to split a single message into multiple messages based on the message content; e.g., material master message sent from SAP ERP for multiple plants is split into multiple messages for each plant.

Correlation workflow is used to merge multiple messages together based on the message content to generate a single message; e.g., production yield confirmation messages sent for the same order multiple times are merged together and sent as a single message to SAP ERP.

However, in OEEINT only standard workflow is currently used for the predefined message workflows. You can access the Workflow Configuration from the MII Admin Menu ➤ ERP Shop-Floor Integration ➤ Workflow Configurations menu as shown in Figure 4-16. For each workflow, the message type is mandatory, and this signifies the name of the message. Based on the workflow type selected, the workflow handler is automatically specified with a standard Java program provided by SAP in MII for OEEINT. A workflow handler parameter is specified to provide input parameters for the handler program. Multiple input parameters can be specified separated by semicolon (;), with the corresponding values either hard coded or set as XPath expressions from the source message. The retry limit (also mandatory) is specified for the number of times the message will be retried in case of error while processing.

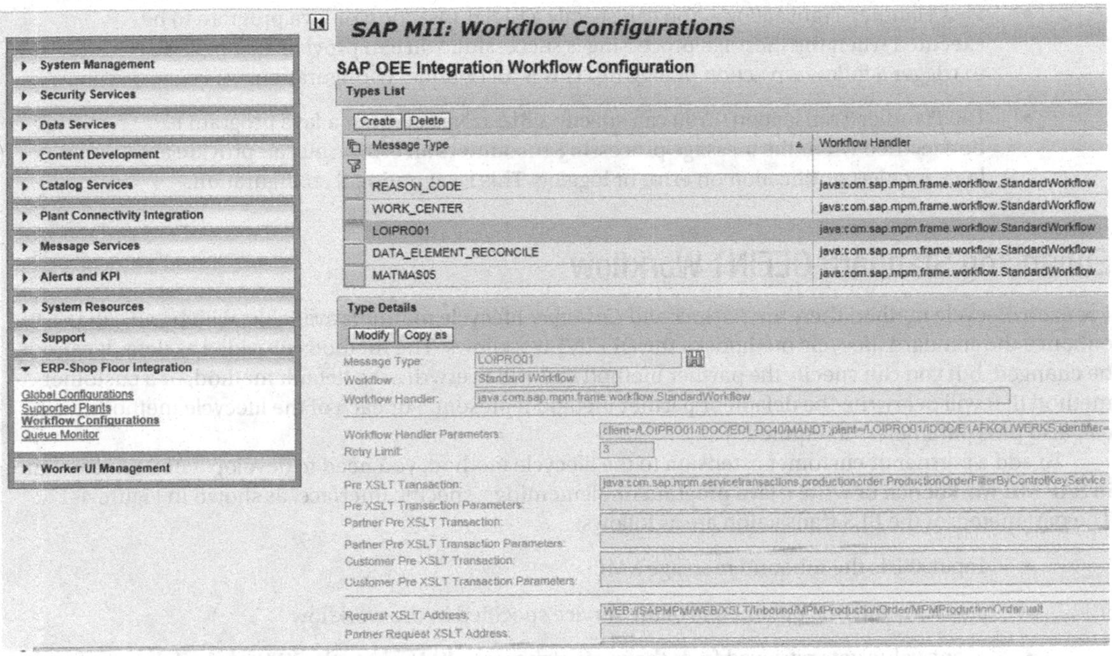

Figure 4-16. *Workflow configurations in OEEINT*

Lifecycle Methods of Standard Workflow

Each message workflow has a few lifecycle methods with which the messages are processed in OEEINT. The lifecycle methods are executed in a sequence, processing the source message or message from the previous step and generating the output message. The source messages, which are XML messages, are queried from the Message Service or OEEINT outbound message queue (database table) and added to the processing queue of OEEINT, from which the corresponding workflow is executed based on the message type. The lifecycle methods are as follows and are executed in the same sequence as shown:

- Pre-XSLT Transaction - You can specify a BLS transaction or a Java program to validate or enrich the source message before transformation. This is an optional configuration.

- Request XSLT Address - You can specify an XSLT file to transform the source message to the target message structure; i.e., IDoc message to OEE message and OEE message to BAPI structure. This is a mandatory configuration.

- Post-XSLT Transaction - You can specify a BLS transaction or a Java program to validate or enrich the transformed message. This is an optional configuration.

- Service Transaction - You can specify a BLS transaction or a Java program to dispatch the message to the destination system; i.e., to SAP ERP by RFC call or to OEE by API call. This is a mandatory configuration.

- Response XSLT Address - You can specify an XML-Style Language Transformation (XSLT) file to transform the response message received from the service executed in the preceding step; i.e., RFC or API call. This is an optional configuration.

- Pass Handler Transaction - You can specify a BLS transaction or Java program to be executed when the message processing is successful. You can provide any logic here to trigger a follow-up action or logging. This is an optional configuration.
- Fail Handler Transaction - You can specify a BLS transaction or a Java program to be executed when the message processing encounters an error. You can provide any logic for alert notification on error or logging. This is an optional configuration.

Enhancing Standard OEEINT Workflow

For each lifecycle method there are *Partner* and *Customer* lifecycle methods available, which you can use to enhance the standard lifecycle methods of the OEEINT workflows. The methods provided as default cannot be changed, but you can specify the partner method that will overwrite the default method, or a customer method that will overwrite the default or partner method if present. For each of the lifecycle methods, you can also pass parameters if required.

To add a partner or customer extension to the lifecycle method, you need to develop a BLS transaction in SAP MII workbench or write a Java program implementing a specific interface, as shown in Figure 4-17. The parameters of the BLS transaction are as follows:

- `inputXML` is the inbound message XML
- `params` is the BLS parameters of the service specified in the workflow
- `plant` value gets retrieved from the queued message XML using the XML path of the plant parameter of the “Workflow Handler Parameters” field.
- `recordId` is a GUID of the message in the SAPMEINT integration queue
- `typeId` is the message type

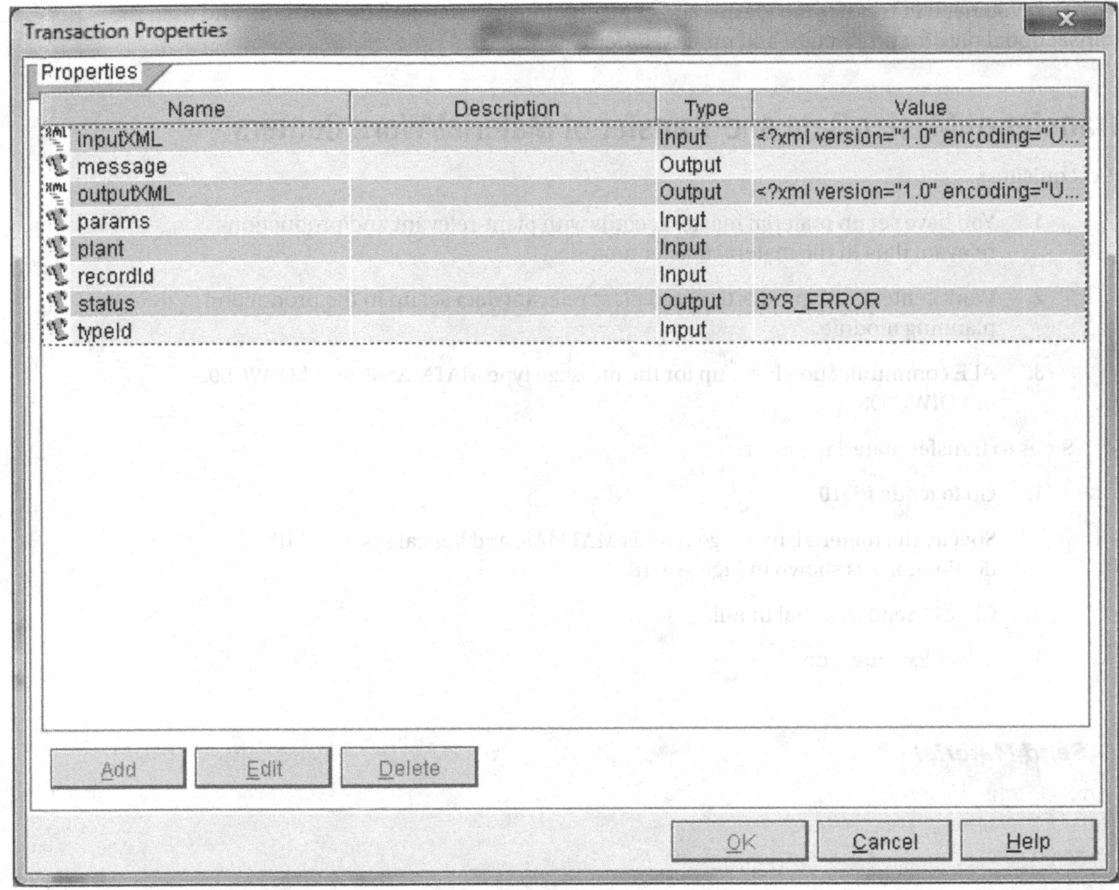

Figure 4-17. BLS transaction interface for OEE lifecycle method

Inside the BLS transaction you need to develop the logic to parse the input XML document, do the required validation and enhancements, and pass the output XML with the enhanced or validated data. If any exception needs to be thrown to signify an error, you need to assign a string with value SYS_ERROR in the output status property. If the processing is successful then you need to specify PASSED.

Most of the services and XSLT for the lifecycle methods of the OEEINT workflows are provided by default, but there may be some scenarios for which you need to enhance the standard lifecycle method of a workflow for an interface to add additional data or validations when transferred from SAP ERP to MII or vice versa some scenarios of which you will learn in Chapter 7.

Transfer of Data from ERP to OEE

To transfer the configuration, master, and transactional data from SAP ERP to SAP MII via the OEEINT framework, you need to log in to SAP ERP and use the specific transactions available there to send the messages to SAP MII. The prerequisite configurations, which you need to do in SAP ERP before you can transfer the data, are explained in Chapter 3, and the configurations in SAP MII are explained in this chapter in an earlier section.

First you need to transfer the master and configuration data required for SAP OEE and then the transactional data for production and process orders.

Transfer of Master Data and Transfer of Material/Work Centers

Prerequisites:

1. You have set up material master records with plant-relevant and production-relevant data in the materal master module.
2. Work centers with production and plant relevant data set up in the production planning module.
3. ALE communication is set up for the message type MATMAS05 and LOIWCS02 or LOIWCS03.

Steps to transfer material master:

1. Go to tcode BD10.
2. Specify the material, message type as MATMAS, and logical system (MII destination) as shown in Figure 4-18.
3. Check "Send material in full."
4. Select Execute icon.

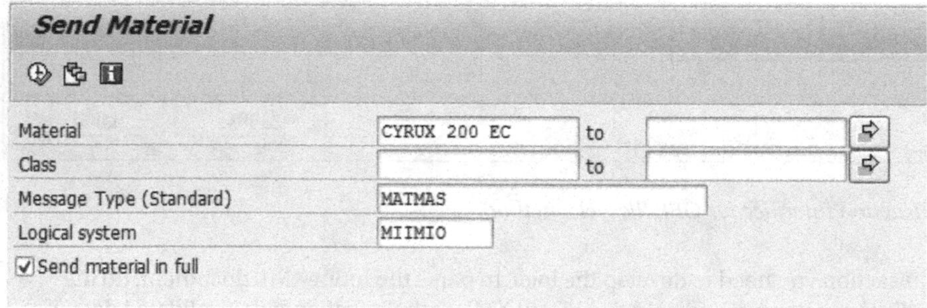

Figure 4-18. *Transfer material to OEE*

5. Go to MII Menu ➤ ERP Shop floor Integration ➤ Queue monitor. Check the message processing status to see if it a success.
6. ERP shop floor integration framework creates or updates the material details in OEE database tables.

Steps to transfer work center master:

1. Go to tcode POIM.
2. Enter the logical system (MII destination).
3. Select the "Work centers for" option and specify the work center to be transferred to OEE as shown in Figure 4-19.

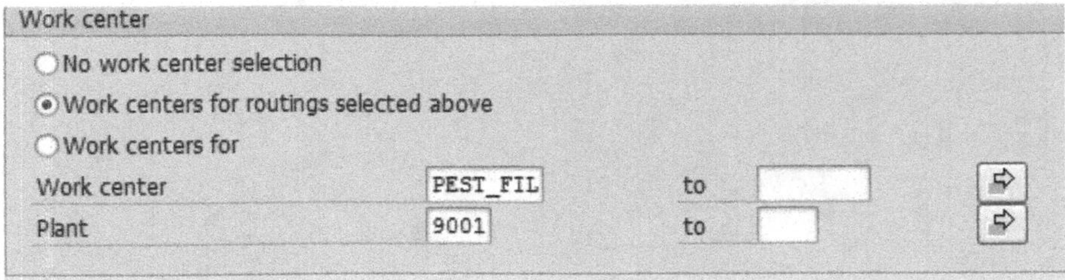

Figure 4-19. *Transfer work center to OEE*

4. Select Execute icon

5. Go to MII Menu ➤ ERP Shop floor Integration ➤ Queue monitor. Check the message processing status to see if it is a success.

6. ERP shop floor integration framework creates or updates the work center details in OEE database tables.

Transfer of OEE Master Data and Transfer of Plant Hierarchy/Reason Codes

Prerequisites:

1. Plant hierarchy with all the node-specific configurations is created.

2. Global and plant reason code configurations from level 1 to level 10 are completed under production ➤ Overall Equipment Effectiveness.

3. ALE communication is set up for the message types /OEE/PLANT01, /OEE/RC01, and /OEE/RC02.

Steps to transfer the data:

1. Go to SAP Menu ➤ Logistics ➤ Production ➤ Overall Equipment Effectiveness ➤ Information system ➤ OEE IDoc selection or go to Tcode - /OEE/BO_IDOC

2. Select the logical system (MII-OEE destination).

3. Select the "All Plant Hierarchy" option to send all the hierarchies configured to OEE, or select "Plant Hierarchy for" and enter the specific plant code to transfer a specific plant hierarchy to OEE, as shown in Figure 4-20.

4. Select "All Plant Reason Code" to send all the reason codes configured to OEE, or select "Reason Code for" and enter the plant-specific reason codes to transfer to OEE, as shown in 4-20.

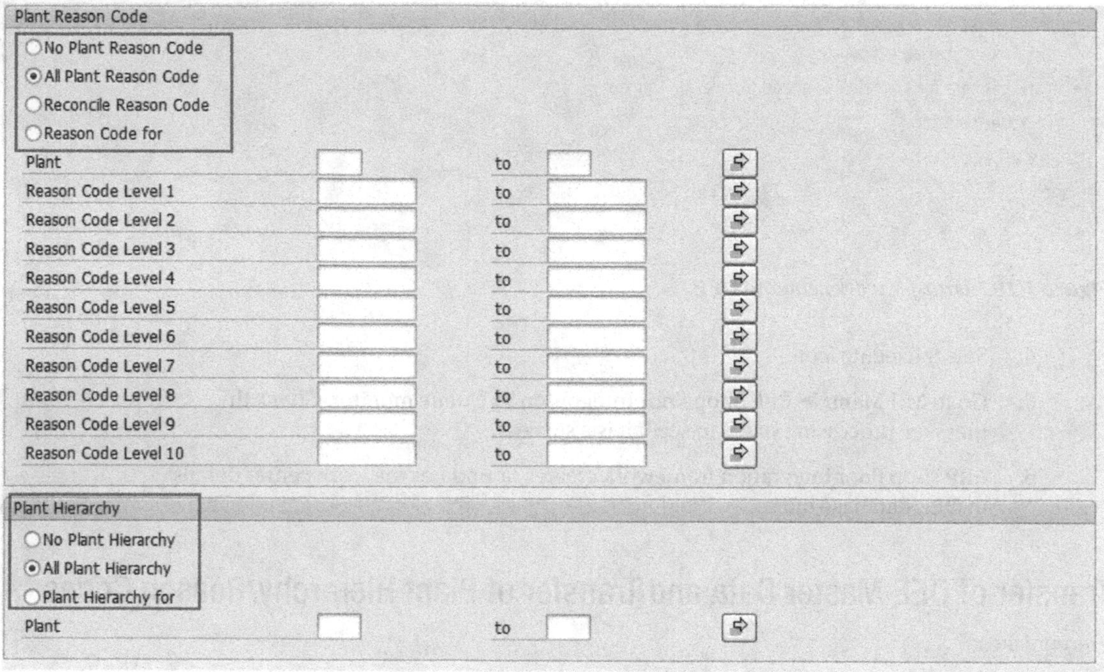

Plant Reason Code

- No Plant Reason Code
- All Plant Reason Code
- Reconcile Reason Code
- Reason Code for

		to	
Plant		to	
Reason Code Level 1		to	
Reason Code Level 2		to	
Reason Code Level 3		to	
Reason Code Level 4		to	
Reason Code Level 5		to	
Reason Code Level 6		to	
Reason Code Level 7		to	
Reason Code Level 8		to	
Reason Code Level 9		to	
Reason Code Level 10		to	

Plant Hierarchy

- No Plant Hierarchy
- All Plant Hierarchy
- Plant Hierarchy for

Plant to

Figure 4-20. *Transfer master data to OEE*

5. Select Execute icon.
6. Go to MII Menu ➤ ERP Shop floor Integration ➤ Queue monitor. Check the message processing status to see if it is a success.
7. ERP shop floor integration framework creates or updates the hierarchy and reason code details in the respective OEE database tables.

Transfer of OEE Configuration data

You can send the following OEE-specific cross-plant configuration data using this transaction:

- KPI
- Data Collection Element Context
- Data Collection Element
- Data Element Type
- Data Elements
- Machine Group
- Production Mode
- Production Activity
- Plant Reason Code

- Plant Hierarchy
- UOM and Dimensions
- Shift
- Classifications
- Standard Value Key and Formula Parameters

Prerequisites:

1. All the OEE-specific configuration data are created and maintained in the OEE add-on.
2. ALE communication is set up for all the message types of configuration data. Refer to chapter 3 for message types of OEE configuration data.
3. Material and work center are transferred to OEE.
4. Plant hierarchy is configured with the material, routing, operation, bottleneck machine, KPIs, classification, and so on for each work center. Hierarchy is published and transferred to OEE.

Steps to transfer the data:

1. Go to SAP Menu ➤ Logistics ➤ Production ➤ Overall Equipment Effectiveness ➤ Information system ➤ OEE IDoc selection, or go to Tcode - /OEE/BO_IDOC
2. Select the logical system (MII-OEE destination).
3. Select either the "All" option or select specific configuration data to send only that data; select the "Reconcile" option when the data already transferred is changed or deleted in SAP ERP, as shown in Figure 4-21.
4. Select Execute icon.
5. Go to MII Menu ➤ ERP Shop floor Integration ➤ Queue monitor. Check the message processing status to see if it a success.
6. ERP shop floor integration framework creates or updates the OEE configuration data details in the respective OEE database tables.

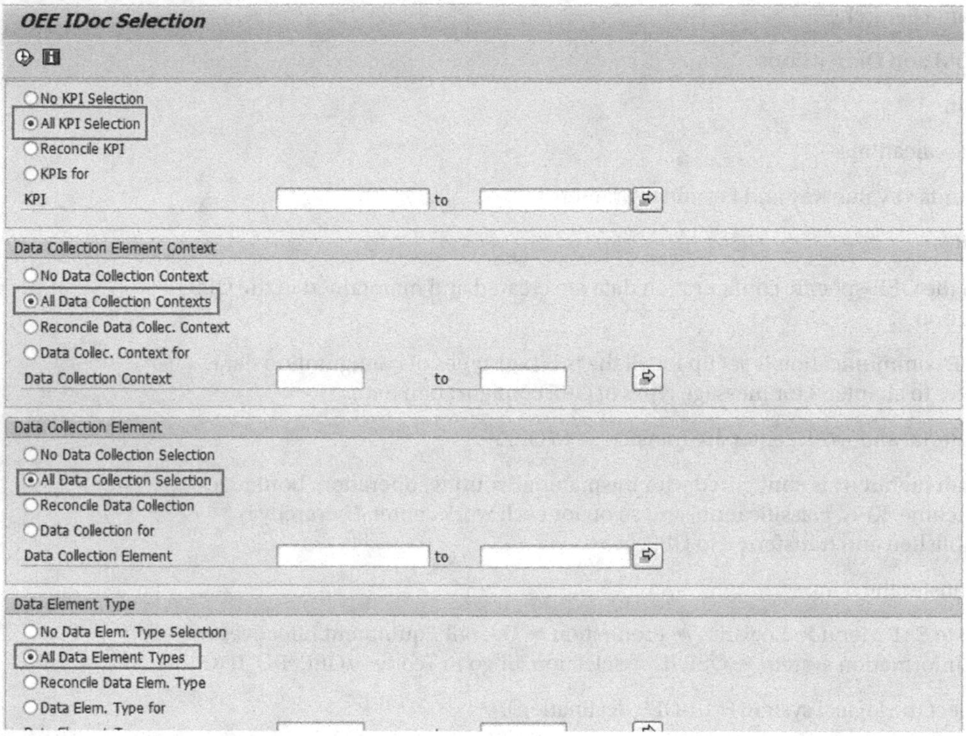

OEE IDoc Selection

No KPI Selection
All KPI Selection
Reconcile KPI
KPIs for
KPI to

Data Collection Element Context
No Data Collection Context
All Data Collection Contexts
Reconcile Data Collec. Context
Data Collec. Context for
Data Collection Context to

Data Collection Element
No Data Collection Selection
All Data Collection Selection
Reconcile Data Collection
Data Collection for
Data Collection Element to

Data Element Type
No Data Elem. Type Selection
All Data Element Types
Reconcile Data Elem. Type
Data Elem. Type for

Figure 4-21. *Transfer configuration data to OEE*

Except for the shift, UOM, and plant hierarchies, all other workflows for OEE-specific configuration and master data have additional workflows with different message types for data reconciliation. As you execute the transaction, IDoc messages will be generated and will be transferred to SAP MII to the OEEINT framework, where they will be processed by the corresponding OEEINT workflows.

You can transfer the process order or production order data from SAP ERP to SAP MII (OEEINT) using the transaction code POIT or the SAP Easy Access menu:

Logistics ➤ Central Functions ➤ Supply Chain Planning Interface ➤ Production Optimization (POIT) ➤ Send Movement Data

Similarly, as in the previous transactions, you need to specify the logical system for SAP MII, and optionally the plant and date range, with the production order selection to send the data to SAP MII to be processed by OEEINT.

Queue Monitor

You can view the messages transferred through OEEINT in the Queue Monitor provided in SAP MII as part of OEEINT, which you can access from MII Admin menu ➤ ERP Shop Floor Integration ➤ Queue Monitor. From the Queue Monitor you can monitor the individual messages sent from ERP or MII for OEE, as shown in Figure 4-22. You can search by specific message name (Document Type), timestamps, process status, identifier, or correlation key.

You can display the messages that are processed by OEEINT with their attributes. A message is retried automatically if it fails in processing depending on the number of retries specified in its corresponding workflow.

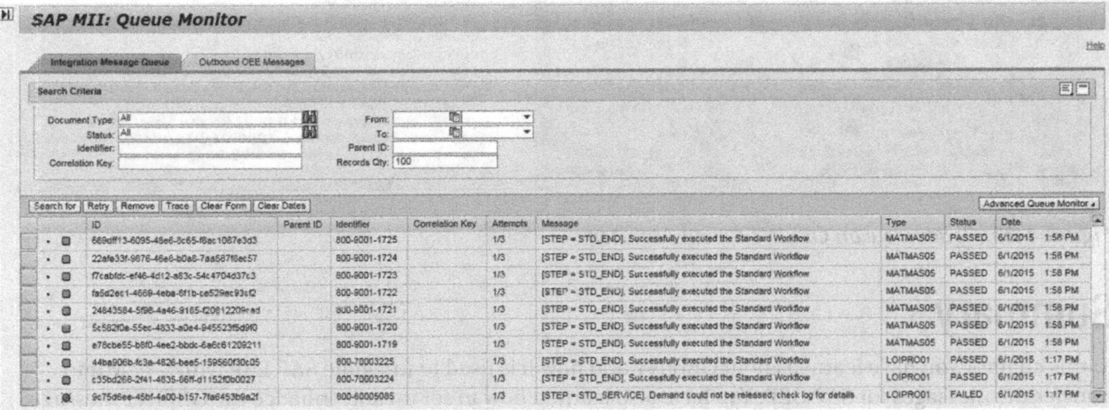

Figure 4-22. OEEINT Queue Monitor

For each message, you can view the message content XML as well by selecting the message and clicking on the Trace button. It displays a pop-up with the different messages generated during the processing, such as the source message or the original document received in MII, the request message generated by OEEINT, and the response message received from ERP or OEE. You can select one of the messages and click the View button to display the message XML, as shown in Figure 4-23. You can also retry processing a message by clicking the Retry button, which will execute the workflow for the selected message.

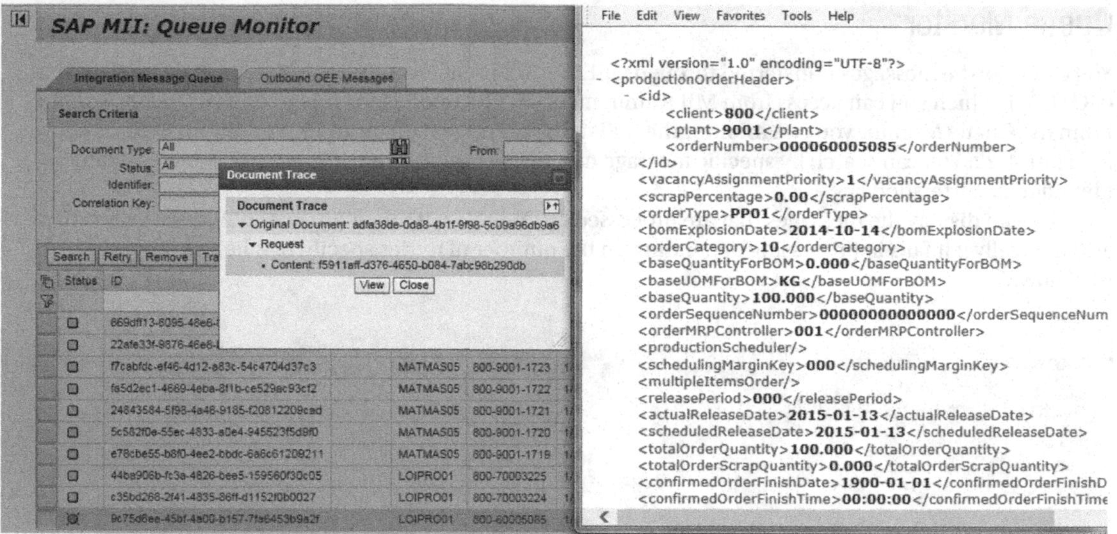

Figure 4-23. *Trace view on OEEINT Queue Monitor*

Summary

In this chapter you have learned about OEEINT and how it is used to integrate SAP ERP with SAP MII to transfer the messages for SAP OEE. You have also learned how to set up and enhance the OEEINT message workflows and their related monitoring activities.

In the next chapter you will learn about the SAP OEE component in SAP MII and how to configure and use it for OEE dashboards.

CHAPTER 5

OEE Configurations in SAP MII

In the last chapter, you learned how MII acts as an integration platform between SAP ERP and OEE components in SAP MII and the OEE CTC configurations for setting up OEE integration.

As a continuation of Chapter 4, this chapter will cover the various roles and authorizations and OEE configurations in SAP MII OEE component required to execute OEE standard functionality.

User Roles and Authorizations

Every action that a user is allowed to perform is governed by the role they are assigned. Hence, you need to create the user roles as per the plant requirements and assign the required actions to these roles.

User roles and authorizations in OEE are configured in three systems:

- SAP ERP
- OEE Integration and Services (NetWeaver Java/SAP MII)
- SAP HANA

User Roles for SAP ERP

Refer to Table 5-1, which lists the authorizations required in SAP ERP to work on OEE-related data management. Each authorization object is assigned an authorization type to execute specific OEE transactions.

D. Saha et al., *Manufacturing Performance Management using SAP OEE*,
DOI 10.1007/978-1-4842-1150-2_5

Table 5-1. User Roles and Authorizations for OEE in SAP ERP

Authorization type	Authorization object	OEE Transactions	OEE Activities
Cross application authorization object	S_TCODE	/OEE/BO_IDOC: OEE IDoc Selection report /OEE/GLOBAL_HIER: Creating Global Hierarchy/OEE/PLANT_HIER: Creating Plant Hierarchy/OEE/PLANT_RC: Creating Plant Reason Codes/OEE/RC_EXCELUPLOAD: Uploading Reason Codes Through MS-Excel	
Basis: Administration	S_TABU_DIS	authorization on maintenance views	Display and change
	S_TABU_LIN	Authorization of organizational criterion on maintenance views	Create, change, display, and delete
OEE Authorization Check		/OEE/C_MGH - Authorization on global hierarchy. /OEE/C_MPH - authorization on plant hierarchy. /OEE/IDOC - OEE IDoc Selection report. /OEE/C_PRC - reason codes using MS-Excel upload	Create, change, display, and delete Execute Create, change, display, and delete

User Roles for OEE Integration Services in SAP MII

SAP OEE, similar to SAP MII, utilizes the authorization concept provided by SAP NetWeaver where users are assigned specific roles. Each role has specific actions assigned.

By default, SAP OEE delivers the following roles, and each role can perform specific OEE actions:

- OEE_OPERATOR
- OEE_SUPERVISOR
- OEE_INTEGRATOR
- OEE_ADMIN
- OEE_SUPERADMIN
- OEE_READ_ONLY

In SAP OEE, the users are authorized for OEE-related actions specifically for a plant–client combination in SAP ERP. Users can perform OEE operations only for the plant and SAP client, which he or she is responsible for. In addition to this, you can define the default SAP client, plant, dashboard, and work center that the user would like to view upon logging on to the system.

To configure this, go to Identity Management ➤ Configuration in SAP NetWeaver UME (`http://<host>:<port>/useradmin`). Choose the User Admin UI tab and select Modify Configuration. Specify "SAPOEE:DEFAULT CLIENT; SAPOEE:DEFAULT PLANT; SAPOEE:DEFAULT WORKUNIT; SAPOEE:DEFAULT POD; SAPOEE:ERP PERSONNEL NUMBER" in Administrator Managed Custom Attributes field and save the entries. Once this configuration is done, for each user you can set the values for client, plant, work unit, and dashboard in the Customized Information tab, as shown in Figure 5-1. Now when the user logs in to the OEE system, the default SAP client and plant will be displayed, while other clients and plants can also be selected, if configured for the user.

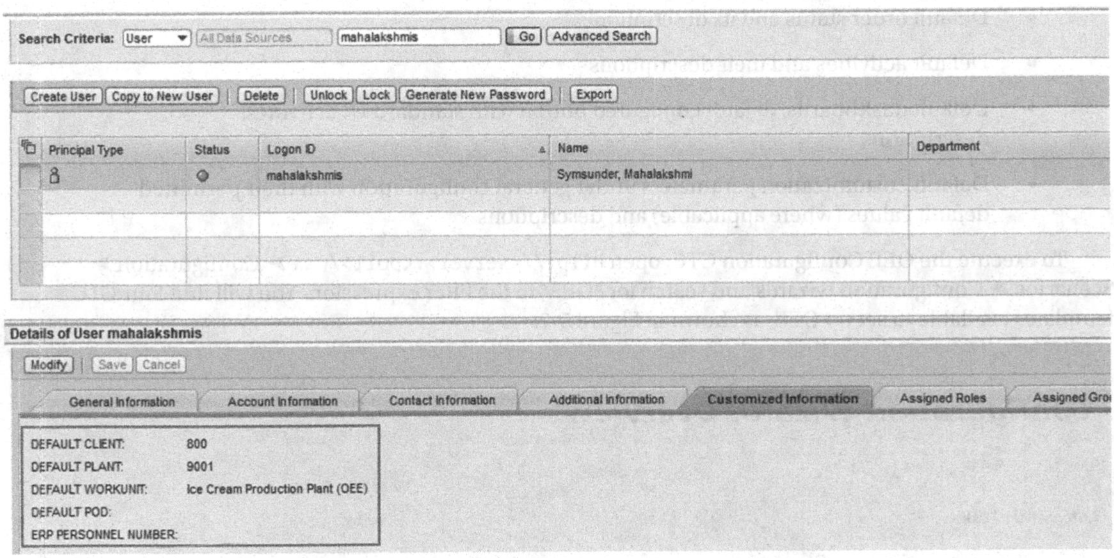

***Figure 5-1.** Configure OEE default values for user*

Default client and plant do not have to be mandatorily mentioned in the Customized Information tab from MII15.0 SP05 release onwards (if the OEE Dashboard is invoked by URL directly and not from MII menu), as these details can also be sent via URL parameters directly–for example, (http://<host>:<port>/OEEDashboard/WorkerUI.jsp?client=<client id>&plant=<plant id>)–but the user group to which the particular user belongs should be assigned to a particular plant, which can be done in the General Configuration tab. Refer to the section on "General Configuration" later in this chapter for details.

User roles and authorizations for the HANA layer will be explained in Chapter 9.

SAP OEE CTC Wizards

In Chapter 4, you learned that configurations of OEE are performed using CTC wizards. You also learned about using SAP OEE NetWeaver Configuration CTC and SAP OEE Integration Configuration CTC to set up the integration component between ECC and OEE. In this section, you will learn the SAP OEE Configuration CTC and SAP OEE Migration CTC, which are used to set up the entire configuration as well as migration from earlier releases, when required, in SAP MII.

In addition to the above-mentioned CTCs, additional CTCs are introduced, such as SAP OEE Demo Plant Master Data Setup CTC and SAP OEE Demo Plant Order Data Setup CTC.

The SAP OEE Demo Plant Master Data Setup CTC creates ERP-related master data in SAP MII and, together with SAP OEE Demo Plant Order Data Setup CTC, provides a sample OEE framework that you can use for demo purposes without setting up data and configurations in SAP ERP. Refer to chapter 8 to set up the demo plant.

SAP OEE Configuration CTC

SAP OEE Configuration CTC setup creates the following OEE configurations in SAP's supported languages:

- Default order status and its description
- Default activities and their descriptions
- Default dashboards, default configured button with standard UI activities, descriptions
- Default customization parameters under general configuration with their permitted default values (where applicable) and descriptions

To execute the OEE Configuration CTC, open `http://<server>:<port>/nwa` ➤ Configuration ➤ Scenarios ➤ Configuration wizards and search for *OEE* in the filter expression. You will find four CTC templates available to set up OEE, as shown in Figure 5-2.

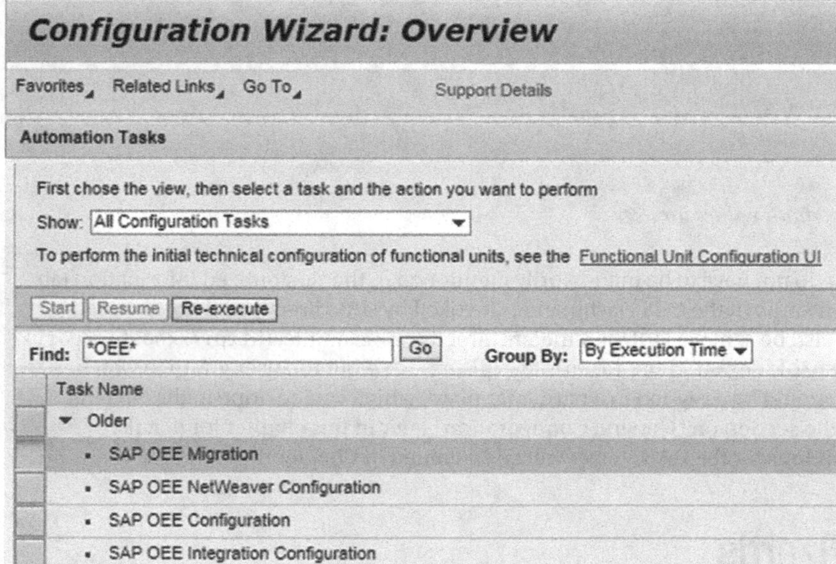

***Figure 5-2.** SAP OEE configuration CTC: step 1*

You need to execute this CTC for every new plant-client setup in SAP ERP. Select "SAP OEE configuration" from the list and click on Start (if executing for the first time) or on Re-execute if you are executing it again. Specify the SAP ERP client and the plant (plant needs to exist in SAP ERP) and click on Next, as shown in Figure 5-3.

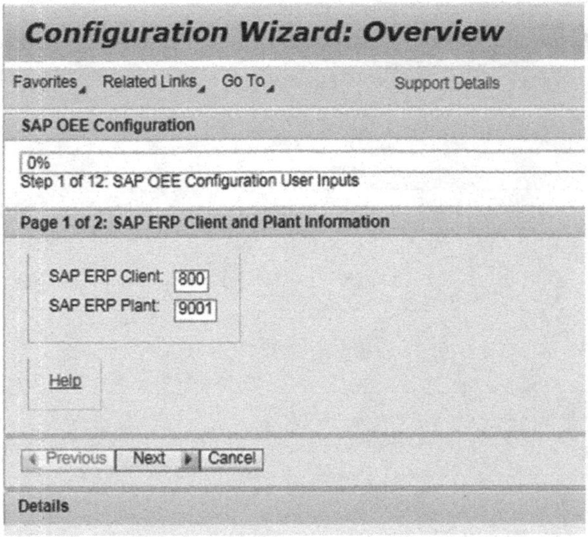

Figure 5-3. *SAP OEE configuration CTC: step 2*

All the OEE configurations are created in this step; click on Next, as shown in Figure 5-4.

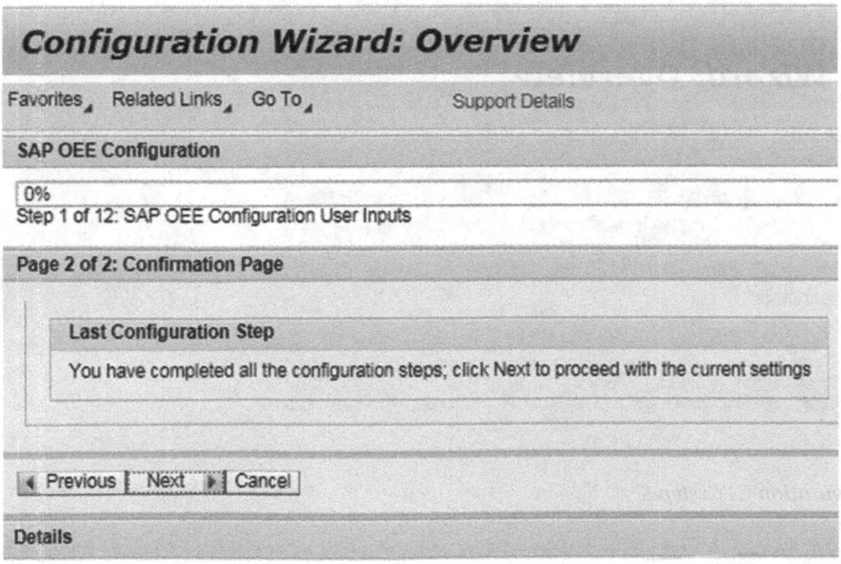

Figure 5-4. *SAP OEE configuration CTC: step 3*

Click on Next as shown in Figure 5-5 to complete the configuration.

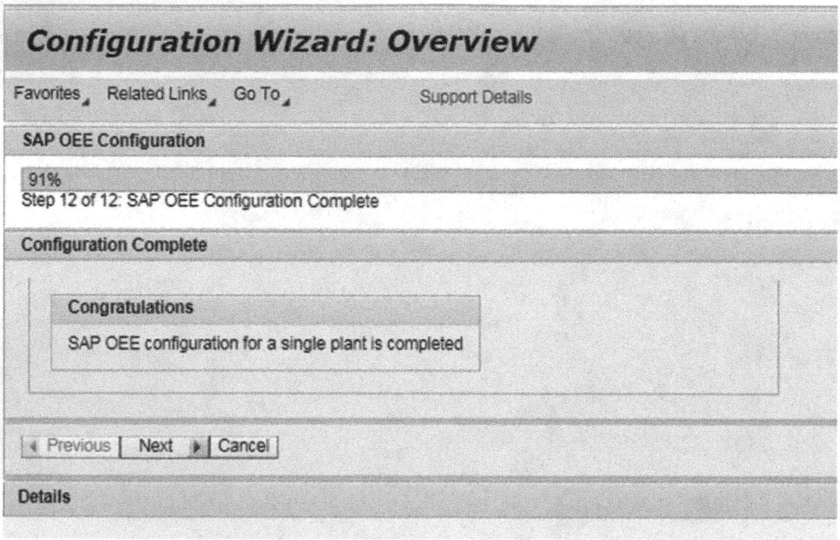

Configuration Wizard: Overview

Favorites Related Links Go To Support Details

SAP OEE Configuration

91%

Step 12 of 12: SAP OEE Configuration Complete

Configuration Complete

Congratulations

SAP OEE configuration for a single plant is completed

Previous Next Cancel

Details

Figure 5-5. *SAP OEE configuration CTC: step 4*

Refer to Figure 5-6. The CTC is executed successfully. You can select the "View Log" option to check the details for each of the steps executed in this CTC.

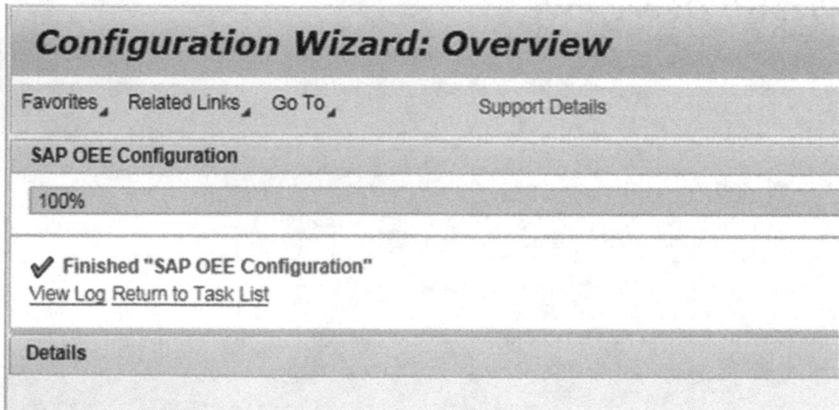

Figure 5-6. *SAP OEE configuration CTC: step 5*

SAP OEE Migration CTC

You would need to execute OEE Migration CTC after a version or service pack upgrade of SAP MII.

Select SAP OEE Migration CTC as shown in Figure 5-7.

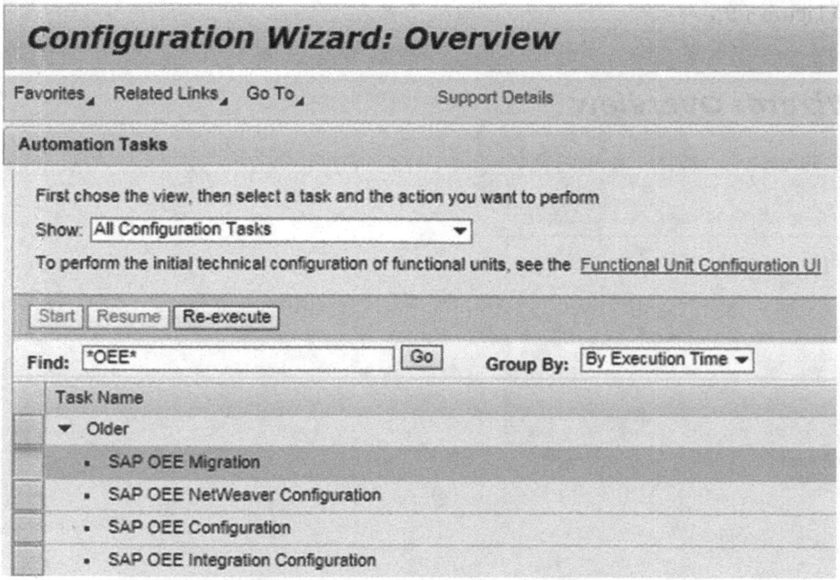

Figure 5-7. *SAP OEE Migration CTC: step 1*

Click Start or Re-execute to get the screen shown in Figure 5-8.

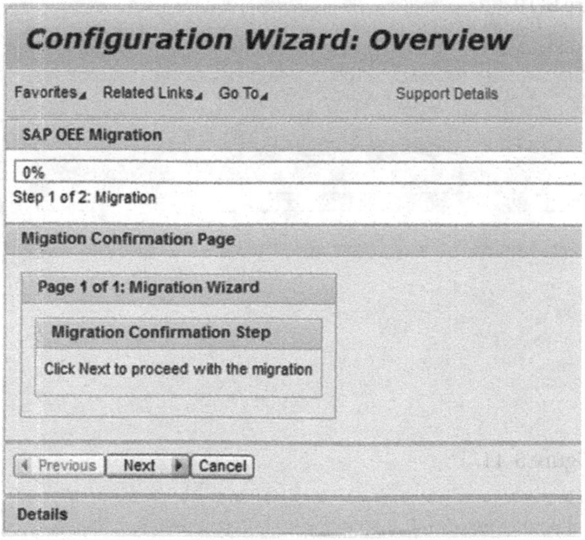

Figure 5-8. *SAP OEE Migration CTC: step 2*

Click Next, as shown in Figure 5-9.

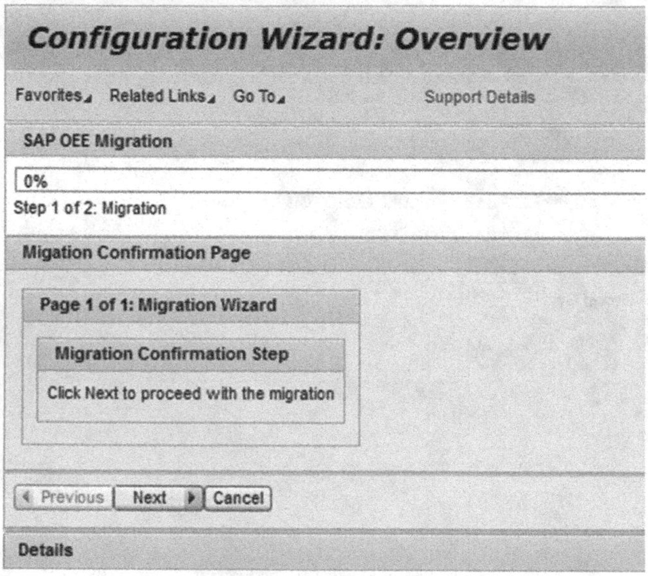

Figure 5-9. *SAP OEE Migration CTC: step 3*

Click Next again to get the screen shown in Figure 5-10.

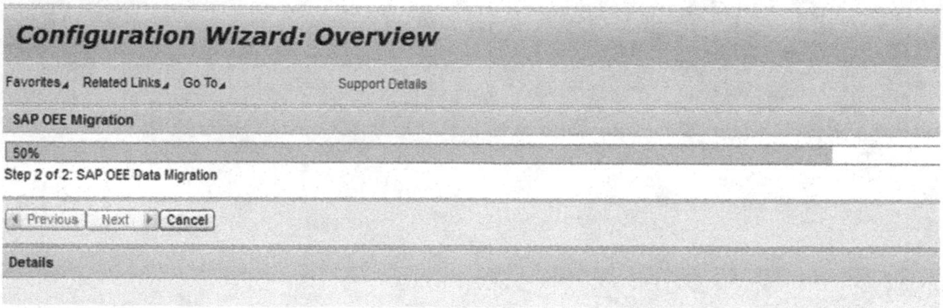

Figure 5-10. *SAP OEE Migration CTC: step 4*

Click Next to bring you to the screen shown in Figure 5-11.

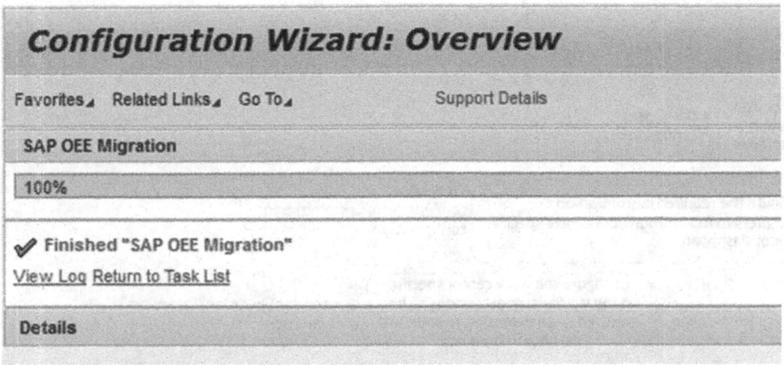

Figure 5-11. *SAP OEE Migration CTC: step 5*

Once the CTC is executed, you can select the "View Log" option to check the details for each of the steps executed in this CTC.

SAP MII Configurations for SAP OEE

SAP OEE uses operator dashboards as a single window for the different OEE users–namely, operator, supervisors, planner–to perform their operations. You can configure these dashboards to suit your shop-floor requirements. To do this, SAP OEE provides the following set of worker UI configurations to maintain the data required for order execution and KPI calculations:

- Display ERP system data
- General configuration
- Activity configuration
- Dashboard configuration
- Modify order status description
- Scheduled downtime maintenance
- Order dispatch
- Review shift
- Review order

As shown in Figure 5-12, you can learn how the various worker UI configurations contribute to framing the OEE dashboard. You need to maintain these configurations using the respective worker UIs in order to develop the desired operator dashboard.

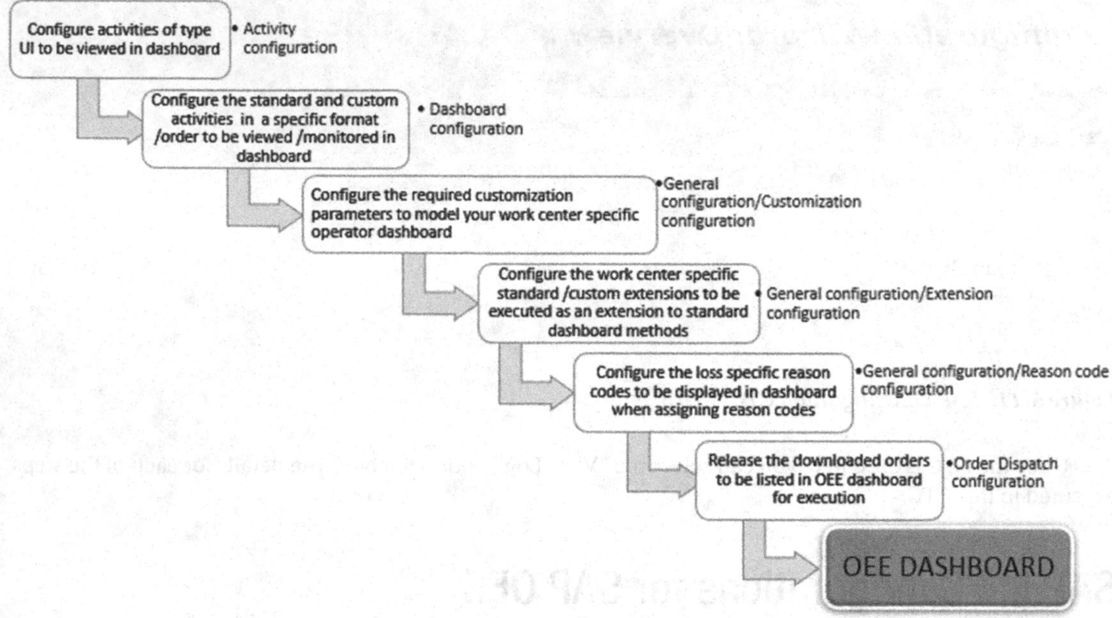

Figure 5-12. *Worker UI configurations for OEE dashboard*

All the preceding configuration menus are available in SAP MII Admin Menu ➤ Worker UI Management menu group, as shown in Figure 5-13.

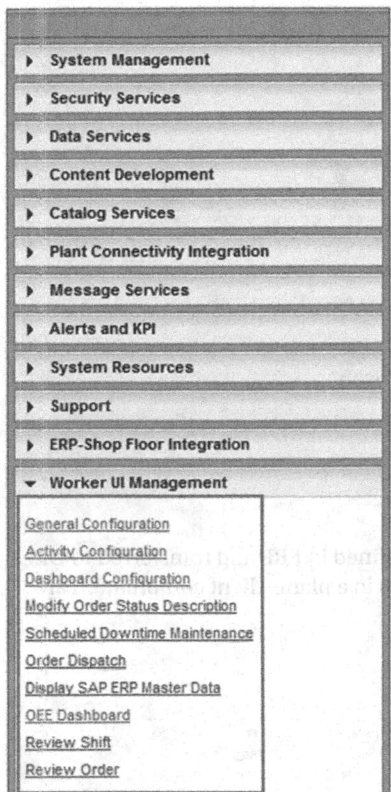

Figure 5-13. *Worker UI configurations menu*

SAP MII 15.1 provides additional menu for Worker UI Configuration which is explained in Chapter 8.

Display ERP System Data

You can access Display ERP System Data to view the plant hierarchy, with node-specific configurations, that was configured in the SAP ERP OEE add-on module. It is non-editable and acts as a reference for OEE-specific master and configuration data. For example, the ERP System Data worker UI is a ready reckoner of plant-client-specific configurations, such as the hierarchy nodes, KPIs defined, standard rates defined for each line, list of machines, bottlenecks, work center and its capacity details, and so on, as shown in Figure 5-14.

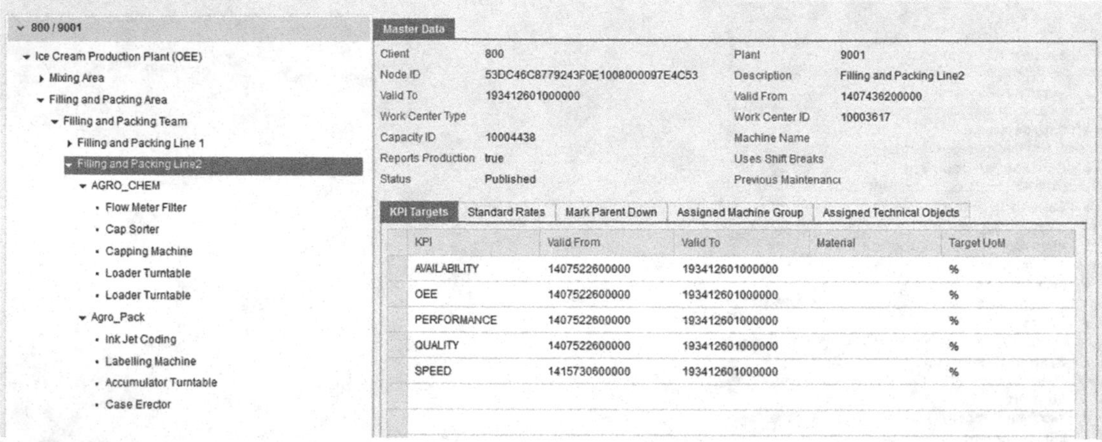

Figure 5-14. *Display ERP System Data: line node*

Refer to Figure 5-15 to see the plant hierarchy structure, which is defined in ERP and transferred to OEE. If the MII server is configured for multiple plants, then all the hierarchies in a plant-client combination are displayed here.

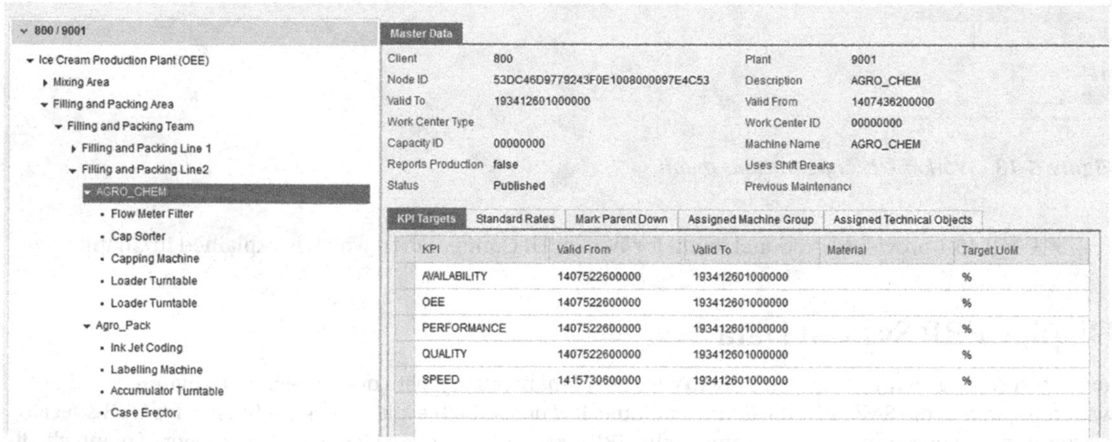

Figure 5-15. *Display ERP System Data: machine node*

Each node is displayed with a unique node ID, which is created whenever the plant hierarchy is transferred to SAP OEE for the first time. This node ID reference is essential for all OEE scenarios and to work on any custom developments specific to each node. You can view these node ID references during the Display ERP System Data configuration. For example, to report a downtime, you need a machine's node ID reference. To report a production count, you need the line node ID reference.

Against each node, there is a set of properties displayed. The top pane refers to the Details tab of the plant hierarchy in the OEE add-on. All the other tabs are displayed in the bottom pane. The Bottlenecks tab defined against the machine node in the plant hierarchy is displayed here within the Mark Parent Down tab.

In SAP OEE, a line (parent node of a machine) is reported as down automatically when a bottleneck machine(s) is down. A line can be reported as down for a single or multiple bottleneck scenarios, which is user defined and based on the configuration of a customization parameter.

General Configuration

General configuration is one of the key worker UI configurations to use when defining your dashboard functions; it has the following four sections:

- User-group dashboard assignment
  - Assignment of operator dashboards to a specific user group responsible for a work center; alternatively, from MII 15.1 user can assign dashboard at plant-level node and all work centers under that plant will get the same operator dashboard assigned
- Customization configuration
  - Define various customizations to achieve the standard OEE functionalities
- Reason code configuration
  - To assign loss-specific reason codes for easy reason-code assignment in operator dashboard
- Extension configuration
  - To assign the standard extensions or custom enhancement logics as an extension, or to hook points to standard OEE service methods

Dashboard Assignment to User Group

It is an essential requirement in manufacturing plants to define role-specific operator dashboards. Each operator or supervisor is responsible for specific activities, and hence must use specific dashboards for order execution. This varies from work center to work center. SAP OEE works using the user-group concept. All users, such as operator, supervisor, plant manager, planner, and so on, may have to perform specific role-based actions in the OEE dashboard. In the following section, you will learn how the users who are part of OEE user groups are assigned OEE dashboards.

User Administration in SAP OEE

In Chapter 4 you learned about the various OEE-specific roles created by the SAP OEE NetWeaver CTC execution in NetWeaver UME–`OEE_SUPERADMIN`, `OEE_ADMIN`, `OEE_OPERATOR`, and `OEE_SUPERVISOR`, as shown in Figure 5-16. Each of these OEE roles are by default assigned with specific OEE actions.

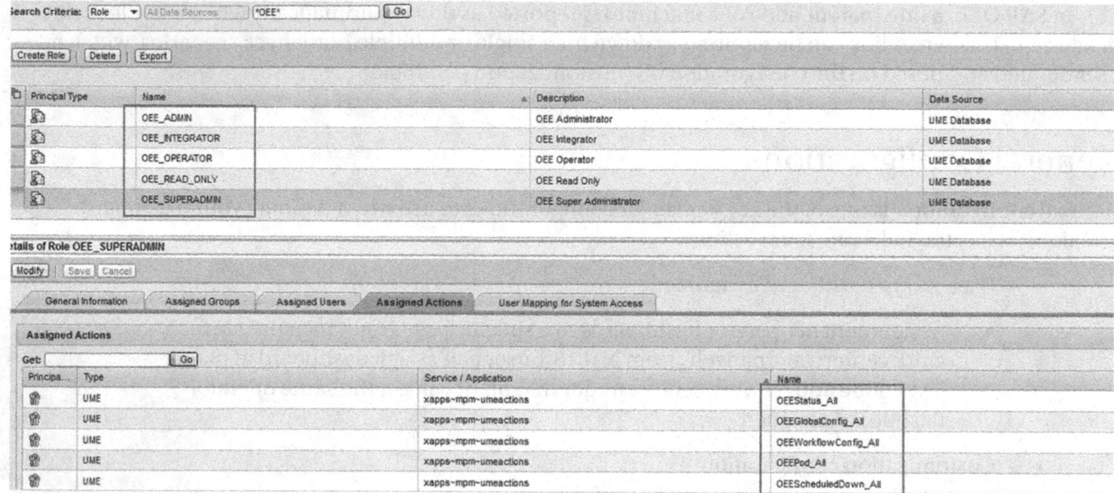

Figure 5-16. *Identity management: OEE roles*

There are a few user groups for SAP OEE, which get created by the CTC wizard in NetWeaver UME, as shown in Figure 5-17.

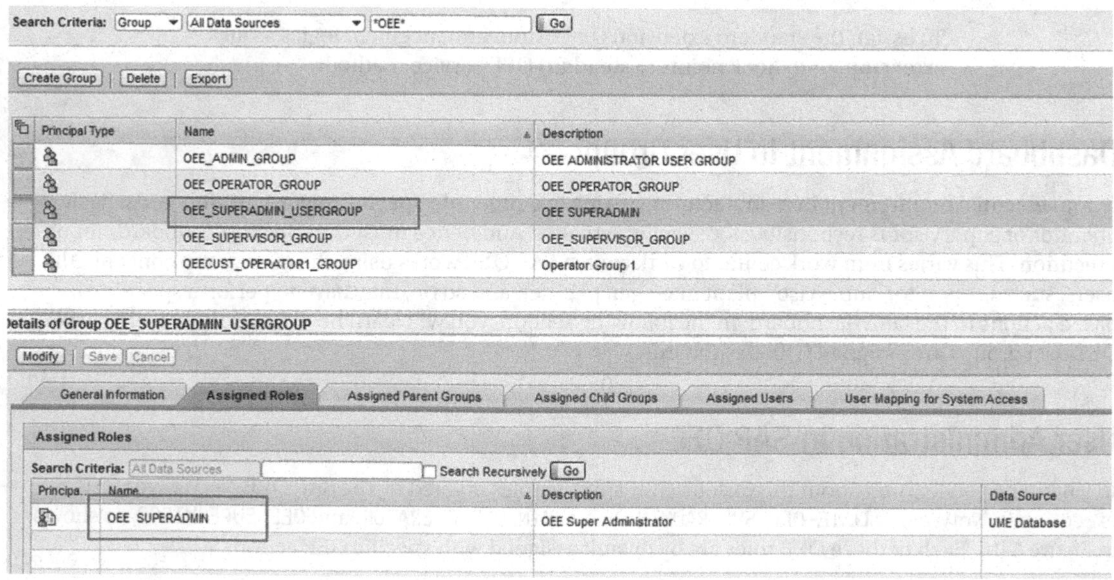

Figure 5-17. *Identity management: OEE user groups*

Dashboard Assignment in OEE

SAP OEE allows the assignment of dashboards based on user groups only. For each user group, assign specific OEE roles as discussed in the previous section, which in turn are assigned with specific OEE actions. Custom OEE roles can also be defined with permission to perform specific OEE actions. A work center node under a plant hierarchy, which executes an order-operation and reports data, can be configured with a user group and a dashboard for that user group.

Since SAP MII Release 15.1 it is also possible to assign a dashboard to a plant-level node; if this is done then the user will have access to all work centers of that plant from the OEE dashboard.

■ **Note** Only unique user groups with different dashboards can be assigned to a work center node. Using different dashboards, a user can report data or monitor data at the work center node. Hence, if a user has multiple roles, say, supervisor and operator, he must be assigned to both those OEE user groups to access a dashboard for a work center.

You can create, edit, and delete the configured user-group dashboard assignments.

Configure user group dashboard assignment:

1. In the SAP MII Menu page, go to Worker UI Management ➤ General Configuration. Select the work center node and select the User Group Dashboard Assignment tab.
2. Click Add.
3. Refer to Figure 5-18. Click the Filter button. The SAP UME user group and Dashboard drop-downs appear. The SAP UME user group drop-down lists all the user groups available in NetWeaver UME. The Dashboard drop-down lists the all standard and custom-configured OEE dashboards available in the system. You will learn about OEE dashboard configurations in the next chapter.

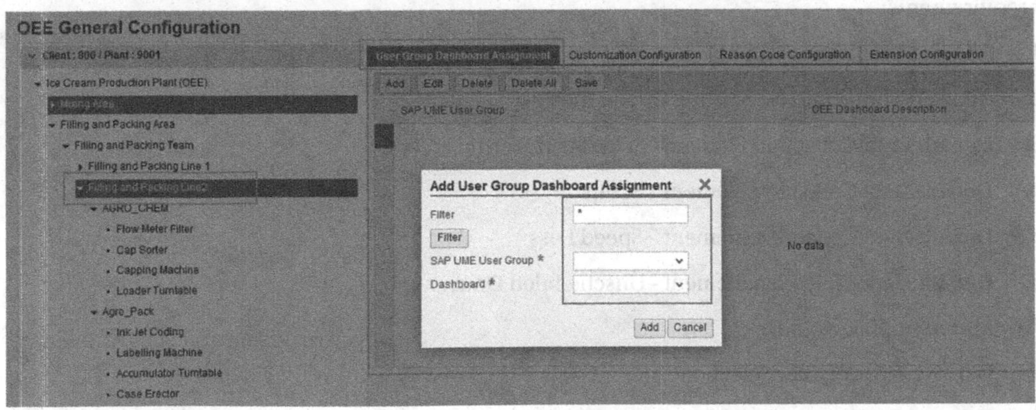

Figure 5-18. User group dashboard assignment: add dashboard

4. Select the desired user group and select the dashboard.
5. Click Add, and the user group dashboard assignment is added. Save the assignment as shown in Figure 5-19.

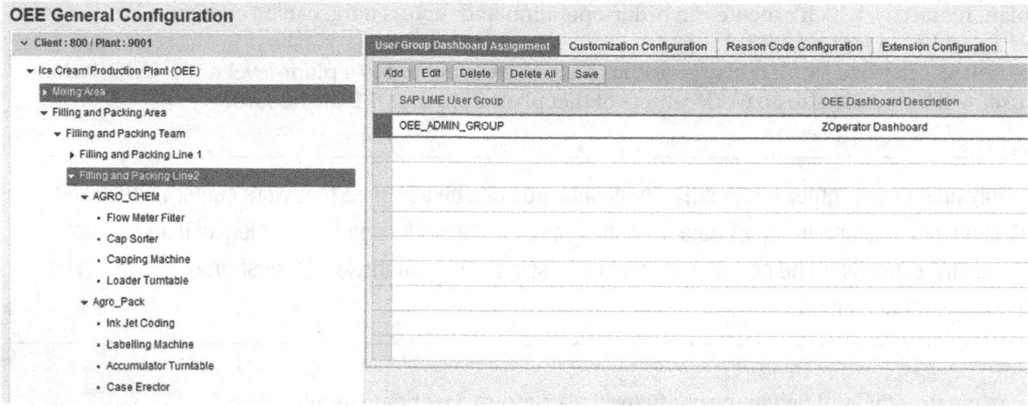

Figure 5-19. User group dashboard assignment: save dashboard

All the users belonging to the `OEE_ADMIN_GROUP` user group will now be able to access the assigned dashboard when selecting the specific production line.

Customization Configuration

SAP OEE, for the benefit of users, has provided 26 customization parameters that can be used to customize the way you perform the node-specific operations and display data in the OEE dashboard. By default, these parameters are assigned with a default value (wherever applicable) when all OEE master and configuration data are downloaded from ERP. Later, you can set the custom values for each of the following parameters as per your requirements:

1. Allowed Modification Limit
2. Allowed Time Limit for Starting Ord. in the Past
3. Default Data Collection Element - Scheduled Down
4. Default Data Collection Element – Scrap
5. Default Data Collection Element – Speed Loss
6. Default Data Collection Element - Unscheduled Down
7. Minor Stoppage Limit
8. Date Range for Order Selection
9. Relevant Production Activity
10. Retention Time for SAP HANA Replicated Tables
11. Retention time for non-SAP HANA replicated tables
12. Unit of Measure Conversion Transaction
13. Batch Number Is Mandatory for Batch-Managed Material
14. Decimal Value Precision
15. Order Start in the Future Is Allowed

16. Serial Number Is Mandatory for Reporting Production
17. Show Completed Orders on Dashboard
18. Order Completion When Accounted Time Exists
19. Shift Handover Available Before Shift End
20. Allow Modification of Automation Records
21. Minor Stoppages Should Be Included in Availability
22. Irrelevant for OEE Calculations
23. Enable Periodic Confirmations
24. Shrinking Order Duration Allowed
25. Unaccounted Speed Loss Limit
26. Line Behavior
27. Allow Multiple Orders to Start at Same Time
28. PM Notification Type
29. Allow Automatic Trigger of PM Notification
30. Offline-Online Mode Change Transaction
31. Online-Offline Mode Change Transaction

Customization configuration helps you set up how you want to monitor the OEE dashboard and in some backend logic and calculations.

For example, the Minor Stoppage Limit parameter helps you to set the duration limit of how long a machine downtime or line downtime event must be for it to be considered minor. The Minor Stoppages Should Be Included in Availability parameter, when set to *Yes*, ensures the backend KPI calculations include minor stoppage durations in the Availability KPI.

Customized values can be set for any of the nodes. When they are set at the plant-node level of the hierarchy, they are by default applicable to any child nodes. Upon defining customized values for child nodes, these values take precedence over the customization value set at parent node. Customized values can be set as being specific for material or as being non-material specific. Refer to the appendix for the details of each of these customization parameters.

Reason Code Configuration

Reason codes are OEE master data created in the SAP ERP OEE add-on and transferred to SAP OEE. Reason codes are defined for each of the hierarchy nodes and data collection elements (DCE) of loss types. In Chapter 3, you learned about the reason code configuration for plant levels, which appear as a hierarchical structure. When these reason codes are transferred to OEE, they are displayed as the complete hierarchy in OEE dashboard. Hence, the operator has to pass through the complete hierarchy to select the right reason code, while assigning it to an event such as machine downtime or material scrap declaration.

Reason code configuration allows you to configure the most applicable reason code for each data collection element and for each machine and work center node that is reporting production. From the whole of the reason code hierarchy, you must select the relevant subset of reason codes to be assigned. These configurations are reflected on the OEE dashboard when assigning reason codes for data collections of loss types. This helps the operator to choose the right reason code quickly.

To configure reason codes for dashboards follow these steps:

1. On the SAP MII main menu, choose Worker UI Management ➤ General Configuration ➤ Reason Code Configuration tab
2. Select the work center or machine node and select "Add"
3. Select the data collection element from the drop-down for which you need to define the reason code. These are listed from the data maintained in the ERP OEE add-on. Refer to Figure 5-20.

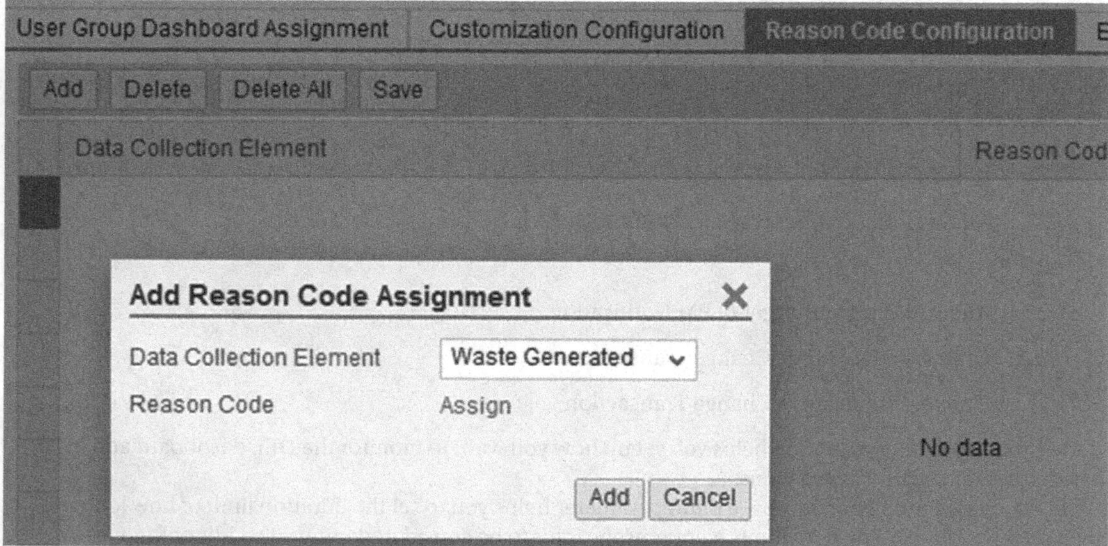

Figure 5-20. *Reason code configuration: add DCE*

4. Click on the "Assign" link and select the level, that which is more relevant, as shown in Figure 5-21.

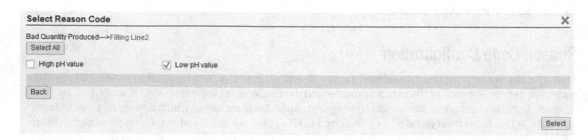

Figure 5-21. *Reason code configuration: assign reason code*

5. Click Add and then Save.
6. The data collection element–specific reason code is configured as shown in Figure 5-22.

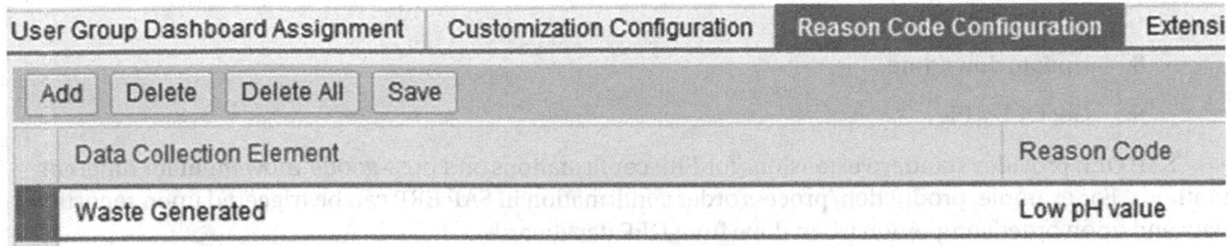

Figure 5-22. Reason code configuration: save reason code assignment for DCE

7. Now, in the OEE dashboard, when you report the waste DCE and click on the "Assign" link to assign the reason code, you will find only the above-configured reason code available for assignment, as shown in Figure 5-23.

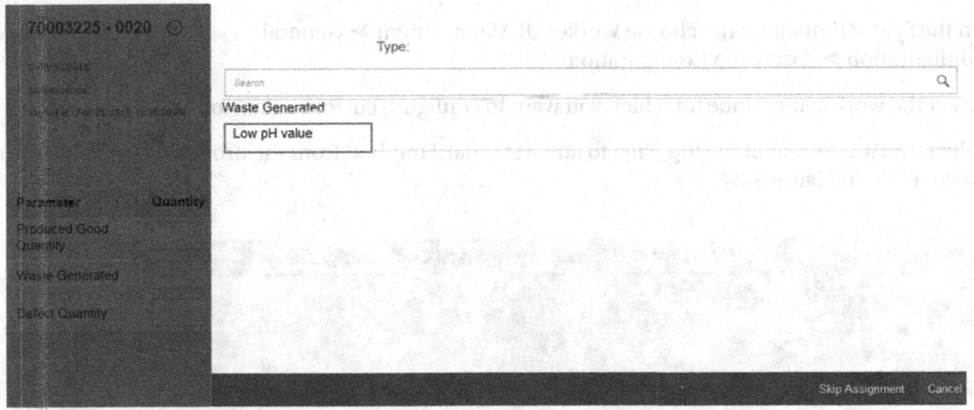

Figure 5-23. OEE dashboard: assign reason code

Extension Configuration

In SAP OEE, there are certain standard process events for OEE dashboard activities called methods that perform standard OEE functionalities like order start, order complete, report data, and so on. Extensions are hooks that are added to these methods to trigger standard/custom logic, when it occurs.

In SAP OEE, methods are standard functionalities assigned to hierarchy nodes that report production; for instance, they could be assigned to a work center node.

The standard methods in SAP OEE are as follows:

1. Start order-operation
2. Stop order
3. Report data
4. Resume order-operation
5. Complete order
6. Close shift

7. Create downtime
8. Update downtime
9. Get OEE KPIs

SAP OEE provides standard extensions for ERP confirmations and post-goods-movement for different methods. For example, production/process order confirmation in SAP ERP can be triggered upon reporting data and upon order completion when done from OEE dashboards.

Custom extensions are configured by creating a custom logic developed on SAP MII (BLS transaction) and hooked to a standard method. These extensions are executed as an extension to these standard methods.

The execution can happen as pre, post or on exception events to these methods. As the OEE extensions work as extensions to the existing standard methods/logics, the standard methods pass the relevant data in the form of XML to the standard/custom logic configured as an extension.

Refer to the appendix to understand the Input/output XML structure to be followed when using extensions.

Configure extensions:

1. On the SAP MII main menu, choose Worker UI Management ➤ General Configuration ➤ Extension Configuration
2. Select the work center node for which you want to configure custom extensions.
3. Select the Add button in the top pane to add a standard method from the drop-down. Refer to Figure 5-24.

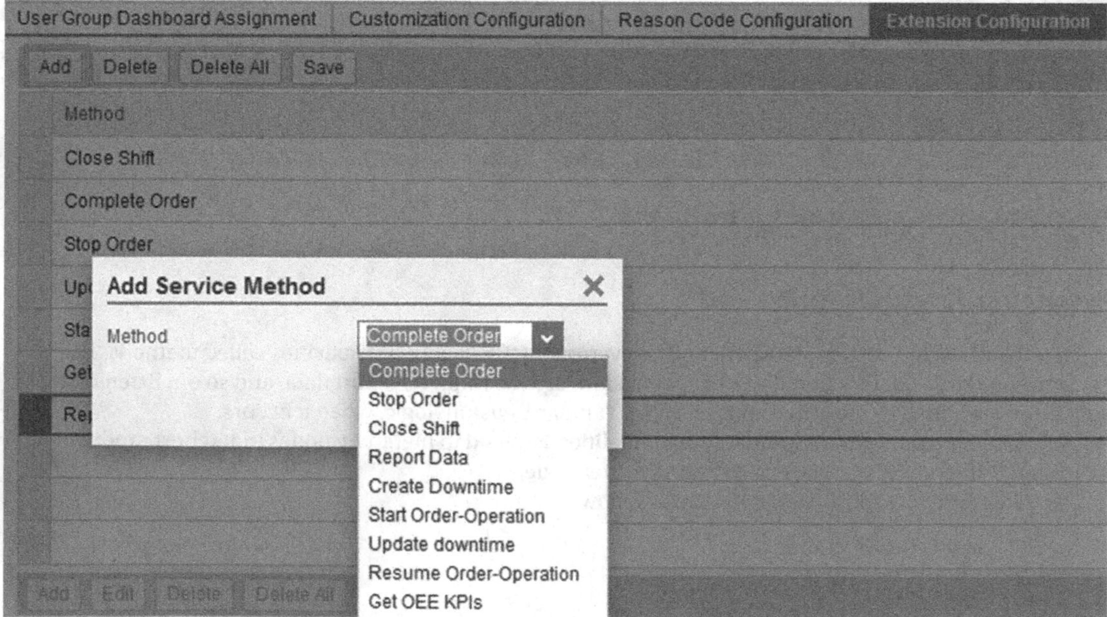

Figure 5-24. *Extension configuration: add service method*

4. Select the method and from the bottom pane click the Add button.

5. Add the extension type as PRE/POST/EXCEPTION.
   - PRE: Extension logic is executed before the execution of standard method.
   - POST: Extension logic is executed after the execution of standard method.
   - Exception: Extension logic is executed upon exception of standard method.
6. Select the standard or a custom activity and add an extension sequence.
7. Check "Enabled" and click the Add button to select the language option.
8. Select the language and add the extension description, then click Add.
9. Save the configurations.

You will learn more about the usage of extensions in OEE dashboards in Chapter 6 (OEE Dashboards) and Chapter 7 (Custom Developments on SAP OEE).

Activity Configuration

Activity configuration in OEE enables you to create activities of different types that are executable components in OEE dashboard. Any OEE functionality like a UI control in OEE dashboard or extension logics is using an OEE activity.

OEE activities are of four types:

- UI
- Transaction
- Extension
- Java class
- External App
- UI Component

By default, a set of standard activities is delivered in SAP OEE; these are assigned to the client and plant of the logged-in user. The standard activities are created when you execute the SAP OEE Configuration CTC wizard.

Also, based on specific requirements, you can create custom activities. The custom development details of each type of activity will be explained in Chapter 8.

- UI: It is an activity required in order for a user interface to provide a section or button actions on the OEE dashboard. UI-type activities can only be provided by utilizing web content developed using SAP UI5 following an MVC approach.
- Transaction: It is an activity where you execute an MII transaction from a standard or custom OEE dashboard.
- Extension: It is an activity to be used when you need to extend the standard OEE functionality. Being an extension, the required input parameters will be passed to the extension logic from the SAP OEE standard application. Extension details are explained in the "Extension Configuration" section. For example, an extension can be a custom logic that you want to execute as an extension to the order start or order complete logic of standard SAP OEE.

- Java Class: A logic component developed on Java that is used to execute any custom logic or services provided by SAP OEE.
- External App: This is an activity type which should be used to view any custom dashboard belonging to third party application within the OEE standard dashboard. The complete URL of the UI page of external application should be configured as the URL.
- UI Component: It is a type of UI activity but used for configuring UI objects in Application launch pad. From 15.1, Goods Movement (GI and GR) can be executed using an Application launch pad. To configure any UI object on this launch pad, the activity should be defined as UI component.

■ Note

1. A custom activity can be used in a standard OEE dashboard, but a standard activity cannot be used in a custom OEE dashboard.
2. From SAP MII 15.0 SP03 onward, custom activity of type UI should use XML views in place of JS views, as all the standard OEE dashboards are redesigned with XML views.

Activity Configuration Options

1. On the SAP MII main menu, choose Worker UI Management ➤ Activity Configuration.
2. You can create a new activity or change an existing activity.
3. To create a new activity, enter the Activity ID. This is a unique ID that should be meaningful to understanding the purpose of the activity.

■ Caution Activity ID should not have any spaces.

---

4. On the Main tab, enter the class or URL to the activity, which is deployed in SAP NetWeaver WebAS. The class or URL is the reference pointing to the actual executable activity code or logic. For standard activities, this field is pre-filled and cannot be edited. For custom activities, you need to fill it in with the right URL based on the activity type being created. URL is different for each kind of activity.
    - Standard OEE activities of type UI start with `sap.oee.ui`. For example, `sap.oee.ui.oeeReviewOrder` is the class/URL for Review Order functionality.
    - Standard activities of type Extension start with `com.sap.xapps.oee.extension.extensions`. For example, `com.sap.xapps.oee.extension.extensions.ErpConfirmationOnDCExtension` is the extension for ERP confirmation on reporting data collection.
    - Pre-delivered standard activities belong to activity types UI or Extension. Refer to Chapter 7 to learn how to configure a custom activity and the class/URL for activity of types UI and Transaction.

5. On the Activity Description tab, maintain the description of the activity in the languages that you want. Currently, eight languages are supported and configured in OEE.

6. Standard activities cannot be deleted and edited, whereas custom activities can.

7. On the Options tab, you can maintain option name, description, and its value. The Options tab is used by a UI activity to define the UI fields in the dashboard to collect the data. It can be localized. You can group similar data elements under a single activity and display them in an ordered sequence with an associated label, and the same is displayed in the operator dashboard for data collection.

   For example, you can define multiple custom data collection elements in OEE add-on and transfer them to OEE. Then, you can create a single custom activity of type UI and add all those custom data collection elements under the Options tab value section. By doing this, all these custom data collection elements are displayed under that activity in the OEE dashboard.

   For example, you can create a custom activity to collect custom data collection elements.

Example to Create an Activity

1. On the SAP MII main menu, choose Worker UI Management ➤ Activity Configuration.

2. Enter a meaningful name for the activity. For example, if you are creating an activity to collect line speed set at the shop floor, then you can enter the activity name as `Z_SET_SPEED`.

3. On the Main tab:

   a. In the Class or URL field, enter `sap.oee.ui.oeeGenericDataCollection`. This is an SAP-delivered activity for collecting custom data collection elements.

   b. In the Activity Type field, select UI.

4. On the Activity Description tab, choose Add to enter a description for the activity in the required languages. The description given here appears on the dashboard.

5. On the Options tab, choose Add to enter the option name, option description in the required languages, and the option values, as shown in Figure 5-25.

   For this example, specify the option name as `DCELEMENT`.

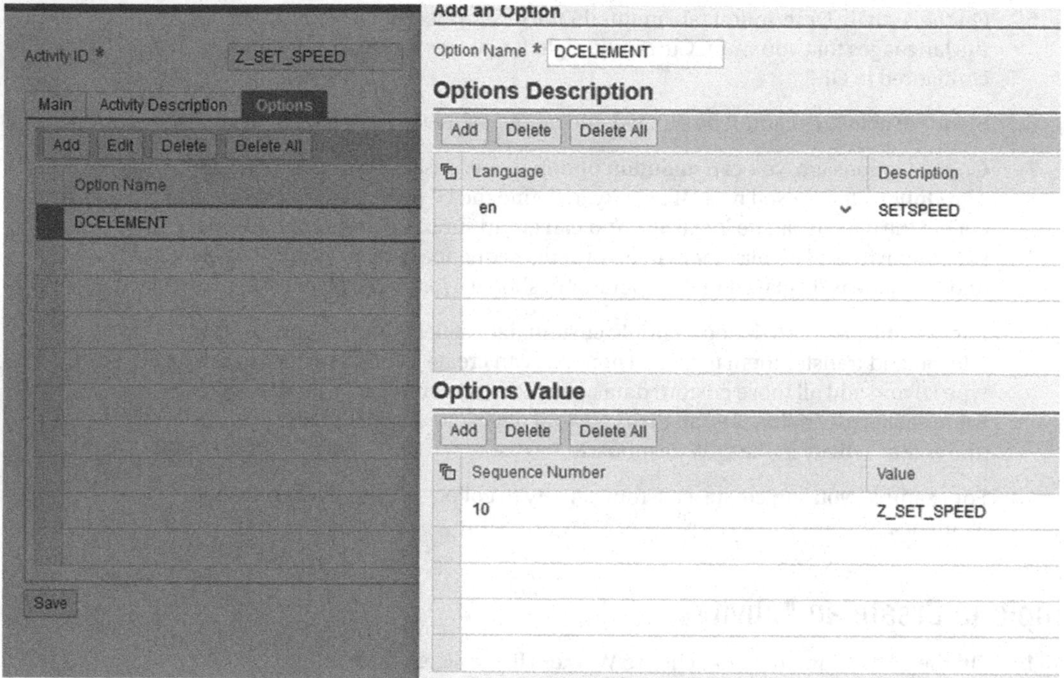

Figure 5-25. Activity configuration: Option tab

6. In the Options Value section, enter the data collection elements that you want to use to collect data from the dashboard. To do this, enter a sequence number and the data collection element that you have already configured in OEE add-on. You can add multiple data collection elements; however, use a different sequence number for each data collection element.

7. Save the activity, and the activity will be listed under the Activity configuration screen as shown in Figure 5-26.

Activity Configuration

Create Activity | Display | Change Activity | Delete

Activity ID	Class or URL	Activity Type
ReportStandardValue	OEEEnhancement/StandardValueReporting/StandardA...	Transaction
ReportWaste_test	OEEEnhancement/BLS_TEST	Transaction
SCRAP_COMP_DC_GM_EXT	com.sap.xapps.oee.extension.extensions.ErpScrapped...	Extension
SCRAP_COMP_GM_EXT	com.sap.xapps.oee.extension.extensions.ErpScrapped...	Extension
TEST_ACT	OEEEnhancement/DownTimeOrderTagging/BLS/TestB...	Transaction
ZMANAGE_DC	XMII/CM/OEEEnhanc...	UI
Z_SET_SPEED	sap.oee.ui.oeeGenericDataCollection	UI

Figure 5-26. Activity configuration: create custom UI activity

If a data collection element has the context raw material (`RAW_MAT`), then it is recommended that you add only one data collection element in the Options Value section for that activity.

Standard OEE activities

With activity configuration you can

- view the pre-delivered standard activities of type UI and extension; and
- create, edit, and delete a custom activity.

Refer to the appendix for the list of standard activities supported by SAP OEE.

Standard OEE activities source code can also be downloaded from MII 15.1 and be reused to develop custom UI activities for use in the OEE dashboard. Refer to chapter 8 for the steps to download and reuse it.

■ Note Activity of type Extension should be added to a node method under General Configuration ➤ Extension Configuration for each line as per the requirements. For example, if your requirement is to confirm yield quantity to ERP after every yield report in the OEE dashboard, then the extension has to be configured and enabled.

Order Status Description Configuration

When a production or process order is executed in OEE, the order operation takes a different status, such as NEW, ACTIVE, HOLD, CMPL, and REV.

NEW: The order is downloaded in OEE from ERP.

ACT: The order is started and being executed in OEE.

HOLD: The order is placed under hold or paused.

CMPL: The order is completed.

REV: The order spans across shifts; i.e., an order is started in one shift, runs beyond the current shift, and may be completed in the future shift, in which case the order needs to be reopened in the next shift. REV status is planned to be enabled in future SPs.

OBS: An order that is sent by mistake to OEE, or an order that no longer needs to be executed or is marked as obsolete on the shop floor, can be marked as obsolete in OEE. An order, once marked obsolete, can no longer be made active, and an order can go to the obsolete state only from the hold state.

Modifying the order status description configuration helps you to change the order status description as per the requirements. It is a simple configuration where you can edit the status description for a specific plant and client in a particular language.

Order Dispatch

Orders (LOIPRO IDocs) are downloaded to SAP OEE from SAP ERP using the OEEINT framework. The downloaded orders are by default auto-released and ready for execution in OEE. At times, the plant may require a manual release of order quantities based on the shop-floor requirements.

Order dispatch UI enables you to do the manual release of partial order quantities to specific work centers of OEE. To enable the manual release you must add the following line of code in the Request XSLT transaction at the end, for the LOIPRO workflow in OEEINT:

```
<automaticRelease>false</automaticRelease>
```

The downloaded orders then will not be automatically released when passing through OEEINT and are listed with the order and its quantity in Order Dispatch worker UI.

The order can be selected and a partial quantity to be released can be specified in the "Enter quantity to release" textbox, as shown in Figure 5-27. If the order corresponds to a single unique work center, then the order is released to that particular work center, after which the order is ready for execution. Sometimes, an order is dispatched to a work center that corresponds to more than one node in the plant hierarchy.

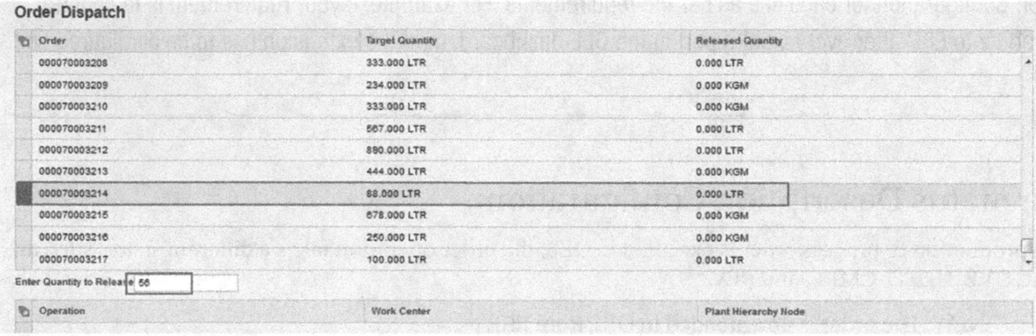

Order Dispatch

Order	Target Quantity	Released Quantity
000070003208	333.000 LTR	0.000 LTR
000070003209	234.000 LTR	0.000 KGM
000070003210	333.000 LTR	0.000 KGM
000070003211	567.000 LTR	0.000 LTR
000070003212	890.000 LTR	0.000 LTR
000070003213	444.000 LTR	0.000 KGM
000070003214	88.000 LTR	0.000 LTR
000070003215	678.000 LTR	0.000 KGM
000070003216	250.000 LTR	0.000 KGM
000070003217	100.000 LTR	0.000 LTR

Enter Quantity to Release 56

Operation	Work Center	Plant Hierarchy Node

Figure 5-27. *Order dispatch configuration: release partial quantity*

For example, let's take a scenario where a material X is produced by passing through machines A, B, and C. For a specific variant of the same material X, it has to pass through machines A, B, C, and D. In this case, two different work center nodes can be created in the plant hierarchy that are assigned to the same PP work center. The first work center node is configured with three machines, A, B, and C, and is assigned to a PP work center. Another work center node is configured and assigned to same PP work center but has four machines, A, B, C, and D.

In this scenario, material X is configured for both work centers in the plant hierarchy, and when an order for material X is created and dispatched, the order dispatch UI displays it as corresponding with two work centers/operations/nodes. Here, you can select the desired work center and do the partial order release.

Order dispatch worker UI is applicable when the orders are dispatched and executed based on the current demand, material, and labor availability, or when there are material variant options.

Scheduled Downtime Maintenance

Scheduled downtime is a planned maintenance time for a resource. Downtime for the purpose of maintenance is scheduled as a part of the manufacturing day and, in some cases, as an integral part of the manufacturing process. It also includes performing routine actions that keep the device in working order. The goal is to restrict emergency and unscheduled maintenance to a minimum.

The scheduled downtime maintenance worker UI in OEE enables you to maintain the planned downtime as part of plant-specific maintenance activities, downtimes, and public holidays. The UI displays the plant hierarchy where you can create your scheduled downtime for a particular client and plant and for a specific line. The downtime can be created for the work center node.

Create Scheduled Downtime

1. Select the work center node in the plant hierarchy for which you want to create the scheduled downtime.
2. Click *Create* button and specify the time period during which the line will be down.
3. Assign the reason code by clicking the "Assign" link. The reason code configured for the data collection element `Scheduled_down` in OEE add-on for the specific plant and client are displayed here.

View Existing Scheduled Downtimes

1. Click on Retrieve button after selecting the required time period in the drop-down. All the created downtimes for the selected time period are displayed
2. The Load from calendar button option pulls all the scheduled downtimes created from the factory calendar. The factory calendar configuration data can be transferred as an IDoc to OEE from ERP.
3. All the created scheduled downtimes can also be deleted and edited.

■ **Note** Scheduled downtimes cannot be created in an overlapped time period. Scheduled downtimes can be created using this worker UI or using the OEE dashboard, which will be dealt in the next chapter.

OEE Configurations Transport

SAP OEE stores various configuration data required for the solution, as explained earlier. You can transfer these data to a different MII environment using the "Transport OEE configurations" option.

To transport the OEE configuration, go to MII Main menu ➤ System configuration ➤ Configurations.

Select the configuration data that are related to OEE, as shown in Figure 5-28. You can select the OEE configuration data in addition to the MII configurations and click on Export. Each configuration is converted into an XML file. Select the required configurations, enter the pass phrase, and choose Export. Select the client and plant for the source and target systems from the popup. The created XML files are zipped. With the export method "File System," the zip file needs to be saved in the desired location in your local client. You can then import the saved zip file into the target system. For export method "CTS+" the zip file is transferred to the CTS+ system, from which the file is imported into the target system automatically.

☐ Dashboard and Activity Configuration	☐ Activity Configuration
☐ Order Status Description	☐ Workflow Configuration
☐ User Group Dashboard Assignment	☐ Customization Configuration
☐ Reason Code Configuration	☐ Extension Configuration

Figure 5-28. *Transport OEE configurations*

Summary

In this chapter, you have learned about User roles and authorizations, OEE-specific CTC executions, and OEE's pre-delivered components such as worker UI configurations that are required to set up OEE dashboard.

In the next chapter, you will learn about the SAP-provided OEE dashboard, how to configure the dashboard, and how the manufacturing-plant floor users can use the OEE dashboards for order execution and data collection based on which OEE KPIs can be generated.

CHAPTER 6

SAP OEE Dashboard

In the previous chapter, you learned about the various worker UI configurations that influence the modeling of OEE dashboards. In this chapter, you will learn the purpose of and the steps to configure OEE dashboards and their detailed descriptions.

The OEE dashboard is the user interface for the users–operator, supervisor, planner, and so on–in a plant to monitor, view, and analyze the shop-floor operations and events. SAP OEE is pre-delivered with a few standard dashboards. These dashboards can be enhanced with additional UI options, and new, customized dashboards can be configured using the worker UI dashboard configuration.

Dashboard Configuration

Dashboard configuration is the worker UI configuration through which you can edit and configure the standard OEE dashboard or create your own customized OEE dashboard. An OEE dashboard is built using OEE activities of type UI. The UI activities can be standard (pre-delivered by SAP) or custom. As per your requirements, you can develop your own UI page, create a custom activity of type UI, and use it in the standard OEE dashboard.

To view, edit, or create an OEE dashboard, go to MII Admin Menu ➤ Worker UI ➤ Dashboard Configuration. The worker UI displays all the plant-client combinations for which you are authorized to edit or configure the dashboards.

The pre-defined dashboards can be viewed by selecting the dashboard under Dashboard ID and clicking the Display button. To configure or customize an existing dashboard, you need to copy the standard dashboard and perform the required changes. You cannot directly edit SAP-delivered dashboards.

- To view a dashboard, click Display.
- To edit a dashboard, click Change.
- To copy a dashboard, click Copy.
- To delete a dashboard, click Delete.
- Click Clear to reset the dashboard selections.

Dashboard Configuration Elements

OEE Dashboard ID: A unique ID for each dashboard; should not have spaces

OEE Dashboard Name: OEE dashboard description

OEE Dashboard Layout: Defines the layout of the dashboard. Currently available options are L1 and L3.

D. Saha et al., *Manufacturing Performance Management using SAP OEE*,
DOI 10.1007/978-1-4842-1150-2_6

OEE Dashboard Description Tab

This tab is to define the description of the dashboard in different OEE-supported languages. This is the description that will be displayed every time you access the dashboard; hence, it should be meaningful and understandable.

You can add and delete entries for different language options.

Dashboard Section Content

This section displays the entries based on the layout type selected. For L1, one layout entry can be selected (there is no L2 layout, so only L1 and L3 are available), and for the L3 type, three entries can be selected, as shown in Figure 6-1. Within each content section, the standard and custom activities of UI type are listed. You can select the required OEE activities, which will be displayed in OEE dashboard in the order they are configured here.

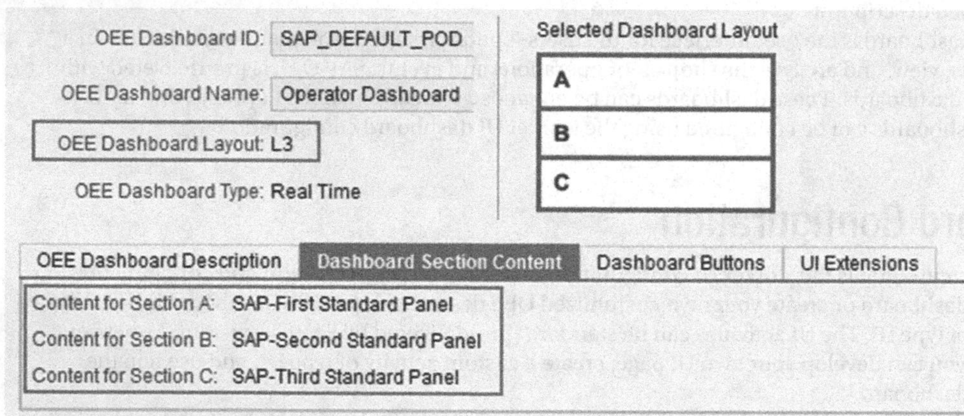

***Figure 6-1.** Dashboard configuration: dashboard section content*

Dashboard Buttons

Apart from the layout, you can define the dashboard buttons that appear in the footer of OEE dashboard, which would open another activity page linked to it. Refer to Figure 6-2, the dashboard button tab of dashboard configuration to edit, delete and configure buttons. You can use "Add Entry" to add a dashboard button to add an entry. Buttons can be normal or group type. Normal buttons have a single activity assigned and group buttons have multiple activities assigned.

OEE Dashboard Description | Dashboard Section Content | Dashboard Buttons | UI Extensions

Button ID	Activity Assigned	Button Sequence	Button Type	Location
DT	SAP-Manage Downtimes	20	Normal	Bottom
ORDER	SAP-Manage Orders	10	Normal	Bottom
RPT_QTY	SAP-Report Produced or Rejected Quantity	30	Normal	Bottom
RVW_SFT	SAP-Review Shift	50	Normal	Bottom
SL	SAP-Report Speed Loss	40	Normal	Bottom

***Figure 6-2.** Dashboard Configuration: dashboard buttons*

Dashboard Button Options

- Button ID: Unique ID for the button being created
- Activity Assigned: Standard or custom OEE activity to be assigned here from the activity list
- Button Sequence: Defines the sequence of the buttons in the footer. The sequence is shown in ascending order for same-level buttons, while for group buttons, the sequence starts for the group entries in the same ascending order.
- Button Type: normal or group
    - For group type, do not assign any activity. Once the entry is created, select the row and a new screen will be opened where you can add a list of standard or custom activities.
- Location: Bottom (all buttons are placed only at the bottom irrespective of this configuration, so this is ignored)
- Language & Description: Give a meaningful description in the desired language.

The UI Extensions tab is obsolete from version 15.0 SP03 onward.

Types of OEE Dashboard

In this section, you will learn the detailed functionalities and features of each of the pre-delivered OEE dashboards.

The standard OEE dashboards are available for use once the OEE-MII component is deployed on MII and configured using the OEE configuration CTC. These dashboards are built based on the metadata defined in the master data and hierarchy definitions. For instance, OEE dashboards are created and maintained specific to a plant and a client. Similarly, master data such as plant hierarchy and reason codes are also maintained as plant and client specific. This relationship ensures the display of correct plant-client data in standard OEE dashboard. SAP OEE dashboards support the Gregorian calendar.

Every dashboard–be it standard or custom–is a collection of logically grouped UI activities (refer to UI activities in "Activity Configuration" in the appendix) required to perform the role-specific actions. For example, a supervisor may be authorized to review the orders executed during the shift, so he would need access to the "Review Order" and "Review Shift" UI activities. Similarly, an operator who manages the order and data collection would need access to the "Manage Order" and "Report Production" UI activities. Hence, based on the user's role, the dashboard is to be configured with the required and restricted authorizations to these UI activities.

To configure the OEE dashboard for specific user groups, refer to the "General Configuration" section in chapter 5.

Let's now look at the SAP-delivered standard dashboards.

Plant Monitor Dashboard

The plant monitor dashboard helps you to monitor the plant by monitoring the status of all the configured work centers in the plant. You can monitor the status of each work center and its performance with respect to an active order running. It also provides all the information about the active order, such as material details, order quantity, remaining quantity to be produced, and the quantity produced in the current shift. The Details icon navigates to the line monitor dashboard. Refer to Figure 6-3.

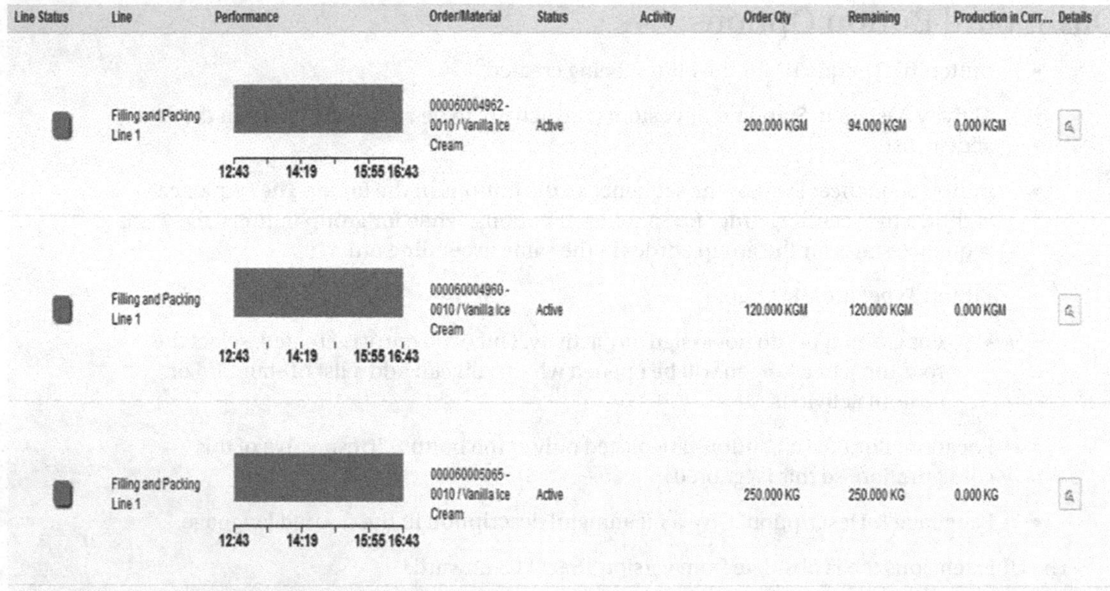

Line Status
Line
Performance
Order/Material
Status
Activity
Order Qty
Remaining
Production in Curr...
Details
Filling and Packing Line 1
000060004962 - 0010 / Vanilla Ice Cream
Active
200.000 KGM
94.000 KGM
0.000 KGM
12:43 14:19 15:55 16:43
Filling and Packing Line 1
000060004960 - 0010 / Vanilla Ice Cream
Active
120.000 KGM
120.000 KGM
0.000 KGM
12:43 14:19 15:55 16:43
Filling and Packing Line 1
000060005065 - 0010 / Vanilla Ice Cream
Active
250.000 KG
250.000 KG
0.000 KG
12:43 14:19 15:55 16:43

Figure 6-3. *OEE dashboard: plant monitor*

The plant monitor dashboard is available as a single UI activity under the activity configuration worker UI `ACT_PLANT_MONITOR`.

Line Monitor Dashboard

The line monitor dashboard helps you to monitor line-specific updates such as the line's availability, machine downtimes that occurred in the shift for the respective line or work center, the reason codes for each machine downtime, and the current shift KPI. Also, this dashboard can be viewed from the plant monitor dashboard when you want to monitor a specific line for a drill-down report. Refer to Figure 6-4.

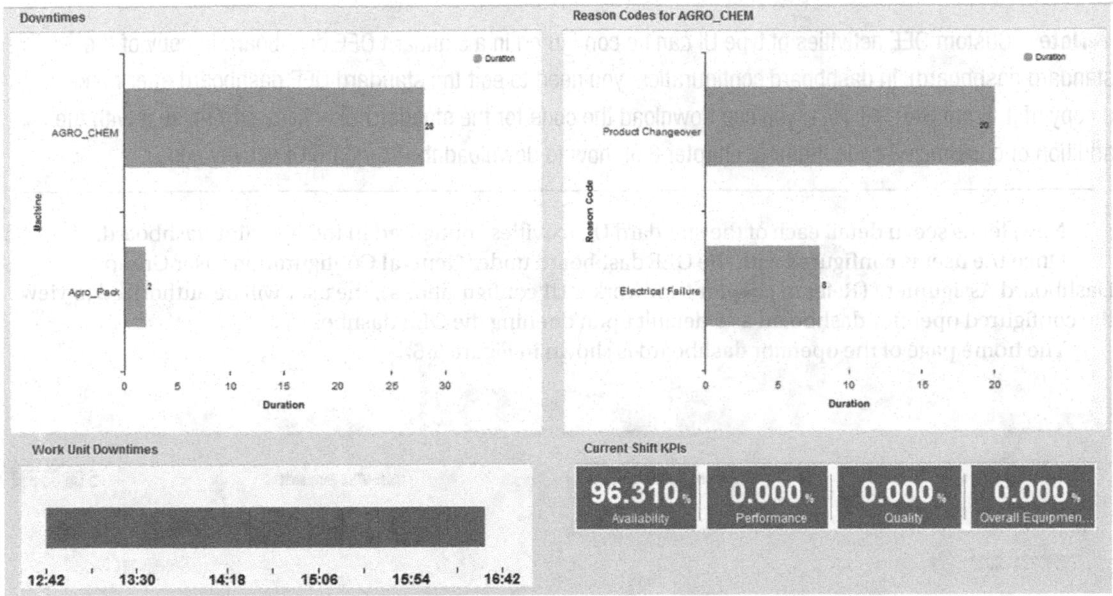

Figure 6-4. *OEE dashboard: line monitor*

The line monitor dashboard is available as the single UI activity `ACT_LINE_MONITOR`. Note the following:

- When the line monitor dashboard is used to drill-down from the plant monitor dashboard, it displays the real-time status of the selected line in the plant monitor.
- When the line monitor is directly accessed by selecting it from the dashboard menu, then the line detail is picked from the global context. Global context is the way OEE provides all its parameter values for use in OEE dashboard. For more details on global context, please refer to chapter 7.

Operator Dashboard

When using the operator dashboard, you can perform all the following operations as an operator:

- Manage orders: start, hold, and completed an order-operation
- Perform parametric data collection
- Manage machine and line downtimes
- Assign reason codes for all production losses
- Many other data maintenance tasks, such as updating production information for an order in the shift

The operator dashboard is a key dashboard that contains all the UI activities necessary for an operator to work with during his or her shift. This dashboard can be enhanced with other standard UI activities as per your requirements. It can also be customized by adding new dashboard buttons, which can be used to navigate to a custom OEE dashboard. In this way, the operator gets to view both the standard and customized OEE activities from the single UI.

■ **Note** Custom OEE activities of type UI can be configured in a standard OEE dashboard (a copy of the standard dashboard). In dashboard configuration, you need to edit the standard OEE dashboard after making a copy of it. From SAP MII 15.1, you can download the code for the standard UI activity and reuse it with the addition of customized code. Refer to chapter 8 on how to download the standard UI activity code.

Now, let us see in detail each of the standard UI activities configured in the operator dashboard.

Once the user is configured with the OEE dashboard under General Configuration/User Group Dashboard Assignment (Refer to chapter 5 for worker UI configurations), the user will be authorized to view the configured operator dashboard as a default upon opening the OEE dashboard.

The home page of the operator dashboard is shown in Figure 6-5.

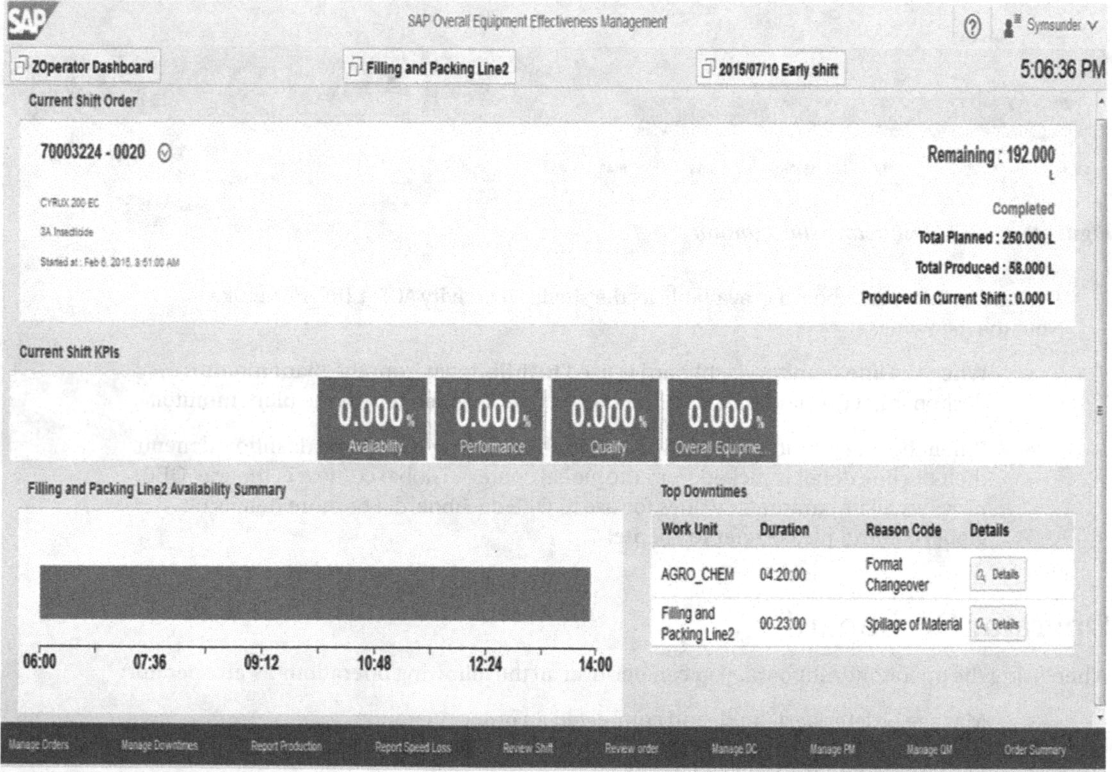

Figure 6-5. *OEE dashboard: operator dashboard*

Any OEE dashboard will have the following options as a default:

- Home icon to navigate to the home page of the dashboard from other screens
- Logged-in user name
- Back arrow button to navigate to the previously accessed dashboard page
- Dashboard selection

- Work center selection
- Shift and date selection

The three drop-down options for dashboard selection, line selection, and shift selection appear by default in a standard dashboard and when navigating to a custom UI from a standard OEE dashboard. This pane displays the current shift, dashboard, and the work center that are selected and provides the option of changing the selections from any activity page.

Dashboard Selection

Upon clicking of the dashboard look-up, you get a pop-up with all the configured dashboards for the logged-in user, as shown in Figure 6-6.

Select the dashboard for which you want to monitor or perform an action.

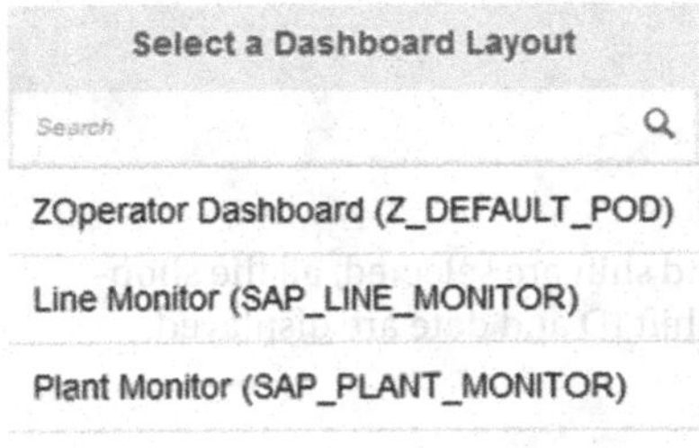

Figure 6-6. *OEE dashboard: dashboard selection*

Line or Work Unit Selection

Upon selection of the line look-up, you get a pop-up list of the work units (the production lines in a plant hierarchy) for which the logged-in user has authorization, as shown in Figure 6-7.

Select the line from the list.

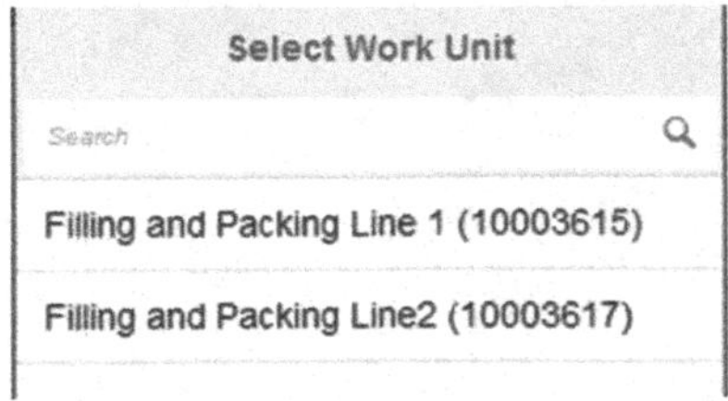

Figure 6-7. *OEE dashboard: work unit selection*

Shift Selection

The shift selection look-up lists all the shift intervals configured for the selected work center. The shift configurations are maintained in ERP, assigned to an OEE work center node of the plant hierarchy using OEE add-on, and then transferred to OEE through an IDoc. Refer to Figure 6-8.

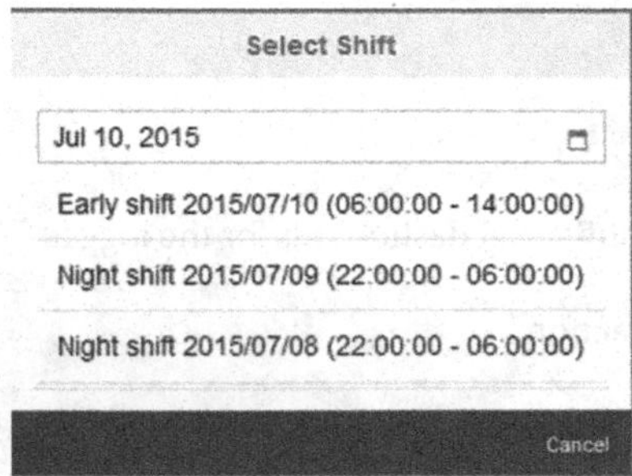

Figure 6-8. *OEE dashboard: shift selection*

You can select any shift interval for a particular date. Once a date and shift are selected, all the shop-floor data collected and the order-operations executed for the selected shift ID and date are displayed.

Current Shift Order

The current shift order pane is an order card (refer to Figure 6-9) that displays information about the active or completed order-operation, such as the following:

- Order-operation number
- Material number
- Material name
- Order-operation start date
- Order status - Active/Completed
- Remaining quantity to be produced
- Planned or total order quantity with UOM
- Total produced quantity with UOM
- Produced quantity in the current shift with UOM
- Production activity
- The names of capacities on which the order is started if the "Line Behavior" customization is set to multi-capacity single-line scenario

Associated Activity (Refer to Figure 6-9) of type UI: ACT_ORDER_CARD

Figure 6-9. *OEE dashboard: order card*

Current Shift KPIs

Current shift KPIs (refer to Figure 6-10) display real-time updates of the OEE KPIs, such as availability, performance, quality, and OEE. In instances of a current shift selection, the shift KPIs displayed would be real-time current KPI values. For the selection of past shifts, the KPI values displayed would be calculated for the whole shift. The KPI monitor can also be configured to display additional custom KPIs, and the same can be viewed by moving left and right.

Associated Activity (Refer to Figure 6-10) of type UI: ACT_KPI

Figure 6-10. *OEE dashboard: KPI monitor*

Line Availability Summary

The line availability summary displays the real-time availability of the selected line based on downtimes logged for it. The performance strip shows the timeline from the shift duration. For example, if the shift selected is Early Shift with the Shift Interval set as 06:00 to 14:00, for the selected shift the strip displays a green color for "line available" and red for "line down." The downtime and uptime are updated in real-time at the refresh rate of the operator dashboard. Refer to Figure 6-11.

The line down can be due to the following:

- physical line down raised manually or automatically
- bottleneck machine down

By keeping the cursor on the red portion of the performance strip, you will be able to see the approximate downtime durations occurred.

Associated Activity (Refer to Figure 6-11) of type UI: `ACT_WC_STRIP`

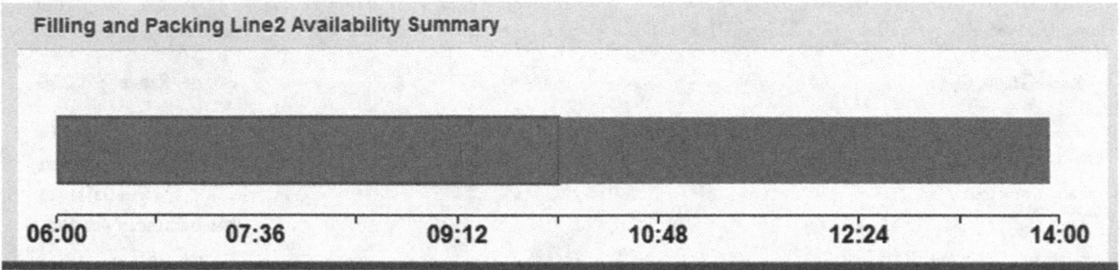

Figure 6-11. *OEE dashboard: line availability*

Top Downtimes

The top downtimes activity displays all the downtimes with a longer downtime duration, as shown in Figure 6-12. Each downtime is displayed with its reason code. On selecting the Details icon, the hierarchy of the reason code is displayed, as shown in Figure 6-13.

Associated Activity (Refer to Figure 6-12) of type UI: `ACT_TOP_DT`

Top Downtimes

Work Unit	Duration	Reason Code	Details
AGRO_CHEM	04:20:00	Format Changeover	Details
Filling and Packing Line2	00:23:00	Spillage of Material	Details

Figure 6-12. *OEE dashboard: top downtimes*

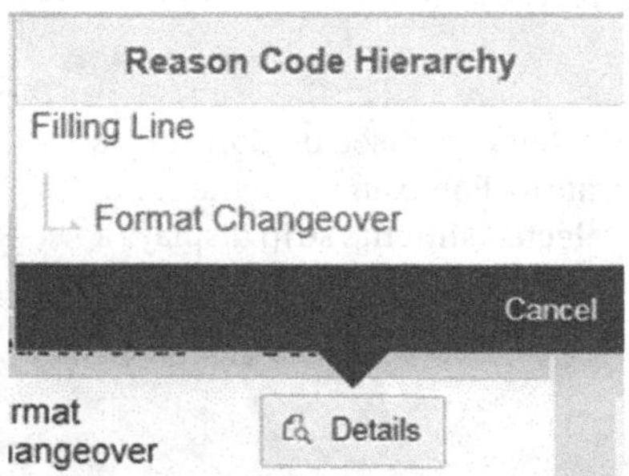

Figure 6-13. *OEE dashboard: reason code hierarchy*

Now let us look into the details of each dashboard button found at the bottom of the dashboard.

Dashboard buttons: Manage Orders

Upon clicking the Manage Orders button, a new UI is opened on the same page.

The purpose of this UI is to do the following:

- Manage orders–List the downloaded and released order-operations from SAP ERP

  This UI screen lists all the order-operations, which are downloaded from ERP and released in OEE for the selected work center

  1. *Associated customization configurations: Date range for order selection*:

     This parameter decides the time duration for which the order should be listed in the dashboard. For example, if the selected duration is ten days, then the dashboard displays the order whose planned start date is ten days before or after the current date.

  Associated Activity: ACT_ORD

Search for an order using fuzzy logic. Refer to Figure 6-14.

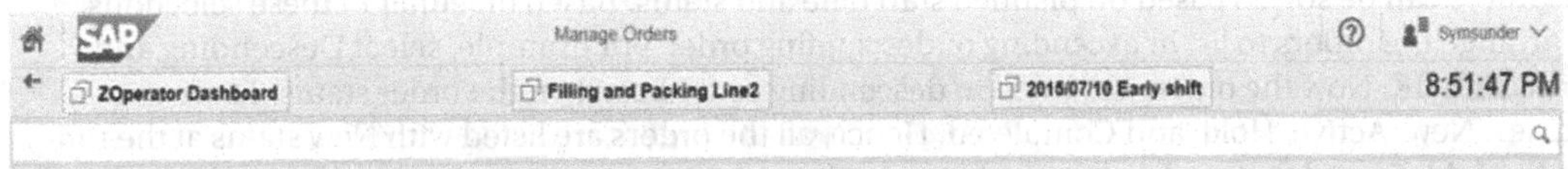

Figure 6-14. *OEE dashboard/manage orders: search orders*

The search box is enabled with fuzzy logic whereby an order can be searched for based on any of its parameters, such as order-operation number, material number, quantity, UOM, status, start date, planned start date, and activity. For example, by entering 78 in the search field, you get the following results because of the search term's match with quantity or any other matching field, as shown in Figure 6-15.

Manage Orders

Symsunder

ZOperator Dashboard | Filling and Packing Line2 | 2015/07/10 Early shift | 8:53:58 PM

78

New ☑ Active Hold Completed

Order	Operation/P...	Material	Quantity	UOM	Status	Actual Start	Planned Start			Activity	Details
70003305	0020 / Filling Process 0010 / Transfer of Filling Process	CYRUX 200 EC 3A Insecticide	78.000	LTR	Active	2015/05/30 20:10	2015/05/12 13:42	HOLD	Complete	Assign	Details
70003215	0020 / Filling Process 0010 / Transfer of Filling Process	CYRUX 200 EC 3A Insecticide	678.000	LTR	Active	2015/07/02 17:57	2014/12/03 13:30	HOLD	Complete	CONSU...	Details

Figure 6-15. *OEE dashboard/manage orders: search orders*

- Sort and refresh the orders. Refer to Figure 6-16.

Manage Orders

Symsunder

ZOperator Dashboard | Filling and Packing Line2 | 2015/07/10 Early shift | 8:55:49 PM

New ☑ Active Hold Completed

Figure 6-16. *OEE dashboard/manage orders: sort and refresh*

Upon selection of the Sort icon, you get the following pop-up from which to select the sort options, as shown in Figure 6-17.

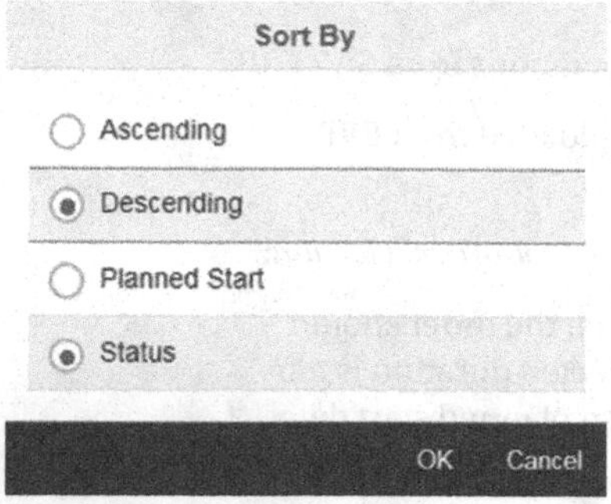

Sort By

- ○ Ascending
- ◉ Descending
- ○ Planned Start
- ◉ Status

OK Cancel

***Figure 6-17.** OEE dashboard/manage orders: sort options*

The orders can be sorted based on planned start date and status. Based on either of these selections, you can arrange the orders to list in ascending or descending order. For example, select Descending and Status and click OK. Now the orders are listed in descending order based on the order status. There are four statuses: New, Active, Hold, and Completed. Hence, all the orders are listed with New status at the top followed by Hold, Completed, and Active, as shown in Figure 6-18.

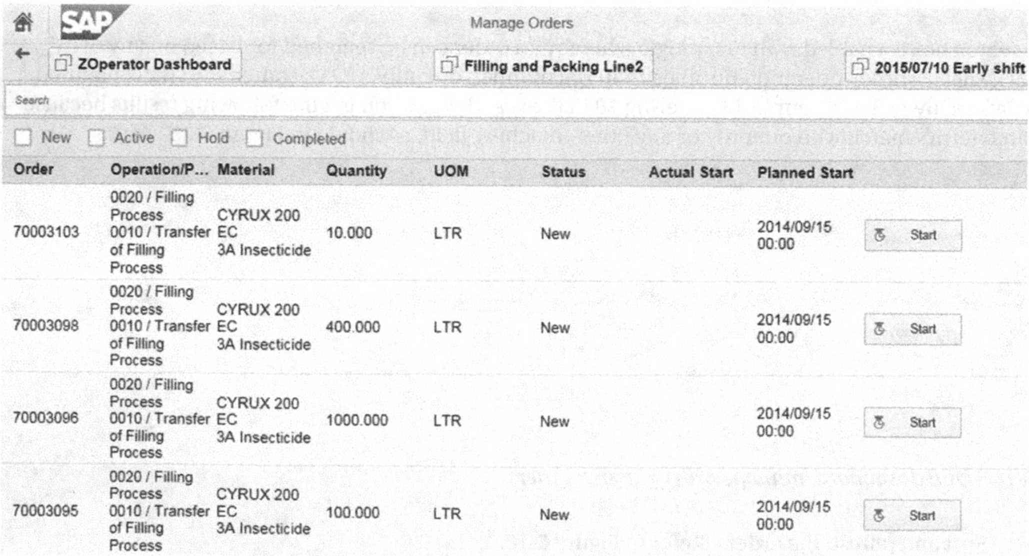

SAP Manage Orders

ZOperator Dashboard | Filling and Packing Line2 | 2015/07/10 Early shift

Search

☐ New ☐ Active ☐ Hold ☐ Completed

Order	Operation/P...	Material	Quantity	UOM	Status	Actual Start	Planned Start	
70003103	0020 / Filling Process 0010 / Transfer of Filling Process	CYRUX 200 EC 3A Insecticide	10.000	LTR	New		2014/09/15 00:00	Start
70003098	0020 / Filling Process 0010 / Transfer of Filling Process	CYRUX 200 EC 3A Insecticide	400.000	LTR	New		2014/09/15 00:00	Start
70003096	0020 / Filling Process 0010 / Transfer of Filling Process	CYRUX 200 EC 3A Insecticide	1000.000	LTR	New		2014/09/15 00:00	Start
70003095	0020 / Filling Process 0010 / Transfer of Filling Process	CYRUX 200 EC 3A Insecticide	100.000	LTR	New		2014/09/15 00:00	Start

***Figure 6-18.** OEE dashboard/manage orders: sorted orders*

■ **Note** When you sort based on order status, the "Status" option should be unchecked. Otherwise, the sorting will happen for the filtered orders based on the "Status" radio button being selected.

The Refresh icon refreshes the UI page to accommodate new orders when downloaded from ERP.

- Filter the orders with status

Refer to Figure 6-19, where you can see four checkboxes for four types of order statuses. You can filter the orders by checking the desired order status checkbox.

- Start an order-operation

Figure 6-19. *OEE dashboard/manage orders: order status filter options*

Select an order-operation that you want to start for execution. Select the "New" checkbox and sort the orders based on planned start date in ascending order. Refer to Figure 6-20.

Order	Operation/P...	Material	Quantity	UOM	Status	Actual Start	Planned Start	
70003212	0020 / Filling Process 0010 / Transfer of Filling Process	CYRUX 200 EC 3A Insecticide	890.000	LTR	New		2014/12/03 13:30	Start
70003211	0020 / Filling Process 0010 / Transfer of Filling Process	CYRUX 200 EC 3A Insecticide	567.000	LTR	New		2014/12/03 13:30	Start

Figure 6-20. *OEE dashboard/manage orders: order-operation start*

Select the Start button to start an order-operation. The current server date time is taken as the order-operation start time. You can also select an order-operation in the past and in the future. The required customization parameter should be configured under general configuration/customization configuration worker UI for the selected line.

Associated customization configuration:

- Allwd time limit for starting ord. in the past

■ **Caution** The order start in the past should be within the current shift duration.

- Hold an order-operation

You can place an order-operation on hold for various reasons. The manage orders UI helps you to both hold and resume an order-operation.

To hold an order-operation, select the Hold button for an active order. Refer to Figure 6-21. The order is placed on hold, with the order status updated to Hold from Active.

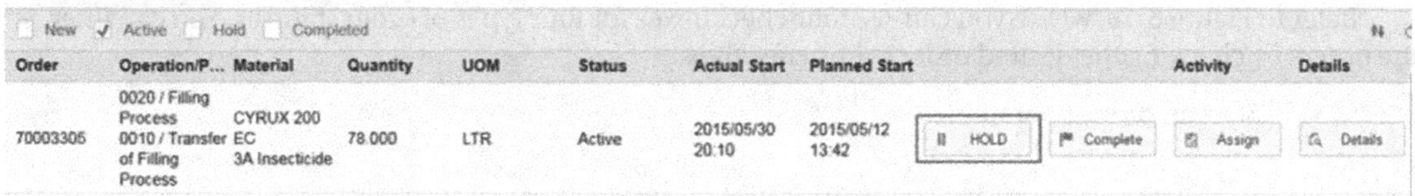

☐ New ☑ Active ☐ Hold ☐ Completed

Order	Operation/P...	Material	Quantity	UOM	Status	Actual Start	Planned Start		Activity		Details
70003305	0020 / Filling Process 0010 / Transfer of Filling Process	CYRUX 200 EC 3A Insecticide	78.000	LTR	Active	2015/05/30 20:10	2015/05/12 13:42	HOLD	Complete	Assign	Details

Figure 6-21. OEE dashboard/manage orders: hold orders

■ **Note** Production and loss data can be reported only for an active order.

To resume an order-operation, select the Resume button for an order that is in Hold status. Now the order status is updated from Hold to Active, and now you can continue with your order execution. Refer to Figure 6-22.

☐ New ☐ Active ☑ Hold ☐ Completed

Order	Operation/P...	Material	Quantity	UOM	Status	Actual Start	Planned Start	
70003224	0020 / Filling Process 0010 / Transfer of Filling Process	CYRUX 200 EC 3A Insecticide	250.000	LTR	Hold	2015/02/06 08:51	2015/01/30 05:13	▶ Resume

Figure 6-22. OEE dashboard/manage Orders: resume orders

- Abort an order

An order can be aborted if it is obsolete on the shop floor and is no longer meant to be executed in OEE dashboard. An order can only be aborted if it is set to Hold status. To set an order as obsolete, go to Manage orders ➤ Filter the Hold order ➤ Order details ➤ click on Set to Obsolete.

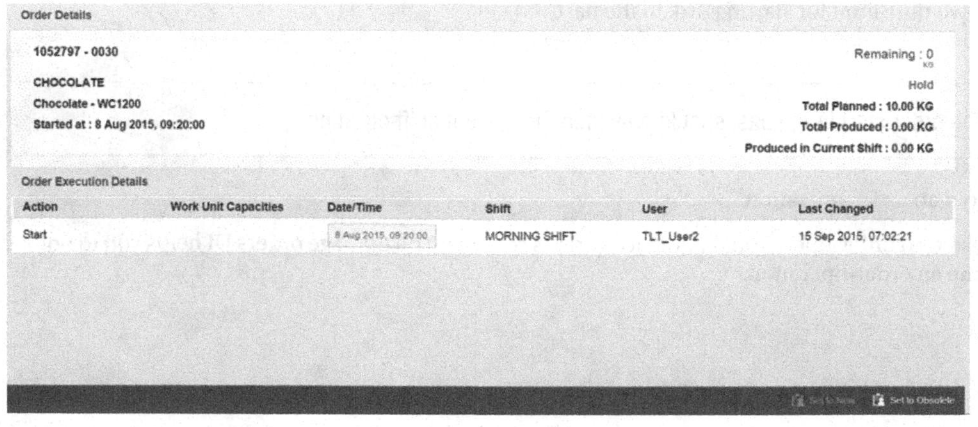

Order Details

1052797 - 0030

CHOCOLATE

Chocolate - WC1200

Started at : 8 Aug 2015, 09:20:00

Remaining : 0 KG

Hold

Total Planned : 10.00 KG

Total Produced : 0.00 KG

Produced in Current Shift : 0.00 KG

Order Execution Details

Action	Work Unit Capacities	Date/Time	Shift	User	Last Changed
Start		8 Aug 2015, 09:20:00	MORNING SHIFT	TLT_User2	15 Sep 2015, 07:02:21

Set to New Set to Obsolete

- Change the production activity for an order-operation

An order-operation may pass through multiple activity phases, such as consumption and production. In such cases, while starting an order-operation, you can start and change over to different production activities that are configured for a work center, as shown in Figure 6-23. Production activities are explained in chapter 3 section Production Activities.

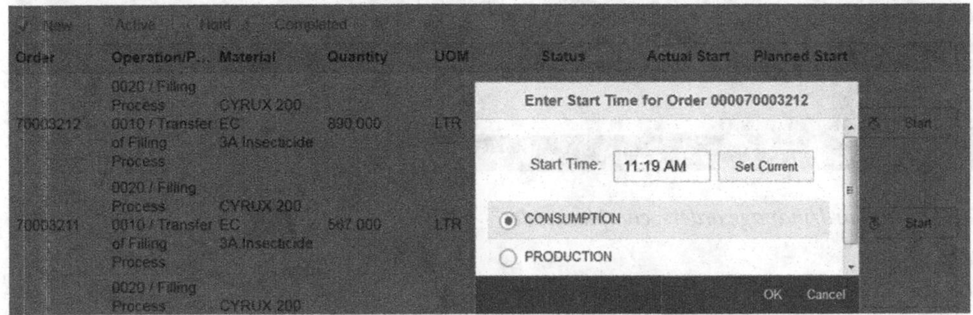

Figure 6-23. *OEE dashboard/manage orders: select production activity*

On starting an order-operation, and if the production activities are configured, you get a pop-up with the configured activities available. You can now select the required activity and click OK.

To change over from one activity to another, select the current activity for an active order; you get the pop-up with the configured activities. Now you can change over to another activity, as shown in Figure 6-24.

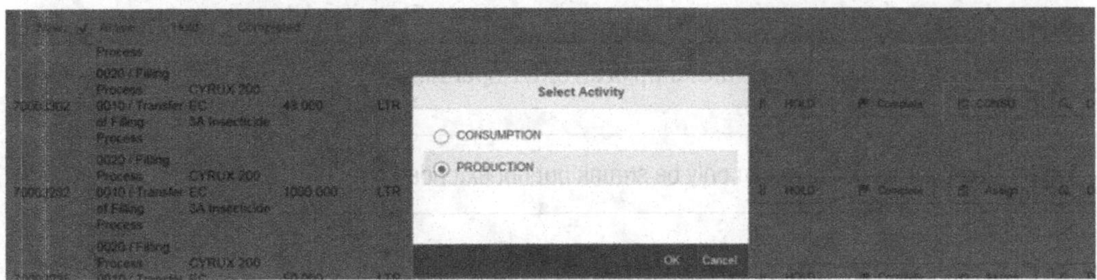

Figure 6-24. *OEE dashboard/manage orders: change over production activity*

■ **Note** Refer to chapter 7 on how to configure custom production activities and use in OEE.

Associated customization configuration:

- Relevant Production Activity
- Complete an order-operation

The manage orders UI also helps you to complete an order-operation. Select an active order and then click the Complete button. Refer to Figure 6-25.

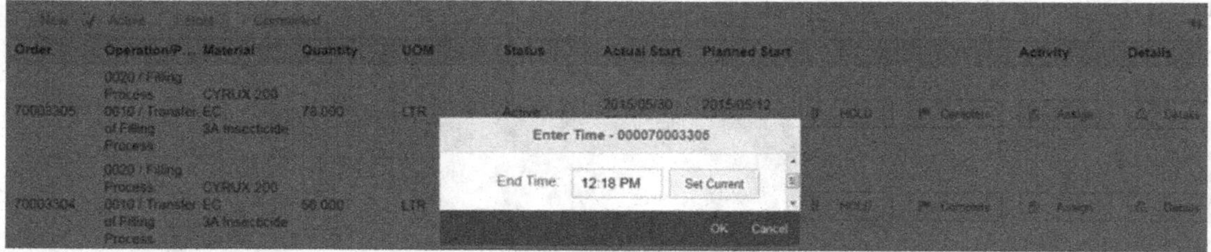

***Figure 6-25.** OEE dashboard/manage orders: complete order*

- View the order details

  The Details icon navigates to a new screen containing all the order-operation details, such as the following:

  - Order overview
  - Order execution details: You can edit the start and completion date time of the order-operation. Also, you can monitor the user details.
  - Activity details: View the activity details in terms of start and end timestamps.

    Associated customization parameter: Shrinking Order Duration Allowed. Using this parameter, you can shrink or shorten the order duration by editing the start or end timestamp of an order-operation.

■ **Note** Within a shift, order duration can only be shrunk but not extended.

Dashboard buttons: Manage Downtimes

Manage downtime is the UI activity to handle time loss for machines or production lines–i.e., downtimes. Downtimes can be reported manually or automatically by API calls in an integrated solution.

From the manage downtime UI, you can do the following:

- Report...
  - unscheduled machine downtimes
  - unscheduled line downtimes
  - scheduled downtimes
  - flow time
- View and edit saved downtimes
- Assign reason codes for downtimes
- Delete a downtime
- Split downtimes and assign reason codes for the split downtimes

The search field is used to search the saved downtimes. The search box is similar to the one in the manage orders UI where a downtime can be searched based on any of its parameters, like work unit, downtime type, user ID, and reason code.

For example, by specifying "Pack" in the search field, you get the following downtimes. Refer to Figure 6-26.

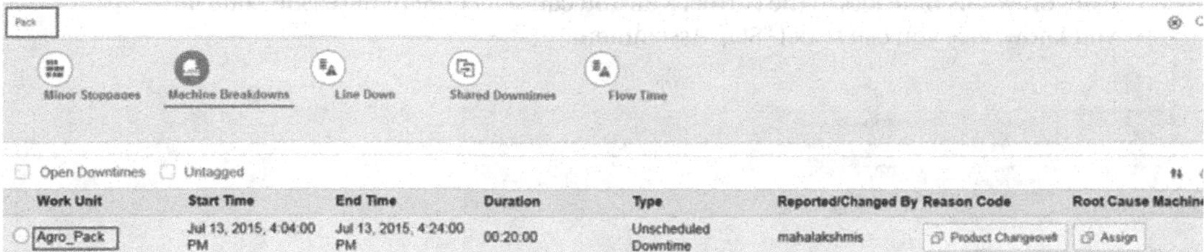

Figure 6-26. OEE dashboard/manage downtimes: search downtimes

Minor Stoppages

Minor stoppages are those stoppages that are categorized as non-critical components for the Availability KPI calculations. The categorization is defined based on the downtime duration.

Associated customization parameter: Minor Stoppage Limit. It is set as ten minutes by default.

For example, any stoppage whose duration is less than ten minutes is considered to be a minor stoppage.

Minor stoppages should be included in availability you can define whether a minor stoppage should be included as part of the availability KPI or not using this customization parameter.

How to create a minor stoppage:

1. Minor stoppage limit for the selected work center is set, for example, to five mins.
2. To report a minor stoppage manually, select the Minor Stoppages tab and select "Report New" option at the bottom .
3. A pop-up lists the work center and the machines that are part of this work center. The bottleneck machines are highlighted and differentiated from the non-bottleneck machines. Refer to Figure 6-27.

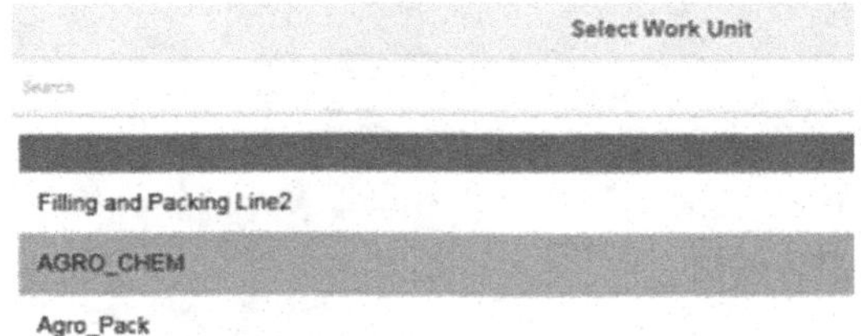

Figure 6-27. OEE dashboard/manage downtimes: report minor stoppage

4. Select the line on which to create the line minor stoppage or select a machine from the list to create a machine minor stoppage. In the Type drop-down, you get the list of data collection elements created to capture the type of downtime loss. Refer to Figure 6-28. By default, unscheduled downtime is the data collection element used. The data collection element acts as an identifier for the system to categorize this time loss to the correct KPI. You can select the right reason code if you know, else you can select "Skip Assignment."

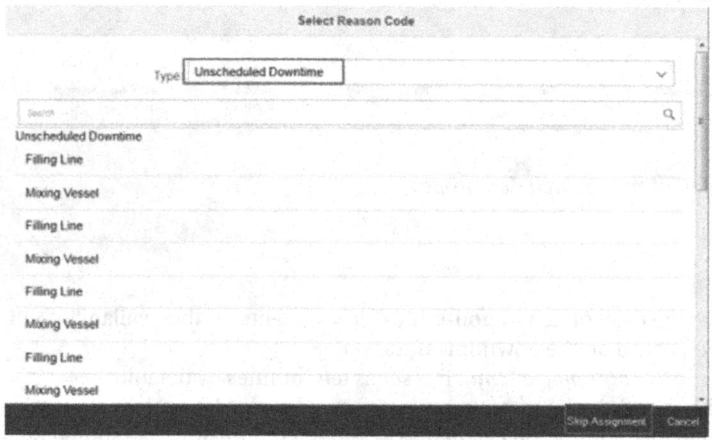

Figure 6-28. *OEE dashboard: select data collection element*

5. Specify the start time and end time (if it's a past downtime), or select the start time for an open downtime by selecting the start and end time textboxes. The "Set current" option allows you to directly set the current time. Once the start and end times are specified, the duration is automatically calculated, or you can define the start time and set the duration by which the end time is calculated, and it will be set automatically. Enter comments, if any. Select OK, and the downtime is saved under Minor Stoppages tab. Check "Mark Line Down" if you feel this machine (whether bottleneck or not) affects the line's availability, as shown in Figure 6-29 and Figure 6-30.

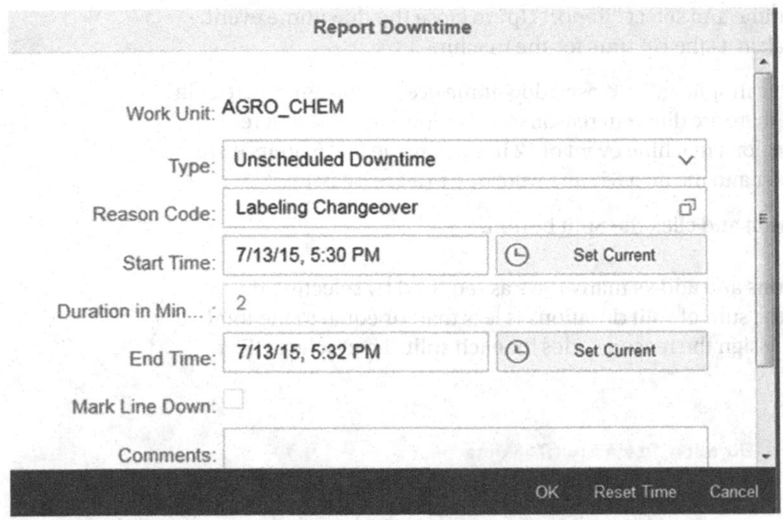

Figure 6-29. *OEE dashboard/manage downtimes: report minor stoppage*

☐ Untagged

Work Unit	Duration	Reason Code	Details
○ AGRO_CHEM	00:03:00	Labeling Changeover	Details

Figure 6-30. *OEE dashboard/manage downtimes: minor stoppage reported*

You can select the created downtime and split it to assign reason codes for each split downtime. Minor stoppages cannot be edited and deleted.

Check the "Untagged" checkbox to filter and list the downtimes that are yet to be assigned a reason code.

Machine Breakdowns

This tab is displayed by default when the manage downtime UI is loaded. You can create machine downtimes using the "Report New" option. When the downtime duration is less than or equal to the minor stoppages limit set, the downtime is saved under the Minor Stoppages tab. If not, it can be viewed under the Machine Breakdowns tab. The saved downtimes can be edited for changes in downtime duration and reason codes. You can also assign a root-cause machine for a downtime if the root-cause machine selected is the root cause of this line going down. The root-cause machine assigned may or may not be down. You can even report the root-cause machine as down during this assignment.

> **Filter options**: Open downtimes and Untagged downtimes
>
> **Sorting**: Sort criteria are start time, end time, and duration, and sort order is ascending or descending. Select the criteria and the order to sort the downtimes as per your requirements.
>
> Search Field enabled with fuzzy logic enables you to search a downtime on any of its parameters, such as work unit, downtime type, reported/changed by, and reason code.

Select an open downtime and select "Report Up" to close the downtime event. The current time is taken as the Up time for the machine.

Split downtimes: You can split only a closed downtime event. Downtimes are split ideally when you feel there are different reasons for the downtime for different intervals. For example, for a machine event of 12 hours, say the first 6 hours were due to label changeover and the next 6 hours were due to a grease issue.

Select a downtime event and click the Split button.

Enter the split durations and add as many rows as required by selecting the Split button. Ensure the sum of split durations is less than or equal to the total downtime duration. Assign the reason codes for each split. Then select OK. Refer to Figure 6-31.

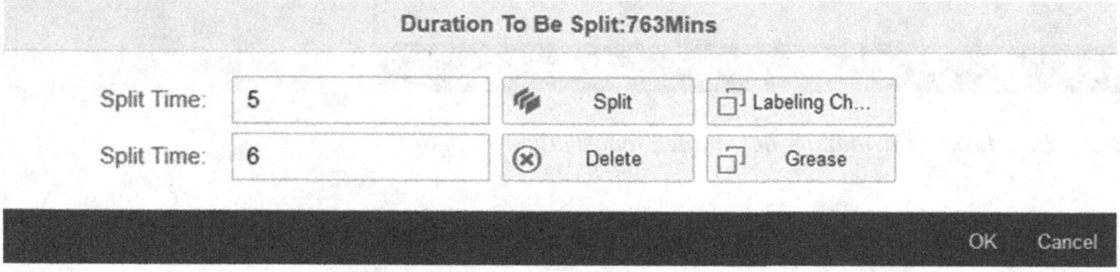

Duration To Be Split:763Mins

Split Time: 5 Split Labeling Ch...

Split Time: 6 Delete Grease

OK Cancel

Figure 6-31. *OEE dashboard/manage fowntimes: split downtimes*

The downtimes are split, and if there is any remaining unsplit duration, then that duration remains as a separate entry.

You can also delete a downtime using the Delete button.

Line Down

Line down is the unavailability of the production line or work center for production purposes. Line down can happen in two ways in OEE:

- Manual/automatic reporting of a line down

  To create a manual line down, follow the same steps as described in the previous section for reporting a machine down. In this case, select the line instead of a machine, and for its respective data collection element say "Line_Stoppage" or "Unscheduled_downtime." For this type of line down, a physical record exists in the OEE standard tables with a corresponding data collection element. This record is displayed in the OEE dashboard under the Line Down tab, and you can assign a reason code.

- A bottleneck machine down

  Report a bottleneck machine down, and based on the customization parameter set for "Line Behavior," the OEE system displays the bottleneck machine that is down as a line down.

  For example, say AGRO_CHEM machine is a bottleneck machine. On reporting AGRO_CHEM down, the Line Down tab displays this bottleneck machine as down, which signifies it as a line down. Refer to Figure 6-32. For this type of line down, the OEE standard table does not have any record signifying the line is down, unlike in the previous line-down scenario. Hence, reason codes can only be assigned for the bottleneck machine that is down, which signifies the reason code for line down as well.

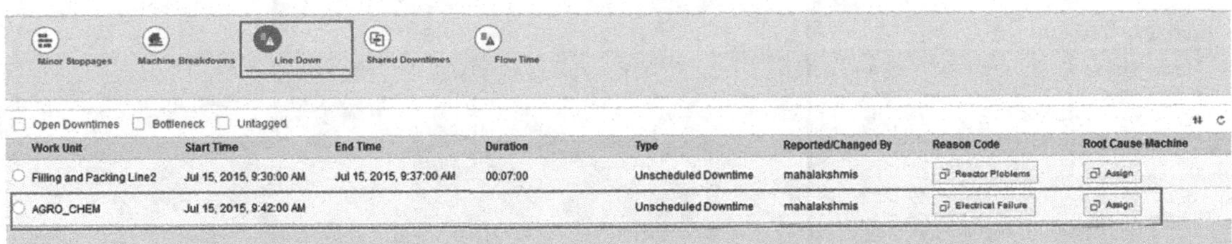

Figure 6-32. *OEE dashboard/manage downtimes: line down*

■ **Note** The line down works based on the customization parameter "Line Behavior." Please refer to customization configuration in chapter 7.

Line downs can be

- deleted;
- assigned a root-cause machine;
- filtered based on open downtimes, bottleneck, and untagged;
- edited for the start and end time timestamps and the reason code;
- split in a similar fashion to machine breakdowns; if the split duration is less than or equal to the minor stoppage limit, then the split line down will appear under minor stoppages; and
- sorted

Shared Downtimes

In OEE, downtimes are independent of order-operations. The operator on the shop floor is the right person to know whether a downtime will affect an order-operation's KPI or not. As an operator, you can use the Shared Downtime tab to assign the order-operation the downtime.

OEE allows you to allocate a downtime to either a single order or all orders, if multiple orders exist. On allocation of downtimes to an order-operation, the order-specific KPIs are affected accordingly, and there is no change to shift KPI.

Create Shared Downtimes

Select the Shared Downtime tab If only one order exists or you want to assign the downtime to only one order, select the downtime and select the "Assign to order" option. A pop-up appears with all the existing active orders for the selected line. Refer to Figure 6-33.

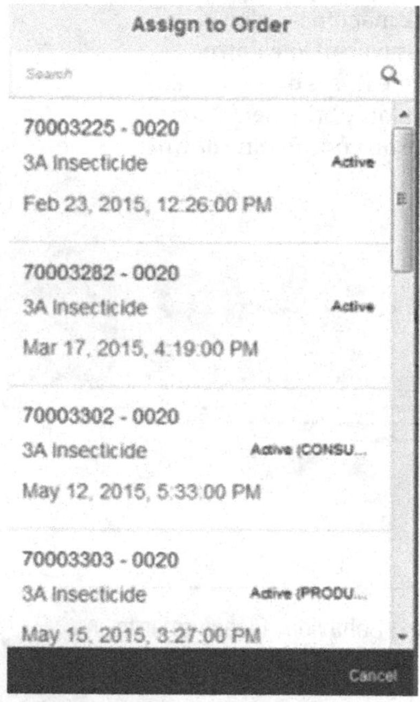

Figure 6-33. *OEE dashboard/manage downtimes: select order for downtime event assignment*

Select a single order and click OK. The assigned order-operation is displayed against the downtime. Refer to Figure 6-34.

Work Unit	Start Time	End Time	Duration	Type	Reported/Changed By	Reason Code	Root Cause Machine	Assign to Order (
Agro_Pack	Jul 15, 2015, 9:43:00 AM			Unscheduled Downtime	mahalakshmis	Product Changeover	Assign	70003225 - 0020

Figure 6-34. *OEE dashboard/manage downtimes: event assigned to order*

Flow Time

Flow time is the time duration for a product to reach to end of line after the start of production. It is non-productive time which is not part of the loading time. Sometimes, you may need to measure the flow time to understand the non production time as otherwise the total time from start to end of line will include this non production time which needs to be measured and corrected to get accurate KPI., which helps you to understand the performance or capacity of the line producing the product.

Dashboard buttons: Report Production

Production is a data collection element of type Yield that collects the actual production and yield data from the shop floor. This element directly affects the performance KPI.

Good production without any speed loss leads to 100 percent performance KPI.

Report production is a standard OEE activity of type UI that collects the production data manually through the operator dashboard. The report production UI displays the following:

- Order summary
- Report production with UOM
- Report waste
- Report quality defects

To report production/yield, enter the yield quantity and the UOM. All the alternate UOMs for the material are listed here. The UOMs come from the UOM T006 table in SAP ERP and are transferred to MII. You can select the desired UOM, and if the UOM happens to be not the standard material UOM defined in the order, the UOM conversion can be enabled using the global configuration parameter `SAP_UOM_CONVERSION_TXN`. Save the reported production.

You can report other material losses like waste/scrap and quality defects along with production/yield. Similar to production, enter the waste quantity and UOM, assign the reason code (if known), add comments (if any), and save the entries. You can select the Details button to view the reported production and the material losses. Refer to Figure 6-35.

Parameter	Quantity	UOM	Reason Code	Comments	Details	Reported Qty per ...	Last Reported D...
Produced Good Quantity	4	L			Details	0.000 BT	
Waste Generated	1	L	Wrong Mixing	Add	Details	0.000 BT	
Defect Quantity	1	L	High pH value	Add	Details	0.000 BT	

Figure 6-35. *OEE dashboard: report production*

Once the production is reported, you will see a change in performance KPI value, and once a quality defect is reported, the quality KPI is affected.

Associated activity: `ACT_REP_QTY`

Dashboard buttons: Report Speed Loss

Speed loss is a time loss–production at nominal speed taken from production at actual speed. Nominal speed is the rated speed at which a product can be produced in a particular work center. This is defined in SAP ERP for a material at a work center and is also defined in the plant hierarchy for a work center node.

Actual speed/set speed is the speed at which a product is actually being produced. Normally a speed is set for each line, which ideally should be the nominal speed. Sometimes that may not be the case, and could be greater or lesser than the nominal speed.

When the actual speed is lesser than the nominal speed, it is a speed loss, and hence the performance of the line goes down or underperforms. In this case, the line should be monitored and decisive action should be taken.

Speed loss = Production at actual speed - Production at nominal speed

In OEE, the time loss due to speed is indicated as an open speed loss in the report speed loss UI. The operator needs to assess the situation and accordingly report a speed loss using Report Speed Loss button in operator dashboard.

For example, refer to Figure 6-36, where you can see an open actual speed. There is an open time loss of 7 hours and 5 minutes. With this, the operator is aware of what length of time was due to a speed loss. You can split the total available duration and report a desired speed loss.

	Downtime	Target Quantity	Reported Quantity	Reported Actual Speed	Open Actual Speed	
07:05:00	00:00:00	28332.220 BT	0.000 BT	00:00:00	07:05:00	Split

Reported Speed Loss

Speed Loss	Reported by	Reason Code	Root Cause Machine	Associated Events
		No data		

Figure 6-36. OEE dashboard: report speed loss

To report speed loss, select the "Split" option, enter the time duration in minutes, assign the reason code for speed loss, and click OK. The speed loss is reported and displayed here. For a reported speed loss, you can attach a root-cause machine if you feel the cause of the speed loss is a machine. You can also link other downtime events to this speed loss. This helps in analyzing the history of similar losses so as to take a corrective action. Refer to Figure 6-36.

Associated activity: ACT_SL

Dashboard buttons: Report Standard value parameter

As part of a process/production order, six standard activities can be defined which are captured during order execution as part of production information. These standard value parameters are production activities and are captured as time duration which has a production contexts. These standard value activities can be setup time, machine hours, labor hours etc as per the business requirements. In OEE, there is a standard activity to capture the values manually in the dashboard.

To enable the standard activity reporting you need to configure the standard activity ACT_STD_VAL in dashboard configuration as a dashboard button. In operator dashboard on clicking the Report Standard Activity, you can report the values defined the selected work center as in Figure 6-37.

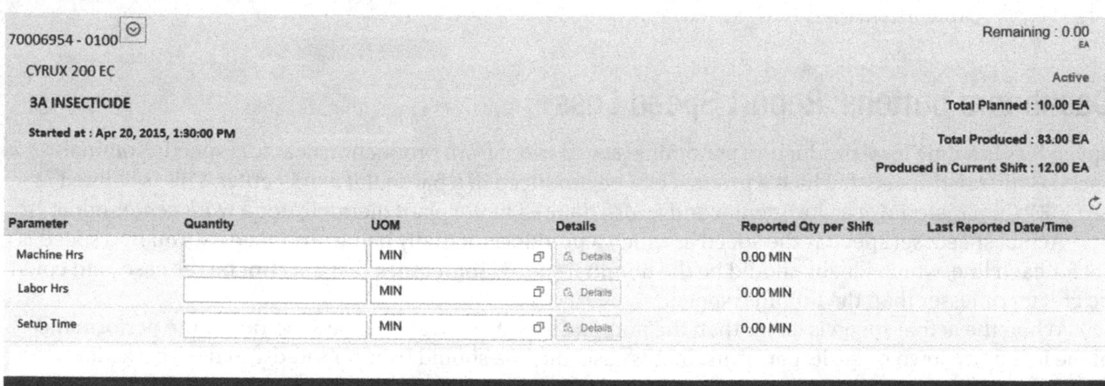

Figure 6-37. OEE dashboard: report standard values

Once reported, these values are stored in MPM_PROD_RUN_DATA along with other order specific data collections. When the standard order confirmation extension is triggered, these reported values are automatically mapped to the ORDER_CONFIRM_BAPI workflow and are updated in ERP.

Dashboard buttons: Review Order

Review order is a standard OEE activity of type UI where you can view and edit the history of an order-operation.

Review order displays order-operation details for all the shifts for which it was active. It displays the following details:

- Order overview
- Order-specific data collections with tagged and untagged quantities and option to view their details
- Order-independent data collections with tagged and untagged quantities and option to view their details
- Top downtimes that occurred during the order-operation execution with their durations, reason codes, and further exploded views
- List of all downtimes that occurred during the order-operation execution with their untagged durations
- Top five reasons for the downtimes
- Line availability in real-time
- Machine availability in real-time
- Current order-specific KPIs

  Associated activity: `ACT_REV_ORD`

Dashboard buttons: Review Shift

Review shift is a standard OEE activity of type UI where you can review and edit all the order-operation details that are active or completed for the selected shift.

Review shift displays the following details:

- Order overview
- Order-specific data collections with tagged and untagged quantities and option to view their details
- Order-independent data collections with tagged and untagged quantities and option to view their details
- Top downtimes that occurred during the order-operation execution with their durations, reason codes, and further exploded views
- List of all downtimes that occurred during the order-operation execution with their untagged durations
- Top five reasons for the downtimes
- Line availability in real-time

- Machine availability in real-time
- Current order-specific KPIs

You can edit or assign reason codes for all the time and material losses reported for the selected order-operation and shift. You can also share the downtime with an order-operation by assigning the downtime to the selected order.

Associated activity: `ACT_REV_SFT`

OEE dashboard can be bookmarked for a specific screen, and from there you can easily navigate to other screens. In addition, you can directly launch the specific screen of the OEE dashboard if you know the activity name.

For example, the URL to launch the OEE dashboard is
`http://<server>:<port>/OEEDashboard/WorkerUI.jsp`

From the dashboard page, when you navigate to the Manage Orders screen, the URL you will get is
`http://<server>:<port>/OEEDashboard/WorkerUI.jsp#/activity/ACT_ORD`

You can bookmark the preceding URL as Manage Orders and directly launch it next time when you want to work on the Manage Orders screen.

Standard Functionalities of SAP OEE

From earlier chapters and the previous sections in this chapter, you have learned the capabilities of SAP OEE and the configurations needed to set up the plant model. To summarize, the following are the functionalities delivered as part of the solution:

- Download and release of order-operation from SAP ERP to MII
- Execution of order-operation, which includes start, hold, resume, and complete an order
- Order-dependent and order-independent data collections
- Downtime handling; managing plant maintenance notifications
- Four KPI calculations in real-time
- Goods Movement in OEE
- Update of order confirmation and goods movement back to SAP ERP
- Real-time monitoring of shop floor through OEE dashboard in SAP MII
- Near real-time replication of OEE transaction data to SAP HANA

You will learn in this section the standard data flow cycle, from the download of an order from ERP to the update of operational information back to ERP. You'll also see how the backend OEE tables are updated with these data.

Download and Release of Order-Operation

OEE KPIs are calculated and monitored at the shift level. Each shift executes order-operation(s). Hence, the first step is to download an order-operation from SAP ERP and release it before its execution.

Prerequisite:

1. ALE customization configuration is configured in SAP ERP to transfer the production/process order.
2. OEE Integration CTC is executed to set up the ERP shop-floor integration framework.
3. Material is created and MATMAS IDoc is transferred to OEE.
4. Work center is created and LOIWCS03 is transferred to OEE.
5. Plant hierarchy is created for the OEE plant, and the work center is assigned to each line node in the hierarchy. Hierarchy is successfully published and transferred to SAP OEE (MII).
6. Production/process order is created using CO01/COR1.

Transfer a production/process order from SAP ERP to SAP MII using tcode POIT. The SAPOEEINT framework processes the order and inserts the data into OEE tables. Next, ensure order processing status is set to Success in the SAPOEEINT queue monitor. By default, all the order quantity is released. You can also partially release an order in the order dispatch worker UI. To do this, you need to disable the auto-release by enhancing the request XSLT transaction for the production/process order. If you want to capture the standard value activities in OEE, then the order needs to be configured with these activities.

Tables involved:

1. `MPM_RELEASED_DMD_HDR`: Order details with partial or full released quantity and status.
2. `MPM_RELEASED_DMD`: Order-operation details along with order status. Initially the status is NEW. Order status is updated from time to time until it is completed and the data is updated back to ERP. Also, this table stores both OEE- and non-OEE-relevant operation details (based on the pre-XSLT parameter configured during CTC execution). OEE dashboard displays only OEE-specific operations. You can use non-OEE-relevant operations for non-OEE-specific enhancements.

Execution of Order-Operation, Which Includes Start, Hold, and Complete an Order

The next step is to execute the downloaded and released order-operation.

Prerequisite:

1. Configure the user group and dashboard assignment for each work center.
2. Order is downloaded and released at the work center.

In the OEE dashboard, go to Manage orders button and select the order-operation from the list that was downloaded. You can start, hold, or complete the order-operation. On start of order-operation, production activity can be selected (if it is configured). In the same Manage Orders screen, the production activity also can be changed from one to another.

The order status changes from NEW to ACT to CMPL. The order takes a Hold status if placed under hold, and will be resumed from the same screen. Once the order is completed, the order-operation confirmation is put into the integration queue if the standard extension ORDER_CONF_EXT_ACT is configured for the "Complete order" method under the Extension Configuration tab under General Configuration worker UI. If it is not configured, the order completion timestamp is updated into OEE tables, Confirmations Enqueuer is a scheduler which at the set scheduler frequency checks for any order related data which are pending for confirmation and the same are pushed to integration queue using ORDER_CONFIRM_BAPI workflow. The ORDER_CONFIRM_BAPI workflow will pick up these messages and update it to SAP ERP through an RFC call.

■ **Note** SAP ERP order confirmations can be configured to be line specific using the customization parameter "Enable Periodic Confirmations" upon order completion or upon reporting the data. When not defined, confirmation for all the work centers will be triggered by the MII scheduler.

OEE database tables involved:

1. MPM_RELEASED_DMD_HDR: Order status is updated with order start details.
2. MPM_RELEASED_DMD: Order status is updated with order start details. If an order is completed, the end date and time are updated along with the timestamp for when the confirmation details were updated to ERP from OEE.
3. MPM_PROD_RUN_HDR: Once an order is started, a new entry is inserted into this table with the status ACT, along with the order start and end times. The entry is given a unique key, RUN_ID, which helps in reading the table data. If an order spans across the shift, the order is automatically marked completed at the end of a shift and started again for the new shift. The status in the old shift is updated to CMPL, and in the new shift its status is set to ACT, and it has a new RUN_ID. Each entry is shift- and work center node-specific.
4. MPM_PROD_RUN_INT: This production interval table stores the interval of a run within a shift; i.e., if a stop gap (hold-resume of an order in a shift) happened in a shift for an order once, two intervals would be created–one from order start to order hold time, then another from order resume to end time for that shift. A change in a production activity also triggers a new interval creation Order-Dependent and Order-Independent Data Collection

During the process of order-operation execution—i.e., after the start and before the completion of an order-operation—shop-floor data are collected either manually (through dashboard) or automatically (enhancement using OEE APIs). The collected data may be order dependent or order independent.

In OEE, the order-dependent data collections are:

- Production yield/goods quantity
- Waste or scrap
- Quality defects
- Speed loss

Order-independent data collections can be any custom data collection element. (The standard product does not deliver any order-independent data collection elements.)

Whether a data collection is dependent or independent is configured in OEE add-on during the configuration of data collection elements (DCE). OEE KPIs are affected by the order-dependent DCEs. For KPI calculations, these DCEs are identified using their names. For example, production count is part of the performance KPI that is identified using its DCE name, say, `GOOD_QUANTITY`, and data element. Order-independent data collection elements are for information purposes and are not part of OEE KPI calculations.

Both order-dependent and -independent DCEs are available as standard activities of type UI within the activity configuration worker UI. Hence, you can use these activities to design your OEE dashboard. In addition, a custom DCE can be configured in the OEE add-on, transferred to OEE, and used in the dashboard.

Refer to chapter 7 for automatic data collection and the configuration of custom data collection elements.

Tables involved:

1. `MPM_PROD_RUN_DATA`: All the data collection elements except for downtimes are stored here, with a quantity UOM for yield and material losses and duration UOM for time losses. This data may or may not be linked with a `RUN_ID` in the `MPM_PROD_RUN_HDR` table.

Order Downtime Tagging

You now know how to trigger a downtime in OEE, and you are aware that line down affects the availability KPI. Line down duration for a shift directly influences the shift availability KPI. To determine the availability KPI at the order level, you need to allocate a downtime event to either a single order or all orders in the line. This is achieved using the Shared Downtime tab under Managed Downtime button in OEE dashboard. Please refer to the "Manage Downtime" section in this chapter to understand how this works. Once you allocate the downtime to one or more orders, you get the order-specific downtime, and accordingly the availability KPI is calculated and displayed at the order-operation level.

The SAP OEE database tables involved are:

1. `MPM_PROD_EVENTS`: Upon your reporting a line down, this table gets an entry for the line down with the assigned reason code and duration. This table has a unique event ID for every event created. The availability KPI at the shift level is calculated from this table.
2. `MPM_INT_EVENT_MAP`: Once the order-operation is allocated a line down, this table gets an entry with the event ID and duration.

Four KPI Calculations in Real-time

You have seen in the previous chapters that OEE by default calculates the four key KPIs, namely availability, performance, quality, and OEE. In this section, you will learn how this is calculated using an example.

Refer to Figure 6-38, a view of a typical shift summary, which displays the loading time, scheduled downtime, unscheduled downtime and so forth happening in a shift.

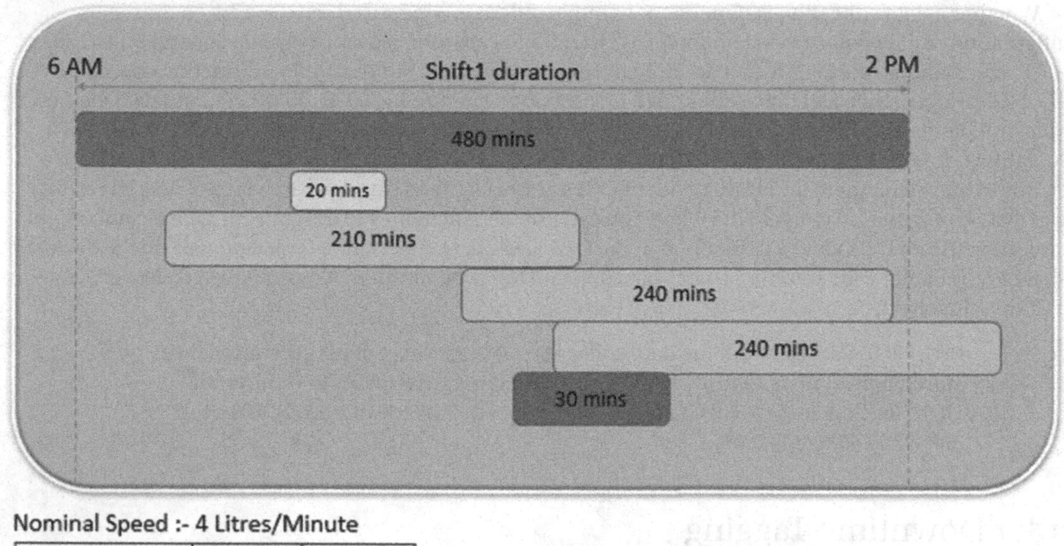

Nominal Speed :- 4 Litres/Minute

Parameters	Order 1	Order 2
Order quantity	840	960
Yield produced	835	950
Quality reject	5	10

Figure 6-38. *Shift summary with order details*

OEE KPI Calculation

Refer to the following formulas of data elements required for KPI calculations. In chapter 3, you learned that every DCE is categorized as a data element, and that a data element is either a reported element or a calculated element. The text in bold is reported elements, and text in italics is calculated elements.

Total production time for a shift	=	*480 mins (8 x 60)*
Scheduled down	=	**20 mins**
Unscheduled down (Line down)	=	**30 mins**
Loading time	=	[∑(Order completed time – Order start time – Order Hold time)] – Scheduled downtime
	=	*[210 + 240] – 20*
	=	430 mins
Net Production time	=	*Loading time – Unscheduled downtime*
	=	*430 – 30*
	=	400 mins
Net Operating time	=	*Net production time – speed loss*
Speed loss	=	**Production time at actual speed - Production time at nominal speed (rated speed)**

(Assume speed loss is 0 and the complete order quantity is produced at the nominal speed)

Net operating time	=	*400 mins*
Quality loss	=	**∑Time taken to produce rejected quantity with production at nominal speed**
	=	**1.25 + 2.5**
	=	**3.75 mins**
Value Operating time	=	*Net Operating time – Quality loss*
	=	*400 – 3.75*
	=	*396.25 mins*

Quality KPI	=	(Value operating time / Net operating time) x 100
	=	*396.25 / 400 x 100*
	=	*99 %*
Performance KPI	=	*(Net operation time / Net production time) x 100*
	=	*(400 / 400) x100*
	=	*100%*
Availability KPI	=	*(Net production time / Loading time) x100*
	=	*(400 /430) x 100*
	=	*93 %*
OEE	=	*Availability x Performance x Quality*
	=	*.93 X 1 X .99*
	=	*92 %*

■ **Note** In SAP OEE, loading time is calculated as the summation of every order-operation duration and not the overall order-operation execution time, considering the possibility of parallel execution durations.

In OEE, KPI values are calculated in real-time and are not stored in OEE database tables. The reported elements and other order-related details are available in OEE database tables, which are replicated to HANA. Both OEE and HANA calculate the KPI in real-time on demand.

OEE database tables involved:

1. `MPM_PROD_RUN_HDR`: provides the order-operation-related details
2. `MPM_PROD_RUN_INT`: has intervals for a run in a shift
3. `MPM_PROD_RUN_DATA`: has the reported elements except for downtime
4. `MPM_PROD_RUN_EVENTS`: has the downtime details

The KPIs monitored in OEE dashboard are shift specific. To calculate the order-specific KPIs, the same formulas and calculations should be used, but for each order.

Goods Movement in OEE

If you are using the 15.0 version, in this section you will learn how goods issue (GI) and goods receipt (GR) are performed using OEE. From 15.1 onward, these are addressed differently through the Goods Issue and Goods Receipt app. Refer to chapter 8 section Goods Movement App.

Goods Receipt

Whenever yield is reported, a goods receipt of the produced yield is mapped to order confirmation BAPI and updated to ERP using the `ORDER_CONFIRM_BAPI` workflow. The ERP order confirmation extension can be triggered as and when data is reported or at the end of order completion.

To trigger a GR for yield, report yield using the report production button in the OEE dashboard worker UI. Ensure the ERP order confirmation is added as an extension to the "Report Data" or "Complete Order" methods in general configuration/extension configuration worker UI.

Goods Issue

Goods issue happens in two ways:

1. Backflush of components: Automatic goods issue during order confirmation
2. Manual goods issue: Report raw material consumption to ERP using OEE dashboard

Backflush of Components

For the backflush scenario, ensure the backflush field is set at either material component level. To do this go to MM02 ➤ MRP2 ➤ set "Always Backflush" for Backflush field. Send the components to OEE using tcode BD10. Refer to Figure 6-39.

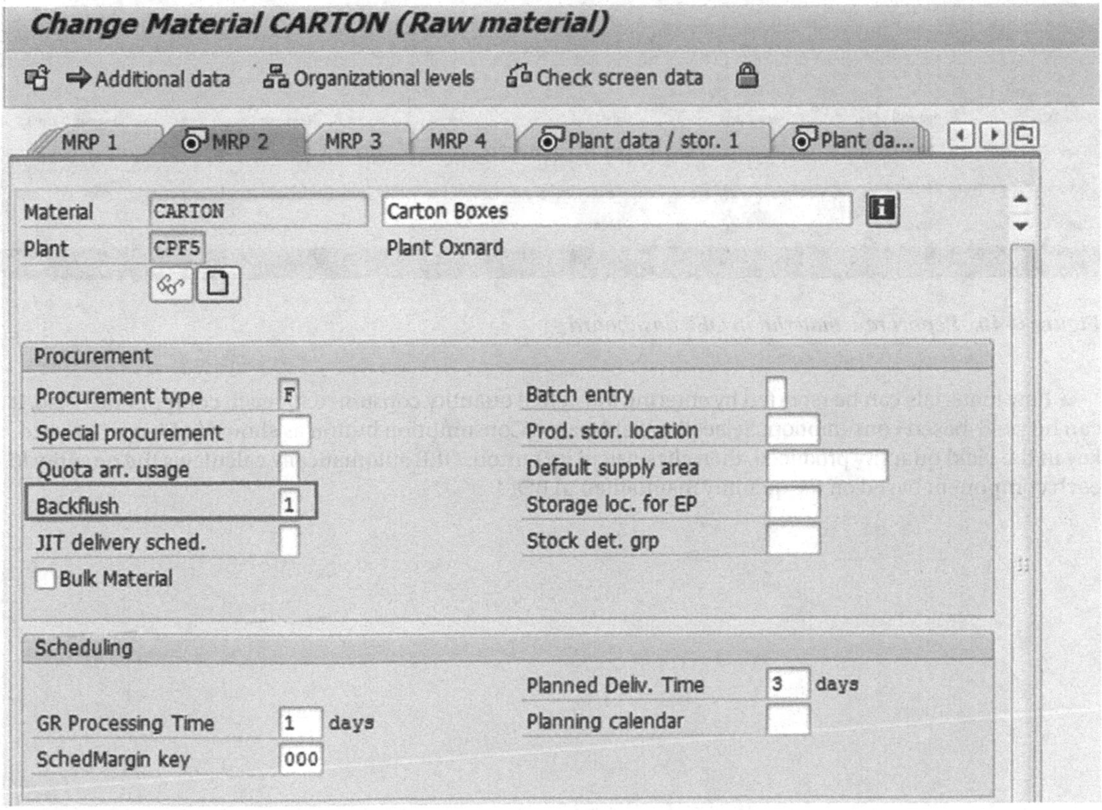

Figure 6-39. *Set backflush using tcode MM02*

Create an order and execute it in OEE. Once the order is completed, as part of ERP, order confirmation GI is triggered for raw material consumption and updated in ERP as movement type 261.

Manual Goods Issue Trigger from OEE

For this scenario, the components material should not be set for backflush. During the order execution, raw materials consumption will be reported manually from the OEE dashboard.

By default, the "Report raw materials" option will not exist in OEE dashboard. You need to add the standard activity (ACT_RAW_MAT ➤ SAP - Report Raw Material Data Collection) as a custom button using the dashboard configuration worker UI. Once this configuration is done, you can report raw materials consumption using the OEE dashboard. Refer to Figure 6-40. The components specific to phase under an operation are displayed here wuth the planned quantity of comsumption. These are picked from MPM_RESBL table.

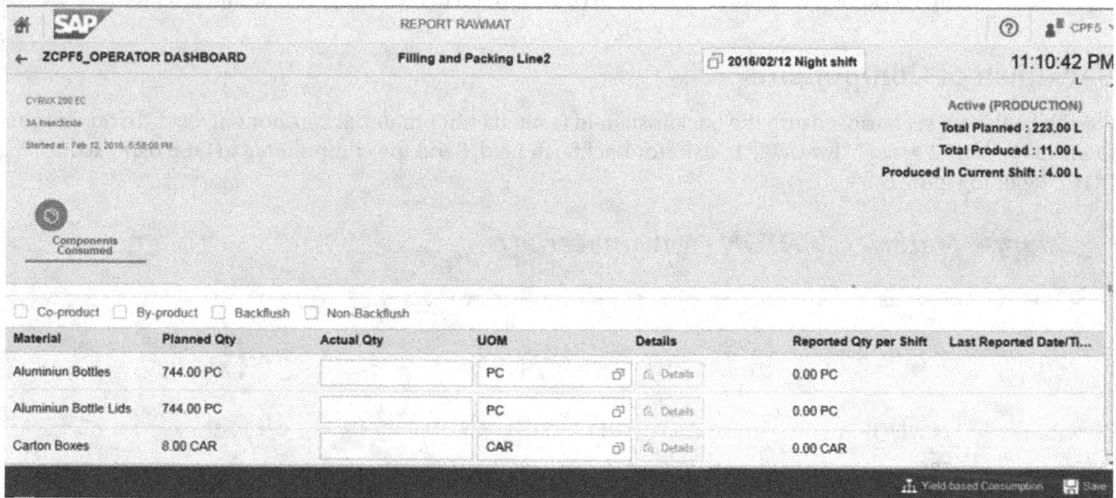

Figure 6-40. *Report raw material in OEE dashboard*

Raw materials can be reported by entering the actual quantity consumed for each components. Also, it can be yield-based consumption. Select the Yield-based Consumption button as shown in Figure 6-41 and key in the yield quantity produced, then click calculate button. OEE automatically calculates the quantity for each component based on the quantity maintained in BOM.

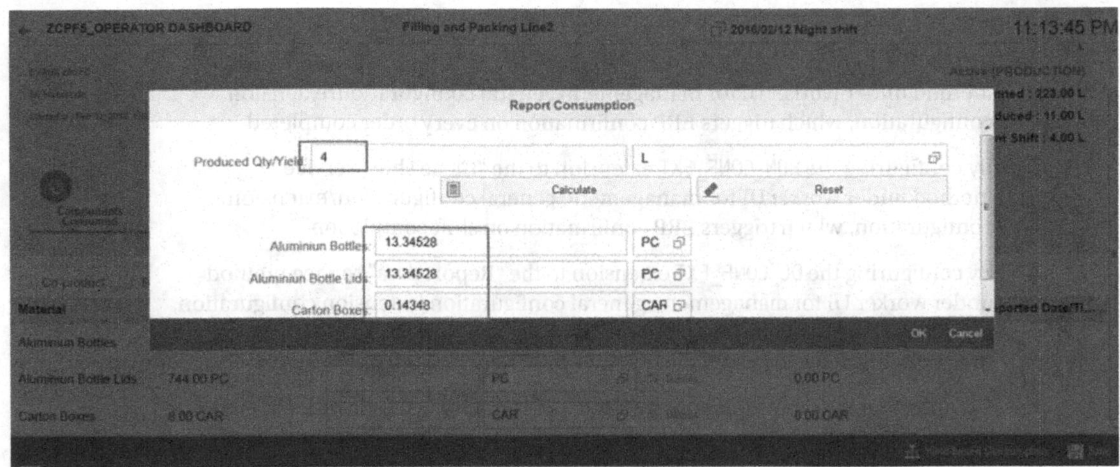

Figure 6-41. Report raw material: yield-based consumption

Raw materials consumption can be also recorded automatically from the shop floor by using OEE action blocks in BLS transactions. Refer to Appendix ➤ Automated data collection to understand these action blocks. Once the raw materials are recorded, either manually or automatically, the ERP order confirmation extension picks these component consumption data for goods issue. Again, the GI can be triggered as and when the data is reported or at the end of order completion.

■ Note As mentioned previously, from 15.1 onward, raw materials consumption recording and goods movement are taken care of using the Goods Issue and Goods Receipt app found in Application Launch Pad. It is recommended you not use the all the standard activity, dashboard option, OEE action blocks mentioned in the previous section (for 15.0 version), as the 15.1 version has a better way of handling it. Refer to chapter 8 to understand more on the Goods Issue and Goods Receipt app delivered through Application Launch Pad.

Update Order Confirmation and Goods Movement to SAP ERP

The order-operation execution flow completes with an operation confirmation uploaded back to ERP. When an order-operation is completed, an outbound OEEINT workflow (`ORDER_CONFIRM_BAPI`) is triggered from OEE, which has the order-operation confirmation, activity confirmation, and goods movement updates for SAP ERP. By default, the input structure of BAPI has all three elements. You can decide to have only the required confirmations in this workflow by enhancing the XSLT transaction. For instance, if you do not want the goods movement update to happen, then you can disable that section. If you want to calculate the standard activities automatically, then the XSLT should be enhanced to pass these activity values. `GOODS_MOVEMENT_BAPI` is another outbound workflow that can be triggered through an OEE extension to report the goods movement of reported waste to SAP ERP.

ORDER_CONFIRM_BAPI workflow can be triggered in the following ways:

1. By configuring the ORDER_CONF_EXT extension to the "Complete order" service method under worker UI for management/general configuration/extension configuration, which triggers ERP confirmation on every order completed

2. By configuring the RUN_CONF_EXT extension to the "Close shift" service method under worker UI for management/general configuration/extension configuration, which triggers ERP confirmation on shift completion

3. By configuring the DC_CONF_EXT extension to the "Report data" service method under worker UI for management/general configuration/extension configuration, which triggers ERP confirmation upon reporting any data collection (production, scrap, quality defects) in OEE dashboard under Report Production button

4. On order-operation completion, the tables are updated with the order status CMPL. Confirmations Enqueuer is the scheduler job, which looks for this order status, executes the ORDER_CONFIRM_BAPI workflow, and enqueues them in the OEE message queue. This scheduler sends the confirmations to ERP, even for the incomplete orders, if the customization parameter "ERP periodic confirmations" in the general configuration/customization configuration worker UI is set to Yes for each work center.

GOODS_MOVEMENT_BAPI workflow can be triggered in the following ways:

1. By following any of the above steps for ORDER_CONFIRM_BAPI. By default, ORDER_CONFIRM_BAPI has the goods movement structure upload to SAP ERP.

2. By configuring the SCRAP_COMP_GM_EXT extension to the "close shift" service method under the worker UI for management/general configuration/extension configuration, which triggers the goods movement of material waste on close of the shift.

3. By configuring the SCRAP_COMP_DC_GM_EXT extension to the "Report data" service method under the worker UI for management/general configuration/extension configuration, which triggers the goods movement of material waste on reporting data in OEE dashboard.

Real-time Monitoring of Shop Floor through OEE Dashboard

By now, you have an understanding of OEE-specific data management, order-operation execution, data collection, and KPI calculations. Ultimately, the aim of SAP OEE is to monitor and visualize these reported and calculated data in real-time on OEE dashboard. You have also learned how to configure and customize OEE dashboard through the dashboard configuration worker UI. OEE dashboard with KPI monitor is updated at a refresh rate that is set for the UI page.

OEE dashboard is used to monitor and visualize in real-time the following:

- View/start/hold/complete status of order-operations
- Data collection summary, which may be OEE- or non-OEE-relevant
- Line and machine availability
- Material and time losses with their reason code and root-cause machines attached to them
- Four standard shift KPIs. Order KPIs can also be viewed under the line monitor dashboard

Apart from this, you can build your own custom dashboards using SAP UI5 and integrate them into the standard OEE dashboard. From SAP MII 15.0 SP03 onward, SAP OEE dashboard works with SAP UI5 XML view only. In cases with a custom dashboard, ensure the view files are developed based on the SAP UI5 XML view.

OEE dashboard can be viewed in real-time or historical. When a real-time custom UI is to be integrated into the standard OEE dashboard, the custom UI expects some input parameters in real-time from the standard dashboard. These are made available through global context. You will learn more about global context and how to use it in the dashboard in chapter 7.

Near Real-time Replication of OEE Transaction Data to HANA

SAP HANA is an optional analytics component with which you can analyze OEE performance. To do this, HANA needs to be replicated with the OEE data in near real-time. The required OEE transaction tables are configured for replication with HANA tables through the SLT (SAP Landscape Transformation) server.

Following are the tables replicated to HANA from ERP and OEE.

OEE Master tables from ERP:

- /OEE/MPH_KPITARG
- /OEE/MPH_LAYOUT
- /OEE/MPH_MRKDWN
- /OEE/MPH_NODE
- /OEE/MPH_NODEAMG
- /OEE/MPH_NODEATO
- /OEE/MPH_NODESTR
- /OEE/MPH_NODET
- /OEE/MPH_CFN

Authorization tables from ERP:

- USRBF2
- UST12

OEE Configuration tables from ERP:

- /OEE/C_DCELEM
- /OEE/C_DCELEMT
- /OEE/C_TIMEELEM
- /OEE/C_TIMEELEMT
- /OEE/C_MCGRP
- /OEE/C_MCGRPT
- /OEE/C_KPI
- /OEE/C_KPIT
- /OEE/C_CLFN

- /OEE/C_CLFNT
- /OEE/C_GRC
- /OEE/C_GRCT
- /OEE/C_PRC
- /OEE/C_PRCT
- /OEE/C_TE_TYPE
- /OEE/C_TE_TYPET

OEE Transaction tables from MII:

- MPM_PROD_RUN_HDR
- MPM_PROD_RUN_INT_EVT
- MPM_PROD_RUN_DATA
- MPM_DATA_AS_MC_EVT
- MPM_SCHEDULED_DOWN

When you use HANA as the analytics component for SAP OEE, you get the HANA Live component. HANA Live for SAP OEE is the real-time operational reporting solution that can be deployed on HANA and provides SAP-delivered content in the form of HANA views and reports. You can also develop custom views and reports for OEE analysis.

By default, HANA Live for OEE delivers the following analytics:

- Loss Analysis report
  - Groups all the reports related to losses, such as unscheduled down, speed loss, and quality loss. The report provides the drill-down view of the reason codes assigned, attached machine events, and so on.
- KPI Analysis report
  - Provides the KPI analysis at the hierarchy level–regional and plant level. You can analyze the KPIs and asset utilization in different trend formats for the nodes that are reporting production.
- Data Collection report
  - Analyze order-dependent and -independent data collection elements data reported in OEE
- Data Elements report
  - Analyze the different data elements, like reported and calculated elements, for different work centers and plants

In HANA, the KPI analysis is done at the work-center level where the production is reported. When the KPI has to be analyzed at the plant level, the KPIs are aggregated from the child node (work center) to the parent node (plant).

You can better understand the KPI aggregation used to calculate the availability KPI with the following example. Refer to Table 6-1.

Table 6-1. *Aggregate KPI Calculations*

Parameter	Line 1	Line 2
Loading time	100 mins	80 mins
Unscheduled downtime	30 mins	20 mins
Availability KPI = Total net production time/Loading time	(100 - 30)/ 100 * 100 = 70%	(80 - 20)/ 80 * 100 = 75%
Availability of plant with line 1 and line 2	([100+80] - [30+20]) / [100+80] * 100 = 72.22%	

Summary

In this chapter, you have learned the purpose of OEE dashboards and how to configure them, as well as seen detailed descriptions of SAP-delivered OEE dashboards and an overview of standard OEE functionalities.

In the next chapter, you will learn about the data model of OEE, its purpose and detailed structure, various customization configurations specific to OEE, in OEE Add-on and different business use cases.

CHAPTER 7

SAP OEE Customizations

This chapter will explain the SAP OEE data model, various configurations of custom data required in OEE, automatic data collection scenarios, and other use cases.

By now, you understand how SAP OEE helps in modeling the plant objects using the plant hierarchy, categorization of losses, KPI calculations, operator dashboard for data collection and order processing, and finally the analytics, which help you to assess your plant performance–which is the ultimate goal of OEE.

During the implementation of SAP OEE, though there are many standard features delivered as part of the product, you may need to do a few enhancements and customizations to fulfill all the business requirements. In this chapter, you will learn the various customizations and enhancements possible for OEE using a use-case scenario. You will also come to understand the detailed data model of OEE and the purpose of each OEE database table.

OEE Custom Actions

As part of the execution of SAP OEE installation, BLS Transaction in SAP MII workbench is provided with additional action blocks that are specific to OEE and help in OEE enhancements and customizations. These action blocks help us to achieve automatically many of the OEE functionalities that are otherwise carried out manually–for example, data collection.

For example, you report production yield using the report production activity in the dashboard. You can achieve the same functionality to get the production data automatically from automation to OEE using the SAP OEE service interface/report production action block. In this section, you will see in detail the purpose of and the required mapping for each of these action blocks.

OEE-specific custom actions can be broadly categorized based on their functionality as one of the following:

- custom actions specific to shop floor data collection in SAP OEE
- custom actions to update data to SAP HANA from SAP OEE
- custom actions to update data to SAP ERP from SAP OEE

Once the SAP OEE component is deployed successfully and you see the OEE menus on the MII home page, you can see the jar file deployed under MII Menu ➤ System Resources ➤ Custom Actions. Refer to Figure 7-1. This jar file is the library of OEE-specific APIs deployed and available in MII workbench under the `SAP_OEE_INTEGRATION` actions menu.

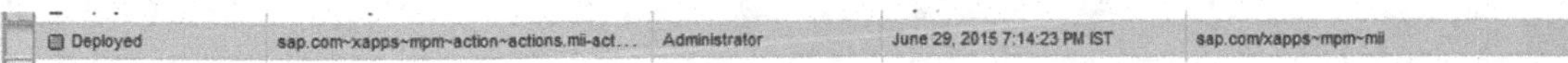

Figure 7-1. *OEE jar file for custom actions*

D. Saha et al., *Manufacturing Performance Management using SAP OEE*,
DOI 10.1007/978-1-4842-1150-2_7

To view the deployed actions, go to MII workbench, open a transaction, and view the Actions menu. Refer to Figure 7-2.

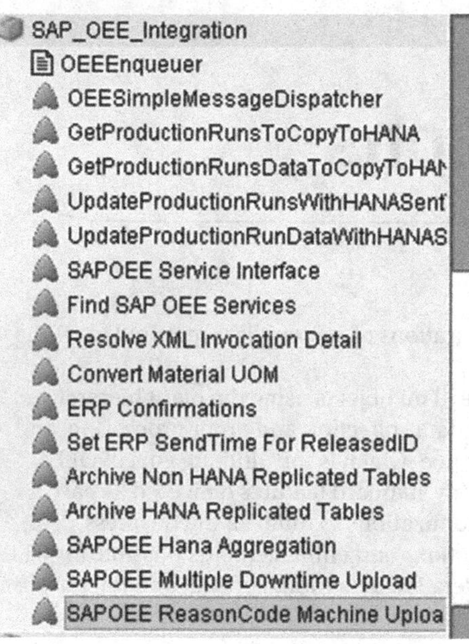

Figure 7-2. *OEE custom action blocks*

Custom Actions for OEE Shop-Floor Data Collection

For every order processed in a shift, various production-related data, such as production volume and time, scrap, quality defects, line speed, and so forth, are collected, which helps in calculating the order and shift KPIs. Again, these data collection elements can be order dependent or order independent, and those are required for OEE and other KPI calculations. These data can be collected manually through the dashboard or automatically using enhancements in MII using OEE APIs.

There are some custom actions deployed as part of OEE component. These custom actions or APIs (Application programming interface) are used to report data collections to OEE, such as yield, scrap, defects, and downtimes, which are required to calculate OEE. It is also used to execute order-related activities, such as start, resume, and complete order-operation.

To understand the purpose of automatic data collection, let us look at an example where you have shop-floor applications such as DCS, SCADA, PLCs, and so on. Each of these applications provides you with particular process data that should be ultimately reported to SAP OEE. For example, you get the machine and line availability from PLCs, process data from DCS, and start/complete information of production orders from SCADA. This information needs to be pushed to SAP OEE in real-time in order for the operators to work on the operators dashboard. You can build your own custom SAP MII transactions using these APIs and make your data collection automatic from the shop floor.

In this section, we will first examine in detail the purpose of some of the OEE action blocks present in BLS Transaction in SAP MII which you need to use for custom developments and its input/output mapping structure for every API or method. You can use these action blocks to develop BLS transactions, which you can use for various scenarios, some of which are explained in section Customization Scenarios in SAP OEE.

1. *Find SAP OEE Services*: This custom action helps to find the list of APIs or services available to report any shop floor-related information to OEE.

2. *Input*: Not Mandatory

3. *Output*: The output XML of the action returns all the OEE APIs specific to shop floor data collection service. Refer to Figure 7-3.


```
- <Rowsets DateCreated="2015-09-13T04:01:22" EndDate="2015-09-13T04:01:22" StartDate="2015-09-13T04:01:22" Version="15.0 SP4 Patch 3 (May 27, 2015)">
  - <Rowset>
    - <Columns>
        <Column Description="service" MaxRange="100" MinRange="0" Name="service" SQLDataType="1" SourceColumn="service"/>
        <Column Description="method" MaxRange="100" MinRange="0" Name="method" SQLDataType="1" SourceColumn="method"/>
      </Columns>
    - <Row>
        <service>ShopFloorDataCollectionService</service>
        <method>getActiveRunsForNodeID</method>
      </Row>
    - <Row>
        <service>ShopFloorDataCollectionService</service>
        <method>pauseProductionRun</method>
      </Row>
    - <Row>
        <service>ShopFloorDataCollectionService</service>
        <method>reportRejection</method>
      </Row>
    - <Row>
        <service>ShopFloorDataCollectionService</service>
        <method>reportSpeedLoss</method>
      </Row>
    - <Row>
        <service>ShopFloorDataCollectionService</service>
        <method>abortProductionRun</method>
```


Figure 7-3. *Response XML of Find SAP OEE Services action block*

SAP OEE Service Interface: This custom action is the one with which you can execute all of OEE's shop floor data collection service methods. You need to configure the credential alias with an SAP MII user who has OEE roles and leave the search filter empty. Then, click on the search button to view the complete list of shop floor data collection service APIs. Refer to Figure 7-4. Select the required data collection methods that you want to use and then provide the required inputs under the Link configuration for the action block.

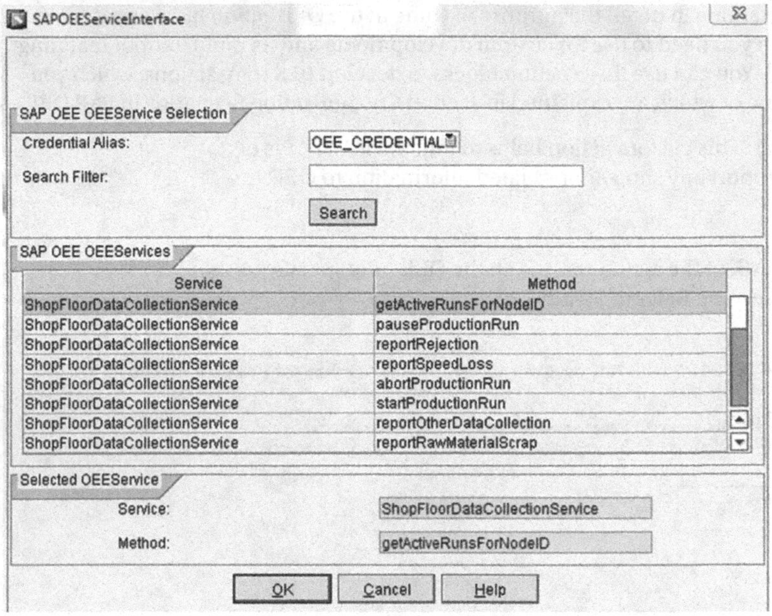

Figure 7-4. *SAP OEE Service Interface Action*

Please refer to Appendix Section 1: Automated Data Collection to view the list of OEE service interfaces for automated shop-floor data collection with their detailed description, request, and response parameters.

SHOP-FLOOR DATA COLLECTION BUFFERING

In SAP OEE, the order-dependent data collection elements can be reported only if an active order exists. Sometimes, the operator may miss starting the order in the SAP OEE dashboard while the actual order production has started on the shop floor. In this scenario, if real-time integration is configured with shop-floor systems and SAP OEE, data collections such as yield, scrap, rework, and so on will get lost, as there is no active order. Real-time shop-floor buffering is the solution for this data collection loss. This buffering framework can be developed in SAP MII with a user interface to monitor the buffered data. The buffered data can then be reported to SAP OEE once the order exists in OEE; this can be achieved through custom extensions. Customization of OEE extensions is discussed in later sections. One such scenario is explained in section Customization Scenarios in SAP OEE.

OEE Data Model

OEE CTC execution deploys the standard OEE tables on the SAP NetWeaver database of SAP MII. OEE custom actions help in performing the shop-floor execution functionalities and the required updates to HANA and ERP automatically. In this section, you will review the structure of OEE data model.

The OEE data model can be broadly categorized into three types for storing the following type of data:

- Master data (OEE related)
- Configuration data
- Transaction data

The following is the high-level overview of the data flow, or data model, of OEE. Refer to Figure 7-5.

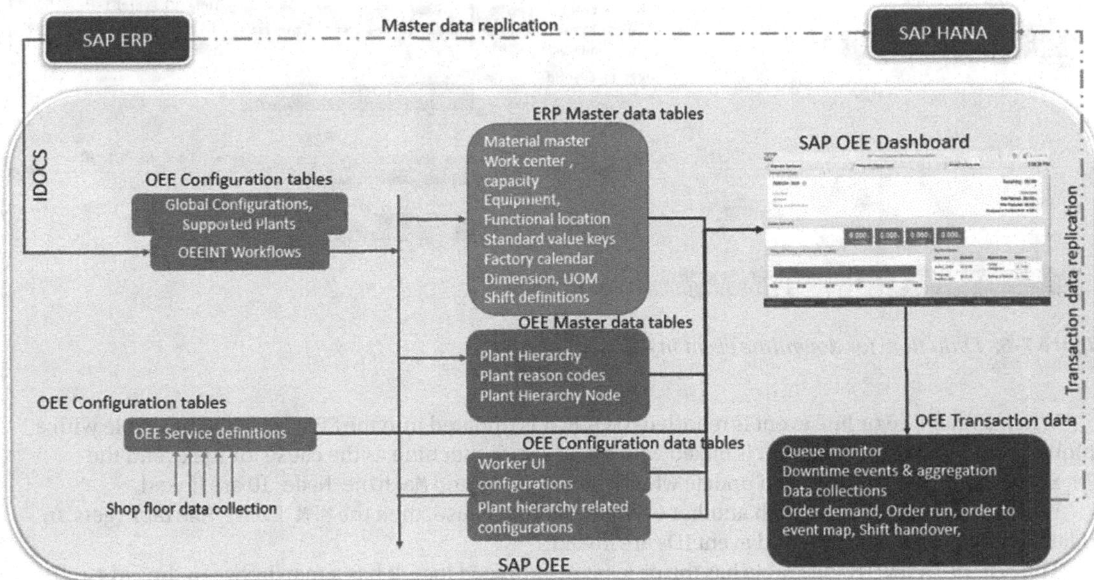

Figure 7-5. *Overview of SAP OEE data model*

In the preceding figure, you can see the different ERP master data, OEE-related master data, and OEE-related configuration and transaction data. All the data are downloaded from SAP ERP in the form of IDocs, and each message is processed by the SAPOEEINT framework for storage in the SAP OEE database.

The transaction data are replicated to SAP HANA from time to time as per the configuration set.

There are 143 standard tables present in SAP OEE. Please refer to Appendix Section 2: OEE Standard Tables to get the list of standard tables and their types, purposes, and descriptions.

There are two key aspects involved when monitoring the OEE KPI, events, and order executions/run. In this section, you will learn what happens when an event is reported to SAP OEE and how it affects the various tables.

Data Model Flow for Events

A downtime event is an order-independent data collection element. Refer to Figure 7-6, which describes how the various event tables are affected when the downtime event flows from the shop floor.

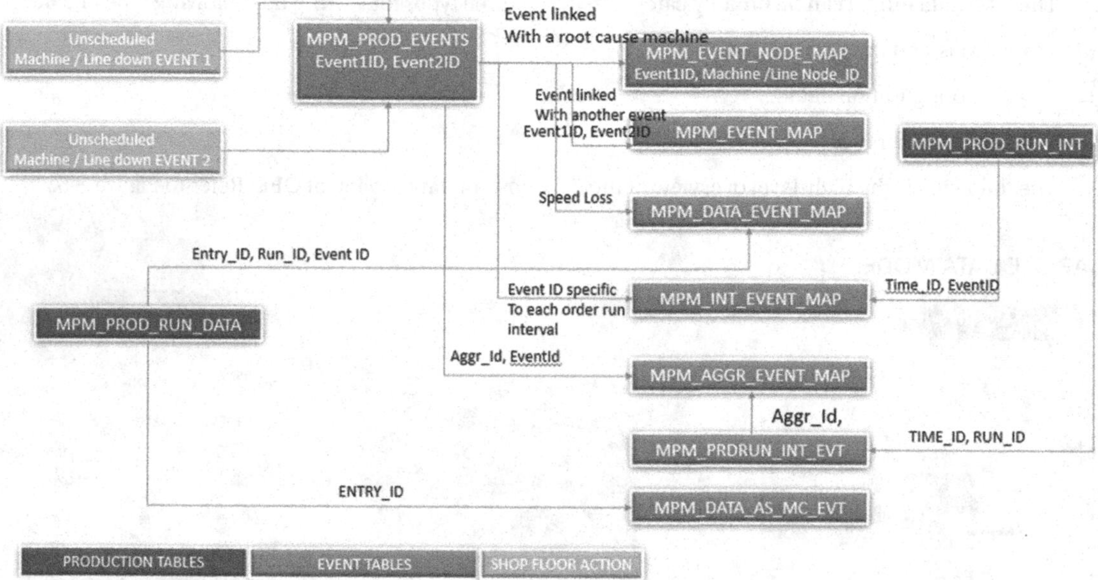

Figure 7-6. *Data flow for downtime event in OEE*

When a machine or line event is reported to OEE, it is updated into the MPM_PROD_EVENTS table with a unique Event_ID. When this event is linked with a root-cause machine as the cause for the event, the MPM_EVENT_NODE_MAP table gets an update where the Event_ID and Machine Node ID are linked.

When this event is linked with another event as the root cause, then the MPM_EVENT_MAP table gets an update where the parent and child event IDs are linked.

The MPM_DATA_EVENT_MAP table has the order specific speed loss. It has a map between the Entry_ID and RUN_ID from production run and event ID. RUN_ID is the unique ID for order in a shift. Entry_ID is the unique for every data collection. Event_ID is the unique ID for every downtime.

The MPM_INT_EVENT_MAP table maps the event with the order run interval by mapping the event ID with the time ID (Time_ID is the unique ID for every order interval) from the MPM_PROD_RUN_INT table. This map happens once an event is assigned to an order-operation using the "Shared downtime" tab under the Manage Downtime button in OEE dashboard.

The MPM_PRDRUN_INT_EVT table has the map of aggregated events and the order run intervals.

The MPM_AGGR_EVENT_MAP table has the map between AGGR_ID and Event_ID.

The MPM_DATA_AS_MC_EVT table has the reference to the machine event that is the root cause for the event; it gets the reference data from a node that reports production. In OEE, two machine events can be linked as one being the root cause for the other machines down. This event to event map is maintained in this table.

Understanding these table structures and their purposes helps during the customization or enhancement of an event scenario.

Data Flow for Order Run

In SAP OEE, production or process order is one of the key elements in determining the KPI and ultimately the performance of the plant. Refer to Figure 7-7, which describes how the various production tables are affected from when the order is downloaded to SAP OEE until it gets completed.

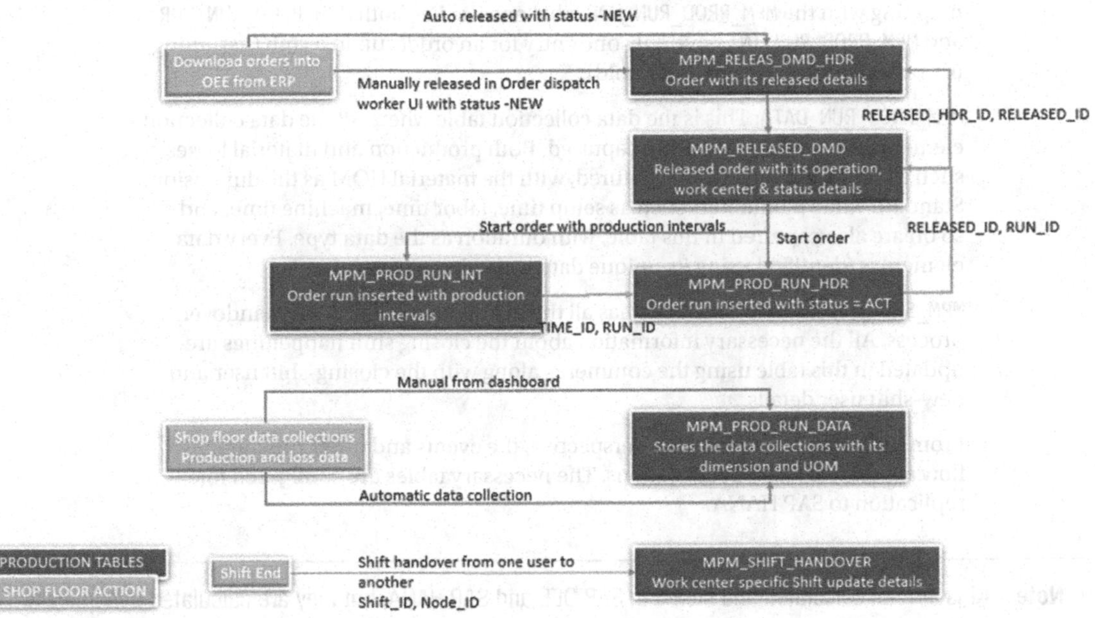

Figure 7-7. *Data flow for data collection in OEE*

In SAP OEE, loading time is one of the key parameters in calculating the OEE KPI. Loading time is the duration of each order run within a shift. In this section, you will learn how production/process order data flows right from its download in SAP OEE to its completion and update of production information back to SAP ERP.

The following are the database tables that are relevant for the production/process order run data flow:

`MPM_RELEASED_DMD_HDR`: Upon download of an order from ERP, it is either auto-released or released manually from the order dispatch UI and gets an entry in this table with the release details and status. It also gets an entry into the `MPM_RELEASED_DMD` table with additional details, such as OEE operation details.

These two tables are linked with their respective unique identifiers, such as `RELEASED_HDR_ID` and `RELEASED_ID`.

`MPM_PROD_RUN_HDR`: This is a key table that stores the complete information of an order, such as status, order start, order complete timestamp, shift ID, material, UOM, and so on. This table gets an entry of an order only after it is started from the dashboard. Every order run has a unique `RUN_ID` for every shift. `RUN_ID` is the key identifier that helps in many customizations to fetch different data from different tables.

MPM_PROD_RUN_INT: In Chapter 3, you learned about configuring production activities. This table captures the changeover of these production activities as an order run interval specific to every RUN_ID. For the order runs configured with production activities, this table has 1 to *n* mapping; i.e., MPM_PROD_RUN_HDR has one entry per shift, and MPM_PROD_RUN_INT has *n* entries for the same order run. If there are no production activities configured, then this table has one-to-one mapping with the MPM_PROD_RUN_HDR table entries; i.e., both MPM_PROD_RUN_HDR and MPM_PROD_RUN_INT have only one entry for an order run in a shift (assuming the order was not placed under hold).

MPM_PROD_RUN_DATA: This is the data collection table where all the data collection elements except downtimes are captured. Both production and material losses such as scrap and rework are captured, with the material UOM as the dimension. Standard value parameters such as setup time, labor time, machine time, and so on are also captured in this table, with duration as the data type. Every data element is identified using its unique data collection element name.

MPM_SHIFT_HANDOVER: This table has all the details about every shift handover process. All the necessary information about the closing shift happenings are updated in this table using the comments along with the closing-shift user and new-shift user details.

From the OEE transaction data perspective, the events and order run data flow are critical for KPI calculations. The necessary tables are configured for replication to SAP HANA.

■ **Note** KPIs are not calculated and stored in SAP OEE and SAP HANA, but they are calculated dynamically whenever required for display in the dashboards.

Customizing OEE Configuration Data

In this section, you will learn how to configure OEE configuration data as well as look at its purpose, or use case.

Customizing Production Activity

Production activities may be required to set up for different activities within the order run, such as after an order is started and before the order is completed. For example, a production or process order may pass through different production phases such as setup time, material consumption time, actual production time, cleanup time, and so on. To capture all these different production time intervals, production activities can be used. This will ensure the capture of each of these durations so as to determine the performance of an order. These time intervals can also be used to determine product costing in SAP ERP.

Let's go over the steps to configure the custom production activity.

In SAP ERP, open T-Code OP7b - Create Formula Parameters. Refer to Figures 7-8 and 7-9 to create the production activities as per your requirements. In this example, two production activities, consumption and production, are configured as formula parameters. You need to configure the right dimensions and standard values for these parameters.

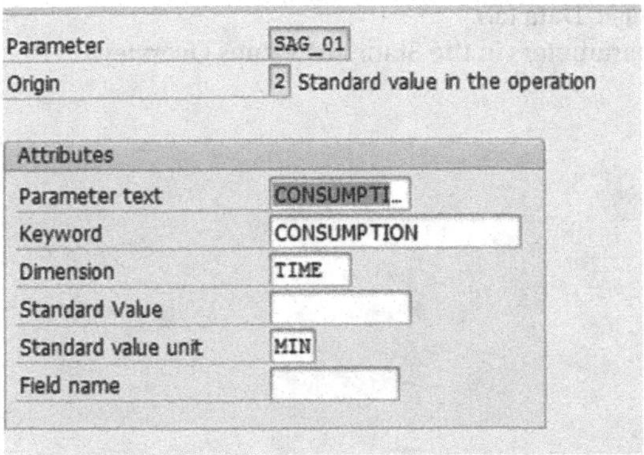

Parameter	SAG_01
Origin	2 Standard value in the operation

Attributes

Parameter text	CONSUMPTI...
Keyword	CONSUMPTION
Dimension	TIME
Standard Value	
Standard value unit	MIN
Field name	

Figure 7-8. *Create formula parameters: activity 1*

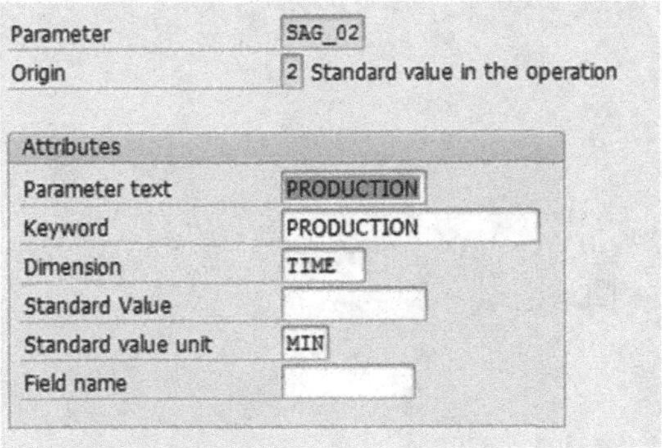

Parameter	SAG_02
Origin	2 Standard value in the operation

Attributes

Parameter text	PRODUCTION
Keyword	PRODUCTION
Dimension	TIME
Standard Value	
Standard value unit	MIN
Field name	

Figure 7-9. *Create formula parameters: activity 2*

Go to T-Code OP19 - Create Standard Value Key and enter the created formula parameters for this key. Refer to Figure 7-10.

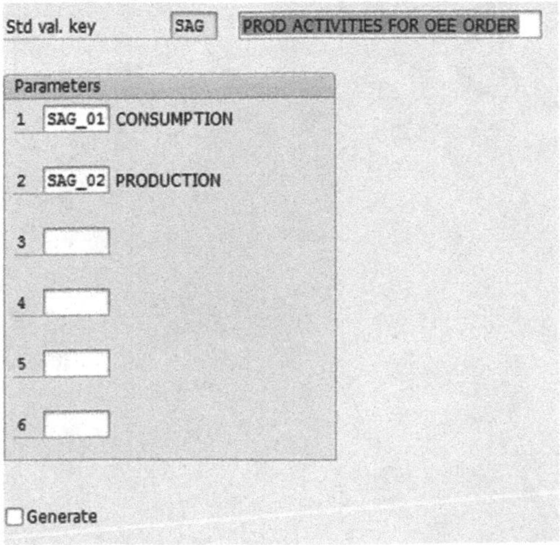

Std val. key SAG PROD ACTIVITIES FOR OEE ORDER

Parameters

1	SAG_01	CONSUMPTION
2	SAG_02	PRODUCTION
3		
4		
5		
6		

☐ Generate

Figure 7-10. *Create standard value key*

Go to T-Code: CR02 - Update Work Center and go to Basic Data tab.

In the Basic Data tab, add the newly created formula parameters in the Standard Values Overview section, as shown in Figure 7-11.

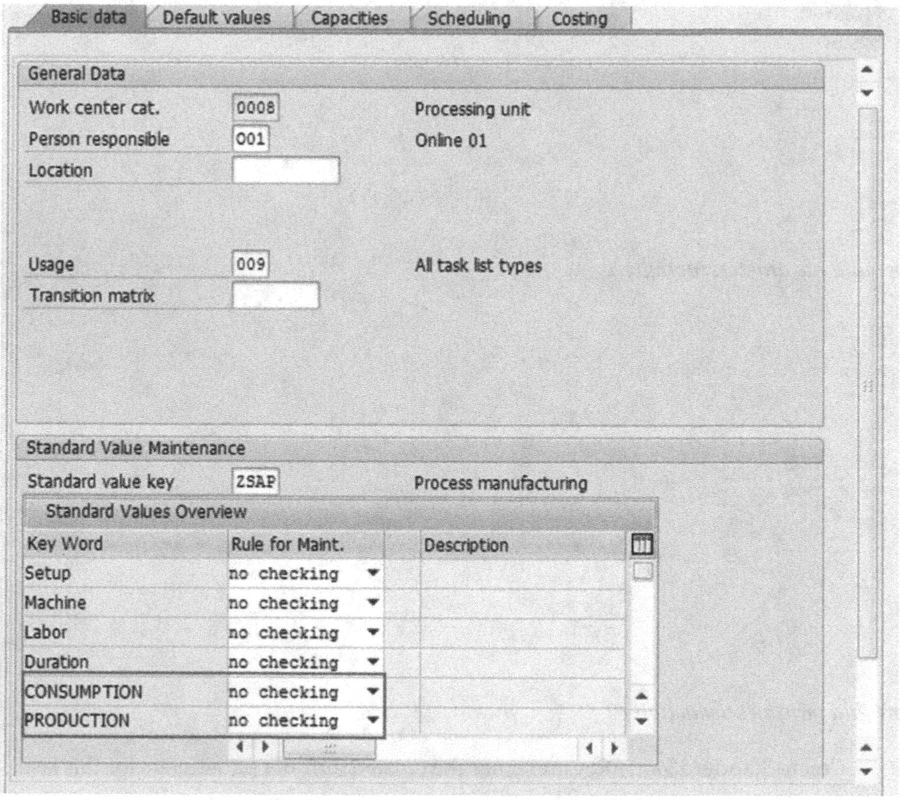

Figure 7-11. *Update work center with standard value keys*

Go to the Costing tab and set the Rec. type group as desired. Refer to Figure 7-12.

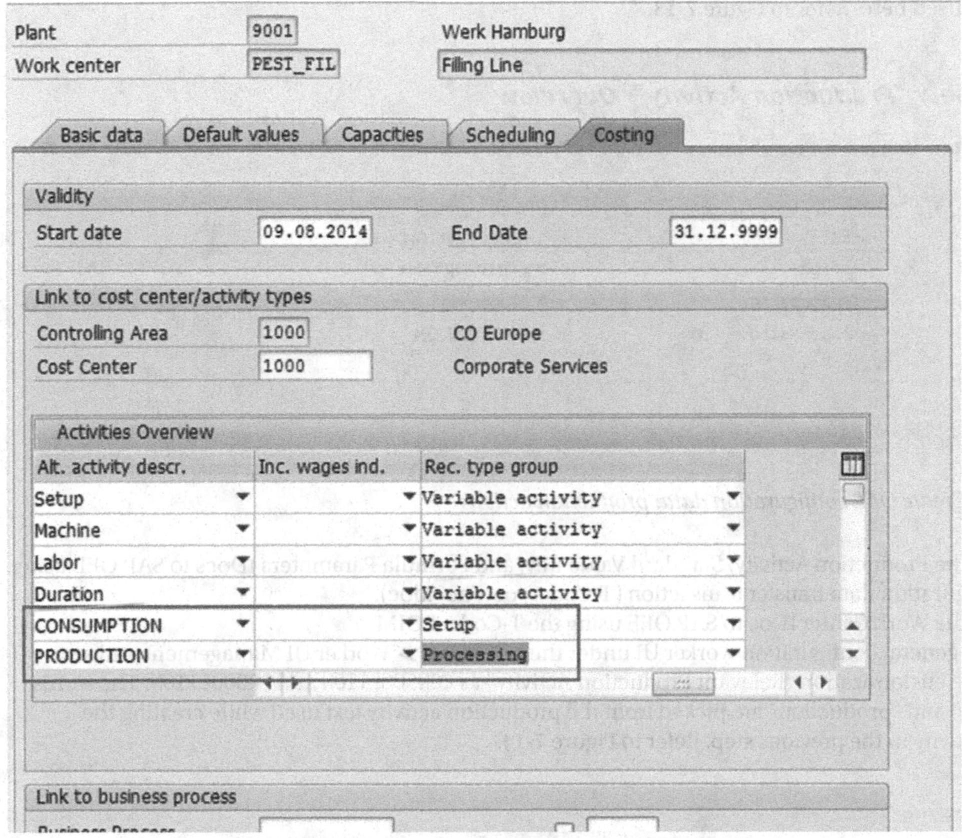

__Figure 7-12.__ Update Rec. type group for the production activity

Go to T Code: SPRO ➤ Production ➤ Overall Equipment Effectiveness ➤ Define Production Activities

Add the newly created formula parameter names here in the production activity column. Ensure the same name is used here. Refer to Figure 7-13.

Change View "Production Activity": Overview

New Entries

Production Activity

Prod. Activity	RecTypeGrp	Production Act Desc
CONSUMPTION	Setup	CONSUMPTION
PROCESSING	Processing	Processing
PRODUCTION	Processing	PRODUCTION

Figure 7-13. *Create OEE configuration data: production activity*

Transfer the Production Activity, Standard Value Key, and Formula Parameters IDocs to SAP OEE using the OEE configuration data transfer transaction (T-Code: /oee/bo_idoc).

Transfer the Work Center IDoc to SAP OEE using the T-Code: POIM.

Open the general configuration worker UI under the MII Menu ➤ Worker UI Management and set the value of the customization "Relevant Production Activity" as `CONSUMPTION` and `PRODUCTION`. The words "consumption" and "production" are picked from the production activity text used while creating the production activity in the previous step. Refer to Figure 7-14.

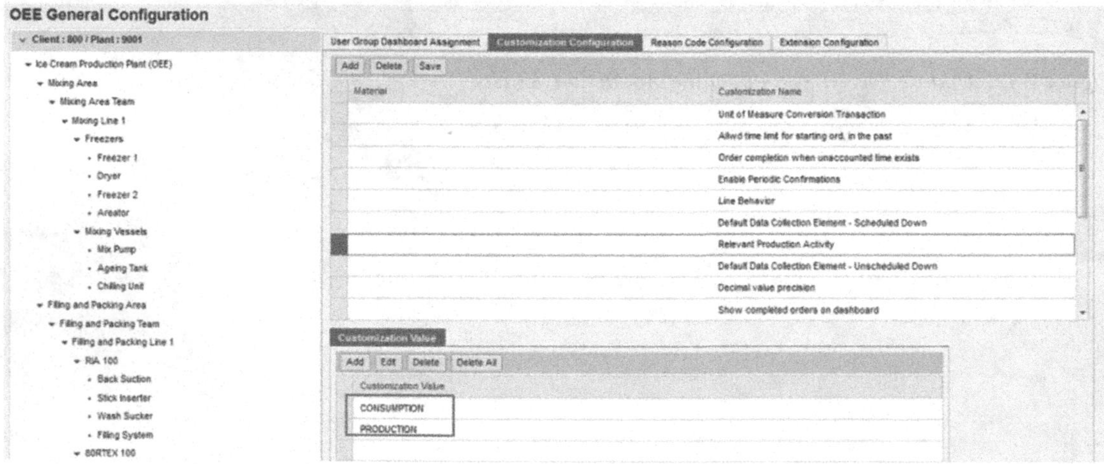

Figure 7-14. *Configure production activity in OEE*

Go to the manage orders activity of the OEE operator dashboard to see that the Assign button for each order has these two production activities. Now you can select the desired activity once you start the order; this is not mandatory though. You can also select the Assign button to change from one production activity to another. Refer to Figure 7-15.

***Figure 7-15.** Configured production activities in OEE dashboard*

■ **Note** Change Production Activity is available as an OEE service interface (Shop Floor Data Collection service in SAP OEE Service Interface action block in workbench; refer to Section OEE Custom Actions) but is not available as a standard method under the extension configuration in the dashboard. Hence, no custom extension can be added to the Change Production Activity functionality from the SAP OEE dashboard.

Customization of OEEINT Workflow Configurations

In Chapter 4, you learned about the OEEINT workflow configurations, which primarily process the inbound and outbound messages to and from SAP OEE. In this section, you will see few use-case scenarios for customization of these workflows.

1. Workflow message: `LOIPRO01`

   Orders when downloaded can be auto-released or manually released as per the requirements. By default, auto-release is enabled for LOIPRO. To enable manual release, add the following line of code in the Request XSLT file at the end for the LOIPRO workflow. Then add the customized request XSLT filepath to the LOIPRO workflow under workflow configuration.

   ```
   <automaticRelease>false</automaticRelease>
   ```

   This customization ensures the orders are manually released using the order dispatch worker UI.

2. Workflow message: `ORDER_CONFIRM_BAPI`

   This is an outbound order confirmation message from SAP OEE to SAP ERP. This message calls the standard BAPI for order confirmation (Internally OEE decides the right BAPI based on the order type. i.e., `BAPI_PRODCONF_CREATE_TT BAPI` for Production order and `BAPI_PROCCONF_CREATE_TT BAPI` for Process order) and passes the mandatory inputs, such as yield quantity, scrap quantity, rework quantity, and standard value activities, such as setup time, labor time, machine time, and so on, as configured in the production order. The Order confirmation using standard extension can be triggered at different instance based on the requirement

At the end of every data collection reported (Yield, Scrap, Rework)

At the end of every order-operation completion

At the end of every shift/day/week/monthly using the confirmations scheduler by configuring the scheduler frequency accordingly.

There may be a requirement where the yield confirmation needs to be sent after the order is complete and the activity confirmation needs to be sent at the end of shift. In this scenario, the Request XSLT transaction can be customized to pass the required data and remove the data that are not be passed.

Customization Scenarios of OEE Extensions

In Chapter 5, you learned about extension configuration under the general configuration worker UI. In this section, you will learn the possible scenarios for custom extensions.

Extension configuration lists the standard SAP OEE methods that are intended for specific dashboard functionality, such as start order, complete order, report data, report downtime, and so on. Sometimes, the functionality achieved by these standard methods may not be sufficient and has to be customized as per the plant requirements. In such a scenario, custom transactions are developed, configured as a custom activity, and then hooked to extension configuration.

The following are some of the use-case scenarios for custom extensions for standard OEE methods:

1. Start order-operation
    - When the operator misses starting an order and to avoid the loss of order-dependent data collections, these data collections can be buffered at the SAP MII layer. A custom transaction needs to be developed that can be hooked to the "Start Order-Operation" method under extension configuration in POST mode. On order start, this custom transaction will be executed from the OEE dashboard to pick the buffered data collections and assign them to the right order and then report it to SAP OEE.
    - Upon the start of an order-operation in SAP OEE dashboard, a custom extension can be executed to transfer this information to the shop-floor SCADA system for data synchronization in real-time.
2. Report data
    - After reporting quality waste from the SAP OEE dashboard, a custom extension transaction can be executed to trigger a quality maintenance notification to ERP.
3. Order complete
    - Upon selection of "order complete" in OEE dashboard, a custom extension transaction can be executed as a PRE option that will calculate all the standard activities like setup time, machine time, labor time, and report it to OEE. In this way, the standard values are calculated automatically at the end of order completion and a manual entry is avoided. These reported standard activities are included as part of the standard extension "order confirmation" and reported to SAP ERP.
4. Create downtime
    - After reporting a machine's downtime, a custom extension transaction can be executed to trigger a plant maintenance notification to SAP ERP.

5. Close shift

    - If there is any unaccounted for yield/scrap/waste that could not be reported to SAP OEE due to the absence of an order, after the close of the shift, these data collections can be reconciled automatically using a custom extension transaction.

■ **Note** Custom extensions can be used only when the standard methods are used in the OEE dashboard. For example, a custom extension hooked to the "Order Complete" method will be executed only when order completion is done from OEE dashboard and not from the custom OEE actions performed by BLS Transaction in the background.

Access Global Context from Standard SAP OEE Dashboard

In Chapter 6, you learned about the standard OEE dashboard and how it utilizes a set of parameters for its functionality, such as shift details, active order, selected dashboard, work center, and so forth.

When you want to configure a custom OEE dashboard and consume it within the standard dashboard, you need the many parameters for achieving custom dashboard functionality, such as the current shift, plant, client, order under execution, and so on, dynamically. All these parameters with their current values are made available as global context. In this section, you will learn how to access the global context parameters and use these in your custom OEE dashboard.

Prerequisites

Develop a SAP UI5-based application using XML view. Add a custom activity of type UI under the activity configuration worker UI. Add the custom activity to a button of a standard OEE dashboard using the dashboard configuration worker UI.

Global context comes with nine main contexts that are further classified into sub-contexts. The main contexts are the high-level data such as KPI, node, and so on, and the sub-contexts are a drill-down of main context information, such as the different KPI values in the case of KPI context and current work center node ID and capacity ID for the node context.

Please refer to Appendix Section 6: Global Context to view the list of main contexts and their sub-contexts.

To retrieve the main contexts, add the following piece of JavaScript code to the beginning of your custom UI activity code developed using SAPUI5:

```
this.appComponent = this.getView().getViewData().appComponent;
this.appData = this.appComponent.getAppGlobalData();
```

To get the value of the context elements, say, node ID, plant order number, and so on, use the following code:

```
Var NodeID = this.appData.node.nodeID;
(Here node is the main context and nodeID is the sub context)
Var plant = this.appData.plant;
Var ordernumber = this.appData.selected.order.orderNo;
```

SAP MII–Based OEE Analytics

As SAP HANA is an optional analytics component, and in the event that SAP HANA component is not available, SAP MII can be leveraged to build the OEE analytics on smaller set of data; e.g., for single plant.

SAP MII's data and visualization services can be leveraged to build the OEE analytics. The custom dashboard can be developed and viewed as an SAP MII portal dashboard or can be merged within the standard OEE dashboard–the standard OEE dashboard and custom OEE dashboard can be merged and viewed in single window with easy navigation for the benefit of the users. Refer to Scenario 4 in Section Customization Scenarios in SAP OEE for the configuration steps and a design example.

The following lists contains some common OEE analytics that can be developed on SAP MII:

- Planned versus actuals report on order execution
- OEE loss report on material losses and time losses
- Shift summary report with a drill-down to data collection, downtime, and KPI report
- Shift and order KPI dashboard
- Cross-plant KPI and loss comparison report

■ **Caution** Proper sizing of the SAP MII (NetWeaver) database should be done for good system performance. MII-based OEE analytics should be aimed for short-term analysis only. Data from SAP OEE should be archived into an external database to store long-term data, which can be SAP BI, if the analysis needs to be done for long-term data in SAP MII.

Customization Scenarios in SAP OEE

In this section, you will review various customization scenarios right from shop-floor data collections and how to view or use the customizations in SAP OEE dashboard.

Scenario 1: Manufacturing Automation Systems' Integration with SAP PCo and SAP MII

A common scenario while implementing SAP OEE is needing the integration of SAP MII with manufacturing automation systems through SAP PCo so as to collect the shop-floor data automatically and report it to SAP OEE.

Refer to Figure 7-16, which represents the overall architecture of how the SAP PCo is connected with SAP MII and SAP OEE for automatic shop-floor data collection. SAP PCo is used to connect to the manufacturing automation systems through OPC or other supported adaptors in order to get the data for the machine status or process parameters either by notification (on-change) or by ad-hoc query from SAP MII. SAP MII then updates the data in SAP OEE by executing the corresponding SAP OEE service.

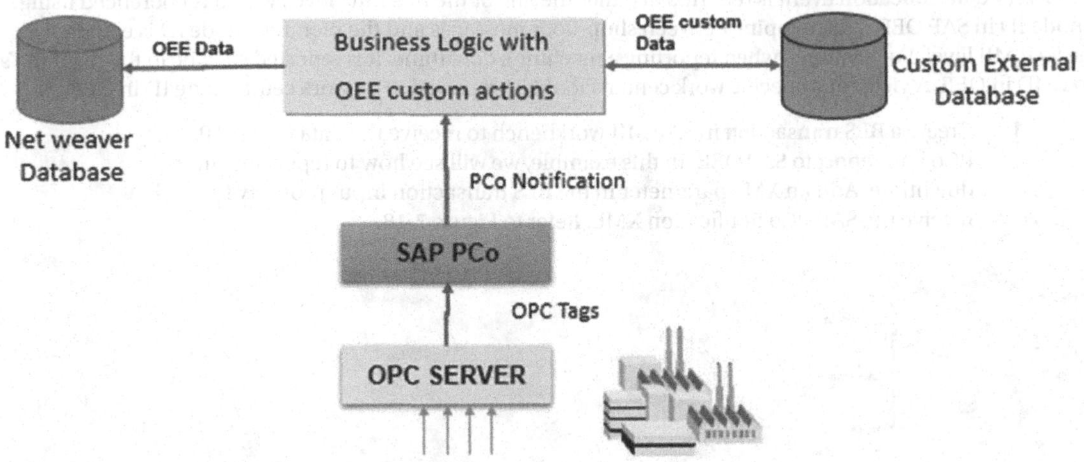

Figure 7-16. Architecture for shop-floor data collection

Prerequisites

SAP PCo is set up with the necessary agents and notifications to trigger the data collection, such as machine event, yield, waste, and so on.

The following is the sample XML structure of a machine event notification configured under the Output tab in SAP PCo Notification. Every data collection should be configured with an SAP PCo notification. Refer to Figure 7-17.

Trigger | Output | Message Delivery | Destinations

Name	Expression
Plant	"9001"
NotifTime	datenow
TagValue	stringif('FillPackLine1_80TREX100'>0,1,0)
TagName	"FillPackLine1_80TREX100"
EventID	"FillPack_VORTEX100"
Sender	"DS_ME_SIM"
NotificationType	FillPackLine1_80TREX100 > 30 || FillPackLine1_80TREX100 <20

Figure 7-17. PCo Notification configuration

Every data collection event is reported at either the line or the machine level, which is referenced using a node ID in SAP OEE. The mapping between shop-floor messages and the hierarchy node ID is essential at the SAP MII level. For example, when reporting a machine's downtime, it is reported specific to the machine's node ID in OEE. A yield for a specific work center should be reported to its work center node ID in OEE.

1. Create a BLS transaction in SAP MII workbench to receive the data from SAP PCo and report to SAP OEE. In this example, we will see how to report machine downtime. Add an XML parameter in the BLS transaction input property to receive the SAP PCo notification XML. Refer to Figure 7-18.

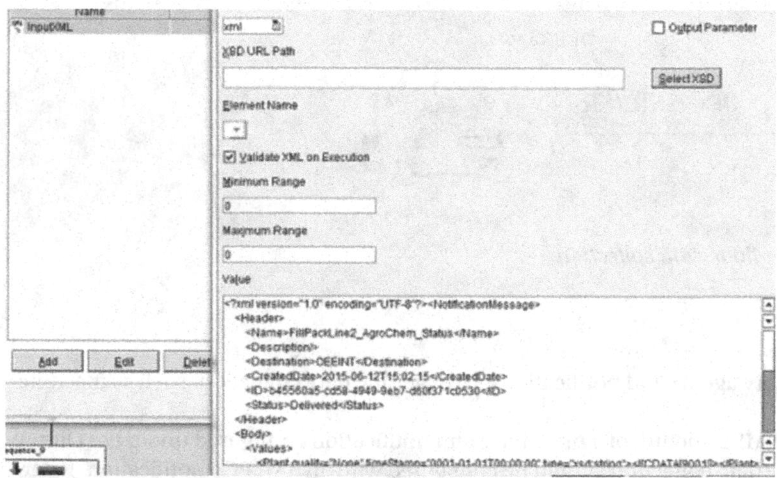

Figure 7-18. SAP MII custom transaction: shop-floor data collection

2. Get the node ID of the machine or line whose downtime is being reported. You should create a custom mapping between the node ID of each SAP OEE object with its respective tag or alias if defined in SAP PCo. Refer to Figure 7-19.

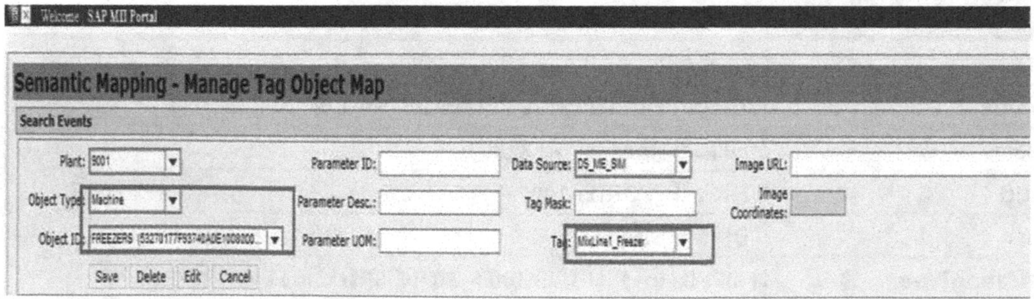

Figure 7-19. Tag versus OEE node ID mapping

This custom tag versus OEE object mapping helps in maintaining the map, which can be queried dynamically, and avoids hard coding at the SAP PCo level.

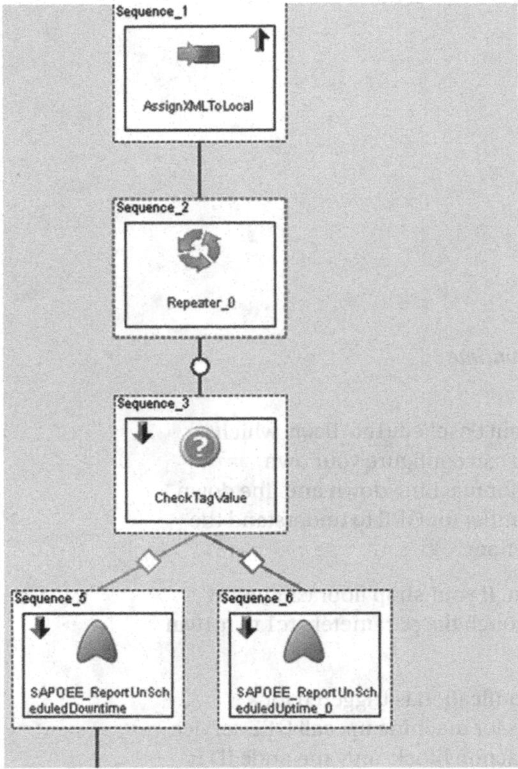

***Figure 7-20.** MII transaction to report machine event to OEE*

3. Configure the preceding BLS transaction as a trigger transaction by specifying it in the destination for each PCo notification of type Machine Event. Refer to Figure 7-20. The notification XML passed from SAP PCo has the tag name, tag value, and timestamp.
4. Get the OEE object node ID from the custom mapping by passing the tag name from the notification XML. This node ID may be for a machine or a line.
5. Get the tag value from the PCo notification XML to check whether the event is for the machine's being up or down. If the event is for machine down, then execute the SAP OEE service interface `ReportUnscheduledDowntime` and pass the inputs as shown next. Refer to Figure 7-21.

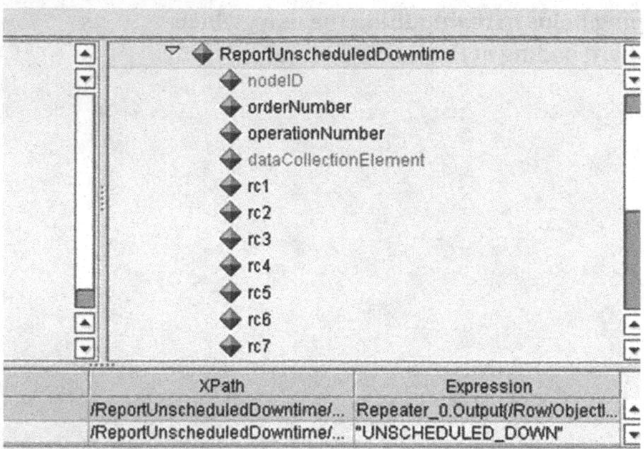

Figure 7-21. *OEE service interface: ReportUnscheduledDowntime*

6. You can use the standard data collection element `Unscheduled_Down`, which is configured as part of standard SAP OEE, or you can configure your own custom data collection element name specific for machine down and line down. This data collection element is the unique identifier for OEE to understand the type of data collection collected from the shop floor.

7. Pass the retrieved node ID to the Node ID input. If your shop floor can report reason codes automatically, you can pass it through the parameters rc1 to rc10 in the service interface.

8. The same transaction is executed when PCo notification is triggered for a machine or line up event. When the tag value is for machine up, call OEE service interface: `ReportUnscheduledUptime`. For this action block, only the node ID is required, as the OEE system checks the open machine or line down for the same node ID and closes that event. Even if a close event comes first, probably because the open event did not reach OEE, then SAP OEE throws an error, as it could not find an open downtime.

Scenario 2: Shop-Floor Data Buffering in SAP MII

Order-dependent data collections such as yield, scrap, rework, and so forth may be collected automatically, which was explained in the previous scenario. For these data, being order dependent, you need to pass order and operation number to the OEE service interfaces in addition to what was explained in the earlier section. Please refer to Appendix Section 1: Automated Data Collection to understand the mandatory inputs to be passed for OEE service interface methods.

Refer to Figure 7-22, which is the typical technical data flow for automatic reporting of order-dependent data collection elements. Similar to the machine event, the PCo notification is triggered on tag-value change, and a custom BLS in SAP MII is executed. A custom SAP MII transaction gets the line node ID from the custom mapping using the tag name (in this case for yield value). The logic checks for the presence of an active order for the selected line node ID. If an active order exists, the OEE service interface to report production is executed and the yield is reported to OEE. Order–operation, line node ID, data collection element (`GOOD_QUANTITY`), material, and the yield quantity are passed to the input parameters of this action block. Similar to a machine status event, data collection element names should be maintained for order-dependent data collection elements as well.

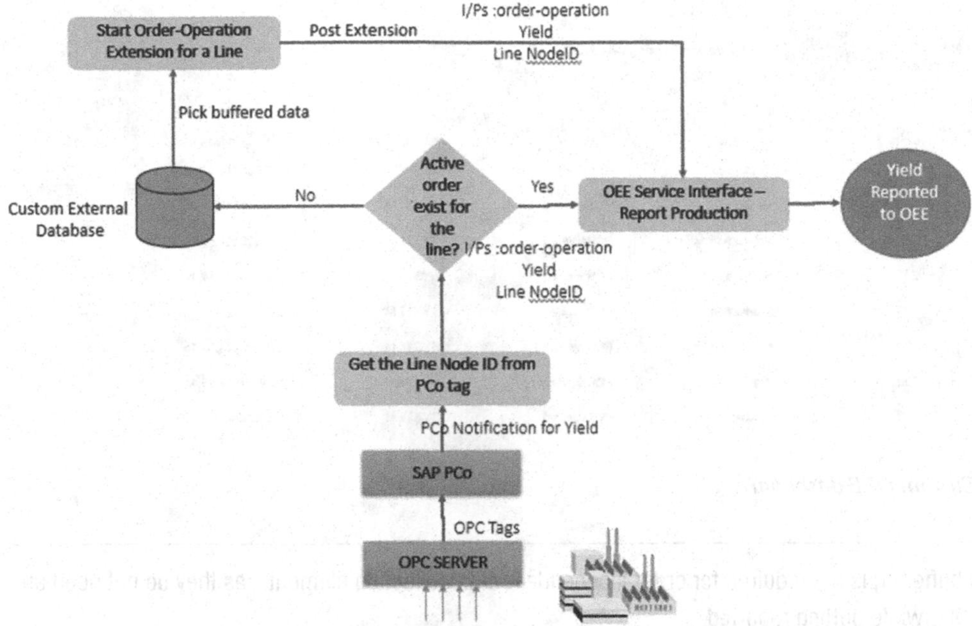

Figure 7-22. *Data flow for shop-floor data buffering*

If there is no active order, the data collection details collected are buffered in a custom database table with details such as tagname, line node ID, timestamp, and yield quantity. An active order may not exist in a scenario where the order is started on the shop floor but is not started in OEE. The processing status of these shop-floor buffered messages can be monitored using a custom data collection monitor user interface. Initially the status of the messages will be "Buffered," which should be changed to "Processed" once reported in SAP OEE. These buffered messages that are not reported to SAP OEE due to the absence of an active order can be processed using a custom extension from the order-operation start event in SAP OEE dashboard.

A custom activity referring to an SAP MII BLS Transaction needs to be added as a post extension to the "Start Order-Operation" method in the general configuration/extension configuration worker UI. Please refer to Chapter 5, "Reason Code Configuration," for details of the configuration. This logic is executed whenever an order operation is started in OEE dashboard. The logic checks the order start timestamp and picks all the buffered messages that are older than this timestamp and reports them to SAP OEE using the OEE interface for reporting production. The operator should ensure that the order start timestamp is started in the past, as this was originally missed, so as to start it at the right time. Refer to Scenario 3 for more details.

The custom data collection monitor (refer to Figure 7-23) can be developed and integrated with the standard OEE dashboard and is where the processing status of each message can be monitored. You can also configure the same monitor to reconcile messages that are no longer required or don't belong to that shift.

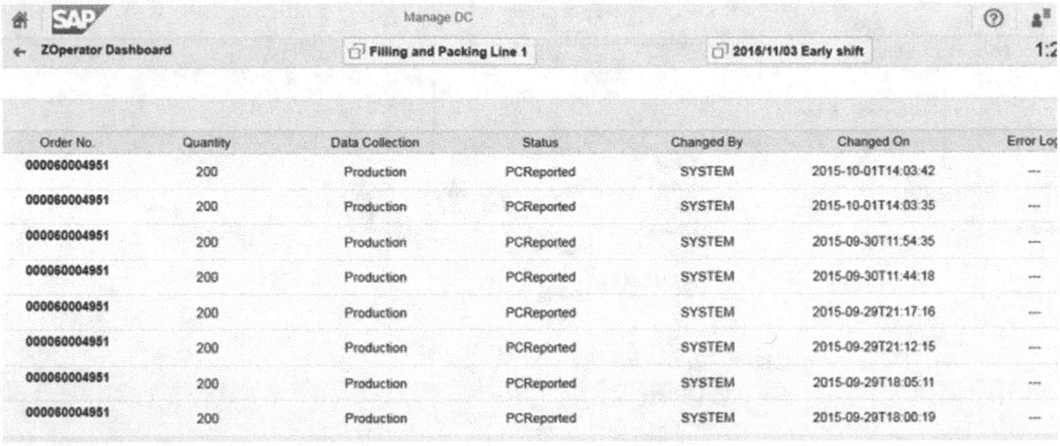

Manage DC

← ZOperator Dashboard | Filling and Packing Line 1 | 2016/11/03 Early shift

Order No.	Quantity	Data Collection	Status	Changed By	Changed On	Error Log
000060004951	200	Production	PCReported	SYSTEM	2015-10-01T14:03:42	---
000060004951	200	Production	PCReported	SYSTEM	2015-10-01T14:03:35	---
000060004951	200	Production	PCReported	SYSTEM	2015-09-30T11:54:35	---
000060004951	200	Production	PCReported	SYSTEM	2015-09-30T11:44:18	---
000060004951	200	Production	PCReported	SYSTEM	2015-09-29T21:17:16	---
000060004951	200	Production	PCReported	SYSTEM	2015-09-29T21:12:15	---
000060004951	200	Production	PCReported	SYSTEM	2015-09-29T18:05:11	---
000060004951	200	Production	PCReported	SYSTEM	2015-09-29T18:00:19	---

Figure 7-23. *Custom OEE dashboard*

■ **Note** Data buffering is not required for order-independent data collection elements, as they do not need an active order in OEE while getting reported.

Scenario 3: Custom Extensions in SAP OEE Dashboard

Custom extensions in SAP OEE are used as an extension to OEE's standard functionality when the standard functionality cannot achieve the complete requirement or there is a need to execute custom logic for specific events in the dashboard. In Scenario 2, the shop-floor messages are buffered at SAP MII as there is no active order. When the order is started, these messages should be picked up and reported to OEE. This is achieved by developing a custom extension and configuring it to the "Start Order-Operation" method under the extension configuration in the SAP OEE dashboard.

Develop BLS Transaction for Custom Extension

1. Develop a custom BLS transaction in SAP MII workbench to handle the processing of these buffered messages, using the following transaction properties:
   - **XMLInputString** DataType: XML Type: Input This XML contains the details the started order-operation
   - **XMLOutputString** DataType: XML Type: Output This XML contains the output structure of the "Start Order-Operation" method
   - **XMLModifiedOutputString** DataType: XML Type: Output. This is the modified version of XMLOutputString when you want to consume the modified output in OEE Dashboard. Refer to Custom KPI section later in this chapter.
2. Get all the order-related details from the `XMLInputString` property to handle the logic inside the transaction.

3. Refer to Appendix Section 5: Extension Configuration to understand the XML structure of each extension method. In this scenario, for the "Start Order-Operation" method, the `XMLOutputString` XML gets all the order-related information, such as `Run_ID`, order-operation number, start timestamp, order number, material, plant, shift ID, and so on, from the start order extension. With this order number and shift ID, the buffered shop-floor messages that are in status "Buffered" are picked up and compared with the order start timestamp. If the data collection timestamp is greater than the time of order start, then these messages can be picked up and processed for reporting production by executing the corresponding SAP OEE service interface. You can also implement your own custom validation logic for reporting buffered production counts. Ultimately, the operator is responsible for accounting yield to the respective order if the yields are not accounted automatically.

Create a Custom Activity

1. From Worker UI Management ➤ Activity Configuration menu choose "Create Activity." On the Main tab, specify an activity ID in uppercase and without any spaces.
2. In the Class or URL field, specify the path of the transaction created in step 1. The format is Project/Folder path/transaction name.

   Example: OEEEnhancement/DownTimeOrderTagging/BLS/BLS_DowntimeMappingForStartOrd
3. Choose Transaction for the activity type.
4. In the Activity Description tab, provide a description in any of the ISO languages. Note: This activity description will be visible to you while creating an extension in the general configuration/extension configuration screen.
5. Click on Save, and the activity creation is complete. Refer to Figure 7-24.

Activity Configuration

Create Activity | Display | Change Activity | Delete

Activity ID	Class or URL	Activity Type
DTTagForCompleteOrd	OEEEnhancement/DownTimeOrderTagging/BLS/BLS_DowntimeMappingForCmpltOrd	Transaction
DTTagForStartOrd	OEEEnhancement/DownTimeOrderTagging/BLS/BLS_DowntimeMappingForStartOrd	Transaction

Figure 7-24. *Custom activity configuration: transaction type*

Configure Custom Extension

1. Open Worker UI Management ➤ General Configuration ➤ Extension Configuration menu
2. Select/Add the method "Start Order-Operation" in the top panel and then click Add in the Extension panel.
3. Specify the extension type as POST and choose the activity from the drop-down that you created in step 5 above.

4. Check the "Enabled" box and add the description in extension description panel in one of the languages.

5. Click Add and Save, and the extension is added.

6. With this configuration set, start an order-operation in OEE; this extension is executed and all the buffered messages are processed and reported to OEE.

Scenario 4: Custom SAP OEE Dashboard

This section will describe the steps for creating an activity of type UI and will use this activity to configure a dashboard button. Scenario 2 described shop-floor buffering. You can develop a custom user interface to monitor the processing status of these shop-floor messages.

1. Create a custom user interface using SAP UI5 following the MVC approach and XML view option only. Other view types are not applicable for SAP OEE.

2. Please note that the view and controller file of the custom UI should be kept in the folder path: `Project/folder name/webContent/customActivity/`. This path is case sensitive.

3. Test the custom UI and get the path of the view file without the extension ".view.xml." For example: `http:<server>:port/Project folder/webContent/customActivity/XMLViewname`. Refer to Figure 7-25.

   Refer to the Appendix for a sample XML view code

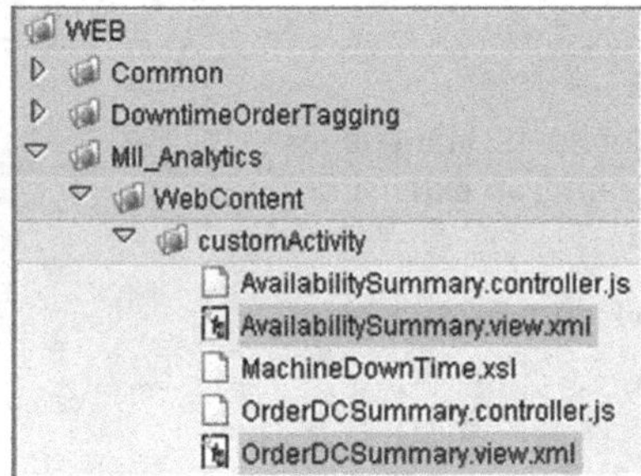

***Figure 7-25.** Custom XML view sample code*

4. Navigate to MII menu page Worker UI Management ➤ Activity Configuration.

5. Choose Create Activity.

6. On the Main tab, specify an activity ID in capital letters and without any white spaces.

7. In the Activity URL specify the relative view path defined in step 3.

8. On the Activity Description tab, provide a description in any of the ISO languages.

9. Click on Save once again after coming out of this window. Refer to Figure 7-26.

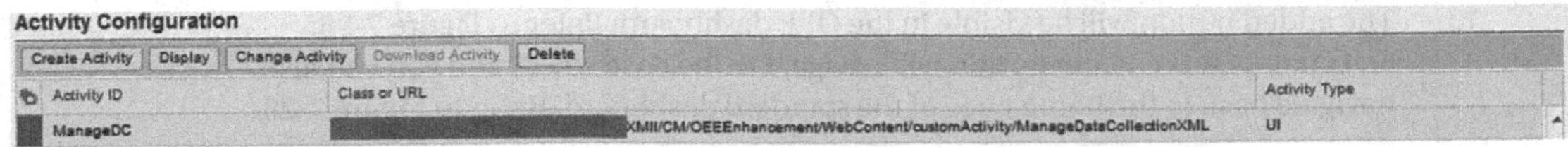

Figure 7-26. Custom activity configuration: UI type

10. Navigate to MII menu page Worker UI Management ➤ Dashboard Configuration.
11. Create your own new dashboard or copy an existing SAP-delivered dashboard and rename it. (Refer to Chapter 5 for how to copy an existing standard dashboard.)
12. Go to the Dashboard Buttons section and choose Add Entry.
13. Specify a button ID in capital letters and without any white spaces.
14. Specify a sequence number for the button; this will determine the relative position of the button with respect to other buttons in the dashboard.
15. In the Activity Assigned drop-down choose the activity description you defined in step 9.
16. Choose the button type as Normal *a*nd leave the location setting to Bottom by default.
17. Provide a description for the button in the bottom panel.
18. Click OK and save the changes. Refer to Figure 7-27.

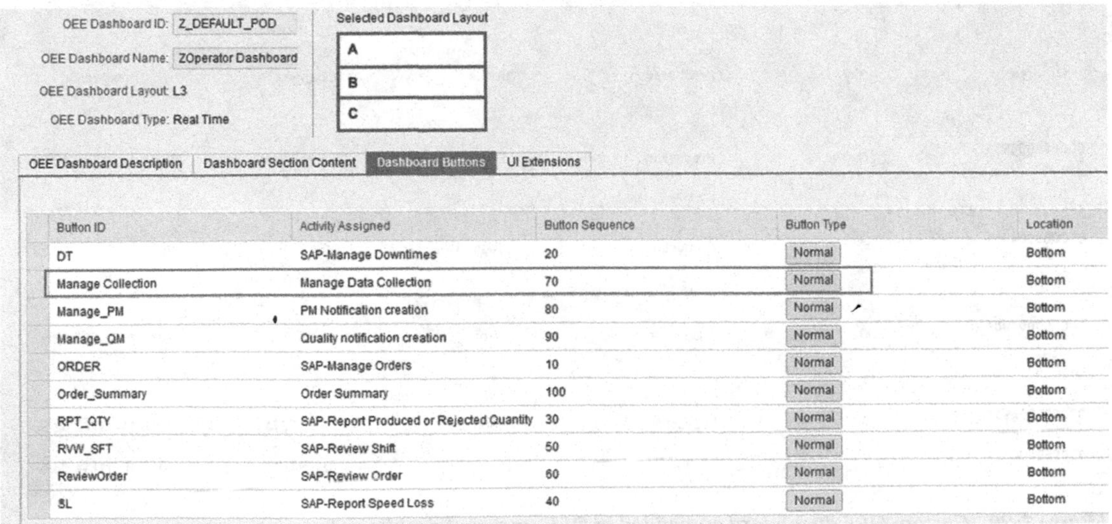

Button ID	Activity Assigned	Button Sequence	Button Type	Location
DT	SAP-Manage Downtimes	20	Normal	Bottom
Manage Collection	Manage Data Collection	70	Normal	Bottom
Manage_PM	PM Notification creation	80	Normal	Bottom
Manage_QM	Quality notification creation	90	Normal	Bottom
ORDER	SAP-Manage Orders	10	Normal	Bottom
Order_Summary	Order Summary	100	Normal	Bottom
RPT_QTY	SAP-Report Produced or Rejected Quantity	30	Normal	Bottom
RVW_SFT	SAP-Review Shift	50	Normal	Bottom
ReviewOrder	SAP-Review Order	60	Normal	Bottom
SL	SAP-Report Speed Loss	40	Normal	Bottom

Figure 7-27. Add dashboard button with custom activity

19. The added button will be visible in the OEE dashboard. Refer to Figure 7-28. Selection of this custom button will navigate to the custom UI, and you can also navigate back to the home page of the standard dashboard. Refer to Figure 7-28.

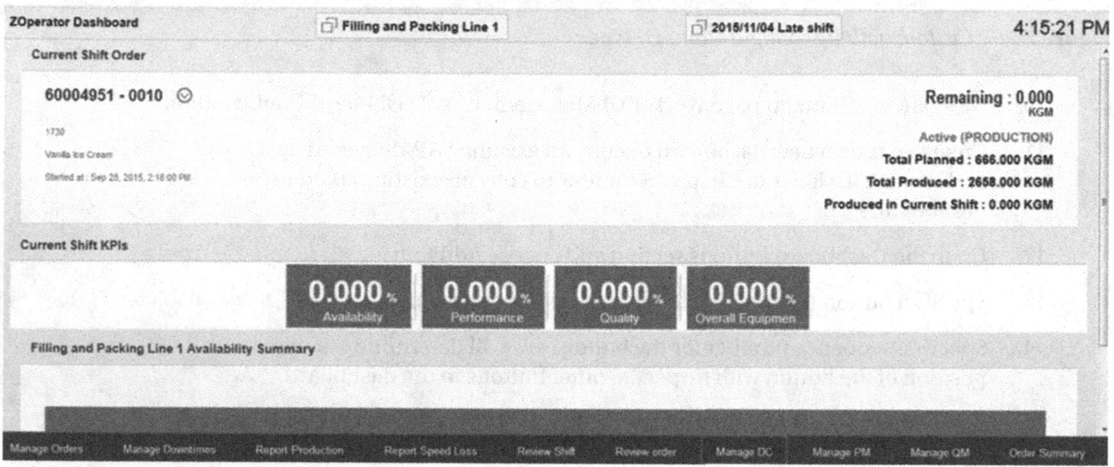

Figure 7-28. *Standard dashboard with custom dashboard button*

Click on Manage DC to open the custom UI as shown in Figure 7-29.

← ZOperator Dashboard | Filling and Packing Line 1 | 2015/11/04 Late shift

Order No.	Quantity	Data Collection	Status	Changed By	Changed On
000060004951	100	Production	Error	SYSTEM	2015-11-04T15:10:21
000060004951	100	Production	PCTagged	SYSTEM	2015-11-04T14:16:39
000060004951	100	Production	Error	SYSTEM	2015-11-03T22:52:59
000060004951	100	Production	PCTagged	SYSTEM	2015-11-03T22:52:59
000060004951	200	Production	PCReported	SYSTEM	2015-10-01T14:03:42

Figure 7-29. *Custom OEE dashboard embedded in OEE standard dashboard*

Scenario 5: Calculate and Monitor Custom KPI

SAP OEE delivers four standard KPIs, such as availability, performance, quality, and OEE. But apart from this, there could be industry-specific KPIs that need to be monitored in a plant. SAP OEE has the placeholder to create, calculate, and monitor customized KPI, which will be covered in this section.

Typically custom KPIs can be the following:

- Planned versus Actuals on
    a. operation costs
    b. order completion as per the promise dates
    c. lead time of different product variants
- Measure the work center capacity
- Measure the line set speed to compare with line's nominal speed, and so on

Line speed is an important data to collect from shop floor. Every production line or work center has a speed-determining machine where the line speed is set by the operator, and it is normally the rated or the nominal speed of the material being produced in the line. This speed is directly proportional to the rate of production. Production is high when the set speed is more than the nominal speed and vice versa. Over-speed causes the wear and tear of the machines as they are made to work more than their rated speed. Under-speed leads to less production. Hence, it is essential to monitor this speed as a KPI in OEE to achieve the planned production goals.

Prerequisites

1. Define a custom KPI in OEE add-on in SAP ERP and transfer it to SAP MII. (Refer to Chapter 3 for the steps to create a custom KPI, which is similar to a standard KPI creation). Refer to Figure 7-30.

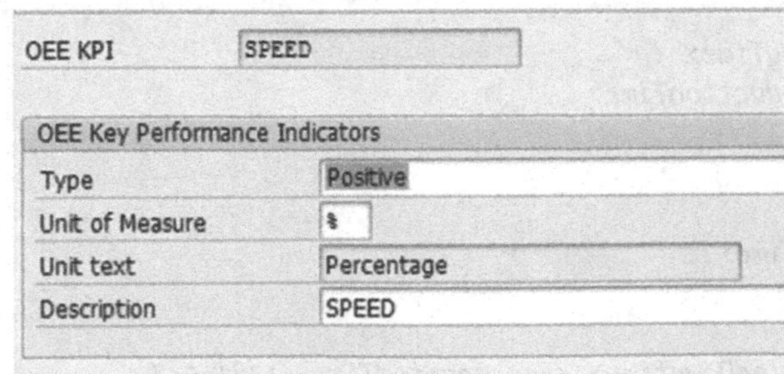

Figure 7-30. *Create custom KPI in OEE add-on*

2. Add the custom KPI to the line node under plant hierarchy where you want to monitor this KPI and also maintain data for the KPI targets, as without targets the KPI data will not be displayed in the OEE dahsboard screen. i.e., in KPI andon of OEE standard dashboard, the KPI actual values are displayed with a color coding set based on the target value range. If the target value are not maintained, display of actual values with color coding will not appear in the dashboard. Refer to Figure 7-31.

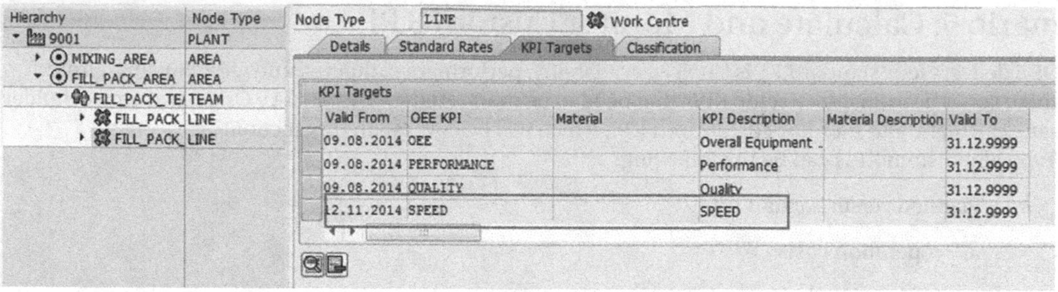
Hierarchy
Node Type
9001
PLANT
MIXING_AREA
AREA
FILL_PACK_AREA
AREA
FILL_PACK_TE/
TEAM
FILL_PACK_
LINE
FILL_PACK_
LINE
Node Type
LINE
Work Centre
Details
Standard Rates
KPI Targets
Classification
KPI Targets
Valid From
OEE KPI
Material
KPI Description
Material Description
Valid To
09.08.2014
OEE
Overall Equipment
31.12.9999
09.08.2014
PERFORMANCE
Performance
31.12.9999
09.08.2014
QUALITY
Quality
31.12.9999
12.11.2014
SPEED
SPEED
31.12.9999

Figure 7-31. *Configure custom KPI in plant hierarchy*

3. Create an MII transaction with the transaction properties as mentioned in Scenario 3. Place the following XML structure in the `XMLOutputString` property.

```
<?xml version="1.0" encoding="UTF-8" standalone="no"?> <ns2:OutputKPIService
xmlns:ns2="com.sap.xapps.oee.dto.kpiservices">
<availability>100.0</availability>
<customKpis>
<entry>
<key>CUSTOM_KPI_1</key>
<value/> </entry> <entry>
<key>CUSTOM_KPI_2</key>
<value/> </entry> <entry>
<key>CUSTOM_KPI_3</key>
value/> </entry> <entry>
<key>CUSTOM_KPI_4</key>
<value/> </entry> </customKpis>
<flowTime>0.0</flowTime>
<loadingTime>11381.0</loadingTime>
<netOperatingTime>0.0</netOperatingTime>
<netProductionTime>11381.0</netProductionTime>
<oee>0.0</oee>
<performance>0.0</performance>
<quality>0.0</quality>
<qualityLossTime>0.0</qualityLossTime>
<speedLossTime>0.0</speedLossTime>
<timeUom>SECOND</timeUom>
<unScheduledDowntime>0.0</unScheduledDowntime> <unaccountedTime>11381.0</
unaccountedTime>
<valueOperationTime>0.0</valueOperationTime>
</ns2:OutputKPIService>
```

4. Custom logic:

   a. Refer to Scenario 1 which explains you the required steps to collect a shop floor data collection element using PCo notification. In this case, it is a line speed.

      Once you get the line speed using a PCo notification, determine the corresponding Line Node ID against which this line speed is collected. Refer to scenario 1 where it talks about the custom mapping to determine this line node ID.

      Using the Line Node ID, get the nominal speed for line and material combination which is configured in plant hierarchy (fetch it from standard table `MPM_MPH_NODESTR`).

      Compare this nominal speed against the collected line speed.

5. Use this formula to calculate the Speed KPI:

   Speed KPI in % = (Collected set speed/nominal speed) x 100

6. In the preceding XML, fields marked in red are placeholders for the custom KPIs, and these values must be dynamically filled from your custom logic. The number of custom KPIs and their positions are dependent on the KPI targets. Normally SAP OEE allows you to configure and display six KPI targets in the dashboard.

7. The result XML is copied to `XMLModifiedOutputString`.

8. Save the MII transaction.

9. Create two custom activities–one for custom extension and another for displaying the custom KPI in OEE dashboard. Please refer to the steps mentioned in earlier scenarios to create a custom activity for adding this transaction (created in step 1) as a custom extension. Refer to Figure 7-32.

Activity Configuration

Create Activity | Display | Change Activity | Delete

Activity ID	Class or URL	Activity Type
Custom_KPI	OEEEnhancement/DataCollection/BLS/BLS_KPIForSpeed	Transaction

Figure 7-32. *Configure custom activity of transaction type*

10. Under Extension configuration, now configure a custom extension using the custom activity created to GetOEEKPI method. The extension type should be post while adding the extension. GetOEEKPI method provides with all the values of four standard KPIs and the inputs required for calculating these KPIs. These values can be used to calculate our custom KPI wherever applicable. For example the GetOEEKPI will provide you the Line Node ID, real time values of downtime and other order related data. Refer to Appendix for understanding the structure of this XML. Refer to Figure 7-33.

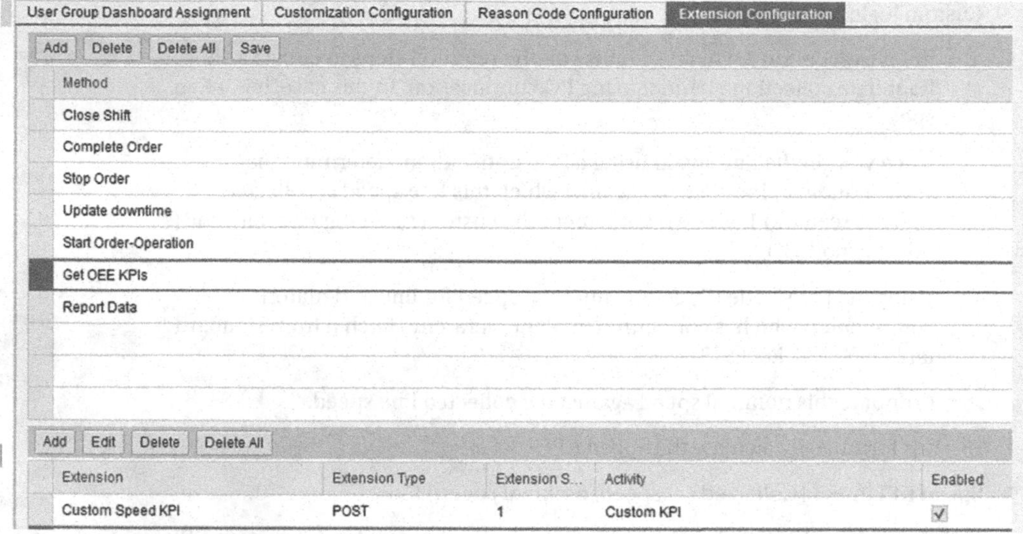

Figure 7-33. *Configure custom transaction as a custom extension*

11. To create a custom activity for KPI display in dashboard, go to activity configuration worker UI and Choose Create Activity.

12. In the Activity URL field, specify the following URL: `sap.oee.ui.oeeKpiTileContainer`.

13. Choose UI for the Activity Type.

14. In the Activity Description tab, provide a description in one of the ISO languages.

15. In the Options tab, click on the Add button.

16. For the Option Name, enter `ALLOWED_KPI`.

17. In the Options Description panel, click the Add button to enter the activity option description.

18. Provide a description for the activity option in one of the ISO languages.

19. In the Options Value panel, click the Add button to enter the list of KPIs to be shown in the KPI AndOn screen (Andon refers to the UI component in home page of OEE dashboard for KPI monitor). This is done to display both standard and custom KPI in the same AndOn.

20. For the Options Value, enter the sequence number and the KPI value to be shown in the AndOn. The same sequence is followed for the display of KPI in AndOn.

21. For the standard OEE KPIs, enter the following text:

```
AVAILABILITY
PERFORMANCE
QUALITY
OEE
```

22. For the custom KPIs, specify the exact KPI names defined in the ERP customization.

23. Click on Save and Click on Save again for the activity. Refer to Figure 7-34.

Activity Configuration

Create Activity | Display | Change Activity | Delete

Activity ID	Class or URL	Activity Type
CUSTOM_KPI_DISPLAY	sap.oee.ui.oeeactivity.configuration.andon	UI

Figure 7-34. *Configure custom activity of UI type*

With all the preceding configurations, a custom speed KPI will be displayed in OEE dashboard. Refer to Figure 7-35.

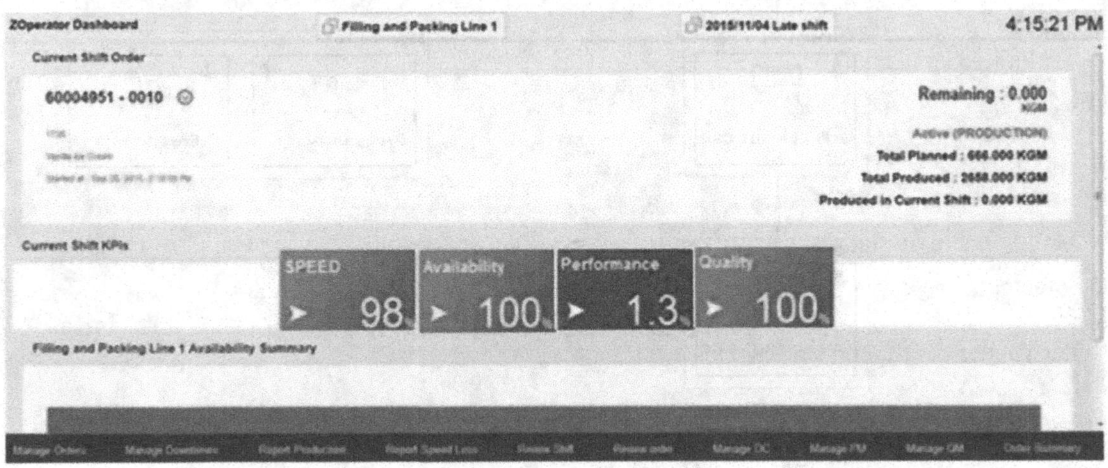

Figure 7-35. *Configure custom activity of UI type*

Scenario 6: QM Notification Handling

This section will describe how SAP OEE can be enhanced to trigger quality notifications in ERP.

Quality defect is one of the data collection elements collected in SAP OEE that affects the quality KPI. Similar to a machine breakdown notification, you can also develop a customization to trigger a quality notification from SAP OEE to SAP ERP that reports a quality defect. The shift- or order-specific quality notifications can be displayed as a report in OEE dashboard for the operators view.

1. Develop a custom OEE dashboard with an option to create quality notifications and to display the created quality notifications.

2. Create a custom activity of type UI with the XML view file under the activity configuration worker UI (refer to Figure 7-36). Follow the steps in Scenario 4 to create a UI activity.

Figure 7-36. *Custom UI activity of custom OEE dashboard for quality notification*

Refer to the appendix for sample XML view code.

3. Develop a custom MII BLS (refer to Figure 7-37) to integrate with SAP QM to create a quality notification.

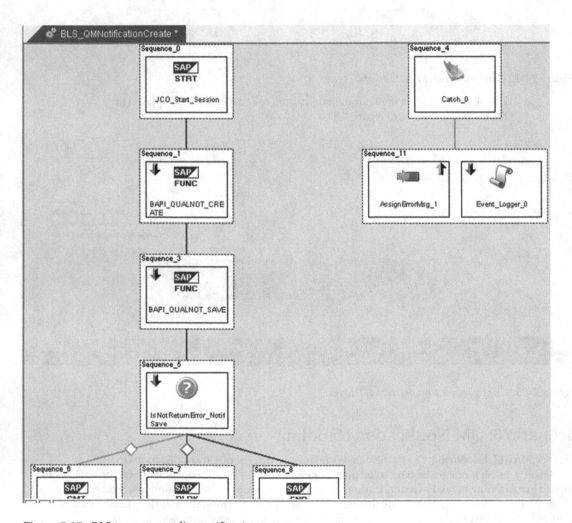

Figure 7-37. *BLS to create quality notification*

4. The preceding BLS can be triggered from the custom dashboard with the Create QM Notification button.

5. Add this custom dashboard to a custom dashboard button using the dashboard configuration worker UI. Follow the steps in Scenario 4 to add the custom button. The custom activity "Manage QM" created in step 2 is assigned to the dashboard button. Refer to Figure 7-38.

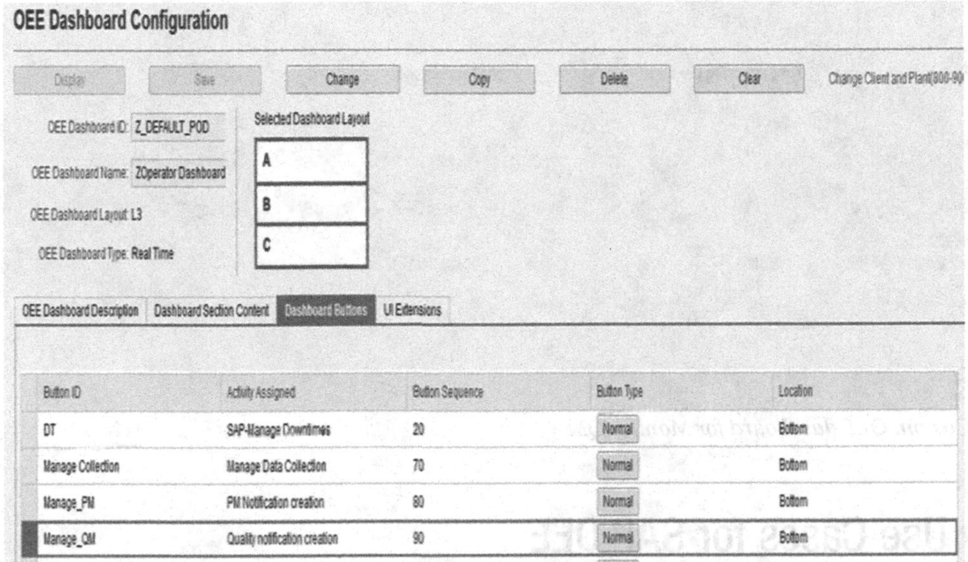

Figure 7-38. *Add "Monitor QM" custom dashboard as a dashboard button*

6. Refer to Figure 7-38, where the preceding configured custom dashboard can be viewed; on selection of this button from the standard dashboard, you can navigate to the custom OEE dashboard. Refer to Figure 7-39.

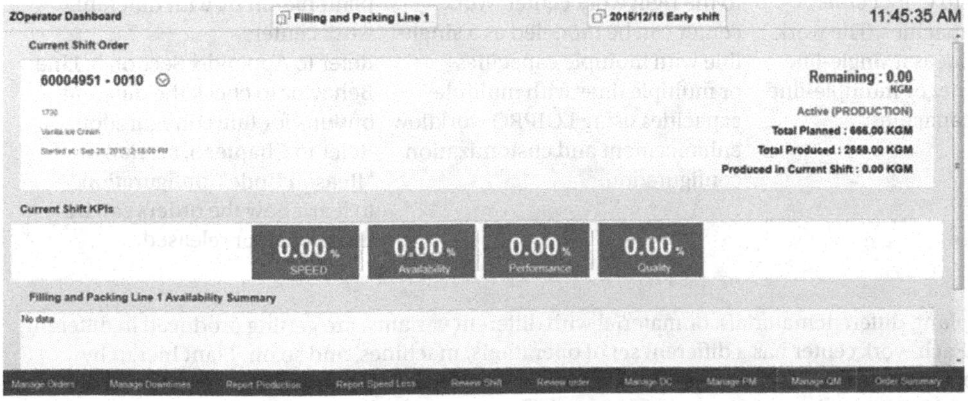

Figure 7-39. *Add "Monitor QM" custom dashboard as a dashboard button*

Refer to Figure 7-40 the Monitor QM custom dashboard screen where you can create and manage the quality notifications. You can customize as per the plant requirements. In this section, it also shows how the custom dashboard is merged into the standard OEE dashboard. Here the Quality notifications are created manually using the custom dashboard or it can be triggered automatically by configuring the custom BLS as an extension to the "Report Data" method (whenever defect is reported) under extension configuration or can be based on your plant requirements.

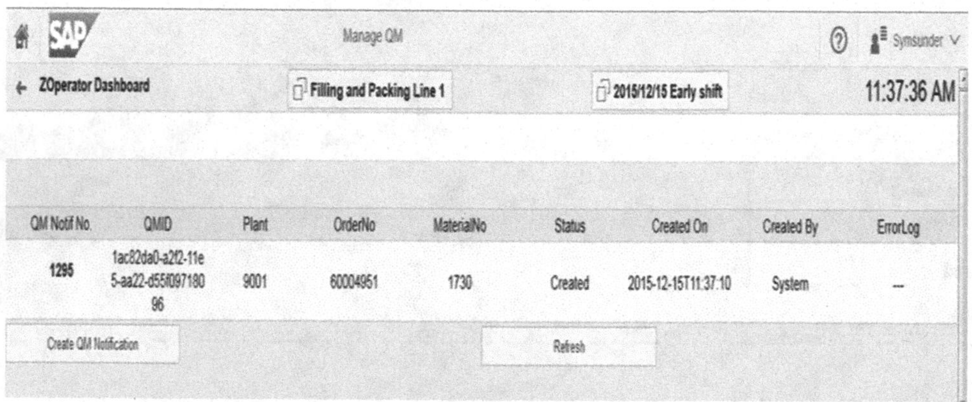

Figure 7-40. Custom OEE dashboard for Monitor QM

Industry Use Cases for SAP OEE

In this section, you will get to know the different use cases for SAP OEE specific to every industry.

1. Use cases for plant floor connectivity, visibility, and shop-floor production execution

Use Case	OEE Functionality	Chapter Reference
Dispatching production orders from SAP ERP to work center/ work center capacities. The work center may work as a single-line multiple capacity or multiple-line and multiple capacities.	Orders are created and dispatched to the right work center. Work center can be modeled as a single line with multiple capacities or multiple lines with multiple capacities using LOIPRO workflow enhancement and customization configuration.	Refer to Chapter 3 to set up the plant hierarchy with different work centers. Refer to Appendix Section 3: Line Behavior to check the different options for line configuration. Refer to Chapter 5, section on "Reason Code Configuration," to learn how the orders can be dispatched or released.

Example:

Typically in a plant, different materials, or material with different variants, are getting produced in different work centers. Each work center has a different set of operations, machines, and so on. Plant hierarchy enables you to define different types of work center models, materials to be processed, and so on, that will be used in SAP OEE. Orders are created in ERP, and when pushed to OEE, they get dispatched to their proper work centers based on the hierarchy configurations.

<table>
<tr><th>Use Case</th><th>OEE Functionality</th><th>Chapter Reference</th></tr>
<tr><td>Data collection and production execution; update order confirmation for yield, scrap and standard activities such as labor time, machine time, setup time, and so on to SAP ERP from SAP OEE.</td><td>All the order-dependent and -independent data collections can be collected manually or automatically in OEE operator dashboard. The collected data are confirmed automatically to ERP using standard workflows.</td><td>Refer to Chapter 6; report production to understand the data collections using OEE dashboard.</td></tr>
<tr><td colspan="3">Example:

Production and material loss data reported in SAP OEE needs to be confirmed to SAP ERP in real-time. You may have different instances that do the order confirmation. ORDER_CONFIRM_BAPI is the standard workflow that does the order-operation-level confirmation in ERP. This confirmation can be done after each data reporting or at the end of order completion using OEE standard extensions.</td></tr>
<tr><td>Goods movement: goods issue and goods receipt</td><td>Goods movement of raw materials and finished goods can be achieved using the Application Launch Pad (available from SAP OEE 15.1).</td><td>Refer to Chapter 6, “Line Availability Summary,” for goods movement functionality.</td></tr>
<tr><td colspan="3">Example:

Goods movement of finished goods is to be updated in ERP in real-time as and when it is produced.</td></tr>
<tr><td>Role-specific operator dashboards for plant/line monitoring and order handling</td><td>SAP OEE delivers three standard dashboards for operators’ action and to monitor plant and line’s performance</td><td>Refer to Chapter 6 to check the standard OEE-delivered dashboards.
Refer to Chapter 5, “User Administration in SAP OEE,” to configure role-specific OEE dashboards.</td></tr>
<tr><td colspan="3">Example:

Each user has specific tasks or responsibilities and accordingly they may have to get the right permissions in the SAP OEE dashboard. A supervisor does an order dispatch based on the line/capacity availability, which an operator is not allowed to do. An operator collects all data from the shop floor, whereas a supervisor should have the permission to edit these collected shop-floor data. SAP OEE enables you to define this role-specific OEE dashboard using a simple configuration map.</td></tr>
<tr><td>SAP ERP to plant floor integration through bidirectional data exchange</td><td>Pre-delivered OEEINT framework in SAP OEE, which ensures seamless integration between SAP ERP and SAP OEE bidirectionally. All the predelivered workflows process the inbound and outbound messages automatically.</td><td>Refer to Chapter 4’s “Workflow Configurations” section.</td></tr>
<tr><td colspan="3">Example:

Any execution system lying in the middle of enterprise and shop-floor systems has the prime responsibility of integrating the two layers in real-time for proper data synchronization and plant visibility. SAP OEE ensures this bidirectional data flow with SAPOEEINT framework. Workflows are delivered by default, which ensures this SAP ERP to plant floor integration.</td></tr>
</table>

Use Case	OEE Functionality	Chapter Reference
Shift handover at the end of production run	SAP OEE delivers a standard shift handover functionality in the operator dashboard, and the time at which shift handover should happen is flexible using a customization configuration.	Refer to Appendix Section 3: Shift Handover Available Before Shift End

Example:

In a typical manufacturing industry, production happens in shifts, and it is essential and critical to hand over the shift-specific tasks to the next shift operators to ensure continuity and a smooth production process. SAP OEE ensures this using a shift-handover screen where you have the option to update all the information about the completed shift.

2. Use cases for complex mixing, filling, and packing lines

Use Case	OEE Functionality	Chapter Reference
Automated data collection of order-specific, OEE-specific, and non-OEE-specific data collections from shop floor through plant floor integration	SAP OEE is pre-delivered with custom actions/APIs that can be leveraged to develop the automated data collection scenarios.	Refer to Chapter 7's Scenario 1 to check the customization required for automated data collection.

Example:

Yield, machine down, line down, scrap, and quality defects are standard data collection elements required for four standard KPI calculations. There may be some non-OEE-specific data collection elements to be collected, like actual line set speed, material-specific custom losses, and so on.

Use Case	OEE Functionality	Chapter Reference
Flexibility in defining the shop-floor area using plant hierarchy in OEE while accommodating the process business rules	SAP OEE add-on component in SAP ERP is a configuration framework to model your plant correctly, from plant as the root node to equipment as the last child node. Plant, area, team, line, machine, and equipment are the nodes that can also be custom ones, as per the specific requirements.	Refer to Chapter 3, "Plant Hierarchy," to check how to configure different plant objects as nodes and use them in OEE for KPI monitoring and data collection. Refer to Chapter 5 section Extension Configuration to understand how extensions can be added to implement business and process rules to work centers and lines.

Example:

Plant hierarchy can be defined with multiple work centers, with each work center having different machine, bottleneck, and material combinations as per the plant requirements. For each configured line, a set of process rules can be developed and configured using OEE extensions. One line may be configured for automated data collection and another for manual data collection. A line may have to update the standard activities automatically to ERP on order completion and another line may not.

Use Case	OEE Functionality	Chapter Reference
Effectively determine speed loss from the machine responsible for a loss in production speed	SAP OEE automatically calculates the speed loss at the end of line production. SAP OEE is also flexible enough to determine the speed loss at the source machine, for example, a bottleneck machine, with few enhancements.	Refer to Chapter 3 section Plant Hierarchy Configuration / Bottlenecks tab to learn how to define bottleneck machines in a plant hierarchy, and refer to Chapter 7's "Customization Scenarios in SAP OEE" section.
Example: SAP OEE determines the speed loss for the end-of-line production counter. If there is a bottleneck machine in a line, and if this is the root cause for the end-of-line speed loss, you can always determine the speed loss when it happens at the bottleneck machine instead of waiting until the production is reported at the end of line. This can be achieved using a customization.		
Define virtual lines, lines sharing same machine, and so on the way you want, and accordingly OEE understands the model	Virtual lines and lines with shared machines can be easily configured using the OEE master data–plant hierarchy	Refer to Chapter 3 section Plant Hierarchy condigurations / Details tab to learn how to define different work center models.
Example: A packing machine may have to be shared between two lines. For example, the products coming out of line 1 and line 2 have to be packed by this machine with its respective order reference. The two lines ideally merge to this sharing machine. This scenario can also be modeled in OEE by creating virtual lines; i.e., two different lines are created in the plant hierarchy, and this machine will be part of both the lines.		
Execute different bottleneck scenarios influencing the line's availability, such as single and parallel bottleneck scenarios	Bottleneck machines can be defined in the plant hierarchy and used in OEE dashboard. Different bottleneck scenarios can be defined to determine the line's availability using customization configuration "Line Behavior."	Refer to Appendix Section 3: Line Behavior to check on different bottleneck scenarios SAP OEE supports.
Example: Based on the line's complexity, there may be one or more bottleneck machines whose availability is directly linked with the line's availability. In SAP OEE, you can configure two bottleneck scenarios. 1) The line is down when the single or any one of the (multiple) bottleneck machines are down. 2) The line is down only when all the bottleneck machines are down. SAP OEE marks the line down automatically based on this configuration set.		
Synchronize shop-floor data with OEE data to avoid manual errors	OEE custom actions enable you to develop simple automatic data-collection scenarios, which ensures real-time data updates to OEE from the shop floor and avoids any manual errors or data manipulations.	Refer to Appendix Section 1 to check how SAP OEE custom actions can be used to collect data automatically from the shop floor.

<table>
<tr><th>Use Case</th><th>OEE Functionality</th><th>Chapter Reference</th></tr>
<tr><td colspan="3">Example:
Though data collection and many order-related activities such as order start/hold/complete can be done manually in an OEE dashboard, it is prone to manual errors, data manipulation, and so forth. In this scenario, all the line operations can be fully automated or partially automated. For example, data collection can be automated and the order start/complete information can be synchronized with the shop floor by triggering this information in real-time using OEE custom actions and extensions.</td></tr>
</table>

3. Use case for KPI monitoring

<table>
<tr><th>Use Case</th><th>OEE Functionality</th><th>Chapter Reference</th></tr>
<tr><td>Calculate and monitor four standard KPIs: availability, performance, quality, and OEE</td><td>SAP OEE delivers calculation and monitoring of four KPIs as a standard feature.</td><td>Refer to Chapter 6's "Four KPI Calculations in Real-Time" section to understand the four standard KPI calculations.</td></tr>
<tr><td colspan="3">Example:
Availability, performance, quality, and OEE are the four KPIs that are critical to measure and monitor so as to analyze the plant performance and to take corrective action.</td></tr>
<tr><td>Flexibility of OEE in defining the different data elements influencing the KPI calculations. For example, industry- and plant-specific losses will have to be defined under a specific loss category, and the OEE KPI is calculated automatically without any customization.</td><td>The SAP OEE add-on configuration framework enables you to define custom data elements and data collection elements, which can be further categorized under a specific loss category. For example, you can define a plant-specific material loss (deviation of finished product weight from the standard weight) as a custom data collection and configure it under the data element DEFECT. Thus, this material loss automatically gets factored into quality KPI calculations.</td><td>Refer to Chapter 3's "OEE Configuration Data in ERP" section to understand SAP OEE configuration data for loss and production data categorization.</td></tr>
<tr><td colspan="3">Example:
As a standard, SAP OEE accommodates yield, scrap, defects, and line downs as the data collection elements with which to calculate the four standard KPIs. But as per the plant requirements, you can configure the plant-specific material and time losses under the specific data elements (production and loss), and this will be automatically considered when calculating the standard KPIs.</td></tr>
<tr><td>Develop, calculate, and monitor industry-specific custom KPIs using the OEE placeholders for enhancement</td><td>OEE extensions allow you to develop custom logic to calculate custom KPI calculations that can be hooked as an extension to a standard method of OEE dashboard.</td><td>Refer to Chapter 7's "Customization Scenarios in SAP OEE" section to understand how custom KPIs can be configured, calculated, and monitored in SAP OEE dashboard.</td></tr>
</table>

Use Case	OEE Functionality	Chapter Reference
Example:		
Each industry may have its process-specific KPIs or additional KPIs to be monitored, such as speed variation (variation between actual set speed and the nominal speed of the line), variation of finished good weight from its standard, and so on. All of these can be customized and monitored.		
Use SAP OEE beyond OEE KPI monitoring by collecting non-OEE-specific data collection elements	SAP OEE collects both OEE-KPI-specific and non-OEE-specific data collection elements.	Refer to Chapter 7's "Customization Scenarios in SAP OEE" section to understand how non-OEE-specific data collection elements can be collected from the shop floor.
Example:		
Line set speed, finished goods weight, labor time, setup time, machine time, and so forth are non-OEE-specific data collection elements that can be configured and collected from the shop floor. SAP OEE is used beyond OEE-specific elements.		

4. Use cases for PM and QM Integration

Use Case	OEE Functionality	Chapter Reference
Integrate with plant maintenance module in SAP ERP to trigger the breakdown notifications from OEE on occurrence of a machine down	SAP OEE can be integrated with the plant maintenance module to automatically trigger the breakdown maintenance for machine events. This is a standard functionality available in SAP MII 15.1.	Refer to Chapter 8.
Integrate with quality management module to trigger the quality notifications from OEE on encountering defects during production	Defects can be reported in OEE. With few enhancements, OEE can be integrated with the QM module to trigger a quality notification.	Refer to Chapter 7, Scenario 6 for QM integration.
Example:		
Quality defect notification can be triggered from SAP OEE to ERP on encountering quality defects.		

5. Use cases for OEE analytics

<table>
<thead>
<tr><th>Use Case</th><th>OEE Functionality</th><th>Chapter Reference</th></tr>
</thead>
<tbody>
<tr><td>Leverage the power of in-memory computing of HANA to build powerful OEE analytics by replicating OEE and ERP data into HANA</td><td>HANA is an optional analytics component for building analytics on plant performance. HANA Live is a default analytics component that is predelivered with analytics on KPI analysis, loss analysis, data collection report, and so on. OEE data is replicated to HANA in near real-time.</td><td>Refer to Chapter 9.</td></tr>
<tr><td>Build simple and short-term OEE analytics in MII</td><td>In absence of a HANA system, MII can be leveraged to build OEE analytics for the short term using MII's data and visualization services.</td><td>Refer to Chapter 7's "Customization Scenarios in SAP OEE" section to review how to develop and configure a custom OEE dashboard.</td></tr>
<tr><td colspan="3">Example:

SAP MII can be leveraged to build OEE analytics such as planned vs actuals, shift summary dashboard, availability dashboard, data collection dashboard, etc.</td></tr>
<tr><td>Integrate with external legacy and third-party applications to pull in data and use it with OEE data for analytics</td><td>MII's data services can be leveraged to connect with external shop floor and enterprise systems like DCS, Historian, MES, and so on for data acquisition and analytics.</td><td>Refer to Chapters 7 and 9.</td></tr>
<tr><td colspan="3">Example:

You may have to view an existing dashboard of an external system in SAP OEE. The external system is integrated to SAP OEE. You can do this using a new activity type, External UI.</td></tr>
<tr><td>Cross-plant analytics to analyze the plant, line, or machine performance; similar in nature to determining the root cause of recurring losses</td><td>Global hierarchy is replicated to HANA from ERP, and plant-specific transaction data are replicated from OEE to HANA. With this data, cross-plant performance analytics can be viewed in HANA. Custom analytics can also be built with this base data.</td><td>Refer to Chapter 9.</td></tr>
<tr><td colspan="3">Example:

HANA Live of SAP HANA helps in comparing the performance of different plants across similar process properties, such as similar production, machines, and so forth.</td></tr>
</tbody>
</table>

6. Use case for mobile goods movement

Use case	OEE Functionality	Chapter Reference
Automatic goods movement: goods receipt and goods issue	Goods Movement App of OEE (available in SAP MII 15.1) ensures the recording of raw material consumption and receipt of finished goods with barcode scanning enabled. This app ensures goods movement irrespective of connectivity with the ERP system by operating in online and offline modes.	Refer to Chapter 8.
Example:		
In the process of products getting manufactured, the raw materials consumption needs to be recorded, and for this the operator may have to move around in scanning different raw materials; i.e., boxes, cartons, pallets, and so on. Hence, there is a need for a recording system that is mobile.		

Summary

In this chapter, you have learned about the OEE data model and different customizations possible in OEE–such as automated data collection, customizations of OEE configuration data, and UI customizations–as well as looked at use cases.

In the next chapter, you will learn about SAP OEE enhancements as part of the SAP MII 15.1 release.

CHAPTER 8

Additional features of SAP OEE Management

This chapter will explain the features that were updated in OEE 15.1 as part of the SAP MII 15.1 release, which include the following:

- Creating PM notification from worker UI
- Line-specific alerts and UI activity to create alerts from OEE dashboard
- Data collection at machine level
- Manual correction of order execution
- Addition of visual icons on dashboard buttons and customer logos in dashboard
- Data maintenance through CSV/XML upload
- Quick setup of a demo SAP OEE plant without having an ERP connection
- Download and reuse the standard UI code for custom development
- Application Launch Pad to launch application goods movement apps (Goods Issue and Goods Receipt) and other custom apps
- SAP Lumira plug-in to create plant-based report on local MII data (covered in chapter 9)

Creating PM Notification from Worker UI

In Chapter 6, you learned how to create a machine downtime using the OEE dashboard worker UI. In some scenarios, operators need to create a PM notification as a follow-up process to machine downtime. This makes addressing the machine or line downtime complete.

From MII 15.1 onward, in the Manage Downtime/Machine Downtime tab (refer ahead to Figure 8-3), you can see a new option: "Report Notification." Report Notification enables the operator to create or trigger a breakdown or maintenance notification from SAP OEE to the PM module of SAP ERP.

Notification can be created for a work center or machine irrespective of the machine's availability; for instance, a notification can be triggered even if the machine is not down, as when preventive maintenance is required. Notification creation triggered by the operator can be controlled by a configuration parameter under the general configuration/customization configuration worker UI, as explained next. The PM notification feature ensures real-time integration of SAP OEE with the plant maintenance module in SAP ERP.

D. Saha et al., *Manufacturing Performance Management using SAP OEE*,
DOI 10.1007/978-1-4842-1150-2_8

Prerequisites

Customization Configurations

1. Go to SAP MII Menu ➤ Worker UI Management ➤ General Configuration ➤ Customization Configuration.
2. Select the customization “PM Notification Type” for plant hierarchy nodes where you want to enable the triggering of notification creation; for example, at the machine and line nodes.
3. Enter the notification types that should available in OEE from the notification types maintained in ERP.

■ **Note** The notification types that are added under customization configuration should be available in SAP ERP, else the notification creation will be incomplete.

---

4. Configure the customization “Allow Automatic PM Notification Trigger.” If this value is set to `NO`, then the system triggers the PM notification to SAP ERP only on an approval (say, by a supervisor) from OEE dashboard. If set to `Yes`, the notification is triggered automatically without an approval process.

Activity Configurations

1. Go to SAP MII Menu ➤ Worker UI Management ➤ Activity Configuration
2. `ACT_PM_NOTIF_LIST`: This is a new activity added for PM notification functionality. The standard OEE dashboard does not have this activity configured by default. You need to configure this activity in your custom dashboard to manage PM notifications. When creating a PM notification, the current shift is considered, and if there is no shift found, the system picks six hours prior to current time as the notification time, or you can overwrite by defining the duration in this activity under Option. i.e., When duration is defined as 4 hours, then the notification time is considered 4 hours past from the current time when no shift is found. Refer to Figure 8-1.

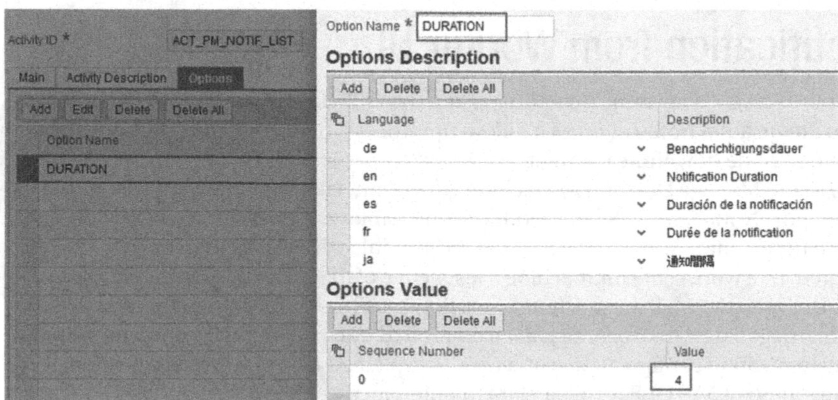

Figure 8-1. *Activity configuration: Duration option: display PM notifications*

3. You can choose to create the PM notification when you are reporting downtime. To get these notification details in the Report Downtime dialog, you need to add the option `ALLOW_PM_NOTIF` to the `ACT_DOWN_LIST` activity. Refer to Figure 8-2.

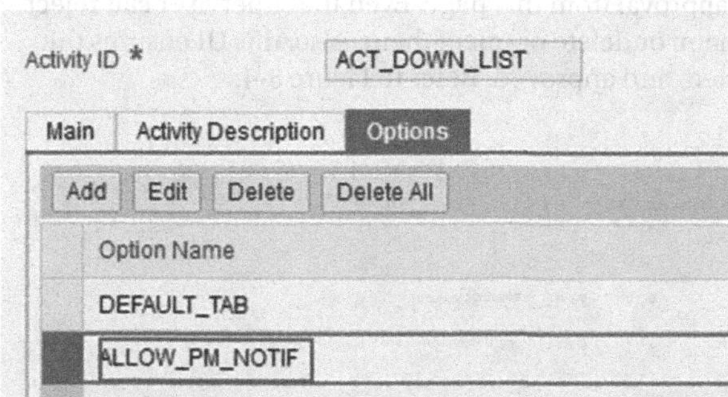

***Figure 8-2.** Activity configuration: PM notification option*

Report Notification in Manage Downtime

Refer to Figure 8-3, where you can see the "Report Notification" option in the Machine Downtimes tab of the OEE dashboard worker UI once step 3 is configured.

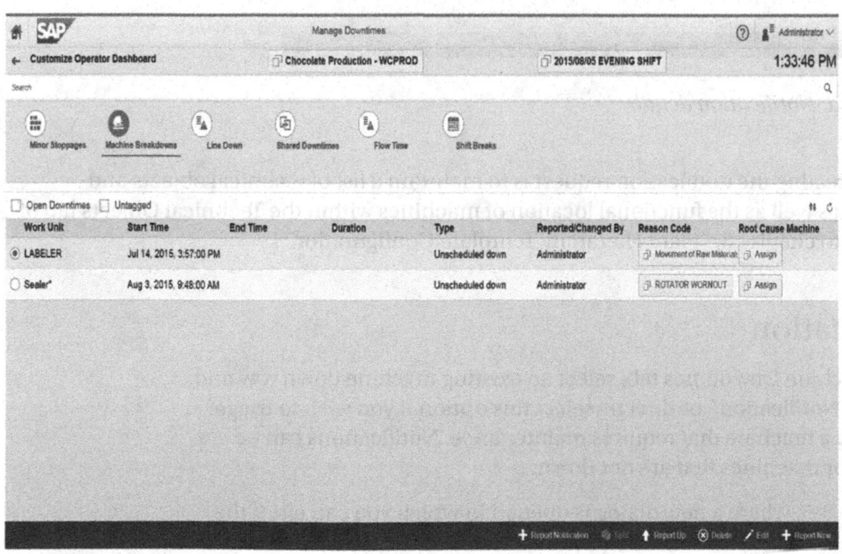

***Figure 8-3.** Manage downtime: report notification*

Once the notification is created, all the notifications are listed in the OEE operator dashboard under Notification details. This UI lists the notification created and waiting for supervisor's approval or rejection. The need for approval is controlled by a customization parameter "ALLOW PM NOTIFICATION TRIGGER". When this activity set to 'Yes,' the notifications are triggered without a need for an approval. When set to 'No,' the notifications are triggered only after supervisors approval from this page. Even the supervisor can reject the notification trigger, pending approval, approve them, or delete or reject them. Also, this UI ensures the tracking of all the notification requests created, rejected, and approved. Refer to Figure 8-4.

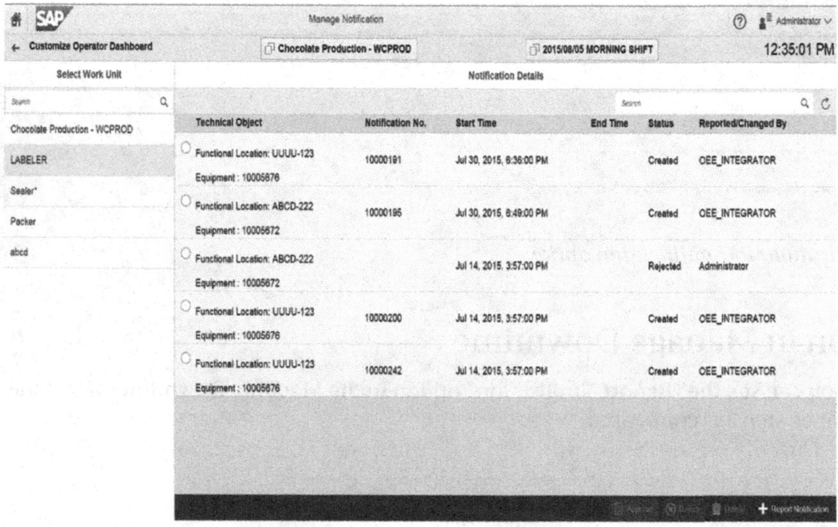

Figure 8-4. *OEE dashboard: Notification details*

The prerequisite for creating the notification request is to maintain a list of technical objects and corresponding equipment as well as the functional location of machines within the Technical Objects tab of the plant hierarchy. (Refer to chapter 3, "Plant Hierarchy Template Configuration").

Create PM Notification

1. Within the Machine Downtimes tab, select an existing machine down row and select "Report Notification," or directly select this option if you wish to trigger notification for a machine that requires maintenance. Notifications can be created even for machines that are not down.

2. Refer to Figure 8-5, where a new dialog is opened in which you can enter the details, such as functional location, equipment, notification type, breakdown/ maintenance start time, and end time (if planned). Check the "Breakdown" checkbox if the notification is of the breakdown type, and finally enter the comments and click the OK button. Now the notification request is created.

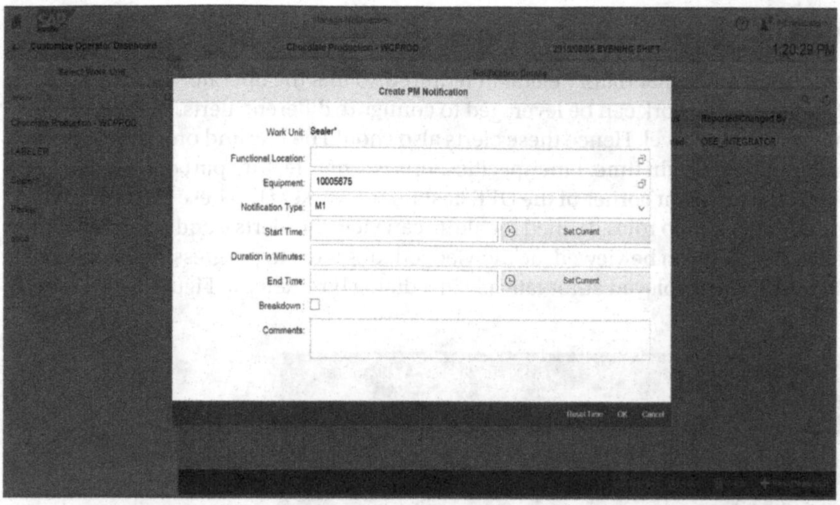

Figure 8-5. *PM notification request creation*

3. The created notification request is listed in the notification details worker UI. Refer to Figure 8-6. The status of the notification request is "Pending Approval."

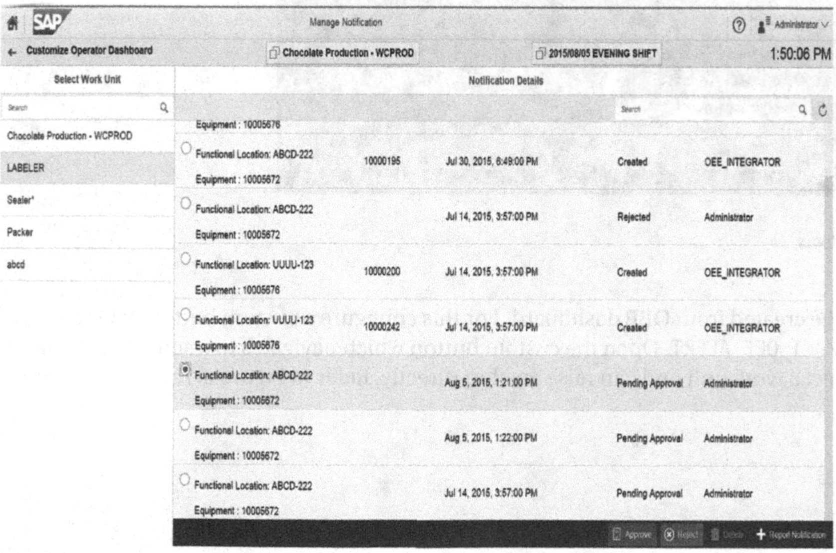

Figure 8-6. *PM notification status details*

The supervisors who have the role-based access to this UI can view and select the notification request and can decide to approve, reject, or delete it.

Any one of the following roles are required for approving the PM notifications:

```
OEE_SUPERADMIN
OEE_SUPERVISOR
OEE_INTEGRATOR
```

Line-Specific Alerts

Alerts on the shop floor are a critical and a mandatory element required so that the operator can act proactively. In OEE, SAP MII's alert framework can be leveraged to configure different alerts. In OEE, everything works at plant hierarchy node level. Hence these alerts also should be line and operator specific so that the right operator is alerted at the right time. Line specific alerts is a new feature part of OEE 15.1.

The alerts are displayed on the top-right corner of the OEE dashboard worker UI. These alerts are role and line specific (Only operators assigned to roles defined for alerts can view the alerts), and selection of the alerts will provide their details. The alert can be viewed, acknowledged, or set to "In progress" from the OEE dashboard. Alerts with high priority are displayed automatically in a dialog box. Refer to Figure 8-7.

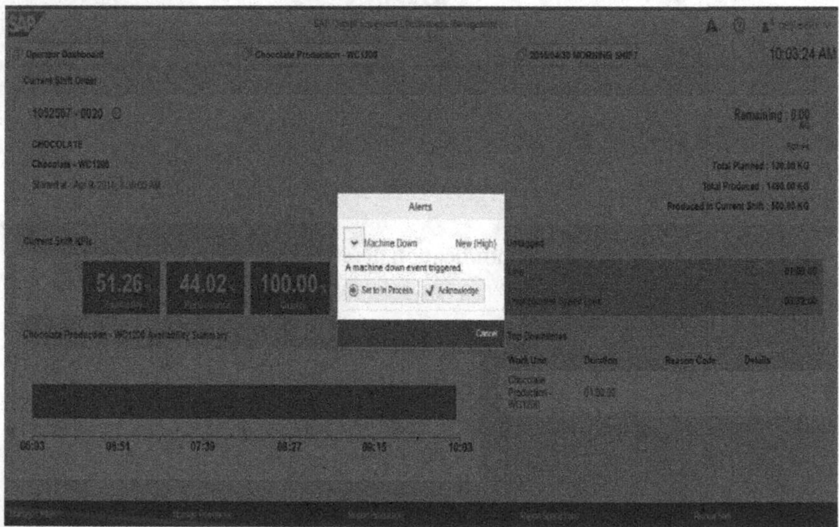

***Figure 8-7.** Line-specific alerts*

The alerts can be also be created from OEE dashboard. For this configure a custom button in OEE dashboard with the activity ACT_OEE_ALERT. Open the custom button which navigates to a screen and from this screen the user can select a work unit and can raise an alert directly. Refer to Figure 8-7a.

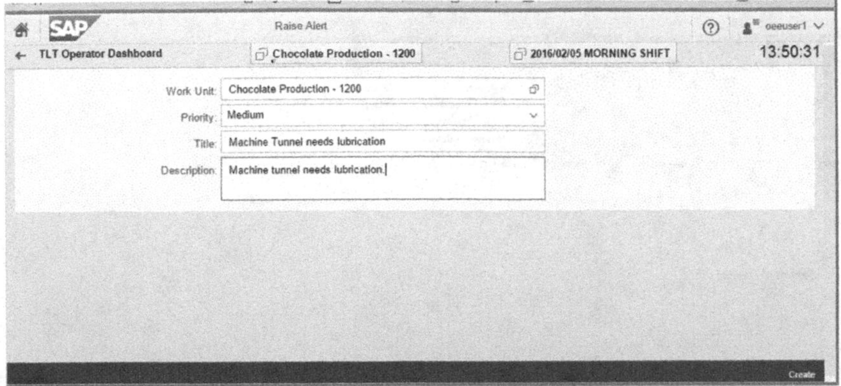

Figure 8-7a. Line-specific alerts using a dashboard button

Data Collection at Machine Level

In previous chapters, you have seen that KPIs are calculated at the node where the production is reported (Report production is enabled in plant hierarchy for this node), and ideally the node is for a line or work center. All the order-dependent and -independent data collection elements, such as yield, waste, defects, speed loss, and any other custom data collection, were reported at the line level except for downtime, which can be created at both machine and line levels. In SAP OEE 15.1, this feature is enhanced and extended to data collection at the machine level as well. Similar to line-level reporting, data collections at the machine level can be handled manually through the operator dashboard or automatically through customizations.

There are three activities that govern this functionality as explained here:

- ACT_RPT_PRD_MAC: This, when configured, allows you to indicate that a reported machine's data affects the line KPI.
- ACT_GENERIC_MAC: This activity allows you to collect machine-specific data.
- ACT_ORD_IND_MAC: This activity allows you to collect data at the machine level that are order independent.

■ **Note** Reporting at the machine level is totally independent to reporting at the line level and does not affect the line KPI, unless the "Impacts Line" checkbox is selected when reporting.

Refer to Figure 8-8, where you can see that the line and its respective machines, which are used for order execution, are listed, and on selection of the line or machine, you can report the different data collections.

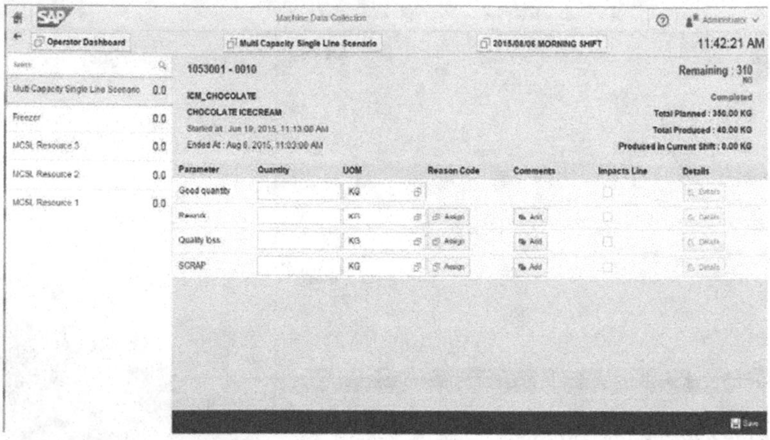

***Figure 8-8.** Machine data collection*

This feature enables the operator to capture the exact version of information from the shop floor at each machine level; these data are otherwise missed when reported at the line level, as the line level data is a consolidation of different data collection elements. Data collection at machine level is a use case when Line Behavior customization parameter is set to multi line multi capacity in General configuration. In this scenario, orders are started at individual capacity level and hence data collections are expected to be collected at machine level.

Manual Correction of Order Execution Data

In previous chapters, you have seen that the start time or the end time of an order can be edited to expand or shrink the order duration. At times, there can be a situation where the order under execution may have to be reverted to its original status of NEW from ACT or to be canceled altogether. It could be that the order was started by mistake, or that due to a decision the order execution is not required.

The Manage Orders screen of the OEE dashboard worker UI enables you to edit the start and end times of the already started order. From SAP OEE 15.1 version onward, this screen enables the operator to change the order status to NEW from ACT or to cancel the order. To do this, select the Details button for that order and then select the Set to New button. Refer to Figure 8-10.

To set the status to NEW, ensure that the reported order-dependent data such as production, scrap, and so on are deleted manually. Please note that the data can be deleted only if they are not confirmed to ERP as an extension of *Report Data* method. To abort an order, the order should be set to Hold first and the data collections are to be deleted. You can manually delete the reported data collections in the Report Production screen of the OEE dashboard for the selected order. Refer to Figure 8-9.

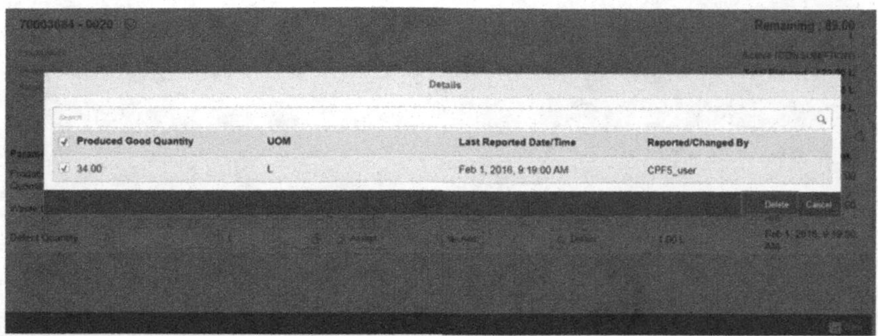

Figure 8-9. *Delete reported data*

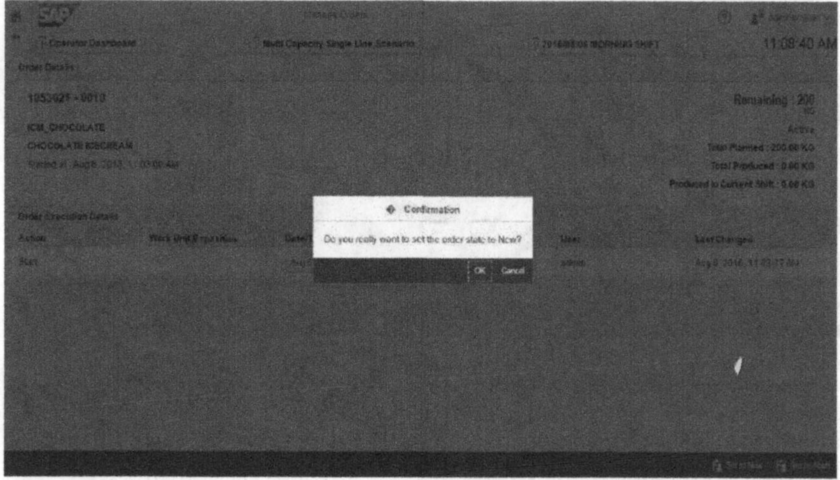

Figure 8-10. *Manual order correction*

Visual Icons and Customer Logo in the Dashboard

Multiple visual icons are added in this new version that can be used in the dashboard configuration worker UI while configuring dashboard buttons.

Refer to Figure 8-11 for a sample OEE dashboard, where you can see the dashboard buttons are configured with visual icons.

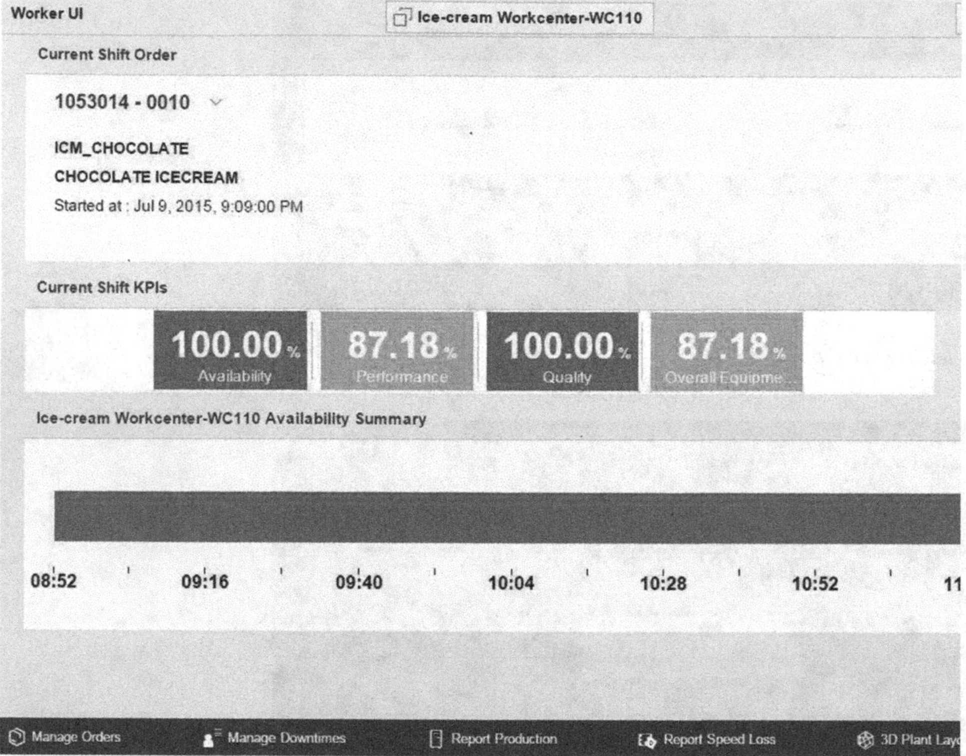

Figure 8-11. *Dashboard buttons configured with visual icons*

The customer's logo can be added in the OEE dashboard worker UI in place of the SAP logo. This is made possible by adding an additional configuration parameter "logo" in the dashboard configuration worker UI.

You need to maintain the image file in the web folder of the MII catalog in workbench and pass the entire URL of the image file to the logo field in the dashboard configuration worker UI. Refer to Figure 8-12.

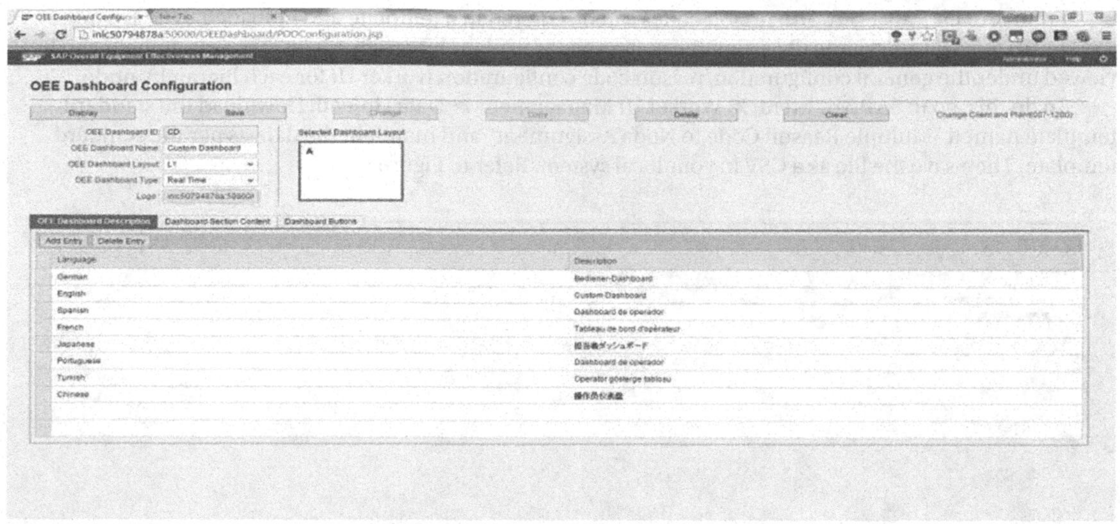

***Figure 8-12.** Dashboard configuration: configure logo*

Refer to Figure 8-13, where the configured customer logo is displayed in place of the SAP logo.

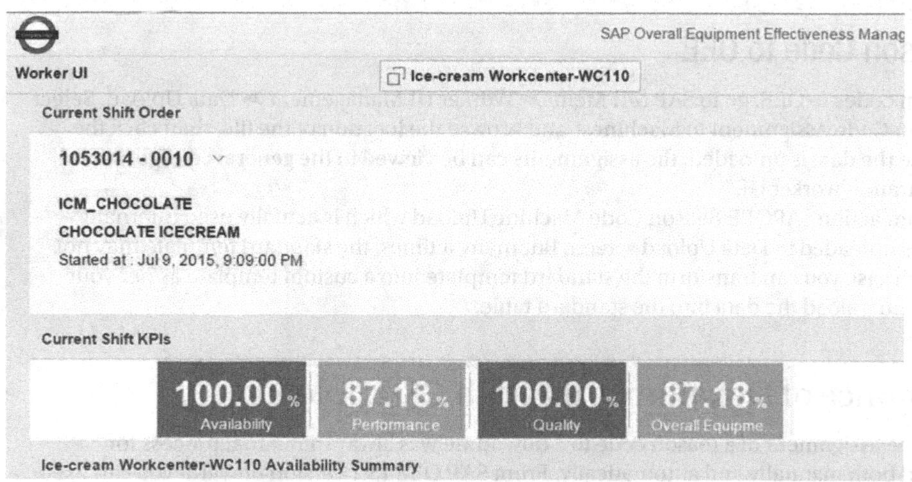

***Figure 8-13.** OEE dashboard: display customer logo*

Data Maintenance through CSV/XML Upload

Data Maintenance of Reason Codes through CSV Upload

In chapter 5, you learnt that specific set of reason codes structure can be assigned for each data collection element under General configuration / Reason code configuration. This basically ease the process of reason code assignment for the operators. Until SAP OEE 15.0, once the reason codes were transferred from SAP ERP to OEE, assignment of reason codes specific to a plant hierarchy node and a data collection element had to be entered manually under the general configuration/reason code configuration worker UI.

From SAP OEE 15.1 onward, reason codes can be entered in a template and uploaded to OEE using a worker UI; this will automatically assign the reason codes to plant hierarchy nodes. This assignment can be viewed under the general configuration/reason code configuration worker UI for each hierarchy node.

To do this, go to SAP MII Menu ➤ Worker UI Management ➤ Data Upload. Download the standard template named "Multiple Reason Code to Node Assignment" and maintain the data as per the standard template. Then save the file as a CSV in your local system. Refer to Figure 8-14.

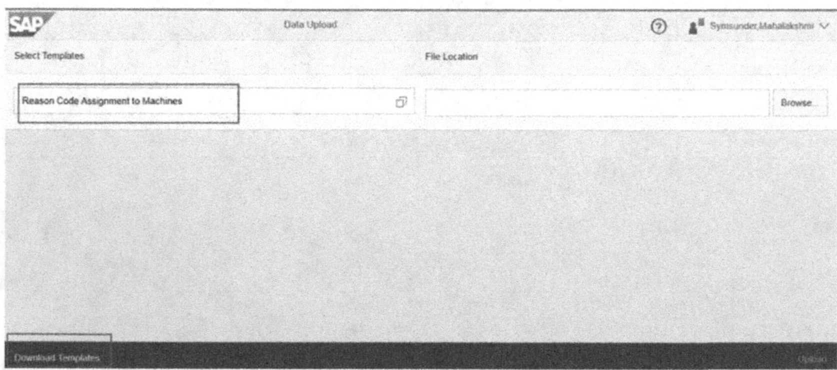

Figure 8-14. *Data upload: download templates*

Upload of Reason Code to OEE

To upload the reason codes to OEE, go to SAP MII Menu ➤ Worker UI Management ➤ Data Upload. Select the template "Reason Code Assignment to Machines" and browse the location of the file, then click the Upload button. Once the data is uploaded, the assignments can be viewed in the general configuration/reason code configuration worker UI.

There is a custom action SAPOEE Reason Code Machine Upload which is actually used internally when the template is uploaded in Data Upload screen. But many a times, the standard template may not be sufficient in which case you can transform the standard template into a custom template as per your requirements and then upload the data into the standard table.

Data Maintenance of Downtimes through CSV Upload

In earlier versions, the assignment of a reason code to a downtime was always a manual process for downtimes collected both manually and automatically. From SAP OEE 15.1 version onward, you can use a standard template to update all the planned and unplanned downtimes for a machine and work center along with the reason codes and then upload it to OEE. This is highly useful for the maintenance supervisor who plans for the scheduled downtimes. They can easily update the template with all the downtimes and upload it at one shot, avoiding the effort of creating the scheduled downtimes and assigning the reason codes individually.

You can download the standard template from SAP MII Menu ➤ Worker UI Management ➤ Data Upload.

In the downtime template, you can maintain machine or line downtimes and any custom data collection element of type time duration and save it to your local system.

Upload of Downtimes in OEE

To upload the downtimes in OEE, go to SAP MII Menu ➤ Worker UI Management ➤ Data Upload. Select the template "Downtimes" and browse the location of the file, then click the Upload button. Once the data is uploaded, the system updates the details in the respective tables. The downtimes can be viewed in the Manage Downtimes screen of the OEE dashboard worker UI. Once the downtime is updated to OEE tables, the respective line downtimes are automatically factored into KPI calculations.

Upload of Reason Code in OEE Add-on

Until SAP OEE 15.0, reason code upload in SAP OEE add-on in SAP ERP allowed you to upload the plant reason codes in CSV/XML format. At a later time, additional rows can be merged or the complete table can be overwritten.

From 15.1 onward, global and plant reason codes can be uploaded separately, and you can also merge or overwrite these reason codes separately. Refer to Figure 8-15.

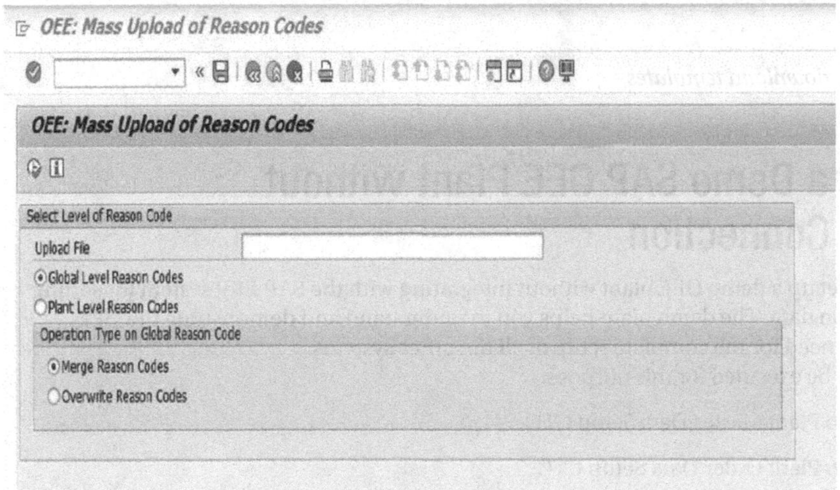

Figure 8-15. *Reason code upload in OEE add-on*

Also, there is the addition of a column for sequence number. Refer to Figure 8-16. This sequence number determines the way the reason codes will be sorted and listed in the reason code hierarchy for the operator to select. You need to determine and define this sequence number based on the way you want the operator to look at the reason codes, which will increase the operator's efficiency in reason-code selection.

Display View "Plant Reason Code Level 5": Details

Plant	0300
Reason Code 1	G1
Reason Code 2	G2
Reason Code 3	G3
Reason Code 4	EPL
Reason Code 5	00400

Plant Reason Code Level 5

Mark for Deletion	
Sequence Number	
Catalog	
Code group	
Code	
Type	UNSCD_DOWN
Description	PALLETIZER
Reason	1

Figure 8-16. *Data upload: download templates*

Quick Setup of a Demo SAP OEE Plant without Having an ERP Connection

In SAP OEE 15.1, you can set up a demo OEE plant without integrating with the SAP ERP system for setting up master and configuration data. The demo plant helps you to understand and demonstrate the OEE functionalities without the need for the complete setup of all the other systems.

There are two CTCs to be executed for this purpose:

- SAP OEE Demo Plant Master Data Setup CTC
- SAP OEE Demo Plant Order Data Setup CTC

SAP OEE Demo Plant Master Data Setup CTC

This CTC sets up the ERP-related master data required to run the OEE system. To execute the CTC, go to Netweaver ➤ Configuration ➤ Scenarios ➤ Configuration Wizard.

Search for OEE CTCs and select "SAP OEE Demo Plant Master Data Setup CTC." Click the Start button. Refer to Figures 8-17 to 8-19.

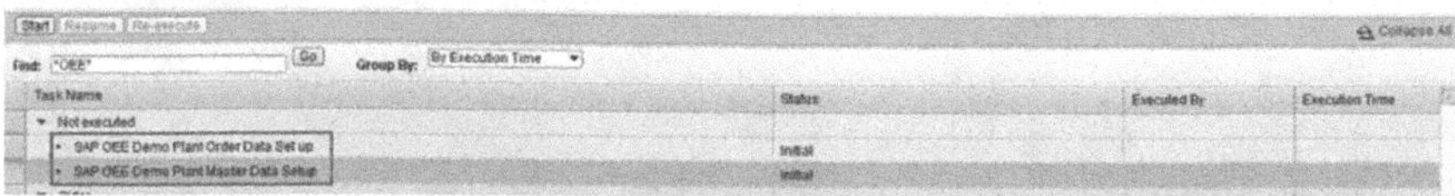

Figure 8-17. *Netweaver configuration wizard*

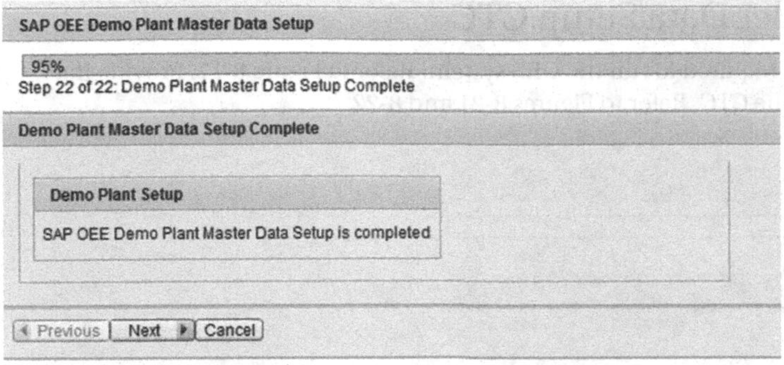

SAP OEE Demo Plant Master Data Setup

95%

Step 22 of 22: Demo Plant Master Data Setup Complete

Demo Plant Master Data Setup Complete

Demo Plant Setup

SAP OEE Demo Plant Master Data Setup is completed

Previous | Next | Cancel

Figure 8-18. *SAP OEE demo plant master-data setup*

SAP OEE Demo Plant Master Data Setup

100%

Finished "SAP OEE Demo Plant Master Data Setup"

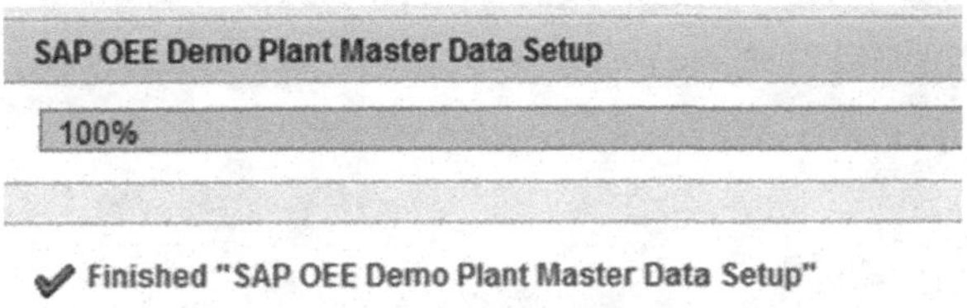

Figure 8-19. *SAP OEE demo plant master-data setup completion*

After this CTC is executed, go to SAP MII main menu ➤ ERP-Shop Floor Integration ➤ Queue Monitor, where you can see that all the master data, OEE-specific master data, and configuration data are queued for processing. Once all these messages are processed successfully, you can see the demo plant hierarchy under the general configuration worker UI. Refer to Figure 8-20.

In General configuration, for the plant node, set the line behavior to "Mark Line Down When Any Bottleneck Is Down." Assign the standard operator dashboard to user group "Everyone" under the general configuration/usergroup dashboard assignment worker UI. With this, all the users will be able to access the dashboard specific to demo hierarchy.

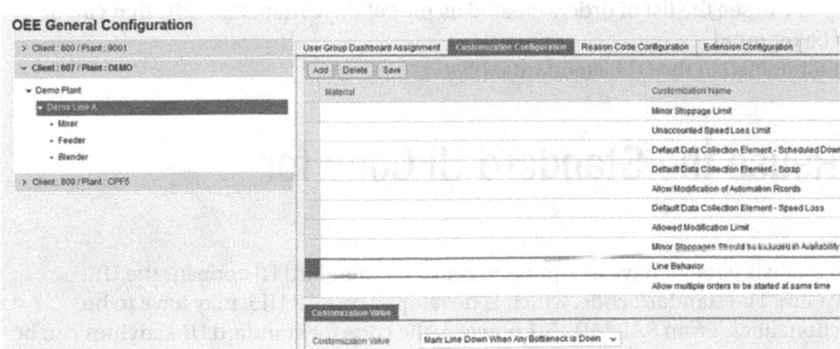

Figure 8-20. *Demo plant hierarchy*

SAP OEE Demo Plant Order Data Setup CTC

This CTC sets up the order-related data required to run the OEE system. Refer to Figure 8-17. Provide the SAP OEE Integrator password and run the CTC. Refer to Figures 8-21 and 8-22.

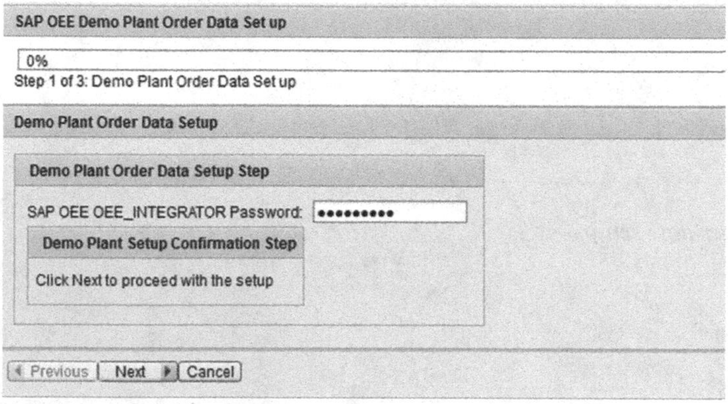

SAP OEE Demo Plant Order Data Set up

0%

Step 1 of 3: Demo Plant Order Data Set up

Demo Plant Order Data Setup

Demo Plant Order Data Setup Step

SAP OEE OEE_INTEGRATOR Password: ●●●●●●●●●

Demo Plant Setup Confirmation Step

Click Next to proceed with the setup

Previous | Next | Cancel

Figure 8-21. *SAP OEE demo plant order-data setup*

SAP OEE Demo Plant Order Data Set up

100%

Finished "SAP OEE Demo Plant Order Data Set up"

View Log Return to Task List

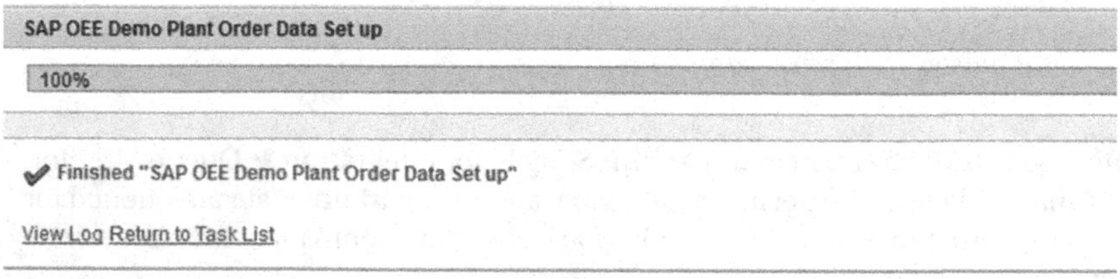

Figure 8-22. *SAP OEE demo plant order-data setup completion*

Once this CTC is executed, you can see a list of orders queued up in Queue Monitor. Once all the orders are processed, the sample OEE dashboard is available for running the system with the demo data setup. On the Manage Orders screen, you can see the list of orders created as part of the Order Data CTC that can be started and whose data can be reported.

The reported data are maintained in the OEE standard tables.

Download and Reuse the Standard UI Code for Customization

Many times, developers feel that it is good to have an option to reuse the standard UI code for the UI activities provided with SAP OEE. The standard code, which is developed on SAP UI5, may have to be enhanced with custom functionalities. From SAP MII 15.1 onward, the code for standard UI activities can be downloaded from the activity configuration worker UI.

To download the UI code, go to SAP MII Menu ➤ Worker UI Management ➤ Activity Configuration. Select a standard UI activity from the list and click the Download Activity button. Refer to Figure 8-23.

Activity Configuration

Create Activity | Display | Change Activity | Download Activity | Delete

Activity ID	Class or URL	Activity Ty
ACT_OPEN_DOWNS	sap.oee.ui.openDownsTile	UI
ACT_ORD	sap.oee.ui.oeeSelectOrder	UI
ACT_ORDER_CARD	sap.oee.ui.orderCardTile	UI
ACT_ORD_DET	sap.oee.ui.orderDetails	UI
ACT_ORD_IND	sap.oee.ui.oeeReportOrderIndependentDataCollection	UI
ACT_ORD_IND_MAC	sap.oee.ui.oeeReportOrderIndependentMachineDat...	UI
ACT_PLANT_MONITOR	sap.oee.ui.plantMonitor	UI
ACT_PM_NOTIF_LIST	sap.oee.ui.oeeNotificationList	UI

Figure 8-23. *Download standard activity*

This will download the `controller.js` and `view.xml` files of the UI code in a new page. The controller has the business logic implemented in the activity, and the XML view file has the XML structure of the view, which controls how the activity is rendered in the dashboard. This functionality ensures high reusability of standard functionality with less development effort.

Application Launch Pad for Goods Movement

Until MII 15.0, SAP OEE handled goods movement as follows:

- Raw material consumption can be collected manually from dashboard or automatically through service interfaces. (From 15.1 onward, these interfaces are obsolete.)
- Goods movement (goods receipt of finished goods and goods issue of raw materials) happens along with order confirmation using the `ORDER_CONFIRM_BAPI` workflow.

From 15.1 onward, goods movement is handled using the Goods Issue and Goods Receipt app available via the Application Launch Pad.

Operators can use this app to do the following:

- Get the raw material batch (for bulk consumption) /handling unit (SSCC) details during Goods issue process
- Post goods issue of raw material consumed
- Reverse raw materials used in the production process
- Generate batch for finished goods during Goods Receipt process
- Post goods receipt against a production or process order available in MII OEE
- Reverse the posted goods receipt and repost it

On the shop floor, an operator mostly has to move around for recording via barcode scanning (if available) the raw materials consumed during the production process. The Goods Movement Application in SAP OEE is device agnostic and can be accessed from any mobile device, so the raw material consumption and goods receipt recording can be done on the move.

This app is available under the worker UI management menu in the SAP MII Menu after the SAP OEE configuration CTC has run.

The app supports the consumption of both HU (Handling Unit) managed and bulk materials consumption. These apps are built in such a way that the UI interface contains backend configurations where a transaction can be configured as per customer requirements. This gives flexibility to customers to use the Goods Issue and Goods Receipt application UI, but also have the backend transactions be configurable.

Configurations Required to Use the Goods Movement App Customization Configuration

At The plant node level, set the customization "SAP OEE Application Transaction Mode" to online or offline in the general configuration/customization configuration worker UI. The Goods Movement App can be integrated with ECC or EWM system. For EWM system, SAP will deliver standard transactions for integration in future release of MII. For ECC integration, custom transactions have to be developed. By default, the value is set to online. When set to online, the system understands that connection is good between OEE and ERP/EWM system. When set to offline, the system understands the presence of a custom transaction and uses the same to post the goods movement. For custom interfaces, custom logic needs to be developed by SAP MII BLS transactions as per the plant requirements. The mode helps to pick up the relevant transactions from the activities. This customization also provides the option to configure the transaction when the mode is changed.

By default, OEE delivers the standard UI and interfaces for goods movement. You can choose to use the standard UI and add custom interfaces as per the plant requirements.

Activity Configuration

You need to configure the following activities in order to configure the apps on the launch pad:

1. Choose "Create Activity."
2. Enter the relevant activity ID (`ACT_STD_COMP_GI` for Goods Issue and `ACT_STD_COMP_GR` for Goods Receipt).
3. Select UI Component as the Activity Type.
4. Enter the URL. For GI, use `sap.oee.m.goodsissue`. For GR, use `sap.oee.m.goodsreceipt`. Refer to Figures 8-24 to 8-26.

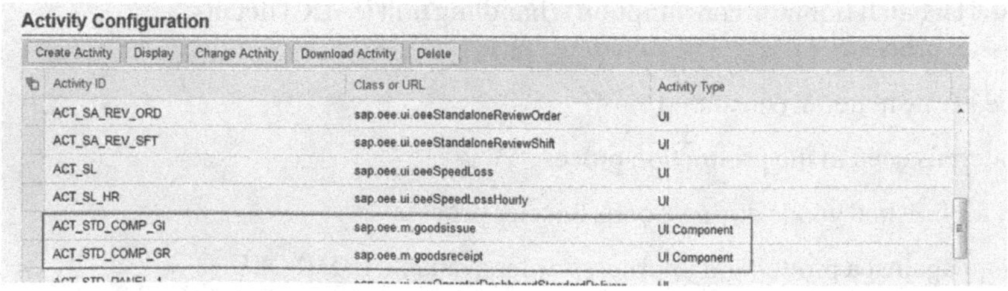

Activity Configuration

Create Activity | Display | Change Activity | Download Activity | Delete

Activity ID	Class or URL	Activity Type
ACT_SA_REV_ORD	sap.oee.ui.oeeStandaloneReviewOrder	UI
ACT_SA_REV_SFT	sap.oee.ui.oeeStandaloneReviewShift	UI
ACT_SL	sap.oee.ui.oeeSpeedLoss	UI
ACT_SL_HR	sap.oee.ui.oeeSpeedLossHourly	UI
ACT_STD_COMP_GI	sap.oee.m.goodsissue	UI Component
ACT_STD_COMP_GR	sap.oee.m.goodsreceipt	UI Component

Figure 8-24. *Goods Movement app activity*

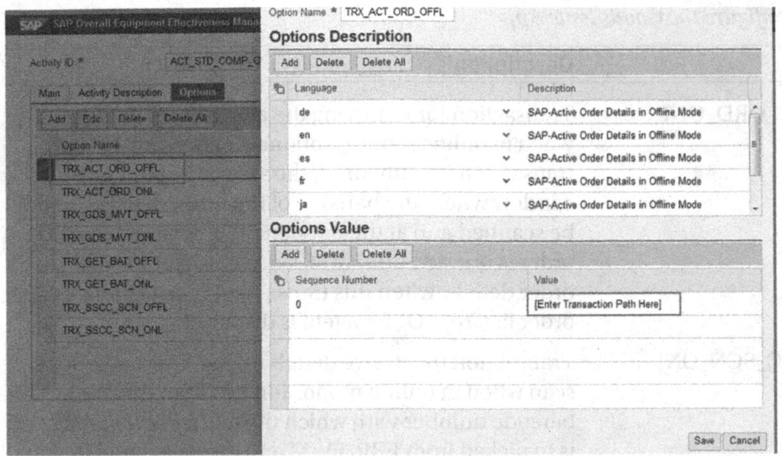

Figure 8-25. *Goods Issue: online/offline transaction options*

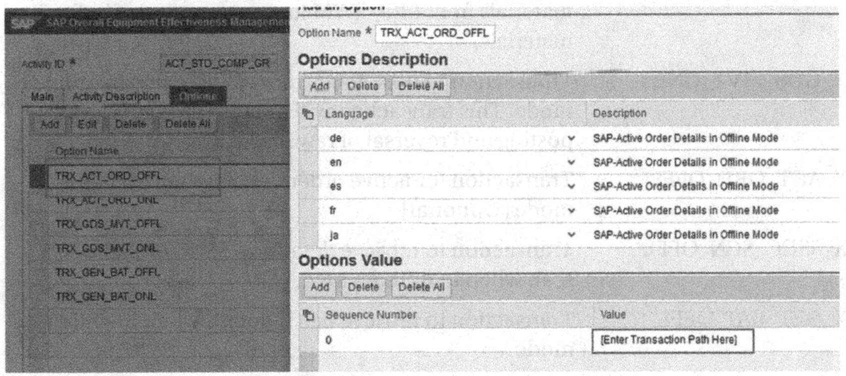

Figure 8-26. *Goods Receipt: online/offline transaction options*

Activity Options to Configure the Goods Issue App

Refer to Table 8-1 to configure the options for the preceding created activities. These options are governed by the customization "SAP OEE Application Transaction Mode." Based on the mode set for this parameter, the respective transactions are called and executed.

Table 8-1. Activity Options to Configure the Goods Issue App

Activity	Options	Description
ACT_STD_COMP_GI	TRX_ACT_ORD_ONL	Transaction for retrieving the active order details when in online mode (Optional). When this custom transaction is configured, the system popup up a window where the barcode of the order details should be scanned and at the back end, the scanned barcode order is queried from MES systemt to display the order details. when this transaction is not configured, order list from OEE system is displayed.
	TRX_SSCC_SCN_ONL	Transaction to retrieve details on SSCC or barcode scan when in online mode. You can scan the SSCC barcode number with which the material availability is to picked from ERP/EWM and displayed for GI posting.
	TRX_GET_BAT_ONL	Transaction to retrieve batch details when in online mode. This transaction is to get the batch number of materials from ERP/EWM for consumption of bulk materials.
	TRX_GDS_MVT_ONL	Transaction to post goods movement when in online mode. This transaction will handle the goods issue posting and reversal of raw materials.
	TRX_ACT_ORD_OFFL	Transaction for active order details when in offline mode (Optional)
	TRX_SSCC_SCN_OFFL	Transaction to retrieve details on SSCC or barcode scan when in offline mode
	TRX_GET_BAT_OFFL	Transaction to retrieve batch details when in offline mode
	TRX_GDS_MVT_OFFL	Transaction to post goods movement when in offline mode
	TRX_GDS_MVT_RPT_ONL	Transaction to generate a report of all goods movement done in online mode. Once the transaction is configured, a button is enabled in GI screen. On click of the button, the custom transaction should return data as a specific output XML, which is displayed in a tabular format on the screen. Refer to Appendix for input and output xml format
	TRX_GDS_MVT_RPT_OFFL	Transaction to generate a report of all goods movement done in offline mode

Activity Options to Configure the Goods Receipt App

Refer to Table 8-2 to configure the activity options for setting up Goods Receipt functionality of Goods Movement App.

Table 8-2. *Activity Options to Configure the Goods Receipt App*

Activity	Options	Description
ACT_STD_COMP_GR	TRX_ACT_ORD_ONL	Transaction for active order details when in online mode (Optional)
	TRX_GEN_BAT_ONL	Transaction to generate batch details when in online mode. This transaction is to call a RFC in ERP/EWM to generate the batch for the finished goods for which the GR is to posted
	TRX_GDS_MVT_ONL	Transaction to post goods movement (posting and reversal of goods receipt) when in online mode
	TRX_ACT_ORD_OFFL	Transaction for active order details when in offline mode (Optional)
	TRX_GEN_BAT_OFFL	Transaction to generate batch details when in offline mode
	TRX_GDS_MVT_OFFL	Transaction to post goods movement when in offline mode
	TRX_GDS_MVT_RPT_ONL	Transaction to generate a report of all goods movement done in online mode. Once the transaction is configured, a button is enabled in GR screen. On click of the button, the custom transaction should return data as a specific output XML, which is displayed in a tabular format on the screen. Refer to Appendix for input and output xml format
	TRX_GDS_MVT_RPT_OFFL	Transaction to generate a report of all goods movement done in offline mode.
	TRX_GDS_MVT_PKG_ONL	Transaction to fetch the package ID in online mode. In GR screen, there is a field package ID which corresponds to "HU_NO" field of MPM_GOODS_MVT_DATA table. If HU_NO is maintained in ERP, you can fetch the details from ERP else you can maintain transaction against this activity option. Refer to Appendix for input and output XML formats.
	TRX_GDS_MVT_PKG_OFFL	Transaction to fetch the package ID in offline mode. In GR screen, there is a field package ID which corresponds to "HU_NO" field of MPM_GOODS_MVT_DATA table. If HU_NO is maintained in ERP, you can fetch the details from ERP else you can maintain transaction against this activity option. Refer to Appendix for input and output XML formats.

In summary the transactions for online mode would ideally make a synchronous RFC call to ERP/EWM for fetching the details and posting of GR and GI. The transactions for offline mode would have to archive all the GM details locally in a custom table for synchronisation only the system connection is restored.

Dashboard Configuration

The default dashboard SAP_APP_LP_POD is delivered as a standard dashboard for the purpose of Application Launch Pad. Using this as a placeholder, you can copy and configure your own custom launch pad under the dashboard configuration worker UI. This dashboard is the placeholder to which to add the standard apps–Goods Receipt and Goods Issue–and also to add custom apps. The apps appear as tiles in the launch pad, and it also shows which activities of type "UI Component" should be configured. From OEE 15.1, "UI Component" is the new activity type added. This is specific for Application launch pad type dashboards. Ensure the custom app is defined as UI component type activity under the activity configuration worker UI before configuring in dashboard configuration.

Configure the Application Launch Pad

1. Copy the default dashboard SAP_APP_LP_POD. Maintain the dashboard type as "Application Launch Pad."

   Only dashboards of this type are displayed on Application Launch Pad.

2. Assign the activities you created for the apps as dashboard buttons.

   1. Select the Dashboard tab and choose Add Entry.
   2. Enter the relevant activity in the Button ID field.
   3. Add the activities created for the apps.

You can add activities of type UI Component or External App.

Goods Movement Process

The Application Launch Pad looks like this when configured with the two apps. Refer to Figure 8-27.

***Figure 8-27.** Application Launch Pad*

Goods Issue

Select the Goods Issue app from the launch pad, and the UI will list all the orders with their details, such as order number, material, material description, planned start, and quantity. Refer to Figure 8-28. If a custom transaction is configured for active order list inGI activity, then scan barcode popup will be displayed when GI tile is launched to scan the order number.

Products for Work Center Line3 for workcenter JK01 — Search: 100036

Order	Material Description	Material	Planned Start	Quantity
1000361	Sweet Muffin	MFG-MUFFIN-2	2016/04/07 00:00	100.00 EA >
1000360	Sweet Muffin	MFG-MUFFIN-2	2016/04/06 00:00	10.00 EA >
1000362	Sweet Muffin	MFG-MUFFIN-2	2016/04/06 00:00	10.00 EA >
1000363	Sweet Muffin	MFG-MUFFIN-2	2016/04/06 00:00	10.00 EA >
1000364	Sweet Muffin	MFG-MUFFIN-2	2016/01/29 00:00	100.00 EA >
1000365	Sweet Muffin	MFG-MUFFIN-2	2016/01/29 00:00	100.00 EA >
1000366	Sweet Muffin	MFG-MUFFIN-2	2016/02/01 00:00	100.00 EA >

***Figure 8-28.** Goods Movement: order selection*

Select an order from the list for which raw material consumption needs to be posted. The orders can be searched using the search box. Refer to Figure 8-29.

Sweet Muffin (1000363) — 10.00 EA

Actual Start Date : 2016/04/06 00:00:00

Material Number : MFG-MUFFIN-2

Material — Search

Material Number	Material Description	Required Qty	Consumed Qty	Status	Action
MFG-BUTTER-2	Butter	10 KG	0 KG	0KG / 10KG	Scan
MFG-EGG-2	Egg	5 EA	0 EA	0EA / 5EA	Scan
MFG-SUGAR-2	Sugar	15 KG	0 KG	0KG / 15KG	Scan

***Figure 8-29.** Goods Movement: component list*

Select the components and enter the quantity manually or scan the SSCC barcode number which fetches the material availability from ERP/EWM and displays it for consumption then post it. Refer to Figure 8-30. The Goods Issue is posted, and the material document number is created and displayed. Refer to Figures 8-30 and 8-31.

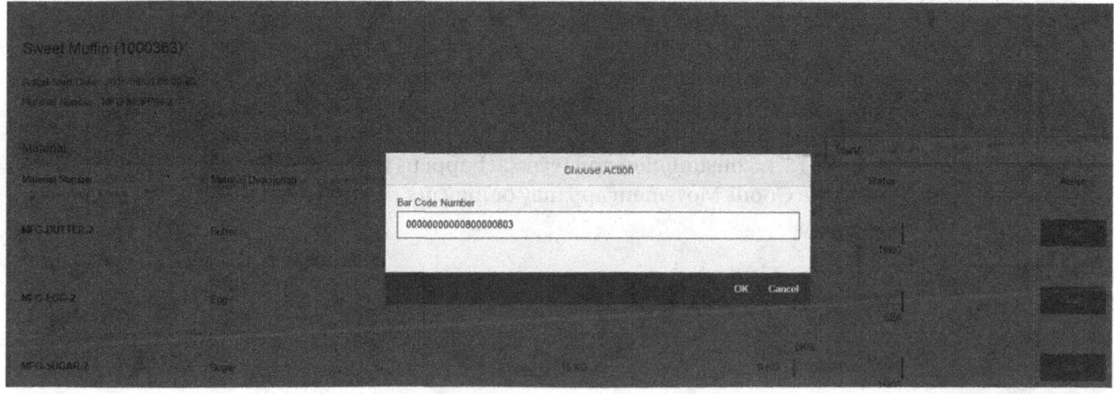

***Figure 8-30.** Goods Movement: scan/enter the quantity*

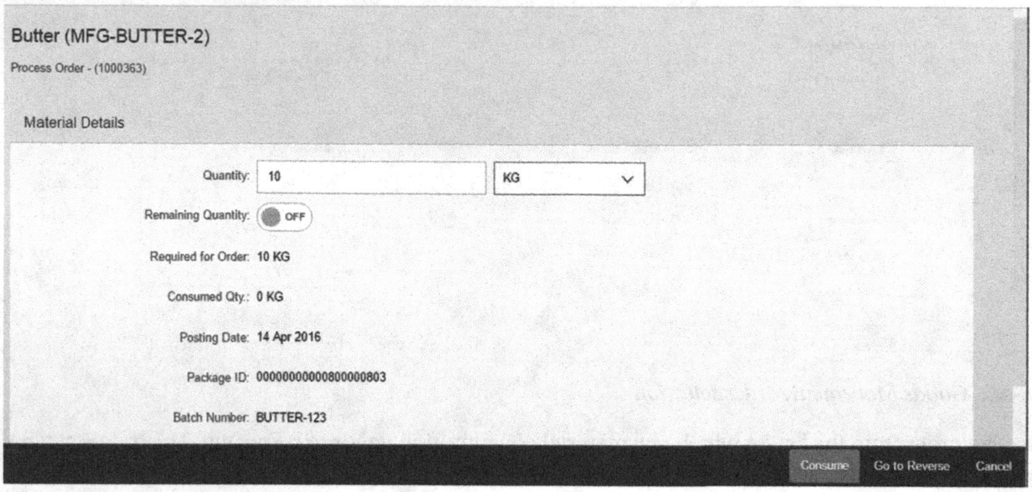

Figure 8-31. *Goods Movement: data posting*

Refer to Figure 8-32 where the consumption is posted and the consumption data is updated visually against the material.

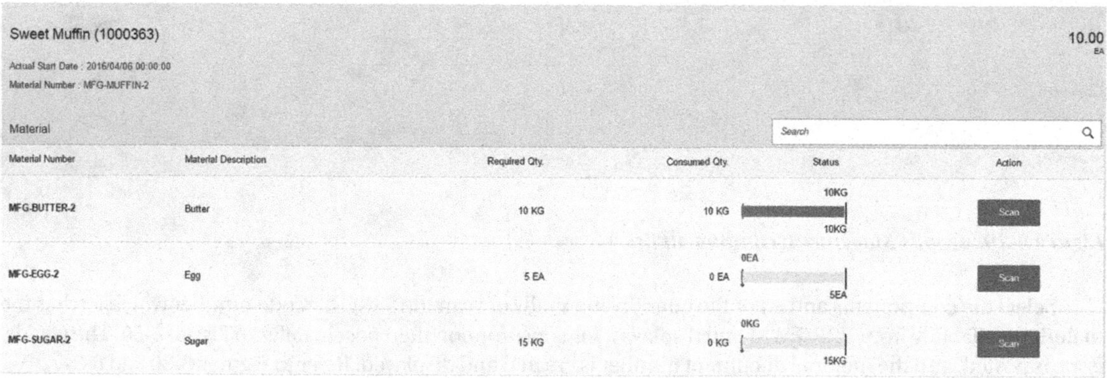

Figure 8-32. *Goods Movement: Consumption posted*

For reversal, scan the SSCC barcode number again and select button Go to reverse and do the reversal of quantities. In case of no SSCC details, select the component material and quantity to be reversed.

From 15.1 SP01, the Declare (consumption) and reverse are placed as separate buttons and can be navigated. In the earlier SP of 15.1, consumption and reversal happens in the same button.

The orders handled in the Goods Movement app may or may not be started in OEE.

Goods Receipt

To post the produced yield, or goods receipt, of finished goods, select an order from the list of those whose finished goods production needs to be posted. Refer to Figures 8-33 and 8-34.

Figure 8-33. *Goods Receipt: list and select orders*

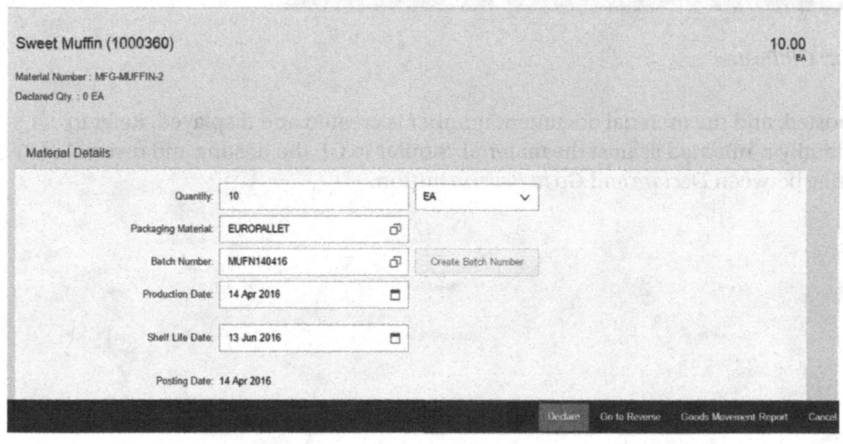

Figure 8-34. *Goods Receipt: list and select orders*

Enter the quantity manually, or it can be scanned (if available for finished goods), then declare it. Refer to Figure 8-34. *Create Batch Number* can be selected to generate a batch number from GR page for the finished goods.

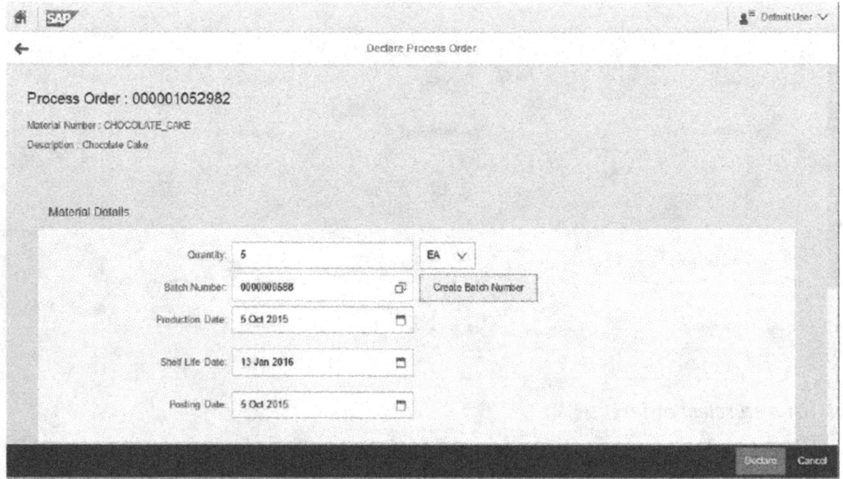

Figure 8-35. *Goods Receipt: GR Posted*

The goods receipt is posted, and the material document number is created and displayed. Refer to Figure 8-36. The posted quantity is updated against the material. Similar to GI, the posting and reversal of GR can be done by navigating between *Declare* and *Go to Reverse* button.

Products for Work Center Line3 for workcenter JK01 — 36

Order	Material Description	Material	Planned Start	Declared Qty.	Status
1000361	Sweet Muffin	MFG-MUFFIN-2	2016/04/07 00:00	13.00 EA	13EA / 100EA
1000360	Sweet Muffin	MFG-MUFFIN-2	2016/04/06 00:00	10.00 EA	10EA / 10EA
1000362	Sweet Muffin	MFG-MUFFIN-2	2016/04/06 00:00	0.00 EA	0EA / 10EA
1000363	Sweet Muffin	MFG-MUFFIN-2	2016/04/06 00:00	1.00 EA	1EA / 10EA

Figure 8-36. *Goods Receipt: material document creation*

Use Case for Goods Movement

The Goods Movement app is suited to working with both SAP ECC update and SAP EWM update.

For both types of update, the app provides you with the standard UI and a placeholder in which to plug custom transactions.

■ **Note** Standard transactions for SAP EWM update are expected to be delivered by SAP in future releases.

Summary

In this chapter, you have learned about the OEE features that were enhanced as part of the release of SAP MII 15.1.

In the next chapter, you will learn about the analytics component of SAP HANA, what HANA Live is, about table replication from OEE to HANA, and how analytics work using SAP Lumira on SAP MII.

CHAPTER 9

SAP OEE: Reporting and Analytics

This chapter will explain the different options SAP OEE provides for reporting and analytics. It will cover the options for both local single-plant-based analytics and global consolidated analytics for the entire corporation.

The whole purpose of SAP OEE as a solution is to support the production operator so as to have one single user interface (the SAP OEE worker UI) for all of his or her computer-related work during the production shift, and also to be the continuous improvement tool for plant performance management team by providing meaningful insights into the data collected from the shop floor.

As we have already learned, to operate on the OEE worker UI, one needs master data, which is retrieved by MII OEE from the SAP ERP system. On the worker UI, the operator reports production-related data (e.g., yield, scrap, rework, and so on) and loss-related data (e.g., downtimes and speed losses), either manually or by automatic means via shop-floor automation. When a loss is reported the system allows the operator to also assign related reasons for the loss. The operators on the production line are the most knowledgeable in identifying the reason for any losses (unless the machines can do that automatically). Hence, the reason codes that are assigned for any losses during a shift are the most accurate way of capturing the root causes at their source. Once these losses and their reasons are captured by the worker UI, OEE reports are used in systematically reviewing the losses to discover any hidden areas for improvement.

The SAP OEE capabilities that provide insight into production performance can be categorized in three ways. Figure 9-1 shows the different reporting and analytics options available with SAP OEE.

D. Saha et al., *Manufacturing Performance Management using SAP OEE*,
DOI 10.1007/978-1-4842-1150-2_9

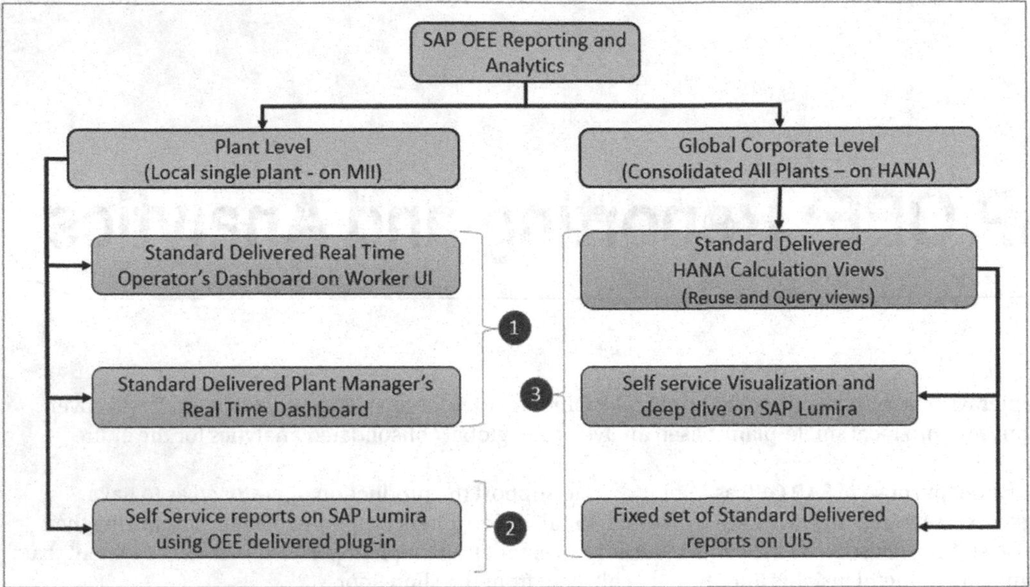

Figure 9-1. *Reporting and analytics options with SAP OEE*

Real-Time Dashboards: Worker UI (Dashboard) and Plant Monitor

When the production worker signs on to the SAP OEE worker UI, by default he is taken to the dashboard of the last work center he was working on. The dashboard shows some real-time KPIs and information to the production operator. SAP OEE delivers a standard set of real-time information on the worker UI dashboard, as follows:

- The active order information (what is being produced and how much is in the current production)
- The open downtimes (if the production line or any of the machines in the line are down)
- The top untagged events (the top losses that still do not have any reason code assigned to them)
- The OEE KPIs (availability, performance, and quality) as percentages for the current shift (combining all the orders that were executed in the current shift)
- The line performance strip showing line status for last four hours
- Top five downtimes in the shift

Figure 9-2 shows the real-time information on the worker UI dashboard.

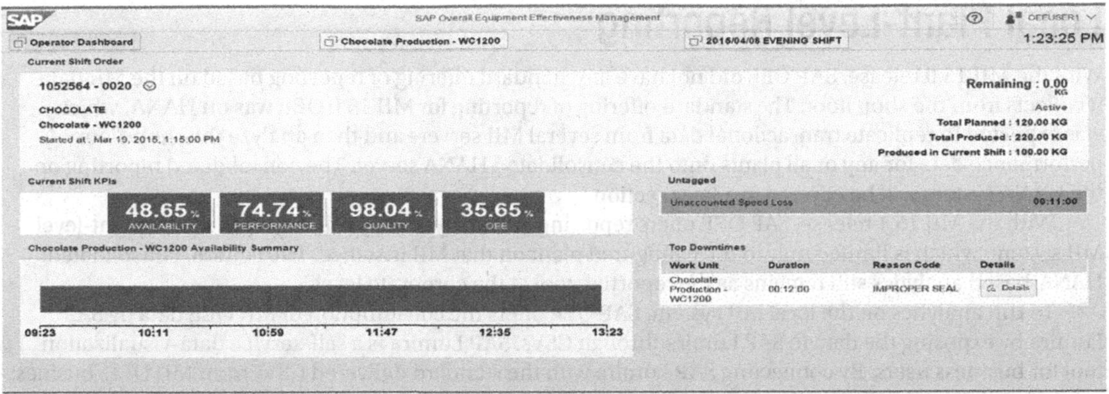

Figure 9-2. *Worker UI standard dashboard*

The SAP OEE also provides a plant monitor (plant manager's dashboard) where all the lines of the plant are shown with their current statuses. On clicking a line, it shows further detailed information on the specific line.

Figure 9-3 shows the real-time information of all production lines on the plant manager's dashboard.

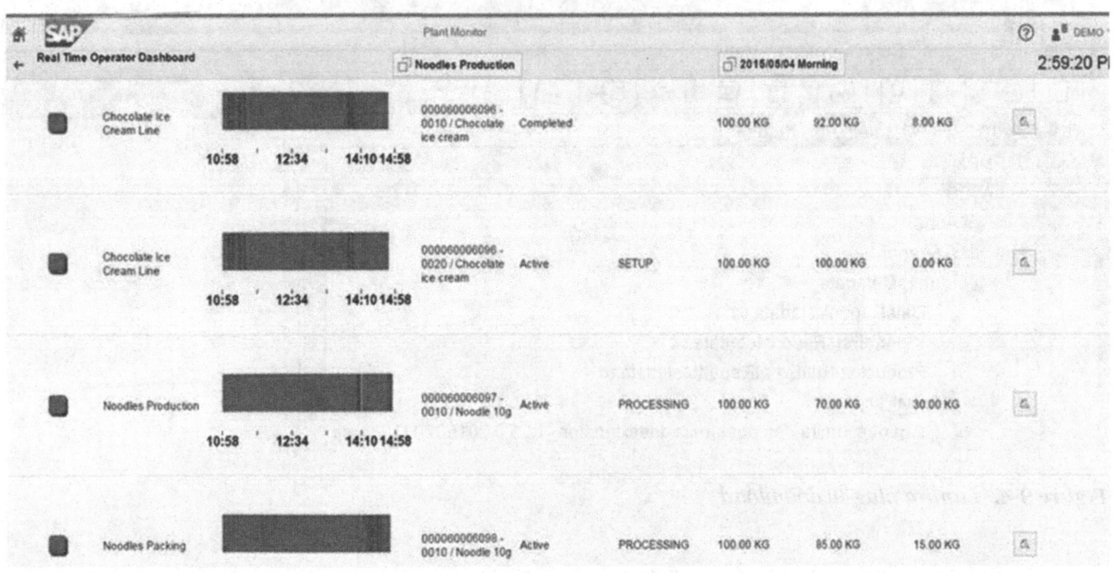

Figure 9-3. *Plant manager's standard dashboard (plant monitor)*

The real-time dashboard and the plant manager's dashboard are the two options delivered as the standard. But you are not limited to these two dashboards. Customers can create their own real-time dashboards through custom development within the SAP OEE framework and plug them in as custom dashboards.

Local Plant-Level Reporting

With the MII 15.0 release, SAP OEE did not have any standard offering of reporting based on the MII data it collects from the shop floor. The standard offering of reporting for MII 15.0 OEE was on HANA, which was expected to replicate transactional data from several MII servers and then analyze the shop-floor performance data for any or all plants onto the consolidated HANA server. The consolidated reporting on the HANA system will be covered in a later section.

With the MII 15.1 release, SAP OEE offers reporting and analytics capabilities on the local plant-level MII system, which is limited only to the configured plant on that MII instance. The central, consolidated, HANA-based analytics still remains as the reporting tool at the corporate level.

To run analytics on the local MII system, SAP OEE offers the consumption of MII OEE data by SAP Lumira by exposing the data to SAP Lumira through CSVs. SAP Lumira is a self-service data-visualization tool for business users. By connecting SAP Lumira with the standard delivered CSVs from MII OEE, business users can compose and visualize their own reports in SAP Lumira.

The following steps need to be done to set up SAP Lumira to connect to SAP OEE data in MII:

- Download Lumira plug-in from MII

Figure 9-4 shows the MII Workbench location at which to download the Lumira plug-in and metadata files. It is present in both the LumiraMetadata and LumiraPlugin folders in the SAPMPM project in the web catalog.

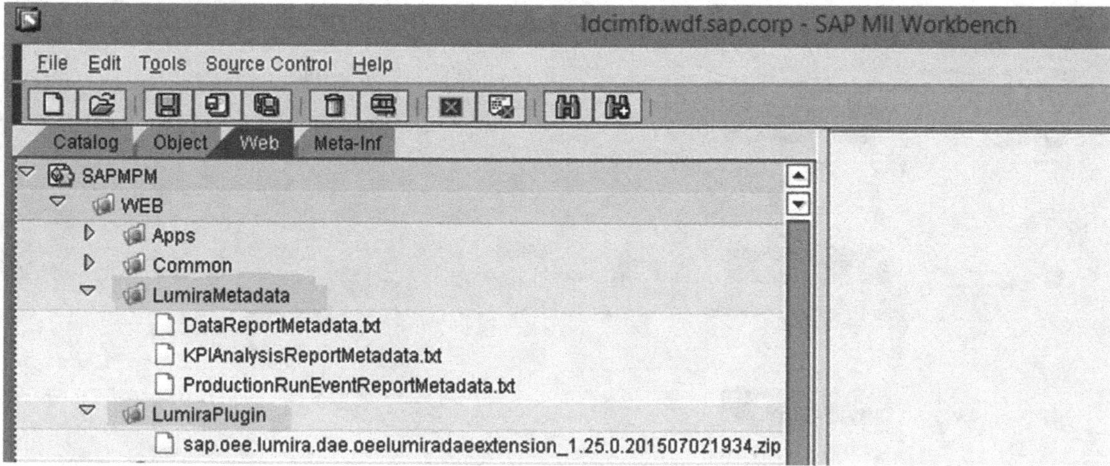

Figure 9-4. Lumira plug-in download

- Install the plug-in on SAP Lumira 1.25 or higher.

Install SAP Lumira desktop and, in the SAP Lumira menu, File ➤ Extensions, Select "Manual Installation" and choose the path for the downloaded Lumira plug-in.

Figure 9-5 shows the installation of OEE plug-in in Lumira.

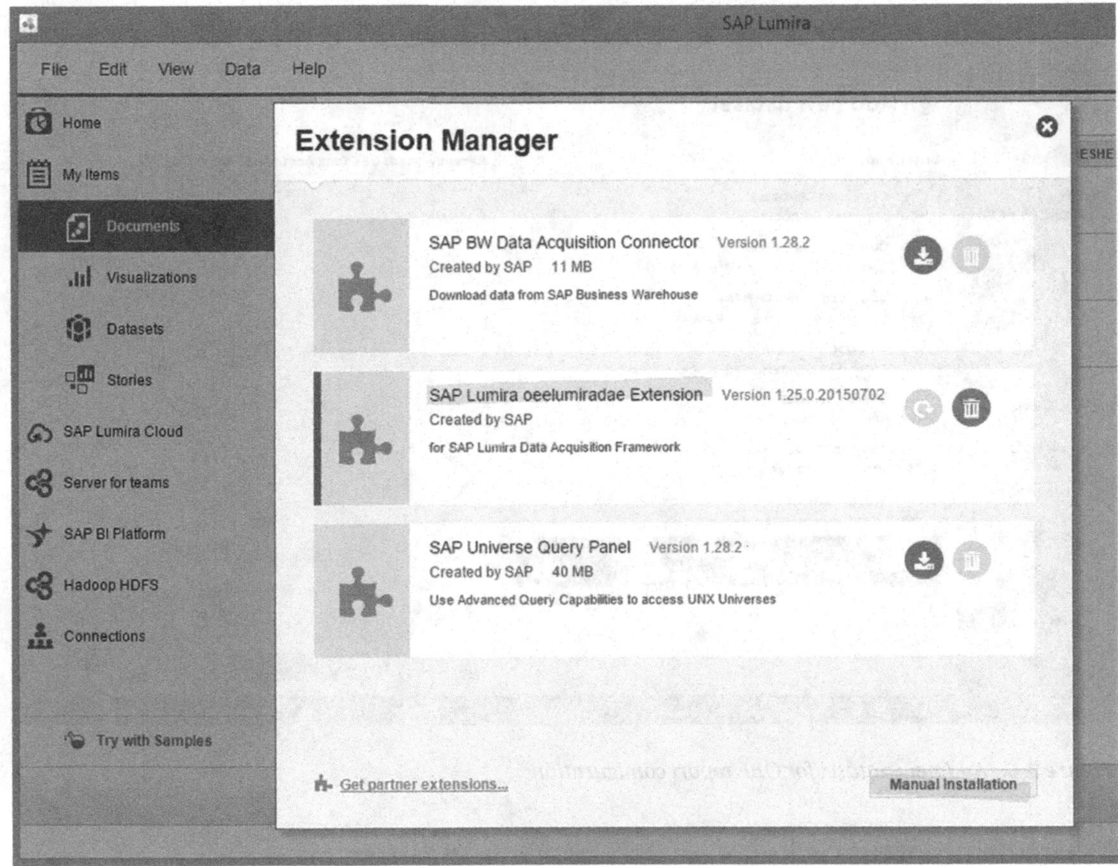

Figure 9-5. *SAP OEE Lumira extension installed*

- Configure Lumira with the OEE data acquisition extension and set the paths to the CSV dataset and the corresponding metadata.

From the Lumira menu, File ➤ New, select the OEE data acquisition extension and configure the path for the metadata and the CSV files. This needs to be done for all the CSV and metadata files.

Figure 9-6 shows adding a new dataset in SAP Lumira and selecting the newly installed extension.

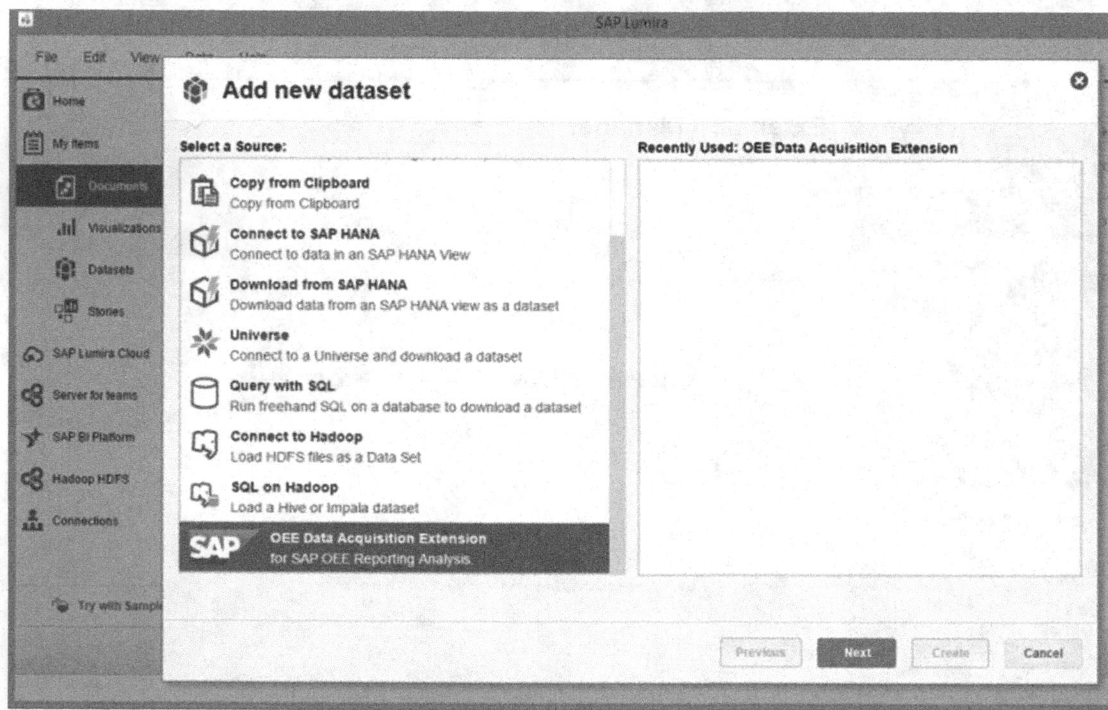

Figure 9-6. *Add new dataset for OEE report configuration*

Figure 9-7 shows the configuration of CSV and metadata files.

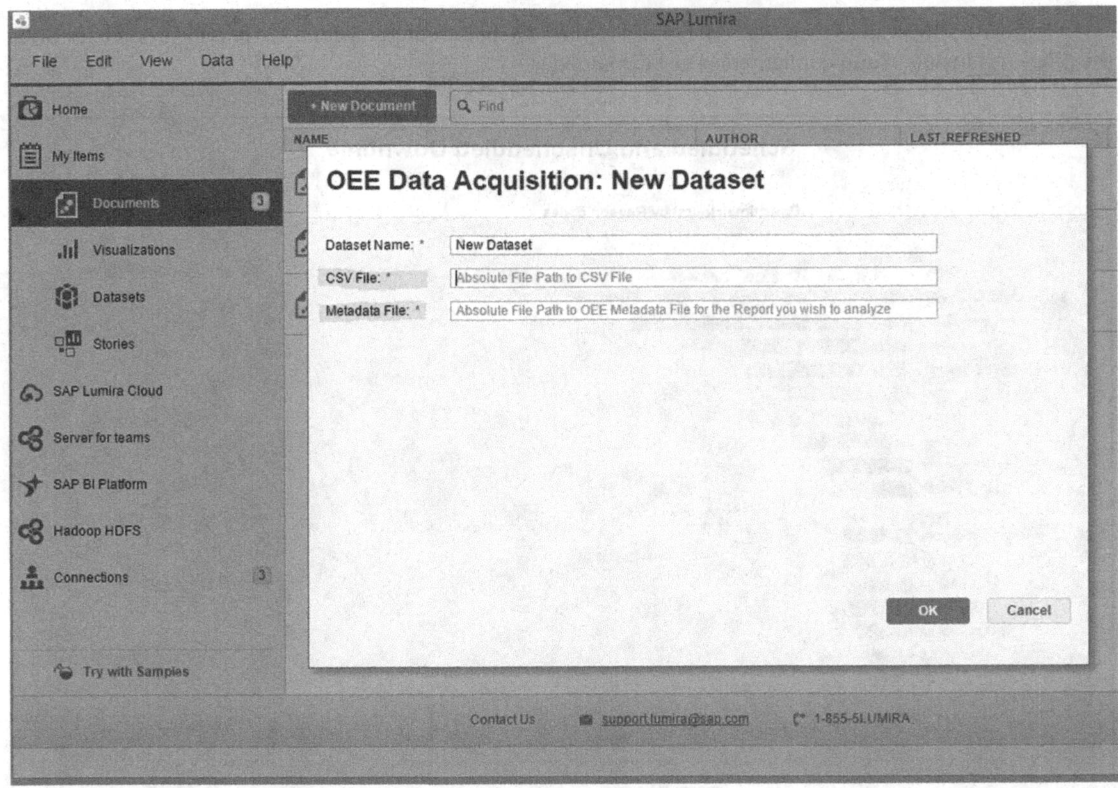

***Figure 9-7.** Configuration of Dateset in Lumira for SAP OEE reports*

- Start analyzing data in Lumira by creating own story boards through self-service by consuming the configured dataset.

Figure 9-8 shows an example of SAP Lumira report which is created through self service by an user, after the plug-in is installed and configured as just explained.

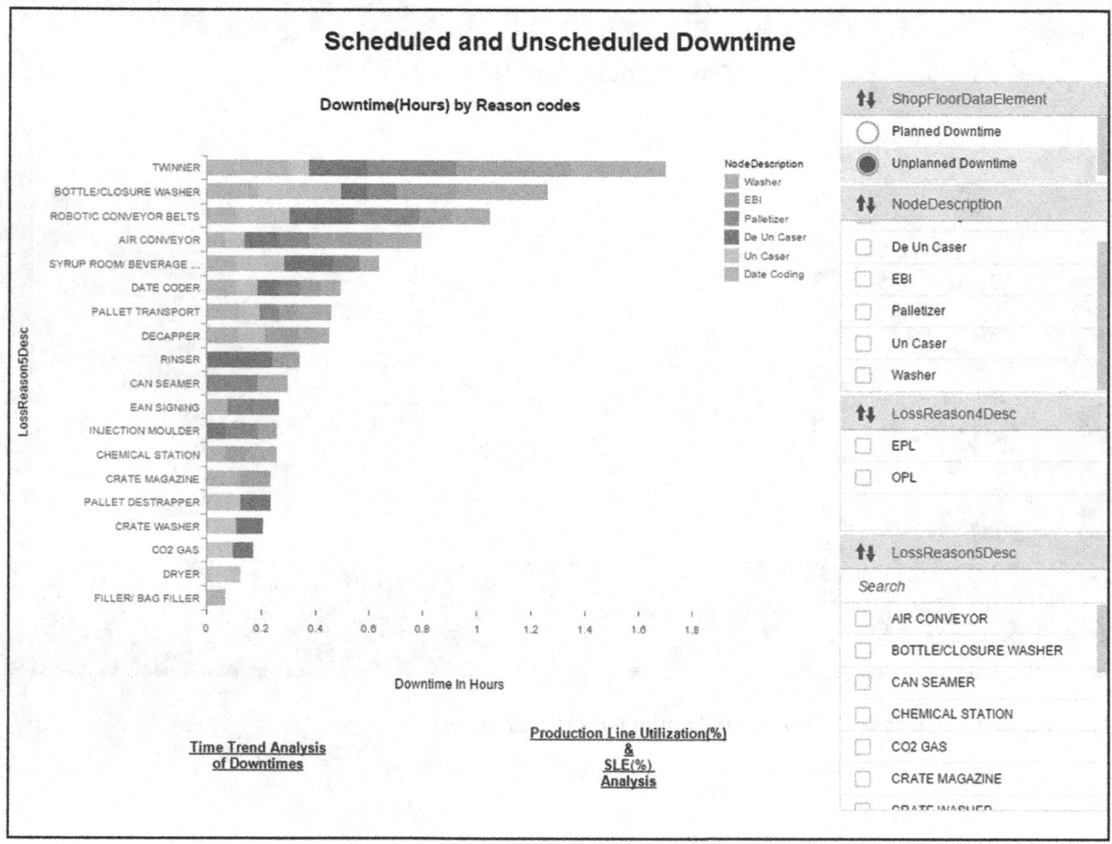

Figure 9-8. *Lumira report with plant-level data from MII*

The end user has to consume the dataset from these CSV files by creating storyboards in Lumira through self-service, as per business needs. The preceding figure shows a sample report (story board) created in Lumira, where the right side of the graph has all the filter criteria and also has navigation links to other reports at the bottom.

For more details about SAP Lumira, please check the `http://saplumira.com/`.

A FTP location and a scheduler needs to be configured so that Lumira is periodically updated with the latest data from MII. The following steps need to be performed to set up the periodic update of the files:

- Set up a folder in the network for the CSV files and configure the folder as an FTP location; provide "read" and "write" permission to the "anonymous" user, so that the scheduler can write the file into the location.
- Configure the scheduler `OEEAutoCsvDownloadForReports`, which gets added to the list after the OEE Integration CTC is run.

- By default, the standard sets the scheduler to run once every 24 hours, but this can be modified as required. Once the scheduler runs, the CSVs will be updated with new records. Currently, the scheduler picks up data for last 90 days.

Figure 9-9 shows the configuration of the scheduler and the FTP location for the CSV files.

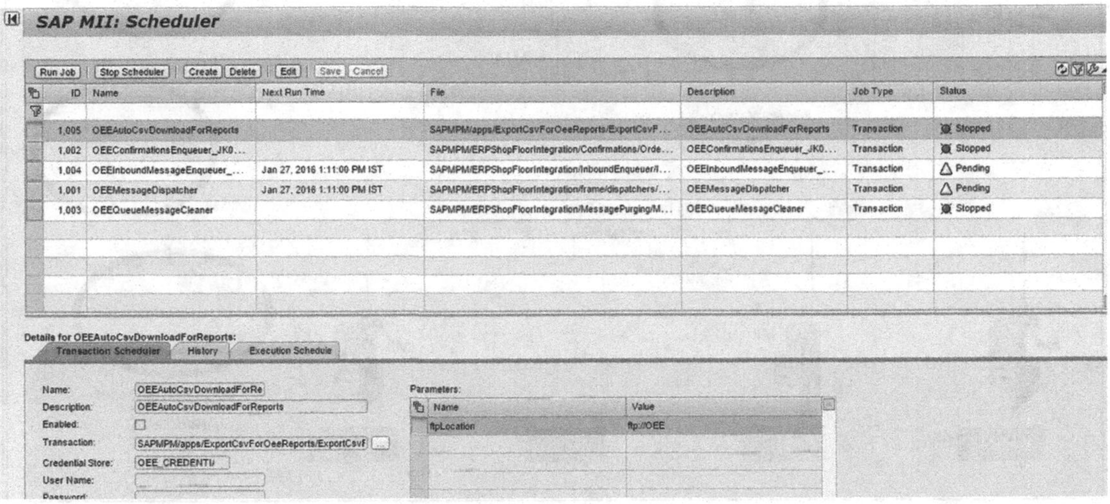

Figure 9-9. *Scheduler OEEAutoCsvDownloadForReports*

Global Consolidated Reporting at the Corporate Level with SAP HANA

As you learned in chapter 2, SAP OEE provides standard content on HANA, where the transactional data from all the plant-level MII servers is replicated. The standard HANA content of SAP OEE provides the capability to have reporting and analytics consolidated at a global level. It comes with a set of standard delivered HANA calculation views and a UI5 application to view the reports. The standard delivered UI5 application provides a limited set of reports to be viewed for any node across the corporation (e.g., corporation, region, country, plant, production line, and machines). But the HANA calculation views can also be consumed through various visualization tools like SAP Lumira, Analysis Office, Design Studio, and so on to deep-dive into the consolidated data exposed through the HANA calculation views. It is also possible to extend both the HANA calculation views and the UI5 application through custom development.

The advantages of such global reporting on HANA are the following:

- All factory data relevant for performance management is available in one single system for the whole corporation or organization.
- It provides the opportunity to run comparisons across plants and production lines, and thus offers support in making business decisions.
- Once data moves to central HANA, the comparatively older data on the local MII servers can be archived as required, but HANA still supports running the reports and analytics for the historical data.

The SAP OEE HANA global reporting system landscape is shown in Figure 9-10.

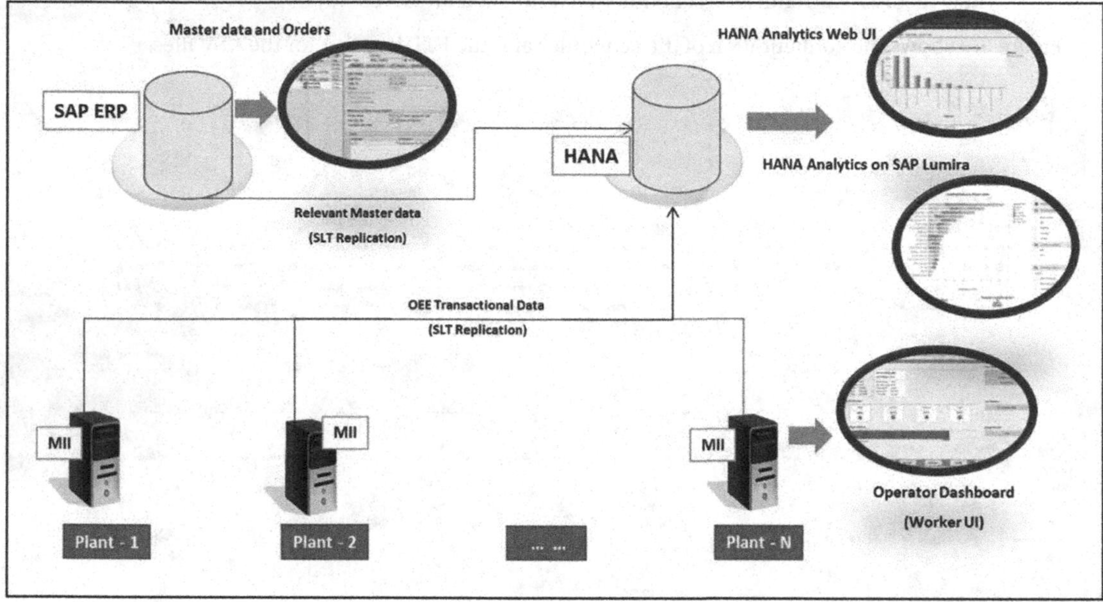

Figure 9-10. *SAP OEE HANA system landscape*

To set up and configure the SAP OEE HANA content, the following steps need to be followed after the ERP configurations, ERP master data, OEEINT, OEE configurations, and worker UI are set up:

1. The components `OEE_ERP` 15.0 SP01 (or higher) and `OEE_MII` 15.1 (or higher) should be installed, configured, and maintained for ERP master data, OEEINT, the OEE configurations, and the worker UI.
2. Set up the SLT replication of tables from ERP and MII systems. The name of the tables to be replicated can be found in SAP Note 1803129. The tables get replicated to a corresponding schema in the HANA system. The replication server (SLT) is positioned for real-time (trigger-based) data replication from SAP and non-SAP sources (SAP-supported databases only).
3. Two delivery units (DUs) `HCO_HBA_OEE` 1.0 SP06 (or higher) and `HCO_HBA_APPS_OEE` 1.0 SP06 (or higher) should be deployed on a HANA Live system. `HCO_HBA_OEE` consists of OEE Reuse and Query Calculation views, which are built on replicated tables from the ERP and MII side. These views are mapped to the replicated tables in the HANA system using schema mapping. These Query Calculation views are exposed to the OEE HANA UI5 application (`HCO_HBA_APPS_OEE`) where a limited number of reports are delivered by SAP OEE HANA for the entire corporation hierarchy. These Query Calculation views can also be consumed by visualization tools like SAP Lumira for deep-dive analytics.
4. Set up access rights to users; once the SLT replications, schema mapping, and OEE components are deployed, the following authorizations need to be set up in order for the users to start working on the calculation views.

a. Read access to schemas where OEE-ERP tables, MII tables, and common master data tables of ECC (e.g., material, shift) are getting replicated. This will enable the views to consume the data from the tables.

b. Read, write, and activate access to `sap.hba.oee` and `sap.hba.apps.oee` packages.

c. Assign the roles `sap.hba.apps.oee.db::BusinessUser` and `sap.hba.apps.oee.db::Admin user`. Also provide read and write access to `SAP_HBA` schema (after the deployment of `HCO_HBA_APPS_OEE`, the schema `SAP_HBA` gets created). This will allow the creation of variants on the UI5 HANA reports.

d. There are additional options to assign analytical privileges. These privileges provide finer control of the data coming from the same view but consumed selectively by different users as per privileges, which means you can provide access to the data of all plants to the users at the corporate office level, but limit the plant users to accessing data only for their own plant.

With the preceding steps set up correctly, the SAP OEE HANA global analytics can now be used for end-user consumption. We will now briefly look into the role of the HANA calculation views (Reuse and Query views).

The standard OEE HANA content delivers a set of calculation views. The calculation views consist of multiple Reuse views and Query views. The Reuse views are a basic set of views that get further used or consumed by the Query views. These views are created in the HANA studio through modeling. Reuse views are the heart of the data model. They expose the business data in a well-structured, consistent, comprehensible way that covers all relevant business data. They are designed for reuse by other views and must not be consumed directly by analytical tools.

To extend the OEE HANA content for specific business needs (e.g., to create a new set of KPIs that are not covered by the standard content) customers can also create their own calculation views. But views delivered by SAP must not be modified by customers. Instead, customers must create views in their own packages (not in the "sap" namespace). The customer-specific views may (and should) refer to Reuse views of the SAP OEE data model. They must not refer to Query views delivered by SAP.

Query views can also be consumed directly by data visualization tools such as SAP Lumira, and reports can be developed with various filter options. SAP Lumira gives users the flexibility to choose from various available visualizations and analyze data on multiple dimensions. Figure 9-11 shows the modeling snapshot of a calculation view in HANA studio.

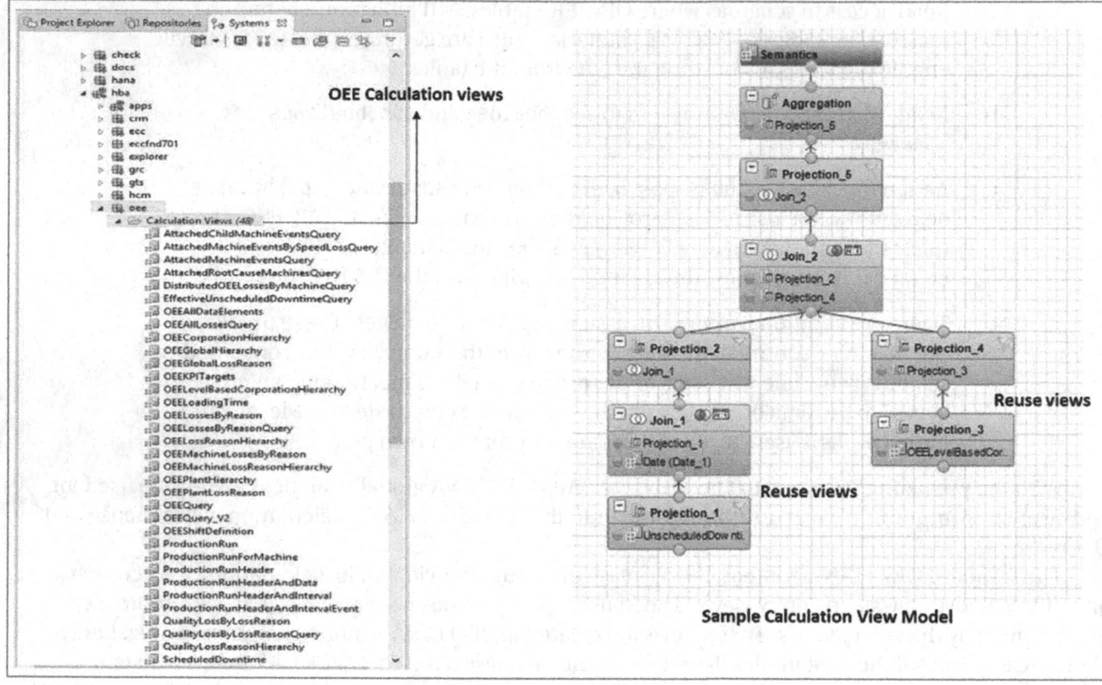

Figure 9-11. *Calculation view model in HANA studio*

Now we will look into the UI5 application, which provides the list of SAP OEE UI5 reports that are delivered as part of the OEE standard content. With all the user authorizations in place, when a user logs in to the browser to access the HANA reports, the reporting screen looks like Figure 9-12.

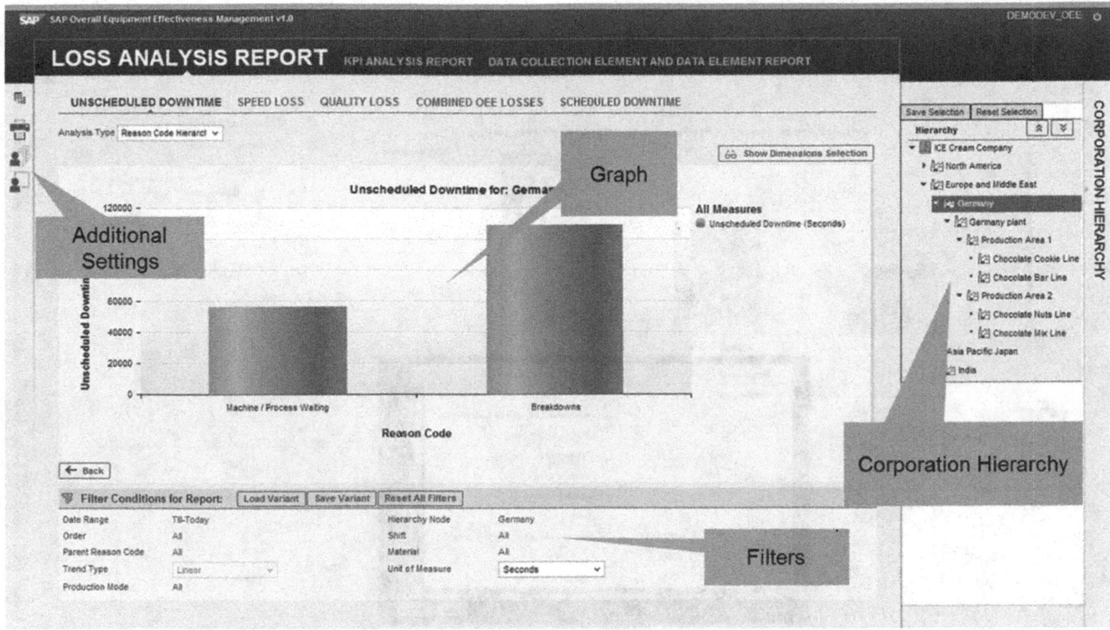

Figure 9-12. *SAP OEE HANA report application on UI5*

The following points describe the different sections and features of the application:

- The right side shows the corporation hierarchy where you can drill down from the corporation at the highest level to a machine at the lowest level. This comes from the global hierarchy and plant hierarchy defined in SAP ERP. The corporation hierarchy on the right can be expanded and collapsed to increase the viewing pane.
- The top left row shows the standard report categories; e.g., Loss Analysis Report, KPI Analysis Report.
- Under the standard report categories, you will see the report sub-categories; e.g., under Loss Analysis Report you will see unscheduled down, speed loss, and quality loss reports.
- Under the main report area, below the main chart, lie the filter criteria that can be applied to the report. There are several filtering options for each report. You can filter unscheduled downtime losses by date range, shift, reason code level, and so on. All the reports will have a date range option that should be selected to see a limited amount of data. Otherwise, the reports will show all the data available. The date range, once selected, can be saved as a variant, allowing you to easily use the same date range again. The date range option is either an absolute range or a relative range. For example, Last One Month is a relative date range. The reason code level filter helps you to set the reason code level you want to view from. Figure 9-13 shows you the reason code filter settings.

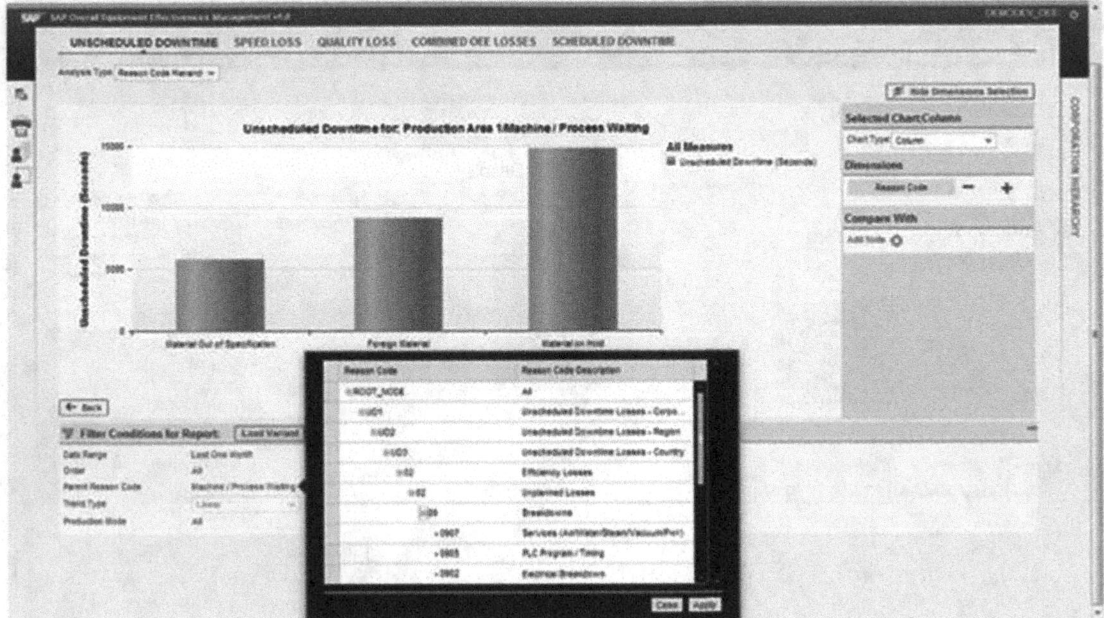

Figure 9-13. Reason code filter settings

- The report can also be viewed in time trend mode by changing the analysis type via the options at the top left of the chart area.
- The chart shows the values of the node that is selected in the hierarchy on the right side.
- More dimension can be added to the chart via the "Show Dimension Selection" option in the right top section of the chart area. With this option, you can view the losses not only for a time range but also by the production shifts. The dimensions are added on the x-axis.
- A user can apply filters and save the individual filters for later use as variants. One of the filters is marked as the default.
- On the extreme left bar there are various options such as viewing the reports in graphical or tabular form, converting the chart into printer-friendly mode, and so on. Figure 9-14 shows the graph in printer-friendly mode. The left bar also provides an option to plug the link of the custom developed package into the application. There is an SAP note (1834144) that details how to add custom reports to the SAP UI5 HANA OEE reports.

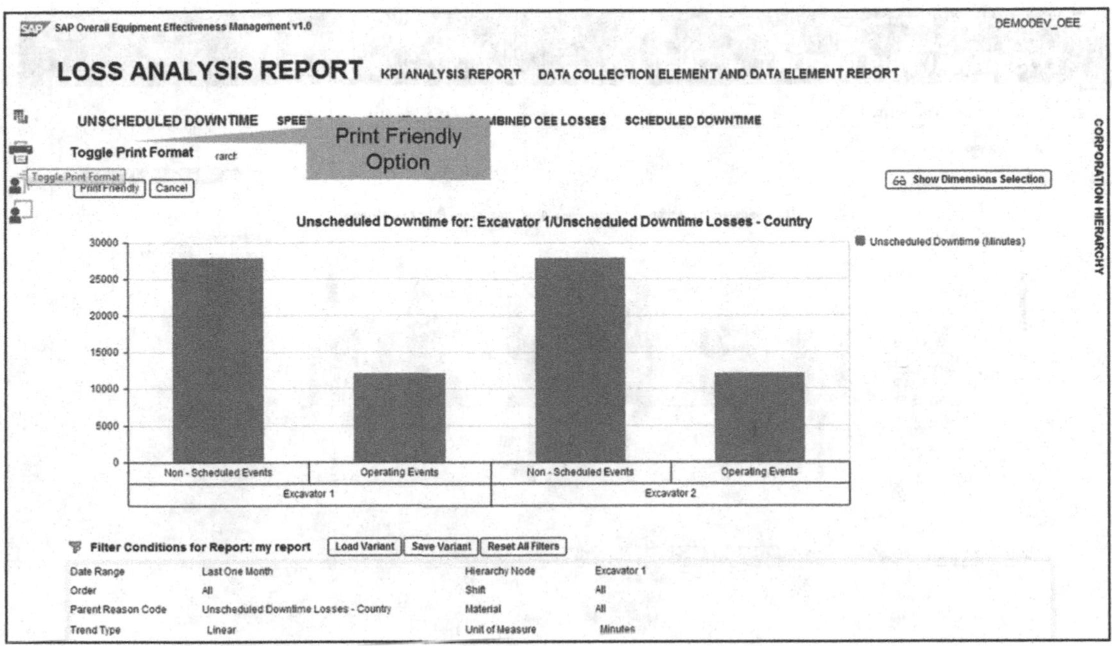

***Figure 9-14.** Graph in printer-friendly mode*

Now that you understand the different types of reporting options available for SAP OEE and the HANA Live component for OEE, let's look into the list of main reports delivered on HANA.

Loss Analysis Report: This report consists of Scheduled Down, Unscheduled Down, Speed Loss, and Rework/Scrap reports. Except for Scheduled Down (which is usually planned), the other three are the basic losses captured by the OEE worker UI (dashboard) and assigned reason codes by the operator on the shop floor during execution. Scheduled downtimes are usually maintained by a super user (or by an operator as well) and assigned with a reason code. The Loss Analysis Report shows the loss reason codes in a sorted manner so as to quickly identify the highest contributing reasons for the losses (Figure 9-15). You can also drill down across the reason code tree to perform a root-cause analysis and find out the most fundamental root cause of the losses. It is also possible to view the losses in time trend mode for a particular reason code level. Figure 9-16 shows the time trend of the unscheduled downtime. You can also compare these losses between two production lines or between two plants from the corporation hierarchy.

Figure 9-15 shows the Loss Analysis Report (Unscheduled Down) with highest to lowest contributing reasons. It also shows the corporation hierarchy panel collapsed so as to increase the view area of the graph. By double-clicking one of the reason codes, you will be taken to the next level of detail for that particular reason code in order to view more detailed reasons for the particular loss.

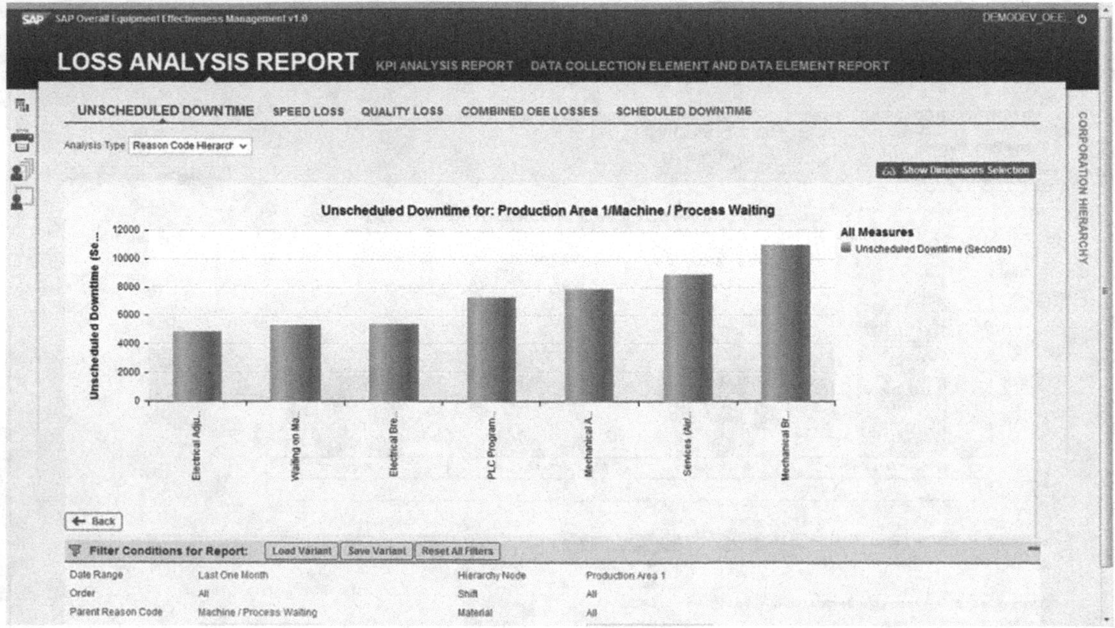

Figure 9-15. *Loss Analysis Report (Unscheduled Downtime)*

Figures 9-16 and 9-17 show the trend of Unscheduled Downtime. The graph type can be either line or bar chart, which is determined by user selection.

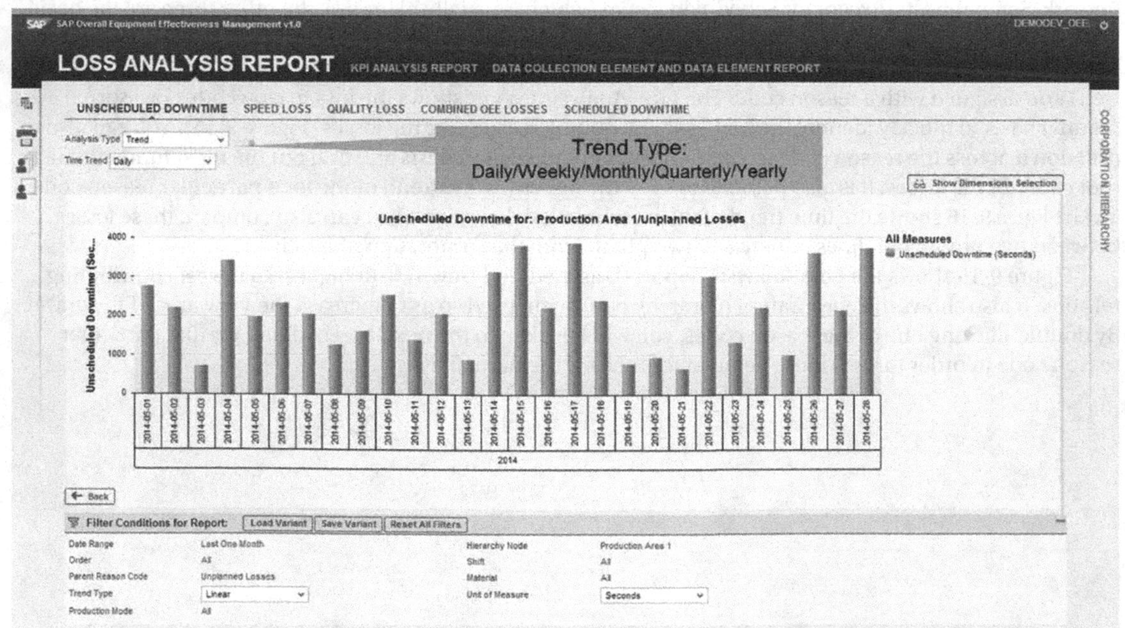

Figure 9-16. *Unscheduled Downtime (time trend, bar chart)*

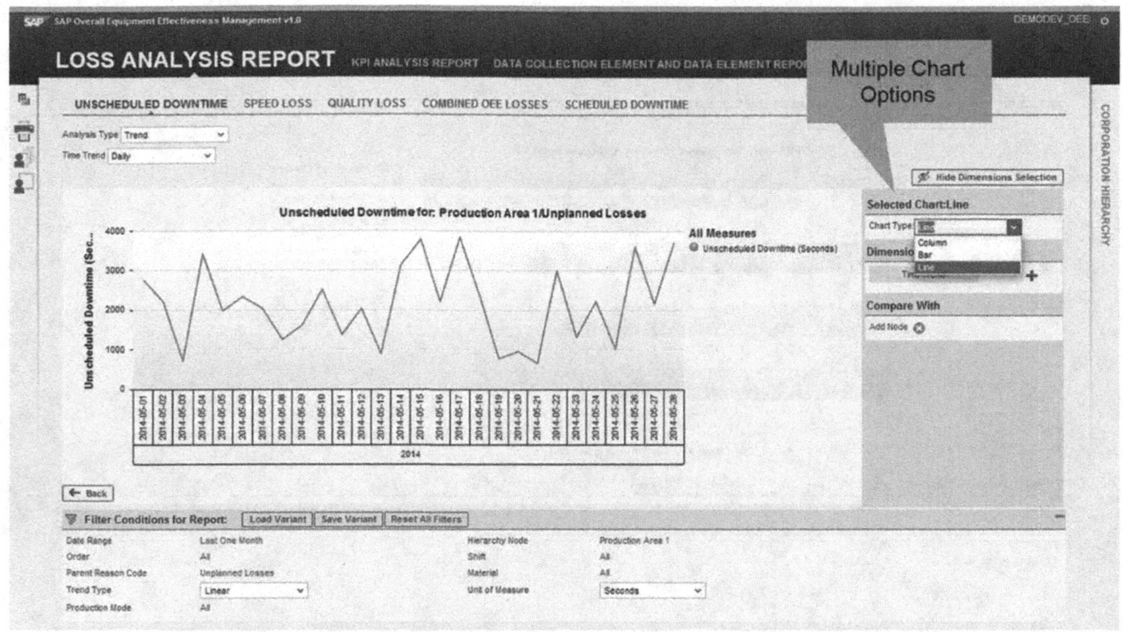

Figure 9-17. Unscheduld Downtime (time trend, line chart)

KPI Analysis Report: This consists of reports of standard KPIs like OEE Analysis, Asset Utilization, and Classic Time Element analysis. The OEE Analysis shows the trend of the OEE KPI and also the trend of availability, performance, and quality KPIs separately. You can also compare these KPIs between two production lines or between two plants from the corporation hierarchy. The Classic Time Element is an important report that shows what, out of the total loading time, is the value operation time remaining, and how the loading time is eaten away by the different losses. Figure 9-18 shows a snapshot of the Classic Time Element Report. Figure 9-19 shows the OEE KPI report for a node.

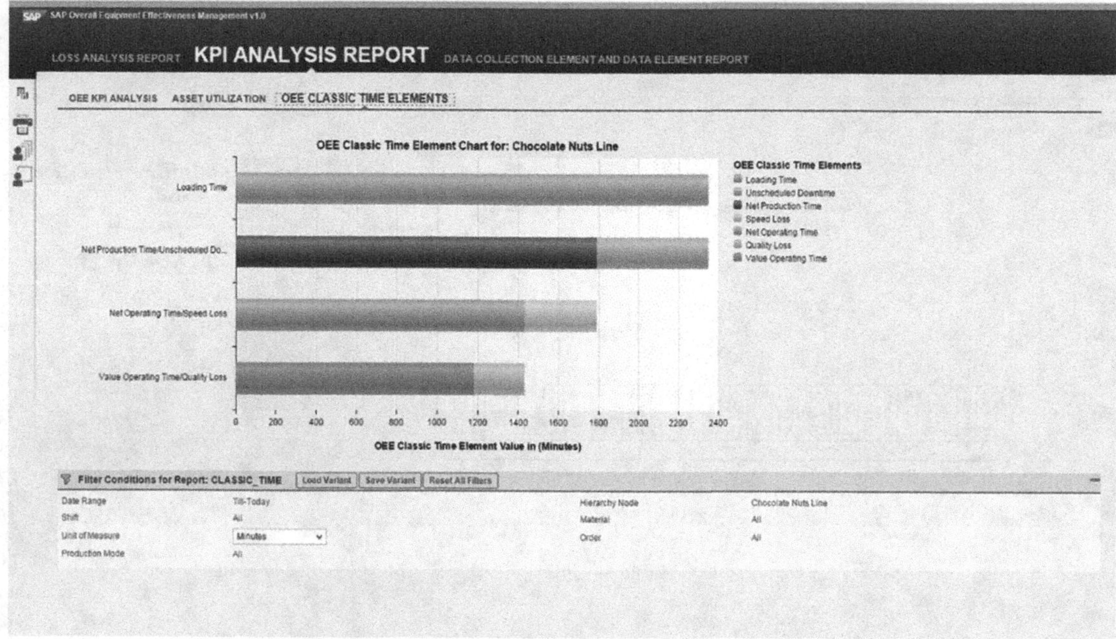

Figure 9-18. *OEE Classic Time Element chart*

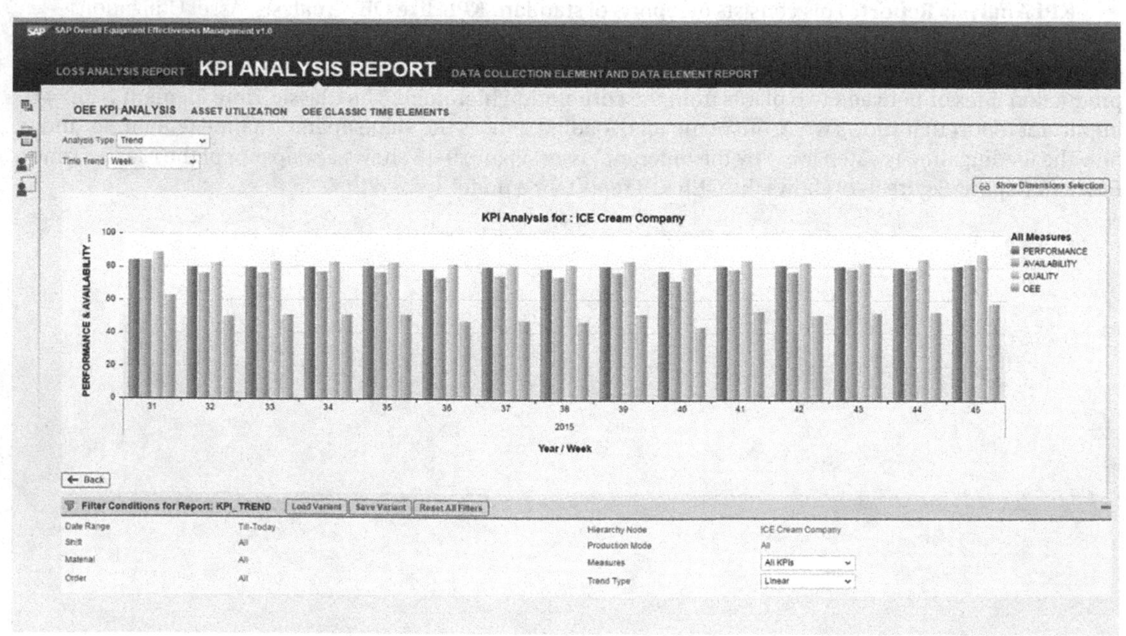

Figure 9-19. *The OEE KPI Analysis Report*

DATA Collection Report: OEE Worker UI allows the operator to collect all relevant production data as it is configured in the OEE ERP add-on configuration. For example, let's say it is configured to collect the overfill per order, additional labor per order, and also the water consumption per shift. When these data are collected during execution, they are also replicated to HANA. The Data Collection Report shows the trend of these data collections. This is a representation of the raw data collected in a time trend. Figure 9-20 provides a snapshot of a sample data collection of Additional Labour.

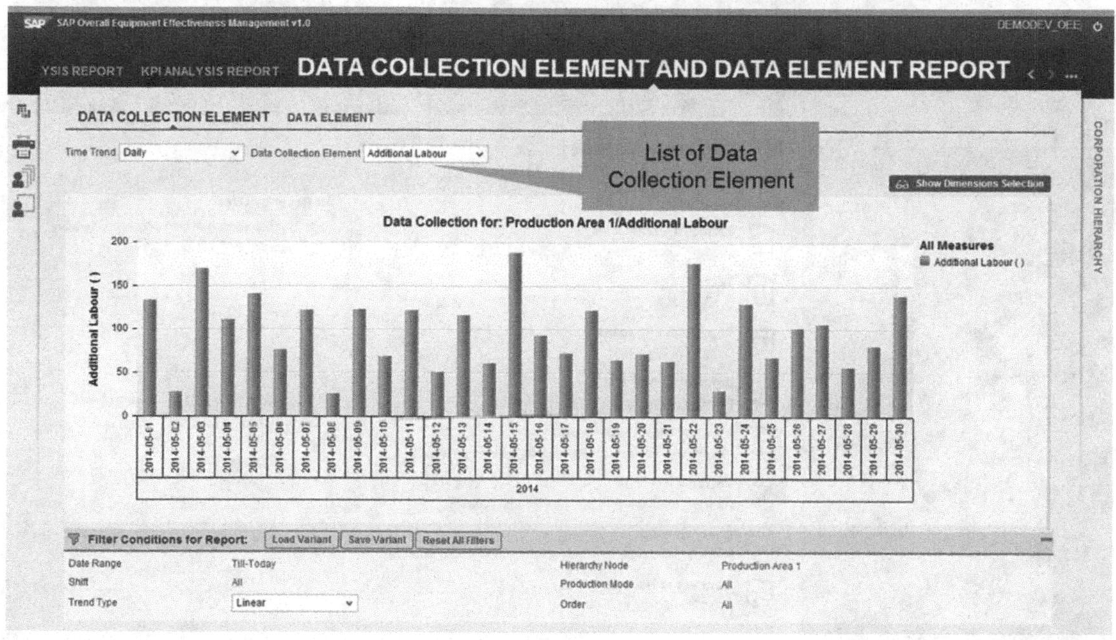

***Figure 9-20.** OEE Data Collection Report*

As you know, the SAP OEE HANA application provides a limited set of reports. But the SAP OEE HANA calculation views can also be accessed through a data visualization tool like SAP Lumira to do self-service reporting and analytics on the HANA views. From Lumira you can connect to HANA by selecting any one of the options (connect to SAP HANA or Download from SAP HANA). Figure 9-21 shows these options on SAP Lumira from menu item File ➤ New.

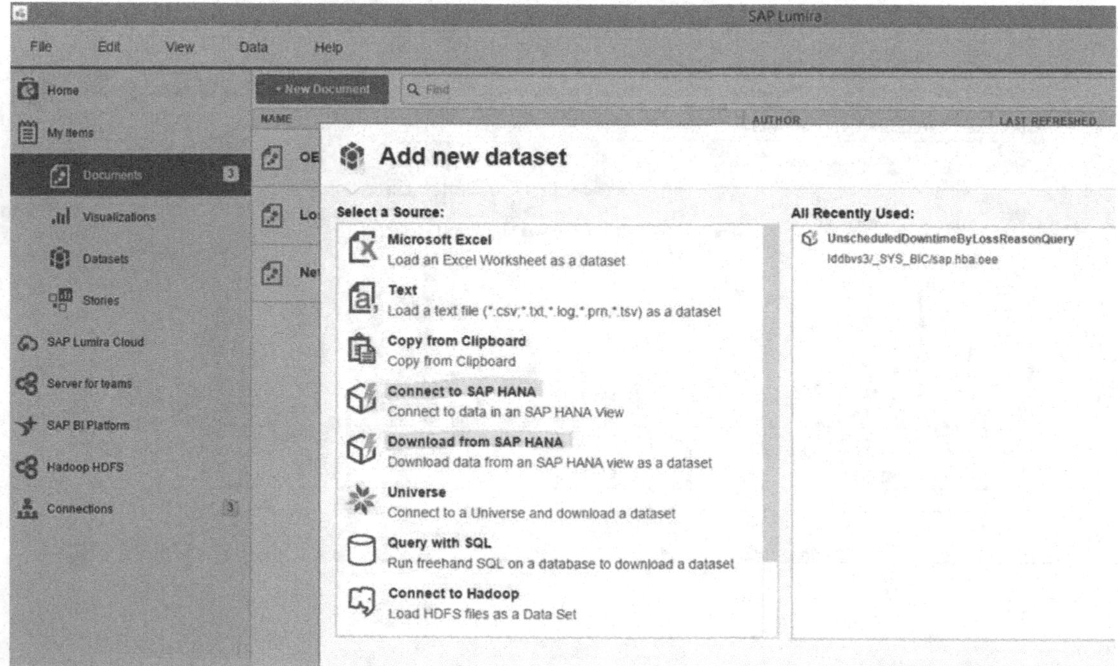

Figure 9-21. *Connecting OEE HANA views with SAP Lumira*

Once the connection is made, in the same way we used Lumira with MII data for local reports, end users can compose their own reports with SAP Lumira for OEE from the HANA views. The options are endless here, depending on how you want to visualize the data compared to the fixed set of UI5 reports we discussed earlier.

Summary

In this chapter you have learned about the different options SAP OEE provides for reporting and analytics. You have learned that the worker UI (dashboard) provides real-time information about the current shift and orders running as well as about corresponding real-time KPIs. For plant-level local reporting, you have seen that SAP OEE delivers a plug-in for SAP Lumira that can be used to connect SAP Lumira with a set of three CSVs, which synchronize the data periodically by downloading from MII. Finally, you have learned that for global consolidated reporting at the corporate level, SAP OEE provides HANA content that delivers a set of calculation views and a UI5 application with a limited set of reports. These calculation views can also be consumed in a visualization tool like SAP Lumira for a self-service deep-dive and analytics. Last, but not the least, you have learned that all these categories can always be extended as per customer needs through custom development.

Appendix

Section 1: Automated Data Collection

D. Saha et al., *Manufacturing Performance Management using SAP OEE*,
DOI 10.1007/978-1-4842-1150-2

SAP OEE Service Interface: SAP OEE Integration

Method	Reference to Standard OEE Dashboard	Description	Mandatory	Optional	Optional/ Recommended	Response XML
getActive RunsForNodeID	Manage orders	Retrieves all the active runs for the node ID	NodeID	ProductionActivity	eventTime isEventTimeInUTC	ActiveRunList
getRunsForNodeID AndTimestamp	Not applicable	Retrieves all the orders that were executed for the Node ID and timestamp passed, irrespective of the order status	NodeID eventTime		isEventTimeInUTC	Production RunList
Complete ProductionOrder	Manage orders	Completes a production order	NodeID OrderNumber OperationNumber	ProductionActivity	eventTime isEventTimeInUTC	status
PauseProductionRun	Manage orders	Holds a production order	NodeID OrderNumber OperationNumber	ProductionActivity	eventTime isEventTimeInUTC	status
Resume ProductionRun	Manage orders	Resumes or restarts a production order that is in HOLD status	NodeID OrderNumber OperationNumber ProductionActivity		eventTime isEventTimeInUTC	status
Abort ProductionRun		Aborts a production order	NodeID OrderNumber OperationNumber			status

ChangeProduction Activity	Manage orders	Changes or moves to the next production activity as configured for a production order	NodeID OrderNumber OperationNumber ProductionActivity	eventTime		status
ReportUnscheduled Downtime	Manage downtime	Reports an unscheduled machine or line down event	NodeID OrderNumber OperationNumber eventTime DataCollection Element	Comments RC1 to RC10 entryType	isEventTimeInUTC	status
ReportUnscheduled Uptime	Manage downtime	Reports an unscheduled machine or line UP event	NodeID OrderNumber OperationNumber eventTime	entryType	isEventTimeInUTC	status
ReportScheduled Downtime	Manage downtime	Reports a scheduled machine or line down event	NodeID eventTime	entryType	isEventTimeInUTC	status
ReportScheduled Uptime	Manage downtime	Reports a scheduled machine or line UP event	NodeID eventTime	entryType	isEventTimeInUTC	status

(*continued*)

Method	Reference to Standard OEE Dashboard	Description	Mandatory	Optional	Optional/ Recommended	Response XML
ReportRejection	Report production	Reports the scrap/ waste /rejected materials for a production order.	NodeID OrderNumber OperationNumber eventTime DataCollection Element reportingQuantity reportingUOM	material Comments RC1 to RC10 entryType serialno batchno	isEvent TimeInUTC	status
ReportSpeedLoss	Report speed loss	Reports speed loss encountered for a production order	NodeID OrderNumber OperationNumber eventTime DataCollection Element reportingQuantity reportingUOM	Material Comments RC1 to RC10 entryType	isEvent TimeInUTC	status
ReportOther DataCollection		Report non-OEE or custom data collection elements configured in OEE	NodeID OrderNumber OperationNumber eventTime DataCollection Element reportingQuantity reportingUOM	Material Comments RC1 to RC10 entryType	isEvent TimeInUTC	status
ReportRaw MaterialScrap	This Service is obsolete as the Application Launch Pad (from SAP MII 15.1) will perform the goods movement for raw material scrap.					

ReportFlow TimeStart	Reports the start of the flow time for a production order. Flow time is a non-production parameter that is not used for KPI calculations and is derived as thestart of the production i.e start of raw material consumption	NodeID OrderNumber OperationNumber eventTime DataCollection Element	Comments RC1 to RC10 entryType	isEvent TimeInUTC	status
ReportFlow TimeEnd	Reports the end of the flow time; i.e., end time of the production i.e end time when the first finished product is out of the line	NodeID OrderNumber OperationNumber eventTime DataCollection Element	entryType	isEvent TimeInUTC	status
ReportStandard ValueParameter	Reports the standard value parameters like machine time, labor time, setup time, etc., as configured in the production order when downloaded from ERP.	NodeID OrderNumber OperationNumber eventTime DataCollection Element reportingQuantity reportingUOM		isEvent TimeInUTC	status

(*continued*)

Method	Reference to Standard OEE Dashboard	Description	Mandatory	Optional	Optional/ Recommended	Response XML
ReportEvent (when an open event exist)		ReportEvent is the new API to report any time loss. It is used to report a new event or an event occured in the past.. If an open event or downtime exists, then this method returns the event's event ID. This may be used in custom developments to know the event ID dynamically.	NodeID	DataCollection Element Comments RC1 to RC10 entryType impactsLine eventStartTime eventEndTime	isEvent TimeInUTC	EventId of the open event
ReportEvent (when no event exist)		ReportEvent can also be used to create a new line or machine event that occurred in the past or that has a start and end timestamp.	NodeID DataCollection Element eventStartTime eventEndTime	Comments RC1 to RC10 entryType impactsLine	isEvent TimeInUTC	EventId of the newly created event

ReportProduction	Report Production	Reports the yield or good quantity for a production order	NodeID OrderNumber OperationNumber eventTime DataCollection Element reportingQuantity reportingUOM	material Comments RC1 to RC10 entryType serialno batchno	isEventTime InUTC	status
ReportRawMaterial Consumption	This service is obsolete, as the Application Launch Pad (from SAP MII 15.1) will perform the goods movement for raw materials consumption.					
getOEEKPIs	KPI Andon display in home page	Returns the real time KPI values along with other parameters like unscheduled downtime, speed loss, loading time, etc. required for the KPI calculations. This can be used in custom development.	nodeID			OutoutKPI Service
Release Demand	Order dispatch worker UI	Releases the demand for a production order that can be started in the dashboard for production.	client Plant OrderNumber releaseQuantity reportingQuantity reportingUOM	isEventTimeInUTC batchno		status

(continued)

Method	Reference to Standard OEE Dashboard	Description	Mandatory	Optional	Optional/ Recommended	Response XML
createPM Notification	Manage Downtimes	This API is to create or trigger the PM notification for a machine down.	client, plant, nodeID, notificationType, technicalObject, startTimestamp, endTimestamp	downtimeMapped, comments, downtimeEventID		createPM Notification DetailsOutput
restartActive RunsInCurrentShift		In OEE, when orders runs across the shift, for every shift, a RUN_ID is created automatically. This happens at the back end only when the dashboard is launched during the shift change. If there is a scenario where the dashboard will not be used, then this API should be used to trigger the restart of the order run when the new shift is started	NodeID			status
updatePM Notification		updates the status of PM notification created	plant, client, notificationNo, oeeNotifyNo, nodeID, status			status

SynchronizePM Notification DetailsInternal	updates the details of PM notification created	client, plant, nodeID, notificationType, breakdown, startTimestamp, endTimestamp.			
Report Quantity	This is a API with which data collection element of type quantity can be reported such as Yield, scrap, rework, standard value parameter etc. So this API can be used in place of individual APIs such as reportProduction, reportRejection, reportStandard ValueParameter, reportOther DataCollection.	runID, client, dcElement, quantity, uom, material, startTimestamp, endTimestamp, nodeID, plant,	rc1 to rc10, comments, startDate, startTime, endDate, endTime, dcElementType, notificationNo, serialNo, batchNo, entryType, impactsLine		ReportQuantity Output

Section 2: OEE Standard Database Tables

Sl.No	Table Name	Description	Type of Data	Details
1	MPM_AFABL	This table maintains the client- and plant-specific AFABL segment of LOIPRO IDoc	Master data	Production order - LOIPRO segment
2	MPM_AFFLL	This table maintains the client- and plant-specific AFFLL segment of LOIPRO IDoc	Master data	Production order - LOIPRO segment
3	MPM_AFKOL	This table maintains the client- and plant-specific AFKOL segment of LOIPRO IDoc	Master data	Production order - LOIPRO segment
4	MPM_AFPOL	This table maintains the client- and plant-specific AFPOL segment of LOIPRO IDoc	Master data	Production order - LOIPRO segment
5	MPM_AFUVL	This table maintains the client- and plant-specific AFUVL segment of LOIPRO IDoc	Master data	Production order - LOIPRO segment
6	MPM_AFVOL	This table maintains the client- and plant-specific AFVOL segment of LOIPRO IDoc	Master data	Production order - LOIPRO segment
7	MPM_C_CLFN	This table maintains the client-specific classification details maintained in plant hierarchy	Master data	Plant hierarchy classification
8	MPM_C_CLFNT	This table maintains the description of classification details maintained in MPM_C_CLFN table	Master data	Plant hierarchy classification description
9	MPM_DIMENSION	This table is the replica of the SAP table T006D for Dimension, which is maintained s client specific with its status (deleted or is used)	Master data	Dimension
10	MPM_DIMENSIONT	This table maintains the list of client-specific dimension contexts created as master data, with descriptions in each language supported by SAP OEE, language code and language ID	Master data	Dimension
11	MPM_FACTCAL	This table stores the factory calendar details like annual and monthly working day and holiday details. These details come through the factory calendar IDoc when pushed from ERP to OEE.	Master data	Factory calendar description

12	MPM_FORMULA_PARAM	This table maintains the client-specific formula parameters created in ECC with its unit, dimension, and other details.	Master data	Formula parameters for order
13	MPM_FORMULA_PARAMT	This table maintains the client-specific description for each formula parameter (parameter_ID) maintained in the MPM_FORMULA_PARAM OEE table (short text and long text) in all the languages supported by SAP OEE.	Master data	Formula parameters description
14	MPM_JSTKL	This table maintains client- and plant-specific production and process order status for header information.	Master data	LOIPRO Order fields
15	MPM_JSTUL	This table maintains client- and plant-specific production and process order status for subprocess information.	Master data	LOIPRO Order fields
16	MPM_JSTVL	This table maintains client- and plant-specific production and process order status for process information.	Master data	LOIPRO Order fields
17	MPM_KBEDL	This table stores the work center–specific capacity requirements for the main process.	Master data	LOIPRO Order fields
18	MPM_KBEUL	This table stores the work center–specific capacity requirements for subprocesses.	Master data	LOIPRO Order fields
19	MPM_MATMAS_ALT_UOM	This table maintains alternate UOM and its associate details for each material master in OEE as maintained in the MARM SAP table.	Master data	Material master
20	MPM_MATMAS_HDR	This table maintains the client-specific material header details as maintained in the MARA SAP table.	Master data	Material master
21	MPM_MATMAS_HDRT	This table maintains the description of materials in the MPM_MATMAS_HDR table in all the languages supported by SAP OEE.	Master data	Material master description
22	MPM_MATMAS_PLANT	This table maintains the client-specific material masters for each plant supported in OEE along with other material details.	Master data	Material master

(continued)

Sl.No	Table Name	Description	Type of Data	Details
23	MPM_MATMAS_STG_LOC	This table maintains the client- and plant-specific material and its associated storage location details as maintained in MARD and T001L SAP tables.	Master data	Material master
24	MPM_MC	OBSOLETE		
25	MPM_MCAEQUI	This table maintains client- and plant-specific equipment name, its ID, validity, and status of usage. This equipment is maintained under the Technical Objects tab of the plant hierarchy.	Master data	Equipment
26	MPM_MCAFLOC	This table maintains client- and plant-specific functional location name, its ID, validity, and status of usage. This equipment is maintained under the Technical Objects tab of the plant hierarchy.	Master data	Functional location
27	MPM_MCAMG	This table maintains client- and plant-specific machine groups maintained under the Machine Group tab of the plant hierarchy.	Master data	Machine group
28	MPM_MCGRP	This table maintains the plant- and client-specific machine group definitions.	Master data	Machine group
29	MPM_MCGRPT	This table maintains the description for equipment maintained in MPM_MCGRP table in the language configured in plant hierarchy.	Master data	Machine group description
30	MPM_MCT	OBSOLETE		
31	MPM_MPH_CFN	This table maintains the list of client- and plant-specific classification data maintained in the plant hierarchy.	Master data	Plant hierarchy classification
32	MPM_MPH_HDR	This table is a core table that contains template information about the OEE plant hierarchy in ERP, but in MII this table is kept for future functionality.	Master data	Plant hierarchy
33	MPM_MPH_HDRT	This table maintains the description of hierarchy header details maintained in the MPM_MPH_HDR table in all the languages supported by SAP OEE.	Master data	Plant hierarchy header description

34	MPM_MPH_NODE	This table lists the details of all the nodes in a plant hierarchy. The node ID is the unique identifier of each node in a plant hierarchy. Node name is the name of each node, parent node ID is the node ID of its parent; for example, for a machine its parent node ID is the work center's node ID. Other details include validity, work center and capacity ID (for work center nodes), node_type (Area/Team/Line/Machine/equipment), and all other configurations as defined in the plant hierarchy.	Master data	Plant hierarchy node
35	MPM_MPH_ NODEAMG	This table maintains the list of machine groups specific to each work center node ID.	Master data	Plant hierarchy machine group
36	MPM_MPH_NODEATO	This table maintains the list of client- and plant-specific technical objects created in the plant hierarchy under all machine nodes. Technical objects are the PM objects; i.e., the associated equipment number and functional location of each machine created under the machine node.	Master data	Plant hierarchy technical objects
37	MPM_MPH_NODESTR	This table maintains the list of client- and plant-specific details maintained under the Standard Rates tab of the work center node in the plant hierarchy.	Master data	Plant hierarchy standard rate
38	MPM_MPH_NODET	This table maintains the description of hierarchy node details maintained in MPM_MPH_NODE table in all the languages configured in plant hierarchy.	Master data	Plant hierarchy node description
39	MPM_NODE_COORDS	FOR FUTURE FUNCTIONALITIES AND CURRENTLY NOT USED		
40	MPM_RC	This table maintains the master data plant reason codes (10 levels) as defined in the ECC OEE add-on specific to time element, client, and plant.	Master data	Plant reason codes
41	MPM_RCT	This table maintains the description of plant reason codes at each level as maintained in MPM_RC table in the language defined in plant reason codes.	Master data	Plant reason codes description

(continued)

Sl.No	Table Name	Description	Type of Data	Details
42	MPM_RESBL	This table maintains the client, plant, material, and prod/process order specific reservation details like reservation number, position, movement type, and quantity.	Master data	LOIPRO Order fields
43	MPM_STD_VAL_KEY	This table maintains the list of ONLY client-specific six standard value keys' parameter names and parameter values maintained in the ECC OEE add-on for an order.	Master data	Standard value keys
44	MPM_STD_VAL_KEYT	This table maintains the description of standard value keys' parameters maintained in MPM_STD_VAL_KEY table in all the languages supported by OEE.	Master data	Standard value keys description
45	MPM_TC37A	This table maintains the list of ONLY client-specific shift definitions as maintained in the SAP master table TC37A.	Master data	Shift definitions
46	MPM_TC37P	This table maintains the list of ONLY client-specific break schedule definitions as maintained in the SAP master table TC37P.	Master data	Shift break schedule
47	MPM_TC37S	This table maintains the list of ONLY client-specific break plan definitions as maintained in the SAP master table TC37S.	Master data	Shift break plan
48	MPM_TC37T	This table maintains the list of ONLY client-specific shift definition text as maintained in the SAP master table TC37T.	Master data	Shift definitions description
49	MPM_UOM	This table maintains the list of ONLY client-specific UOM created as maintained in the SAP master table T006.	Master data	Unit of measurement
50	MPM_UOMT	This table maintains the list of ONLY client-specific UOM created in ECC, and its configured language as maintained in SAP table T006A.	Master data	Unit of measurement description

51	MPM_WC_CAP_AVL_IVL	This table maintains the list of client-specific work center's interval of available capacity details as created in SAP table KAZY.	Master data	Work center capacity availability
52	MPM_WC_DLY_CAP_REQ	This table maintains the list of client-specific work center capacity requirement records maintained as a master in ECC.	Master data	Work center capacity requirement
53	MPM_WRKCTR_CAP_HDR	This table maintains the list of client-specific work center capacity header records maintained as a master in ECC.	Master data	Work center capacity header
54	MPM_WRKCTR_CAP_MAP	This table maintains and holds capacity volume mapping for a work center.	Master data	Work center capacity volume map.
55	MPM_WRKCTR_CAP_SFT	This table maintains the list of client-specific work center capacity shift details as created in SAP table KAPA.	Master data	Work center capacity shift details
56	MPM_WRKCTR_CAP_UOM	This table maintains the list of client-specific work center capacity unit of measurement allocation as created in SAP table KAPE.	Master data	Work center capacity UOM
57	MPM_WRKCTR_COST	This table maintains the list of client-specific work center capacity assignment to cost center details as created in SAP table CRCO.	Master data	Work center capacity cost assignment
58	MPM_WRKCTR_HDR	This table maintains the list of client-specific work center header-level details as created in SAP table CRCA.	Master data	Work center header
59	MPM_WRKCTR_HDRT	This table maintains the list of client-specific work center IDs and their descriptions in language defined in ECC.	Master data	Work center header description
60	MPM_ACTIVITY	This table maintains header data of each activity created under the Main tab of worker UI activity configuration	Configuration data	Activity configuration/Main tab

(continued)

Sl.No	Table Name	Description	Type of Data	Details
61	MPM_ACTIVITY_DESC	This table maintains all the plant- and client-specific activity descriptions for each activity created under activity configuration worker UI in each of its supported languages.	Configuration data	Activity configuration/Activity Description tab
62	MPM_ACTOPTION_DESC	This table maintains all the plant- and client-specific option descriptions for each activity created under activity configuration /Options tab/option description section with all the supported languages.	Configuration data	Activity configuration/Options tab
63	MPM_ACT_OPTION	This table maintains all the plant- and client-specific option names for each activity created under activity configuration/Options tab.	Configuration data	Activity configuration/Options tab/Option Name
64	MPM_ACT_OPTION_VAL	This table maintains all the plant- and client-specific option values and sequences of display for each activity created under worker UI activity configuration/Options tab/options value	Configuration data	Activity configuration/Options tab/Option value
65	MPM_CA_UG_ASSGNMT	This table maintains the client- and plant-specific user groups maintained for a plant that can be seen when the plant node is selected. These user groups will further be used to assign the work center– or line-specific dashboards.	Configuration data	General configuration /admin configuration user group assignment tab
66	MPM_CUST_NM	This table maintains the master list of customization parameters used by SAP OEE along with other information such as version, multivalued or not, its dimension, and its context (data collection element, production activity, raw material, etc.)	Configuration data	Customization configuration
67	MPM_CUST_NMT	This table maintains the description of master list of customization parameters in different OEE-supported languages.	Configuration data	Customization configuration description

68	MPM_CUST_NM_ALVALT	This table maintains all the possible value options for each of the customization parameters maintained under customization configuration in different languages.	Configuration data	Customization configuration/ Parameter alternate values description
69	MPM_CUST_NM_AL_VAL	This table maintains all the possible values for each of the master lists of customization parameters.	Configuration data	Customization configuration/ Parameter alternate values
70	MPM_CUST_NM_VAL	This table maintains the list of plant- and client-specific customization parameters that are configured at different nodes, such as plant, work center, machine. Each entry has a unique ID along with the parameter name, node ID for which it is configured, material (if material specific), and its version.	Configuration data	Customization configuration/ Parameter values
71	MPM_CUST_NM_VALDET	This table maintains the details for the values of each customization parameter, which are maintained in the table MPM_CUST_NM_VAL. Each CUST_VAL_ID of MPM_CUST_NM_VAL has a detail ID CUST_VAL_DETAIL_ID	Configuration data	Customization configuration/ Parameter value details
72	MPM_C_DCELEM	This table maintains the list of client-specific data collection elements, their type (time or quantity), time element, context, UOM, dimension, order independent or not, and status (whether deleted or in use in OEE).	Configuration data	Data collection element
73	MPM_C_DCELEMT	This table maintains, in different languages, the description of data collection elements maintained in MPM_C_DCELEM table.	Configuration data	Data collection element description
74	MPM_C_DCE_CTXT	This table maintains the master list of data collection contexts maintained in ERP client and sent to OEE for use in OEE.	Configuration data	Data collection element context
75	MPM_C_DCE_CTXTT	This table maintains, in different languages, the description of data collection contexts maintained in the MPM_C_DCE_CTXT table.	Configuration data	Data collection element context description

(*continued*)

Sl.No	Table Name	Description	Type of Data	Details
76	MPM_C_PRDMODE	This table maintains the master list of production modes maintained in ERP client and their status (whether deleted or in use in OEE)	Configuration data	Production mode
77	MPM_C_PRDMODEOT	This table maintains the master list of production-related order types (production and process order) maintained in ERP client.	Configuration data	Production mode order types
78	MPM_C_PRDMODET	This table maintains the description of production modes maintained in different ERP clients.	Configuration data	Production mode description
79	MPM_C_TE_TYPE	This table maintains the list of client-specific data elements, their category (production or loss), their status (deleted or is used), and their calculated value (if it's a calculated value or a reported value in OEE).	Configuration data	Data element type
80	MPM_C_TE_TYPET	This table maintains the description of data elements maintained in each ERP client.	Configuration data	Data element type description
81	MPM_EXTENSIONS	This table maintains all the client- and node-specific extensions and their properties (activity_ID, sequence, method_ID, Extension_Type, ASYN or not) created under extension configuration.	Configuration data	General configuration/Extension configuration
82	MPM_EXT_DESC	This table maintains all the extensions with an Extension_ID and their descriptions with a Description_ID in all the languages supported by SAP OEE.	Configuration data	General configuration/Extension configuration description
83	MPM_EXT_FILTER	This table contains the extension filter criteria details.	Configuration data	
84	MPM_EXT_FILTER_ DSC	This table contains the description details of extension filter criteria.	Configuration data	
85	MPM_EXT_FILTER_ OPT	This table contains the options configured in the filter criteria of extension filter criteria.	Configuration data	

86	MPM_GLOBAL_CONFIG	This table maintains the list of global parameters created after the SAP OEE CTC run. By default, three global parameters are created, and their values are maintained in this table.	Configuration data	Global configurations
87	MPM_KPI	This table maintains the list of client-specific standard and custom KPIs created in OEE add-on with its UOM, description, type, and status details.	Configuration data	Display ERP system data
88	MPM_KPIT	This table maintains the description of KPIs maintained in the MPM_KPI table in all the languages supported by SAP OEE.	Configuration data	Display ERP system data
89	MPM_LAYOUT	This table maintains the type of layouts available in standard OEE. L1 and L3 are currently supported.	Configuration data	Dashboard configuration
90	MPM_LAYOUT_PANEL	This table maintains the list of panel IDs of OEE dashboard specific to layout ID. For the L3 layout type, four panel IDs are applicable, including the bottom button panel.	Configuration data	Dashboard configuration
91	MPM_LSTCONF_UPDATE	This table contains the last modified time of all configuration.	Configuration data	
92	MPM_MPH_KPITARG	This table maintains the list of client- and plant-specific KPI definitions and their details, like target values, UOM, and material specific to each node ID (work center) created under the plant hierarchy.	Configuration data	Display ERP system data
93	MPM_MPH_MRKDWN	This table maintains the list of client- and plant-specific machines that are declared as bottleneck machines under the Bottleneck tab of the plant hierarchy. The table stores other details like machine node ID, order-operation key, DC element used for downtime, material, routing name and operation, and the validity.	Configuration data	Display ERP system data

(*continued*)

Sl.No	Table Name	Description	Type of Data	Details
94	MPM_POD	This table maintains the list of client- and plant-specific standard and custom OEE dashboards created with their ID, layout, type, and version.	Configuration data	Dashboard configuration
95	MPM_POD_BTN	This table maintains the list of client- and plant-specific PODs created and the list of dashboard buttons created for each dashboard along with each button's details.	Configuration data	Dashboard configuration
96	MPM_POD_BTN_DESC	This table maintains the list of client-, plant-, and POD-specific button descriptions in all the languages supported by OEE.	Configuration data	Dashboard configuration
97	MPM_POD_DESC	This table maintains the descriptions of dashboards maintained in MPM_POD table in all the languages supported by OEE.	Configuration data	Dashboard configuration
98	MPM_POD_PANEL	This table maintains the client- and plant-specific POD design details like LayoutID, Panel ID, and Activity ID configured under Dashboard section's Content tab.	Configuration data	Dashboard configuration
99	MPM_POD_SIDEPNL_BT	CURRENTLY NOT USED		
100	MPM_POD_SIDE_PANEL			
101	MPM_POD_SPBTN_DESC			
102	MPM_POD_UG_ASSGNMT	This table maintains the list of client- and plant-specific user group dashboard assignments maintained for each work center node ID in a plant hierarchy.	Configuration data	General configuration/User group dashboard assignment
103	MPM_PROD_ACTIVITY	This table maintains the list of client- and plant-specific production activities defined under customization configuration for a work center node.	Configuration data	General configuration/Customization parameters

104	MPM_PROD_ ACTIVITYT	This table maintains the description of production activity details maintained in the MPM_PROD_ ACTIVITY table in the language configured in the plant hierarchy.	Configuration data	General configuration/ Customization parameters/ Production activity description
105	MPM_RC_PH_DCELEM	This table maintains the client- and plant-specific reason codes defined for each node and data collection element.	Configuration data	General configuration/Reason code configuration
106	MPM_SUPPRTD_ PLANTS	This table maintains the list of plants configured in OEE as part of the CTC run between ECC and OEE.	Configuration data	OEE-supported plants
107	MPM_TIMEELEM	This table maintains the list of ONLY client-specific data elements configured in OEE add-on and their associated data elements type.	Configuration data	Data element
108	MPM_TIMEELEMT	This table maintains the list of ONLY client-specific data elements configured in OEE add-on, configured language, and data elements description in configured language.	Configuration data	Data element description
109	MPM_WRKFLOW_ CONFIG	This table maintains for each workflow under workflow configuration, its Type_ID, step_ID in the sequence of execution, along with each parameter's value. This table will basically tell the workflow execution steps.	Configuration data	OEEINT workflow configuration
110	MPM_SEQUENCES	This table maintains the next number for the unique ID/key generation for all OEE transaction tables. For example, the MPM_RELEAS_DMD_HDR table has a unique column RELEASED_HDR_ID whose next value is maintained in this table. For every data insertion to this table, the unique key is incremented and maintained with its value.	Configuration data	OEE transaction data unique ID sequence numbers
111	MPM_VERSION_GEN	This table maintains the list of version keys and the next value to be used. All OEE transaction data has a version number maintained in their respective tables. This version unique value is generated and maintained in this VERSION_GEN table.	Configuration data	OEE transaction data unique ID version numbers

(continued)

Sl.No	Table Name	Description	Type of Data	Details
112	MPM_SERVICES_DEF	This table maintains the list of OEE-related services, their JNDI look-up names, and BEAN details.	Configuration data	OEE service definitions
113	MPM_STATUS	This table maintains the list of client- and plant-specific various order status details.	Configuration data	Order status
114	MPM_STATUS_DESC	This table maintains the status description of client and plant order status maintained in MPM_STATUS table in all the languages supported by OEE.	Configuration data	Order status description
115	MPM_METHODS_DEF	This table maintains the list of method names, their IDs, and their service IDs of extension configuration	Configuration data	OEE configuration/Extension configuration
116	MPM_FILES	This table lists the inbound and outbound messages that can be monitored in the queue monitor. For every message, request and response XML files are stored with a unique file ID with corresponding timestamps. For example, when a LOIPRO is transferred from ECC to MII, the LOIPRO IDoc file, LOIPRO.Req, and LOIPRO.Res file structures are stored.	Transaction data	Queue monitor
117	MPM_INT_CAP_NODE	This table maintains the production run interval event specific to each capacity node.	Transaction data	Capacity-specific order run
118	MPM_PROFILE	This table maintains the profile information for each OEEINT message processed, such as message processed duration and message processing start time for every step ID.	Transaction data	OEEINT message profiler
119	MPM_QUEUE	This table lists the OEEINT messages that are in the integration queue for processing.	Transaction data	Queue monitor
120	MPM_MESSAGE	This table maintains the key columns displayed in the queue monitor (ID, Type, Data Time, Message, Content, and Status).	Transaction data	Queue monitor
121	MPM_MESSAGE_QUEUE	This table maintains all the columns displayed in the queue monitor and additional details for each message queued and processed.	Transaction data	Queue monitor

122	MPM_PROD_EVENTS	This table maintains the list of machine and line downtimes created either manually or automatically from Pco. The table stores the machine node ID, DC element used, start and end timestamps (local and UTC), downtime duration, order correlation, unique event ID, reason codes for 10 levels, and HANA-replicated time.	Transaction data	Machine/line events
123	MPM_EVENT_MAP	This table maintains the map between two events. For instance, when you link a machine/line downtime to another machine downtime, the parent event ID and child event ID (attached) are mapped here.	Transaction data	Event-to-event map
124	MPM_EVENT_NODE_MAP	This table lists any downtime events that are attached with a root-cause machine.	Transaction data	Event-to root-cause-machine map
125	MPM_AGGR_EVENT_MAP	This table has the map between the events and its aggregations. These aggregations are the ones that are replicated to HANA tables.	Transaction data	Event-to-aggregation map
126	MPM_DATA_AS_MC_EVT	OBSOLETE		
127	MPM_DATA_EVENT_MAP	This table maintains the link between the machine event (EVENT_ID) and its associated order (RUN_ID), whether it is a bottleneck or not, and status of downtime (closed or open).	Transaction data	Event-to-RUN map
128	MPM_SCHEDULED_DOWN	OBSOLETE		
129	MPM_INT_EVENT_MAP	This table stores the map of events that happened in a production interval. The TIME_ID of MPM_PROD_RUN_INT table has a map with the EVENT_ID of the MPM_PROD_EVENTS table.	Transaction data	Order-run-interval-to-event map

(*continued*)

Sl.No	Table Name	Description	Type of Data	Details
130	MPM_PRDRUN_INT_EVT	This table stores the aggregated events by reason codes that occurred during the order run. This table gets replicated to HANA for generating events reports for an order/shift, etc.	Transaction data	Aggregated events in order run interval
131	MPM_RELEASED_DMD	This table maintains the client- and plant-specific production and process orders downloaded from ECC with other details like operation number, planned start and end datetimes, dispatched node ID with a unique released ID (specific to OEE) and released header ID.	Transaction data	Released order demand
132	MPM_RELEAS_DMD_HDR	This table maintains the client- and plant-specific header details of production and process order.	Transaction data	Released order demand header
133	MPM_PROD_RUN_DATA	This table maintains all the client- and plant-specific data collection elements that can be order dependent and order independent. Each data collection element has the data collected timestamp in local and UTC, UOM of data collection, material name, HANA-replicated timestamp, and reason codes for data collections of loss type.	Transaction data	Shop-floor data collection
134	MPM_PROD_RUN_INT	This table maintains the duration of each production activity interval for an order run (if prod activities are configured). For orders where production activity is not configured, the complete order duration for the shift is stored as an interval.	Transaction data	Order run interval
135	MPM_PROD_RUN_HDR	This table maintains the list of client- and plant-specific production and process orders, with their release ID, release header ID, release timestamp, node ID, shift ID, shift start and end timestamps, order status, production mode, production activity, reporting shift ID, routing details, target quantity, etc.	Transaction data	Order run header

136	MPM_SHIFT_HANDOVER	This table maintains the list of client-, plant-, and node-specific shift-handed-over details like shift ID, shift datetime, handed over by user, and shift related happenings, etc.	Transaction data	Shift handover
137	MPM_HANA_AGG_QUEUE	This table lists the details of records aggregated to be replicated to HANA from OEE. The details stored are the timestamp and the Time_ID and a confirmation of the replication process.	Transaction data	HANA aggregation queue
138	MPM_PMNOTIFY_HDR	This table stores all the header details of Plant maintenance notification such as breakdown type, machine, functional location, triggered timestamp, PM notification number etc	Transaction Data	PM Notification
139	MPM_GOODS_MVT_RC	This table is available from 15.1 patch 7. This table stores the reason code when you perform GR reversal from GR screen in Application launch pad	Transactiondata	ApplicationLaunchPad
140	MPM_GOODS_MVT_LOGS	This table is for future enhancement. Not used now.	Transactiondata	ApplicationLaunchPad
141	MPM_GOODS_MVT_DATA	This table stores the goods movement data posted from Goods movement app for goods receipt and goods issue. The data stored are material details, order details, posting ID, material document number created, Handling unit number, Reservation number etc	Transactiondata	ApplicationLaunchPad
142	MPM_USR_DFTS	This table stores the default definitions configured for each user in Netweaver identity management. The definitions are default client, plant, Workunit and POD.	Master Data	Netweaver User Management
143	MPM_LSTCONF_UPDATE	Planned for future enhancements		

Section 3: Customization Configuration In General Configurations

Customization Parameter	Description	Values
Allowed Modification Limit	It is the time duration from the current time for which you are allowed to edit the order-specific reported data in the past.	Enter a time duration with a desired UOM. All the time-specific UOMs are listed from MPM_UOM standard table.
Allowed time limit for starting order in the past	A duration in the past within which an order can be started for data-reporting purposes.	Enter a time duration with a desired UOM. All the time-specific UOMs are listed from MPM_UOM standard table. e.g., 1440 MIN (1 day)
Default Data Collection Element - Scheduled Down	Configure the data collection element name used to report scheduled/planned downtime to OEE. This is created in ERP OEE add-on and transferred to OEE.	SCHEDULED_DOWN If you use any custom data collection elements for scheduled down, then you need to configure it here.
Default Data Collection Element - Scrap	Configure the data collection element name used to report scrap to OEE.	SCRAP If you use any custom data collection elements for scrap, then you need to configure it here.
Default Data Collection Element - Speed Loss	Configure the data collection element name used to report speed loss to OEE.	SPEED_LOSS If you use any custom data collection elements for speed loss, then you need to configure it here.
Default Data Collection Element - Unscheduled Down	Configure the data collection element name used to report unscheduled/unplanned downtime to OEE.	UNSCHEDULED_DOWN If you use any custom data collection elements for Unscheduled down, then you need to configure it here.
Minor stoppage limit	Configuration to set a duration for minor stoppages of machines. All stoppages under this will be categorized as minor stoppage and will be listed in Minor Stoppage tab in Manage Downtime screen.	Example: 10 mins
Date range for order selection	Duration in either the past or future from the current time within which an order will be displayed in the OEE dashboard in Manage Orders screen. The orders are displayed based on their scheduled start date time with all different statuses (New, Active, Hold, or Completed).	Example: Value set is 1440 MINS, which is 1 day. Current date: July 5th 2015. All the orders whose scheduled date time are July 4th and July 6th are displayed in the Manage orders button of OEE dashboard.

(*continued*)

Customization Parameter	Description	Values
Relevant Production Activity	Production activities are used in modeling your production line for different activities during order execution. These production activities are configured in ERP add-on and then transferred to OEE. You can configure these activities for each line using this customization parameter.	No default values.
Retention Time for SAP HANA Replicated Tables	Duration for which SAP HANA replicated tables' data in SAP OEE should be retained.	Enter a time duration with a desired UOM. All the time-specific UOMs are listed that are maintained in the MPM_UOM standard table. If you want to retain data for a particular period, then run transaction SAPMPM/apps/ DataArchive/ArchiveHANAReplicatedTables
Retention time for non-SAP HANA replicated tables	Duration for which non-SAP HANA replicated tables' data in SAP OEE should be retained.	Enter a time duration with a desired UOM. All the time-specific UOMs are listed in the MPM_ UOM standard table. If you want to retain data for a particular period, then run transaction SAPMPM/apps/ DataArchive/ArchiveNonHANA ReplicatedTables
Unit of measure conversion transaction	Configure a standard or customized UOM conversion transaction that does the conversion of quantity, in particular for a given material, quantity, and UOM.	SAPMPM/apps/common/ MaterialUOMConversion is the standard MPM transaction. You can also maintain your own customized MII transaction.
Batch Number Is Mandatory for Batch-Managed Material	Batch number can be configured for a line to capture the batch number when reporting production for monitoring purpose.	Yes: System prompts for batch number when reporting Production No: Production can be reported without a batch number in OEE dashboard.
Decimal Value Precision	Configure the precision of decimal values that you want when reporting data collection elements of type quantity on the OEE dashboard.	Example: 2
Order start in the future is allowed	You can configure this if you have a requirement to start an order in the future from current date.	Yes: System allows you to start an order on the future date No: System throws an error when you try to start an order on the future date on the OEE dashboard

(*continued*)

Customization Parameter	Description	Values
Serial Number Is Mandatory for Reporting Production	Serial number can be configured for a line so that the system can capture the serial number when reporting production for monitoring purpose.	Yes: System prompts for serial number when reporting production No: Production can be reported without a serial number in OEE dashboard.
Show completed orders on dashboard	You can configure whether you want to view the completed orders on OEE dashboard under the Manage Orders screen.	Yes: Completed orders are listed on OEE Dashboard. No: Completed orders are not listed on OEE Dashboard.
Order completion when unaccounted time exists	During the order execution, there may be unaccounted for time that is still not reported to OEE in the form of any loss. You can use this parameter to define whether the system should allow the order completion even when unaccounted for time exists.	Allowed: System allows you to complete the order even when unaccounted for time exists. Not Allowed: System does not allow you to complete the order even when unaccounted for time exists.
Shift Handover Available Before Shift End	Shift handover normally happens before the shift end. OEE allows you to configure the time at which shift handover should happen. You can configure a time interval and only when that time is reached, the shift handover button will appear.	Enter a time duration with a desired UOM. All the time-specific UOMs are listed that are maintained in MPM_UOM standard table. If you want to retain data for a particular period, then run transaction SAPMPM/apps/DataArchive/ ArchiveNonHANAReplicatedTables e.g., 10 MIN
Allow Modification of Automation Records	This parameter allows you to configure whether the data collection elements reported automatically from shop floor can be modified or not.	Yes: Automation records are allowed to be modified No: Automation records cannot be modified
Minor Stoppages Should be Included in Availability	You can define here if you want the minor stoppages to be part of availability KPI.	Yes: System considers minor stoppages to affect the availability KPI. No: System does not consider minor stoppages when calculating the availability KPI.
Irrelevant for OEE Calculations	If you have a requirement where you are not measuring KPI at line level, then you can control that using this parameter.	Yes: System considers line-specific reported data collection elements for OEE calculations No: System does not consider line-specific reported data collection elements for OEE calculations

(*continued*)

Customization Parameter	Description	Values
Enable Periodic Confirmations	You can use this parameter if you want to periodically perform order confirmations to ERP at a line level. Note: "ConfirmationsEnqueuer" is the scheduler job that does periodic confirmations for all the lines.	Yes: OEE periodically confirms production data to SAP ERP No: System follows the duration of periodic confirmation set at scheduler job "ConfirmationsEnqueuer" at the plant level
Shrinking Order Duration Allowed	You can edit a completed order's start or completed timestamp to shrink an order using this parameter.	Yes: order duration can be shrunk No: order duration cannot be shrunk E.g., A completed order has start and end timestamps as 3pm and 5pm, respectively. You can edit any of this to shrink the order. Say, 5pm can be edited to 4pm. Caution: When you shrink the order, the production and loss data that were reported between 4pm and 5pm will be lost, which needs to be handled using a customization.
Unaccounted Speed Loss Limit	During the order execution, there may be unaccounted speed loss duration, which is still not reported to OEE as a speed loss. You can use this parameter to define the limit for unaccounted speed loss.	E.g., 10 MIN Enter a time duration with a desired UOM. All the time-specific UOMs are listed from MPM_UOM standard table.
Line Behavior	Mark Line Down if any bottleneck machine is down.	Line will be down when even one bottleneck is down. (Line has multiple bottlenecks.)
	Mark Line Down if all bottleneck machines are down.	Line will be down only when all the bottlenecks of the line are down. (Line has multiple bottlenecks.)
	Multi-capacity single-line	Production is reported at line level with the option to select the number of capacities that will be used for production.
Line Behavior	Multi-capacity multi-line	Line is configured with multiple capacities. Order-operation can be released to different capacities and can be started and completed at each capacity. The data collections are done at capacity level and not at line level. KPIs are calculated at capacity level and hence will look bloated.
SAP OEE Application transaction mode	This parameter signifies if the goods movement app should operarte in online or offline mode.	Online: ERP/EWM and OEE connection is active. The goods movement app posts the GR and GI synchronously to ERP Offline: ERP/EWM and OEE connection is inactive. The goods movement app data should be archived in a custom table and later should be posted to ERP/EWM once the connection is restored

(*continued*)

Customization Parameter	Description	Values
Offline-online mode change transaction:	This transaction would get executed, when you are changing the mode from offline to online. You can use this transaction to take care of some preparatory steps when the mode change happens. For example, you can use this transaction to synchronize/post the archived goods movement data to ERP when in offline mode.	
Online-Offline mode change transaction	This transaction would get executed, when you are changing the mode from online to offline. You can use this transaction to take care of some preparatory steps when the mode change happens.	
Allow PM Notification trigger	This parameter signifies if the plant maintenance notification triggered to ERP requires a supervisor approval or not	No: PM Notification in triggered automatically to ERP without any supervisors approval Yes: PM Notification requires supervisors approval before triggered to ERP
Allow multiple orders to be started at same time	This parameter decides if single or multiple order can be executed in a line.	Yes: You can start multiple orders from the dashboard. No: Only one order/operation can be started and executed at a given point of time. The second order/operation can be started only after completing the first order/operation.
PM Notification type	This parameter signifies the type of notification that you wish to handle in OEE when triggered to ERP.	Example: M1, M2. Ensure the configured notification types exist already in ERP
SAP ERP type	From OEE_MII 15.0 SP06 and OEE_MII 15.1 SP01 onwards, S4Hana is supported in OEE. The corresponding supported OEE_ERP version is OEE_ERP 15.0 SP02. This means if the ERP system is on S4HANA system, OEE would work with Plant Hierarchy creation in S4HANA system and download to MII. There are 3 Options for this customization.	Ehp: ERP is on normal Ehp or Suite on HANA system. Compatibility mode: ERP system is on S4HANA system but running in Compatibility Mode. Target Mode: ERP system is on S4HANA system but running in Target mode.The above enhancement was done to support long material number in S4HANA.

Section 4: Standard Activity Configuration

Activity ID	Class or URL	Activity Type	Activity Description	Options	Options Value	Details
				Description	Sequence /Value	
AC_DOWN_LIST	sap.oee.ui.oeeDowntimeList	UI	SAP-Manage Downtimes	Default Tab	0 /	Displays the list of reported downtimes. Provides the option to report / edit/split/delete downtimes.
					BREAKDOWN	Displays all the breakdowns
					MINOR	Displays minor breakdowns as per the limit set in customization configuration “Minor stoppage limit”
					LINEDOWN	All line downs are displayed
					OVERLAPPING	All the overlapped downtimes are displayed
				ALLOW_PM_NOTIF	0 / TRUE	This enables reporting PM notification directly from Manage Downtime screen
AC_GENERIC	sap.oee.ui.oeeGenericDataCollection	UI	SAP-Generic Data Collection		Optional value:	Displays the list of configured custom data collection elements. Data can be reported against these data collection elements.
					CONTEXT	A DC element context can be defined and all the DC elements with that context will be displayed together when this activity and option are used.
					DCELEMENT	Lists all the DC elements when this activity is used with the option value

(*continued*)

Activity ID	Class or URL	Activity Type	Activity Description	Options	Options Value	Details
				Description	Sequence / Value	
AC_KPI	sap.oee.ui.oeeKpiTile Container	UI	SAP-KPI Tile Container			Displays the list of configured KPI tiles.
				ALLOWED_ KPI	0 / KPI names	Add details about additional custom KPI that needs to be displayed in a KPI container in OEE worker UI
AC_LINE_ MONITOR	sap.oee.ui.lineMonitor	UI	SAP-Line Monitor	AUTO_REF_ TIME_IN_MIN	0 / 1	UI to monitor all the parameters of a specific line with a refresh rate configuration for the UI
				SAP-Auto Refresh Time in Minutes		The refresh time interval can be set as per the requirements
AC_ORD	sap.oee.ui. oeeSelectOrder	UI	SAP-Manage Orders	DEFAULT_ FILTERS	0 / ACT/NEW/ CMPL/HOLD	Displays the list of active orders for a line on Manage Order screen. By default, the orders in active status are filtered and displayed. The filter can be set as per the requirements.
				Default Filters		
AC_ORD_DET	sap.oee.ui.orderDetails	UI	SAP-Order Details			Displays the details of an order on the Manage Order screen.
AC_ORD_IND	sap.oee.ui.oeeReportO rderIndependentDataC ollection	UI	SAP-Order Independent Data Collection			Displays the list of custom data collection elements, which are configured to be order independent.

AC_PLANT_ MONITOR	sap.oee.ui.plantMonitor	UI	SAP-Plant Monitor	AUTO_REF_ TIME_IN_MIN	0 / 1	UI to monitor all the line parameters within a plant with a refresh rate configuration for the UI.
				SAP-Auto Refresh Time in Minutes		
AC_RAW_ MAT	sap.oee.ui.oeeReport Components	UI	OBSOLETE			
AC_REP_QTY	sap.oee.ui.oee ReportQuantity	UI	SAP-Report Produced or Rejected Quantity			Displays all the reported quantities and their UOM on Report Production screen. Quantities can be reported on a shift basis.
AC_REP_ QTY_HR	sap.oee.ui.oeeReport QuantityHourly	UI	SAP-Report Hourly Production			Displays all the reported quantities and their UOM on Report Production screen on an hourly basis.
AC_REV_ORD	sap.oee. ui.oeeReviewOrder	UI	SAP-Review Order			Displays all the consolidated data for an order and its details for the order across all shifts.
AC_REV_SFT	sap.oee. ui.oeeReviewShift	UI	SAP-Review Shift			Displays list of orders executed for the given shift and their associated data.
AC_SA_REV_ ORD	sap.oee.ui.oee Standalone ReviewOrder	UI	Standalone Review Order			Displays the order details, order data collections, other data collections, top downtimes, downtimes, top 5 reasons, line availability summary, machine availability summary, and current order KPIs.

(continued)

Activity ID	Class or URL	Activity Type	Activity Description	Options	Options Value	Details
				Description	Sequence /Value	
PM_NOTIF_ LIST	sap.oee.ui.oee NotificationList	UI	Manage Plant Maintenance Notification			Display the PM notification raised from OEE and also allows user to create, approve, reject, and delete an existing notification.
				DURATION	0/ <number>	This value defines how many numbers of hours the notification should be displayed.
ACT_REV_ ORD_GRAPH	sap.oee.ui.oee Revie OrderGraphical	UI	Review Order Graphical View			Displays in graphical manner the order details, order data collections, other data collections, top downtimes, downtimes, top 5 reasons, line availability summary, machine availability summary, current order KPIs.
ACT_REV_ SFT_GRAPH	sap.oee.ui.oeeRevie ShiftGraphical	UI	Review Order Graphical View			Displays the shift-orders details, order data collections, other data collections, top downtimes, downtimes, top 5 reasons, line availability summary, machine availability summary, current order KPIs, shift-related data collection.

AC_SA_REV_SFT	sap.oee.ui.oee Standalone ReviewShift	UI	Standalone Review Shift	Displays the shift order details, order data collections, other data collections, top downtimes, downtimes, top 5 reasons, line availability summary, machine availability summary, current order KPIs, and shift-related data collection.
AC_SL	sap.oee. ui.oeeSpeedLoss	UI	SAP-Report Speed Loss	Displays the reported speed loss quantity against an order-operation and provides option to report and edit speed loss data.
AC_SL_HR	sap.oee.ui.oeeSpeed LossHourly	UI	SAP-Report Speed Loss Hourly	Shows the reported speed loss quantity for an order and provides option to report and edit speed loss data. Data can be reported on hourly basis.
AC_STD_PANEL_1	sap.oee.ui.oeeOperator DashboardStandardDel iveredActivityForPanel1	UI	SAP-First Standard Panel	Displays the order card and list of open downtimes.
AC_STD_PANEL_2	sap.oee.ui.oeeOperator DashboardStandardDel iveredActivityForPanel2	UI	SAP-Second Standard Panel	Displays the current shift KPIs and list of untagged events.
AC_STD_PANEL_3	sap.oee.ui.oeeOperator DashboardStandardDel iveredActivityForPanel3	UI	SAP-Third Standard Panel	Displays the line availability summary and top downtimes.
AC_STD_VAL	sap.oee.ui.oeeReportS tandardValueDataColl ection	UI	SAP-Standard Value Data Collection	Displays the list of standard value parameters configured for a particular work center against which the data can be collected and updated back to ECC.

(continued)

Activity ID	Class or URL	Activity Type	Activity Description	Options	Options Value	Details
				Description	Sequence / Value	
DC_CONF_EXT_ACT	com.sap.xapps.oee.extension.extensions.ErpConfirmationOnDCExtension	Extension	SAP-ERP Confirmation on Reporting Quantity			This activity performs the yield confirmation to ERP and gets executed as a data collection extension after the yield is reported in OEE dashboard.
SCRAP_COMP_DC_GM_EXT	com.sap.xapps.oee.extension.extensions.ErpScrappedComponentGoodsMovementOnDCExtension	Extension	SAP-GM of Material Waste on Reporting Quantity			This activity performs the scrap confirmation to ERP and gets executed as a data collection extension after the scrap is reported in OEE dashboard.
SCRAP_COMP_GM_EXT	com.sap.xapps.oee.extension.extensions.ErpScrappedComponentGoodsMovementForRunExtension	Extension	SAP-GM of Matl Waste on Order Stop/Shift Complete			This activity performs the scrap goods movement to ERP and gets executed as a data collection extension after the order is stopped or shift is completed
AC_ORDER_CARD	Used internally within the standard operator dashboard by SAP					
AC_UNTAGGED	Used internally within the standard operator dashboard by SAP					
AC_WC_STRIP	Used internally within the standard operator dashboard by SAP					
AC_TOP_DT	Used internally within the standard operator dashboard by SAP					
AC_OPEN_DOWNS	Used internally within the standard operator dashboard by SAP					

ORDER_CONF_EXT_ACT	com.sap.xapps.oee.extension.extensions.ErpOrderConfirmationExtension	Extension	SAP-ERP confirmation on order complete		This activity performs the order confirmation to ERP and gets executed as an extension after order completion in OEE dashboard
RUN_CONF_EXT	com.sap.xapps.oee.extension.extensions.ErpOrderConfirmationForRunExtension	Extension	SAP-ERP confirmation on order stop/shift complete		This activity performs the order confirmation to ERP and gets executed as an extension after the order is stopped or shift is completed in OEE dashboard
ACT_STD_COMP_GI	sap.oee.m.goodsissue	UI Component	Goods Issue		Transaction paths required for the app to operate in online and offline mode for goods issue. (Refer to Chapter 8 for the details on these transactions)
ACT_STD_COMP_GR	sap.oee.m.goodsreceipt	UI Component	Goods Receipt		Transaction paths required for the app to operate in online and offline mode for goods receipt. (Refer to Chapter 8 for the details on these transactions)

Section 5: Extension Configuration

In this section, you will learn about the request and response XML structures of all the OEE standard methods seen under extension configuration. These XML structures are to be followed when developing custom OEE extensions.

In the custom MII transaction, the following three parameters are to be defined as transaction properties. The respective request and response structure is to be utilized. For example, if the custom extension is hooked to the post of the "Order Complete" method, then the `OutputString` XML of the "Complete Order" method should be passed to the `Input` transaction property of your custom MII transaction to get the order completed details. All these XML structures are standard. Similarly, when a custom MII transaction is added to pre of extension, the the XMLInputString is passed with the required values from the standard method.

- Property Name: `XMLInputString`, Data type: XML and Parameter type: Input
- Property Name: `XMLModifiedOutputString`, Data type: XML and Parameter type: Input
- Property Name: `XMLOutputString`, Data type: XML and Parameter type: Output
- You can check the XMLInputString and XMLOutputString structure for each of the extension methods in the below section.

Start Order-Operation InputString


```
<?xml version="1.0" encoding="UTF-8"?><ns2:InputStartProductionRun xmlns:ns2="com.sap.xapps.
oee.dto.releaseddemandservices">
    <releasedHeaderID>41513</releasedHeaderID>
    <releasedID>543</releasedID>
    <reportingShiftID>S-11</reportingShiftID>
    <productionActivity>CONSUMPTION</productionActivity>
    <shiftGrouping>51</shiftGrouping>
    <workBreakSchedule/>
          <runStartDate xmlns:xsi=http://www.w3.org/2001/XMLSchema-instance
               xsi:nil="true"/>
    <runStartTime xmlns:xsi="http//www.w3.org/2001/XMLSchema-instance" xsinil="true"/>
    <runStartTimestamp>2015-07-06T20:14:00+05:30</runStartTimestamp>
        </ns2:InputStartProductionRun>
```


Start Order-Operation OutputString


```
<?xml version="1.0" encoding="UTF-8" standalone="yes"?>
<outputProductionRunBasic>
    <runID>5185</runID>
    <releasedHeaderID>41515</releasedHeaderID>
    <releasedID>545</releasedID>
    <plant>9001</plant>
    <nodeId>53DC46C8779243F0E1008000097E4C53</nodeId>
    <reportingShiftId>S-11</reportingShiftId>
    <shiftGrouping>51</shiftGrouping>
    <workBreakSchedule xmlns:xsi=http://www.w3.org/2001/XMLSchema-instance
          xsi:nil="true"/>
```

```
    <targetQuantity>444.000</targetQuantity>
    <targetQtyUom>L</targetQtyUom>
    <client>800</client>
    <order>000070003213</order>
    <routingOperNo>0020</routingOperNo>
    <material>CYRUX 200 EC</material>
    <productionActivity xmlns:xsi="http://www.w3.org/2001/XMLSchema-instance"
      xsi:nil="true"/>
    <startDate xmlns:xsi="http://www.w3.org/2001/XMLSchema-instance" xsi:nil="true"/>
    <startTime xmlns:xsi="http://www.w3.org/2001/XMLSchema-instance" xsi:nil="true"/>
    <endDate xmlns:xsi="http://www.w3.org/2001/XMLSchema-instance" xsi:nil="true"/>
    <endTime xmlns:xsi="http://www.w3.org/2001/XMLSchema-instance" xsi:nil="true"/>
    <status>ACT</status>
    <grossDuration>0</grossDuration>
    <startDateUtc xmlns:xsi="http://www.w3.org/2001/XMLSchema-instance" xsi:nil="true"/>
    <startTimeUtc xmlns:xsi="http://www.w3.org/2001/XMLSchema-instance" xsi:nil="true"/>
    <endDateUtc xmlns:xsi="http://www.w3.org/2001/XMLSchema-instance" xsi:nil="true"/>
    <endTimeUtc xmlns:xsi="http://www.w3.org/2001/XMLSchema-instance" xsi:nil="true"/>
    <ioStatus>
        <version>0</version>
    </ioStatus>
    <standardRateQty>1000.000</standardRateQty>
    <standardRateUom>BT</standardRateUom>
    <timeQty>15.000</timeQty>
    <timeUom>MIN</timeUom>
    <timeQtyInSeconds>900</timeQtyInSeconds>
    <oeeRelevant>T</oeeRelevant>
    <sequenceNumber>0</sequenceNumber>
    <version>0</version>
    <startTimestamp>2015-07-06T20:40:00+05:30</startTimestamp>
    <endTimestamp xmlns:xsi="http://www.w3.org/2001/XMLSchema-instance" xsi:nil="true"/>
</outputProductionRunBasic>
```

Complete Order InputString

```
<?xml version="1.0" encoding="UTF-8"?><ns2:InputCompleteReleasedDemandList xmlns:ns2="com.
sap.xapps.oee.dto.releaseddemandservices">
    <inputCompleteReleasedDemandList>
        <endTimestamp>2015-07-06T20:15:00+05:30</endTimestamp>
        <releasedHeaderID>41556</releasedHeaderID>
        <releasedID>586</releasedID>
    </inputCompleteReleasedDemandList>
</ns2:InputCompleteReleasedDemandList>
```

Report Data OutputString

```
<?xml version="1.0" encoding="UTF-8"?><ns2:InputCollectDataForDCElementList xmlns:ns2="com.
sap.xapps.oee.dto.productionrunservices">
    <autoCollected>false</autoCollected>
    <client>800</client>
    <inputCollectDataForDCElements>
```

```
        <runID>7792</runID>
        <client>800</client>
        <dcElement>GOOD_QUANTITY</dcElement>
        <quantity>4.0</quantity>
        <uom>KG</uom>
        <material>1730</material>
 <startDate xmlns:xsi=http://www.w3.org/2001/XMLSchema-instance xsi:nil="true"/>
               <startTime xmlns:xsi=http://www.w3.org/2001/XMLSchema-instance
               xsi:nil="true"/>
        <endDate xmlns:xsi="http://www.w3.org/2001/XMLSchema-instance" xsi:nil="true"/>
        <endTime xmlns:xsi="http://www.w3.org/2001/XMLSchema-instance" xsi:nil="true"/>
        <rc1 xmlns:xsi="http://www.w3.org/2001/XMLSchema-instance" xsi:nil="true"/>
        <rc2 xmlns:xsi="http://www.w3.org/2001/XMLSchema-instance" xsi:nil="true"/>
        <rc3 xmlns:xsi="http://www.w3.org/2001/XMLSchema-instance" xsi:nil="true"/>
        <rc4 xmlns:xsi="http://www.w3.org/2001/XMLSchema-instance" xsi:nil="true"/>
        <rc5 xmlns:xsi="http://www.w3.org/2001/XMLSchema-instance" xsi:nil="true"/>
        <rc6 xmlns:xsi="http://www.w3.org/2001/XMLSchema-instance" xsi:nil="true"/>
        <rc7 xmlns:xsi="http://www.w3.org/2001/XMLSchema-instance" xsi:nil="true"/>
        <rc8 xmlns:xsi="http://www.w3.org/2001/XMLSchema-instance" xsi:nil="true"/>
        <rc9 xmlns:xsi="http://www.w3.org/2001/XMLSchema-instance" xsi:nil="true"/>
        <rc10 xmlns:xsi="http://www.w3.org/2001/XMLSchema-instance" xsi:nil="true"/>
        <comments/>
        <dcElementType>GOOD_QUANTITY</dcElementType>
        <notificatioNo xmlns:xsi="http://www.w3.org/2001/XMLSchema-instance"
              xsi:nil="true"/>
        <serialNo xmlns:xsi="http://www.w3.org/2001/XMLSchema-instance" xsi:nil="true"/>
        <batchNo xmlns:xsi="http://www.w3.org/2001/XMLSchema-instance" xsi:nil="true"/>
        <nodeID>53270168F93740A0E1008000097E4C53</nodeID>
        <plant>9001</plant>
        <entryType xmlns:xsi="http://www.w3.org/2001/XMLSchema-instance"
          xsi:nil="true"/>
        <startTimestamp>2015-10-31T14:50:26.534+05:30</startTimestamp>
        <endTimestamp>2015-10-31T14:50:26.534+05:30</endTimestamp>
    </inputCollectDataForDCElements>
</ns2:InputCollectDataForDCElementList>
```


Report Data OutputString


```
<?xml version="1.0" encoding="UTF-8"?><ns2:OutputDataCollection xmlns:ns2="com.sap.xapps.
oee.dto.productionrunservices">
    <client>800</client>
    <productionRunDataList>
        <runID>7792</runID>
        <entryID>2013</entryID>
        <client>800</client>
        <dcElement>GOOD_QUANTITY</dcElement>
        <quantity>4.0</quantity>
        <uom>KG</uom>
        <material>1730</material>
        <startDate>2015-10-31T14:50:26+05:30</startDate>
        <startTime>2015-10-31T14:50:26+05:30</startTime>
```

```
        <endDate>2015-10-31T14:50:26+05:30</endDate>
        <endTime>2015-10-31T14:50:26+05:30</endTime>
        <startDateUtc>2015-10-31T09:20:26+05:30</startDateUtc>
        <startTimeUtc>2015-10-31T09:20:26+05:30</startTimeUtc>
        <endDateUtc>2015-10-31T09:20:26+05:30</endDateUtc>
        <endTimeUtc>2015-10-31T09:20:26+05:30</endTimeUtc>
        <startTimestamp>2015-10-31T14:50:26+05:30</startTimestamp>
        <endTimestamp>2015-10-31T14:50:26+05:30</endTimestamp>
        <createdBy>mahalakshmis</createdBy>
        <changedBy>mahalakshmis</changedBy>
        <creationTimestamp>2015-10-31T14:50:34.019+05:30</creationTimestamp>
        <changeTimestamp>2015-10-31T14:50:34.019+05:30</changeTimestamp>
        <effectiveDuration>4</effectiveDuration>
        <quantityInStandardRateUOM>4.0</quantityInStandardRateUOM>
        <version>0</version>
        <serialNoRelevant>false</serialNoRelevant>
        <batchRelevant>false</batchRelevant>
        <baseUom>KG</baseUom>
        <quantityInBaseUom>4.0</quantityInBaseUom>
        <dataCollectionElementType>GOOD_QUANTITY</dataCollectionElementType>
        <splitAllowed>false</splitAllowed>
        <entryType>M</entryType>
        <noChangeOfDependencies>false</noChangeOfDependencies>
    </productionRunDataList>
</ns2:OutputDataCollection>
```

Create Downtime InputString

```
<?xml version="1.0" encoding="UTF-8"?><ns2:InputDowntimeStartEndList xmlns:ns2="com.sap.
xapps.oee.dto.test">
    <client>800</client>
    <downStartEndList>
        <client>800</client>
        <plant>9001</plant>
        <nodeID>53270189F93740A0E1008000097E4C53</nodeID>
        <startDate xmlns:xsi="http://www.w3.org/2001/XMLSchema-instance" xsi:nil="true"/>
        <startTime xmlns:xsi="http://www.w3.org/2001/XMLSchema-instance" xsi:nil="true"/>
        <dcElement>UNSCHEDULED_DOWN</dcElement>
        <rc1>DWNT_LOSS</rc1>
        <rc2>DWNT_LOSS</rc2>
        <rc3>BREAK_DOWN</rc3>
        <rc4>OEE_FILL</rc4>
        <rc5>PNEU_FAIL</rc5>
        <rc6/>
        <rc7/>
        <rc8/>
        <rc9/>
        <rc10/>
        <comments/>
        <runID xmlns:xsi="http://www.w3.org/2001/XMLSchema-instance" xsi:nil="true"/>
        <endDate xmlns:xsi="http://www.w3.org/2001/XMLSchema-instance" xsi:nil="true"/>
```

```
        <endTime xmlns:xsi="http://www.w3.org/2001/XMLSchema-instance" xsi:nil="true"/>
        <actsAsBottleneck>false</actsAsBottleneck>
        <entryType xmlns:xsi="http://www.w3.org/2001/XMLSchema-instance" xsi:nil="true"/>
        <startTimestamp>2015-10-31T13:03:00+05:30</startTimestamp>
        <endTimestamp xmlns:xsi="http://www.w3.org/2001/XMLSchema-instance" xsi:nil="true"/>
    </downStartEndList>
</ns2:InputDowntimeStartEndList>
```

Create Downtime OutputString

```
<?xml version="1.0" encoding="UTF-8"?><ns2:IOProductionRunDowntimeList xmlns:ns2="com.sap.
xapps.oee.dto.productionrunservices">
    <listOfIoProductionRunDowntime>
        <downID>819</downID>
        <runID xmlns:xsi="http://www.w3.org/2001/XMLSchema-instance" xsi:nil="true"/>
        <client>800</client>
        <plant>9001</plant>
        <nodeID>53270189F93740A0E1008000097E4C53</nodeID>
        <startDate>2015-10-31T13:03:00+05:30</startDate>
        <startTime>2015-10-31T13:03:00+05:30</startTime>
        <endDate xmlns:xsi="http://www.w3.org/2001/XMLSchema-instance" xsi:nil="true"/>
        <endTime xmlns:xsi="http://www.w3.org/2001/XMLSchema-instance" xsi:nil="true"/>
        <createdBy>mahalakshmis</createdBy>
        <changedBy>mahalakshmis</changedBy>
        <rc1>DWNT_LOSS</rc1>
        <rc2>DWNT_LOSS</rc2>
        <rc3>BREAK_DOWN</rc3>
        <rc4>OEE_FILL</rc4>
        <rc5>PNEU_FAIL</rc5>
        <rc6 xmlns:xsi="http://www.w3.org/2001/XMLSchema-instance" xsi:nil="true"/>
        <rc7 xmlns:xsi="http://www.w3.org/2001/XMLSchema-instance" xsi:nil="true"/>
        <rc8 xmlns:xsi="http://www.w3.org/2001/XMLSchema-instance" xsi:nil="true"/>
        <rc9 xmlns:xsi="http://www.w3.org/2001/XMLSchema-instance" xsi:nil="true"/>
        <rc10 xmlns:xsi="http://www.w3.org/2001/XMLSchema-instance" xsi:nil="true"/>
        <comments xmlns:xsi="http://www.w3.org/2001/XMLSchema-instance" xsi:nil="true"/>
        <dcElement>UNSCHEDULED_DOWN</dcElement>
        <eventType>UNSCD_DOWN</eventType>
        <effectiveDuration>0</effectiveDuration>
        <notificationNo xmlns:xsi="http://www.w3.org/2001/XMLSchema-instance" xsi:nil="true"/>
        <version>0</version>
        <quantity>0.0</quantity>
        <uom xmlns:xsi="http://www.w3.org/2001/XMLSchema-instance" xsi:nil="true"/>
        <material xmlns:xsi="http://www.w3.org/2001/XMLSchema-instance" xsi:nil="true"/>
 <quantityInBaseUOM xmlns:xsi=http://www.w3.org/2001/XMLSchema-instance xsi:nil="true"/>
        <baseUom xmlns:xsi="http://www.w3.org/2001/XMLSchema-instance" xsi:nil="true"/>
        <quantityInStandardRateUOM xmlns:xsi=http://www.w3.org/2001/XMLSchema-instance
          xsi:nil="true"/>
        <erpSendTime xmlns:xsi="http://www.w3.org/2001/XMLSchema-instance" xsi:nil="true"/>
        <startDateUtc>2015-10-31T07:33:00+05:30</startDateUtc>
        <startTimeUtc>2015-10-31T07:33:00+05:30</startTimeUtc>
        <endDateUtc xmlns:xsi="http://www.w3.org/2001/XMLSchema-instance" xsi:nil="true"/>
```

```
        <endTimeUtc xmlns:xsi="http://www.w3.org/2001/XMLSchema-instance" xsi:nil="true"/>
        <isBottleneck>F</isBottleneck>
        <actsAsBottleneck>F</actsAsBottleneck>
        <startTimestamp>2015-10-31T13:03:00+05:30</startTimestamp>
        <endTimestamp xmlns:xsi="http://www.w3.org/2001/XMLSchema-instance" xsi:nil="true"/>
        <entryType>M</entryType>
        <effectiveDurationForStartAndEndTime>0</effectiveDurationForStartAndEndTime>
        <noChangeOfDependencies>false</noChangeOfDependencies>
    </listOfIoProductionRunDowntime>
</ns2:IOProductionRunDowntimeList>
```

Update Downtime InputString

```
<?xml version="1.0" encoding="UTF-8"?><ns2:IOProductionRunDowntimeList xmlns:ns2="com.sap.
xapps.oee.dto.productionrunservices">
    <listOfIoProductionRunDowntime>
        <downID>820</downID>
        <runID xmlns:xsi="http://www.w3.org/2001/XMLSchema-instance" xsi:nil="true"/>
        <client>800</client>
        <plant>9001</plant>
        <nodeID>53270189F93740A0E1008000097E4C53</nodeID>
        <startDate xmlns:xsi="http://www.w3.org/2001/XMLSchema-instance" xsi:nil="true"/>
        <startTime xmlns:xsi="http://www.w3.org/2001/XMLSchema-instance" xsi:nil="true"/>
        <endDate xmlns:xsi="http://www.w3.org/2001/XMLSchema-instance" xsi:nil="true"/>
        <endTime xmlns:xsi="http://www.w3.org/2001/XMLSchema-instance" xsi:nil="true"/>
        <createdBy xmlns:xsi="http://www.w3.org/2001/XMLSchema-instance" xsi:nil="true"/>
        <changedBy>mahalakshmis</changedBy>
        <rc1>DWNT_LOSS</rc1>
        <rc2>DWNT_LOSS</rc2>
        <rc3>BREAK_DOWN</rc3>
        <rc4>OEE_FILL</rc4>
        <rc5>ELEC_FAIL</rc5>
        <rc6 xmlns:xsi="http://www.w3.org/2001/XMLSchema-instance" xsi:nil="true"/>
        <rc7 xmlns:xsi="http://www.w3.org/2001/XMLSchema-instance" xsi:nil="true"/>
        <rc8 xmlns:xsi="http://www.w3.org/2001/XMLSchema-instance" xsi:nil="true"/>
        <rc9 xmlns:xsi="http://www.w3.org/2001/XMLSchema-instance" xsi:nil="true"/>
        <rc10 xmlns:xsi="http://www.w3.org/2001/XMLSchema-instance" xsi:nil="true"/>
        <comments xmlns:xsi="http://www.w3.org/2001/XMLSchema-instance" xsi:nil="true"/>
        <dcElement>UNSCHEDULED_DOWN</dcElement>
        <eventType xmlns:xsi="http://www.w3.org/2001/XMLSchema-instance" xsi:nil="true"/>
        <effectiveDuration>0</effectiveDuration>
        <notificationNo xmlns:xsi="http://www.w3.org/2001/XMLSchema-instance" xsi:nil="true"/>
        <version>3287</version>
        <quantity>0.0</quantity>
        <uom xmlns:xsi="http://www.w3.org/2001/XMLSchema-instance" xsi:nil="true"/>
        <material xmlns:xsi="http://www.w3.org/2001/XMLSchema-instance" xsi:nil="true"/>
 <quantityInBaseUOM xmlns:xsi=http://www.w3.org/2001/XMLSchema-instance xsi:nil="true"/>
        <baseUom xmlns:xsi="http://www.w3.org/2001/XMLSchema-instance" xsi:nil="true"/>
 <quantityInStandardRateUOM xmlns:xsi=http://www.w3.org/2001/XMLSchema-instance
  xsi:nil="true"/>
        <erpSendTime xmlns:xsi="http://www.w3.org/2001/XMLSchema-instance" xsi:nil="true"/>
```

```
        <startDateUtc xmlns:xsi="http://www.w3.org/2001/XMLSchema-instance" xsi:nil="true"/>
        <startTimeUtc xmlns:xsi="http://www.w3.org/2001/XMLSchema-instance" xsi:nil="true"/>
        <endDateUtc xmlns:xsi="http://www.w3.org/2001/XMLSchema-instance" xsi:nil="true"/>
        <endTimeUtc xmlns:xsi="http://www.w3.org/2001/XMLSchema-instance" xsi:nil="true"/>
        <actsAsBottleneck>F</actsAsBottleneck>
        <startTimestamp>2015-10-31T15:00:00+05:30</startTimestamp>
        <endTimestamp>2015-10-31T15:06:00+05:30</endTimestamp>
        <entryType xmlns:xsi="http://www.w3.org/2001/XMLSchema-instance" xsi:nil="true"/>
        <effectiveDurationForStartAndEndTime>0</effectiveDurationForStartAndEndTime>
        <noChangeOfDependencies>true</noChangeOfDependencies>
    </listOfIoProductionRunDowntime>
</ns2:IOProductionRunDowntimeList>
```


Update Downtime OutputString


```
<?xml version="1.0" encoding="UTF-8"?><ns2:IOProductionRunDowntimeList xmlns:ns2="com.sap.
xapps.oee.dto.productionrunservices">
    <listOfIoProductionRunDowntime>
        <downID>820</downID>
        <runID xmlns:xsi="http://www.w3.org/2001/XMLSchema-instance" xsi:nil="true"/>
        <client>800</client>
        <plant>9001</plant>
        <nodeID>53270189F93740A0E1008000097E4C53</nodeID>
        <startDate>2015-10-31T15:00:00+05:30</startDate>
        <startTime>2015-10-31T15:00:00+05:30</startTime>
        <endDate>2015-10-31T15:06:00+05:30</endDate>
        <endTime>2015-10-31T15:06:00+05:30</endTime>
        <createdBy>mahalakshmis</createdBy>
        <changedBy>mahalakshmis</changedBy>
        <rc1>DWNT_LOSS</rc1>
        <rc2>DWNT_LOSS</rc2>
        <rc3>BREAK_DOWN</rc3>
        <rc4>OEE_FILL</rc4>
        <rc5>ELEC_FAIL</rc5>
        <rc6 xmlns:xsi="http://www.w3.org/2001/XMLSchema-instance" xsi:nil="true"/>
        <rc7 xmlns:xsi="http://www.w3.org/2001/XMLSchema-instance" xsi:nil="true"/>
        <rc8 xmlns:xsi="http://www.w3.org/2001/XMLSchema-instance" xsi:nil="true"/>
        <rc9 xmlns:xsi="http://www.w3.org/2001/XMLSchema-instance" xsi:nil="true"/>
        <rc10 xmlns:xsi="http://www.w3.org/2001/XMLSchema-instance" xsi:nil="true"/>
        <comments xmlns:xsi="http://www.w3.org/2001/XMLSchema-instance" xsi:nil="true"/>
        <dcElement>UNSCHEDULED_DOWN</dcElement>
        <eventType>UNSCD_DOWN</eventType>
        <effectiveDuration>360</effectiveDuration>
        <notificationNo xmlns:xsi="http://www.w3.org/2001/XMLSchema-instance" xsi:nil="true"/>
        <version>3288</version>
        <quantity>0.0</quantity>
        <uom xmlns:xsi="http://www.w3.org/2001/XMLSchema-instance" xsi:nil="true"/>
        <material xmlns:xsi="http://www.w3.org/2001/XMLSchema-instance" xsi:nil="true"/>
 <quantityInBaseUOM xmlns:xsi=http://www.w3.org/2001/XMLSchema-instance xsi:nil="true"/>
        <baseUom xmlns:xsi="http://www.w3.org/2001/XMLSchema-instance" xsi:nil="true"/>
 <quantityInStandardRateUOM xmlns:xsi=http://www.w3.org/2001/XMLSchema-instance
  xsi:nil="true"/>
```

```
        <erpSendTime xmlns:xsi="http://www.w3.org/2001/XMLSchema-instance" xsi:nil="true"/>
        <startDateUtc>2015-10-31T09:30:00+05:30</startDateUtc>
        <startTimeUtc>2015-10-31T09:30:00+05:30</startTimeUtc>
        <endDateUtc>2015-10-31T09:36:00+05:30</endDateUtc>
        <endTimeUtc>2015-10-31T09:36:00+05:30</endTimeUtc>
        <isBottleneck>F</isBottleneck>
        <actsAsBottleneck>F</actsAsBottleneck>
        <startTimestamp>2015-10-31T15:00:00+05:30</startTimestamp>
        <endTimestamp>2015-10-31T15:06:00+05:30</endTimestamp>
        <entryType>M</entryType>
        <effectiveDurationForStartAndEndTime>0</effectiveDurationForStartAndEndTime>
        <noChangeOfDependencies>false</noChangeOfDependencies>
    </listOfIoProductionRunDowntime>
</ns2:IOProductionRunDowntimeList>
```

GET OEE KPIs InputString

```
<?xml version="1.0" encoding="UTF-8"?><ns2:InputKPIService xmlns:ns2="com.sap.xapps.oee.dto.
kpiservices">
    <client>800</client>
    <endTimestamp>2015-10-31T22:00:00+05:30</endTimestamp>
    <nodeID>53270168F93740A0E1008000097E4C53</nodeID>
    <plant>9001</plant>
    <startTimestamp>2015-10-31T14:00:00+05:30</startTimestamp>
</ns2:InputKPIService>
```

GET OEE KPIs OutputString

```
<?xml version="1.0" encoding="UTF-8" standalone="no"?> <ns2:OutputKPIService xmlns:ns2="com.
sap.xapps.oee.dto.kpiservices">
<availability>100.0</availability>
<customKpis>
<entry>
 <key>CUSTOM_KPI_1</key>
<value/> </entry> <entry>
<key>CUSTOM_KPI_2</key>
<value/> </entry> <entry>
 <key>CUSTOM_KPI_3</key>
value/> </entry> <entry>
<key>CUSTOM_KPI_4</key>
<value/> </entry> </customKpis>
<flowTime>0.0</flowTime>
 <loadingTime>11381.0</loadingTime>
 <netOperatingTime>0.0</netOperatingTime>
 <netProductionTime>11381.0</netProductionTime>
<oee>0.0</oee>
<performance>0.0</performance>
 <quality>0.0</quality>
 <qualityLossTime>0.0</qualityLossTime>
<speedLossTime>0.0</speedLossTime>
<timeUom>SECOND</timeUom>
```

```
<unScheduledDowntime>0.0</unScheduledDowntime> <unaccountedTime>11381.0</unaccountedTime>
 <valueOperationTime>0.0</valueOperationTime>
 </ns2:OutputKPIService>
```

Close Shift InputString

```
<?xml version="1.0" encoding="UTF-8" standalone="true"?>
    <ns2:InputCloseShift xmlns:ns2="com.sap.xapps.oee.dto.productionrunservices">
        <inputCloseProductionRunList>
        <runID>5761</runID>
        <endDate>2013-05-16T19:46:54.049+05:30</endDate>
        <endTime>2013-05-16T19:46:54.049+05:30</endTime>
        <endTimestamp>2013-05-16T19:46:54.049+05:30</endTimestamp>

        </inputCloseProductionRunList>
        <inputCloseProductionRunList>
        <runID>5762</runID>
        <endDate>2013-05-16T19:46:54.268+05:30</endDate>
        <endTime>2013-05-16T19:46:54.268+05:30</endTime>
        <endTimestamp>2013-05-16T19:46:54.268+05:30</endTimestamp>
        </inputCloseProductionRunList>
    <restartRunInNextShift>false</restartRunInNextShift>
    </ns2:InputCloseShift>
```

Close Shift OutputString

```
<?xml version="1.0" encoding="UTF-8" standalone="yes"?>
<outputProductionRunBasic>
        <runID>5802</runID>
        <releasedHeaderID>5694</releasedHeaderID>
        <releasedID>6098</releasedID>
        <plant>1000</plant>
        <nodeId>00163EA724B81ED28E8B2390F5B089EC</nodeId>
        <reportingShiftId>HWS3</reportingShiftId>
        <shiftGrouping>HW</shiftGrouping>
        <workBreakSchedule>HWP3</workBreakSchedule>
        <targetQuantity>1</targetQuantity>
        <targetQtyUom>KGM</targetQtyUom>
        <client>007</client>
        <order>000001001553</order>
        <material>ICM_CHOCOLATE</material>
        <productionActivity>SAP_R2</productionActivity>
        <startDate>2013-05-16T00:00:00+05:30</startDate>
        <startTime>1970-01-01T19:21:58+05:30</startTime>
        <endDate>2013-05-16T19:46:55.774+05:30</endDate>
        <endTime>2013-05-16T19:46:55.774+05:30</endTime>
        <status>CMPL</status>
        <grossDuration>1497</grossDuration>
        <startDateUtc>2013-05-16T00:00:00+05:30</startDateUtc>
        <startTimeUtc>1970-01-01T13:51:58+05:30</startTimeUtc>
        <endDateUtc>2013-05-16T14:16:55+05:30</endDateUtc>
        <endTimeUtc>2013-05-16T14:16:55+05:30</endTimeUtc>
```

```
<ioStatus>
        <client>007</client>
        <plant>1000</plant>
        <status>ACT</status>
        <statusDescDTOList>
                <client>007</client>
                <description>Active</description>
                <language>de</language>
                <plant>1000</plant>
                <status>ACT</status>
        </statusDescDTOList>
        <statusDescDTOList>
                <client>007</client>
                <description>Active</description>
                <language>en</language>
                <plant>1000</plant>
                <status>ACT</status>
        </statusDescDTOList>
        <statusDescDTOList>
                <client>007</client>
                <description>Active</description>
                <language>es</language>
                <plant>1000</plant>
                <status>ACT</status>
        </statusDescDTOList>
        <statusDescDTOList>
                <client>007</client>
                <description>Active</description>
                <language>fr</language>
                <plant>1000</plant>
                <status>ACT</status>
        </statusDescDTOList>
        <statusDescDTOList>
                <client>007</client>
                <description>Active</description>
                <language>ja</language>
                <plant>1000</plant>
                <status>ACT</status>
        </statusDescDTOList>
        <statusDescDTOList>
                <client>007</client>
                <description>Active</description>
                <language>pt</language>
                <plant>1000</plant>
                <status>ACT</status>
        </statusDescDTOList>
        <statusDescDTOList>
                <client>007</client>
                <description>Active</description>
                <language>zh</language>
```

```
                <plant>1000</plant>
                <status>ACT</status>
            </statusDescDTOList>
            <version>0</version>
        </ioStatus>
        <standardRateQty>10</standardRateQty>
        <standardRateUom>KG</standardRateUom>
        <timeQty>10</timeQty>
        <timeUom>MIN</timeUom>
        <timeQtyInSeconds>600.000</timeQtyInSeconds>
        <oeeRelevant>T</oeeRelevant>
        <sequenceNumber>0</sequenceNumber>
        <version>58345</version>
</outputProductionRunBasic>
```

Goods Movement App I/O Structure

This section describes the input and output XML structure for use in Goods Movement App. In chapter 8, you understood how to configure and use Application launch pad to perform goods movement. The activity of GR and GI has some transactions to be configured in online and offline mode. These transaction when integrated with UI needs to get input from UI and send back some output to UI. For this purpose, it follows a certain Input and Output structure.

This Transaction is used to read HU managed stcok

```
Transaction Name : TRX_SSCC_SCN_ONL
 Input Parameter Name
<PackageDetailsInput> <PackageDetailsOutput>
  <language> <items>
  <huNumber/> <item>
  <orderNumber/> <huNumber/>
  <routingOperationNumber/> <client/>
  <parentOperationNumber/> <materialNumber/>
  <plant/> <batchNumber/>
  <client/> <shelfLifeDate/>
  </PackageDetailsInput>
Output Parameter Name
<PackageDetailsOutput>
<items>
<item>
<huNumber/>
<client/>
<materialNumber/>
<batchNumber/>
<shelfLifeDate/>
<stock/>
<uom/>
</item>
</items>

<messages>
<message/>
<status/>
</messages>
</PackageDetailsOutput>
```

This Transaction is used to get available batches for given material
Transaction Name : TRX_GET_BAT_ONL

Input Parameter Name

```
<MaterialDetailsInput>
<materialNumber/>
<plant/>
<client/>
<warehouseNumber/>
<storageBin/>
<storageType/>
<storageLocation/>
<productionSupplyArea/>
</MaterialDetailsInput>
```

Output Parameter Name
No output XML. Output is stored in MII Document and returns as output

Following Documents have been used for this transaction

Doc_Batch
batchNumber
shelfLifeDate

Doc_Error
message
status

Transaction name : TRX_GDS_MVT_ONL

```
<?xml version="1.0" encoding="UTF-8"?><IOReportGoodsMovementDetails>
    <txnPath>OEEEnhancement/GoodsMovement/Test</txnPath>
    <client>800</client>
    <plant>CPF5</plant>
    <nodeID>55D6188B8FAA2290E100800009718168</nodeID>
    <orderNumber>000070003662</orderNumber>
</routingOperationNumber>
</parentOperationNumber>
    <warehouseNumber/>
    <userId>cpf5_user</userId>
    <goodsMovementItems>
        <client>800</client>
        <goodsMovementItem>
            <postingDate>2016-03-01T02:49:36.409-06:00</postingDate>
            <productionDate>2016-03-01T02:49:36.409-06:00</productionDate>
            <huNumber/>
            <materialNumber>CYRUX 200 EC</materialNumber>
            <quantityInReportUom>34</quantityInReportUom>
            <reportUom>L</reportUom>
            <batchNumber/>
            <movementType>101</movementType>
            <packagingMaterial>CARTON</packagingMaterial>
            <documentNumber/>
            <documentYear/>
            <postingID>1</postingID>
            <goodsMovementPostingMessages>
```

```
                <goodsMovementPostingMessage>
                    <status/>
                    <message/>
                </goodsMovementPostingMessage>
            </goodsMovementPostingMessages>
        </goodsMovementItem>
    </goodsMovementItems>
</IOReportGoodsMovementDetails>
```

This Transaction is used to Generate / Create batch for produce material
Transaction Name : TRX_GEN_BAT_ONL

Input Paramteter Name

```
<BatchDetailsInput>
<materialNumber/>
<productionDate/>
<plant/>
<client/>
<materialType/>
</BatchDetailsInput>
```

Output Paramteter Name

```
<BatchDetailsOutput>
<batchNumber/>
<expiryDate/>
<message/>
<status/>
</BatchDetailsOutput>
```

Input

Document Output
Input Parameter

```
<?xml version=""1.0"" encoding=""UTF-8""?>
<PostingDetailsInput>
<language/>
<plant/>
<client/>
<nodeID/>
<orderNumber/>
<routingOperationNumber/>
</PostingDetailsInput>
```

Document Output

isAggregated
material
Description
totalReportedQuantity
plannedQuantity
Uom
storageUnit
batch
variance
status
statusText

Transaction name : TRX_GDS_MVT_PKG_ONL/OFFL

Input Parameter Name

```
<?xml version='1.0' encoding='UTF-8'?>
<packageIdInput>
<client></client>
<plant></plant>
<nodeId></nodeId>
<order</order>
<material></material>
<movementType></movementType>
</packageIdInput>
```

Document Output

```
BATCH_NO
DOCUMENT_NO
HU_NO
POSTING_DATE
QTY_IN_REPORT_UOM
REPORT_UOM
SHELF_LIFE_DATE
```

Transaction name : TRX_GDS_MVT_RPT_ONL/OFFL

Input Parameter Name

```
<?xml version=""1.0"" encoding=""UTF-8""?>
<PostingDetailsInput>
<language/>
<plant/>
<client/>
<nodeID/>
<orderNumber/>
<routingOperationNumber/>
</PostingDetailsInput>
```

Document Output

```
isAggregated
material
Description
totalReportedQuantity
plannedQuantity
Uom
storageUnit
batch
variance
status
statusText
```

Section 6: Global Context

Context	KPI	Context	Current
Sub-Context	availability	**Sub-Context**	material
	oee		description
	performance		id
	quality		operationNo
Context	**Custom KPIs**		order
Sub-Context	kpix		baseUoM
Context	**KPI Targets**		orderNo
Sub-Context	client		orderStatus
	description		ACT
	kpi		CMPL
	kpiType		releasedHeaderID
	material		releasedQuantity
	nodeID		salesOrderNo
	plant		startDate
	targetx		productionActivity
	targetUom		quantityRejected
	validFrom		quantityReleased
	validTo		quantityReleasedUOM
			quantityReported
			releasedID
			runID

Context	Node	Context	PODs
Sub-Context	capacityID	**Sub-Context**	__metadata
	description		type
	nodeID		uri
	workcenterID		button_x
Context	**Shift**		activityAssigned
Sub-Context	description		activityAssignedx
	endDate		activityDescDTOList
	endTime		results
	shiftGrouping		activityId

(*continued*)

Context	Node	Context	PODs
	shiftID		client
	startDate		description
	startTime		language
	workBreakSchedule		plant
Context	UOM Text Cache		activityEnabled
Sub-Context	KGM		activityId
			activityOptionDTOList
			activityType
			client
			description
			enabled
			Plant, urlProgram

Context	PODs	
Sub-Context	version	extensionNodeID
	buttonId	extensionPlant
	buttonSequence	plant
	buttonSize	plantTimezoneOffset
	buttonType	podDescDTOList1
	client	results
	description	client
	hotKey	description
	imageIcon	language
	label	plant
	location	podId
	openAs	podLayout
	parentButtonId	podPanelDTOList
	plant	results
	podButtonDescDTOList1	activity
	results	activityDescDTOList
	podId	results
	subButtons	activityId
	client	client
	description	layoutId

(continued)

Context	PODs	
	extensionClient	panelId
		plant
		podId
		podType
		subButtons
		version

Context	Selected	
Sub-Context	currentSpeed	startDate
	material	startTime
	batchRelevant	timeQty
	description	timeQtyInSeconds
	id	timeUom
	serialNoRelevant	
	operationNo	
	order	
	baseUoM	
	orderNo	
	orderStatus	
	ACT	
	CMPL	
	releasedHeaderID	
	releasedQuantity	
	salesOrderNo	
	startDate	
	productionActivity	
	quantityRejected	
	quantityReleased	
	quantityReleasedUOM	
	quantityRemaining	
	quantityReported	
	releasedID	
	runID	
	standardRateQty	
	standardRateUom	

Sample XML View Code

```
<mvc:View
        controllerName="customActivity.ManageQMNotificationXML"
        xmlns:l="sap.ui.layout"
        xmlns:mvc="sap.ui.core.mvc"
        xmlns="sap.m"
        xmlns:model="sap.ui.model"
        xmlns:table="sap.ui.table">
<Page enableScrolling="true">
        <Table id="ManageQMNotificationTable"
                inset="false"
                mode="SingleSelectMaster"
                selectionChange="rowSelectionChanged"
                items="{
                        path: '/Rowset/Row',
                        sorter: {
                                path: 'Name'
                        }
                }">
                <headerToolbar>
                        <Toolbar>
                        </Toolbar>
                </headerToolbar>
                <columns>
               <Column   width="12em"  hAlign="Center"> <Text text="QM Notif No." /> </Column>
                <Column width="12em" hAlign="Center"> <Text text="QMID" /> </Column>
                <Column width="12em" hAlign="Center"> <Text text="Plant" /> </Column>
                                                <Column width="12em" hAlign="Center"> <Text
                                                text="OrderNo" /> </Column>
                <Column minScreenWidth="Tablet" demandPopin="true" hAlign="Center">
                <Text text="MaterialNo" /> </Column>
                <Column hAlign="Center"> <Text text="Status" /> </Column>
                <Column hAlign="Center"> <Text text="Created On" /> </Column>
                                                <Column hAlign="Center"> <Text text="Created
                                                By" /> </Column>
                                                <Column hAlign="Center"> <Text
                                                text="ErrorLog" /> </Column>
                </columns>
                <items>
                        <ColumnListItem>
                                <cells>
                                        <ObjectIdentifier
                                                title="{NotiFNO}"/>
                                        <Text   text="{QMID}" />
 <Text          text="{Plant}" />
                                        <Text text="{OrderNo}" />
                                        <Text text="{MaterialNo}" />
                                        <Text text="{Status}" />
                                        <Text text="{CreatedOn}" />
```

```
                                            <Text text="{CreatedBy}" />
                                            <Text text="{ErrorLog}" />
                                    </cells>
                            </ColumnListItem>
                    </items>
            </Table>
<FlexBox alignItems="Start" >
        <Button
                text="Create QM Notification"
        id="ButtonQMNotif"
        enabled="false"
                width="250px"
                press="onCreateQMNotificationDialog"
                class="sapUiSmallMarginBottom">
        <layoutData>
            <FlexItemData growFactor="1" />
          </layoutData>
         </Button>
        <Button
                text="Refresh"
                width="250px"
                press="doSearch"
                class="sapUiSmallMarginBottom">
        <layoutData>
            <FlexItemData growFactor="1" />
          </layoutData>
          </Button>
</FlexBox>
</Page>
</mvc:View>
```

Glossary

Term	Definition
Activity	A logical piece or component that can be used in OEE
ALE	Application link enabling
BAPI	Business application programming interface
BLS	Business logic services
Bottleneck	Critical machine for line production
CTC	Central Technical Configuration
UI5 controller	Separates the view logic from the model logic in the MVC concept of UI5
Dashboard	User interface for monitoring production and performance
Data buffer	Data archiving and processing
DCE	Data collection element
DCS	Distributed control system
Distribution model	Model view that stores information on the different IDoc messages flowing from a logical system in ERP to a remote system
Downtime	Unavailability of a machine or work center
Extension	Placeholder to extend the standard functionality with custom logic
Flow time	Duration from the start of an order-operation to the first product or unit produced at the end of a line
Global context	Placeholder that provides OEE-specific UI objects to be used in a custom dashboard
GR and GI	Goods receipt of production Goods issue of raw materials
HANA Live	SAP-delivered package with predefined SAP HANA content
Hierarchy	Relational model composed of systems and sub-systems that represents multiple levels of detail in describing the organization, plant, or production line. It reflects both the structural and process flow characteristics of the plant or production line
IDoc	Container for the application data to be transmitted between two systems

D. Saha et al., *Manufacturing Performance Management using SAP OEE*,
DOI 10.1007/978-1-4842-1150-2

Term	Definition
KPI	Key performance indicator; a metric used to monitor and evaluate the business or system performance
Labor time	Time spent by the laborers to build a product
Logical port	Specifies the way in which IDocs are transferred to the EDI (electronics document interchange) subsystem. This communication is implemented in different ways or via so-called port types
Machine groups	Grouping machines under a common category
MES	Manufacturing execution system
MII	Manufacturing integration and intelligence
MPM	Manufacturing performance management
MTO	Make to order
MTS	Make to stock
Notification	A message to inform that an event happened
OEE	Overall equipment effectiveness
OEEINT	OEE integration
OEE add-on	ERP component specific to OEE to manage OEE-specific data
OPC	OLE (object linking and embedding) for process control
Order confirmation	Update to ERP of the order-related data collected from the shop floor
Partner profile	Defines the different profile parameters, such as partner number, partner type, and so on, by which to identify the unique communication partner
PCo	Plant connectivity
PLC	Programmable logic controller
PP	Production planning
PP-PI	Production planning-process industries
PM	Plant maintenance
Production activity	Different activity specific to production during an order execution
QM	Quality maintenance
Reason code	A string to define the cause for an event or loss that occurred
Reconcile	Update the deleted data sent previously to the OEE system as obsolete
RecTypeGrp	Defines the type of contexts associated with production activity
Rework	A finished product that needs to be worked on or repaired in order to declare it as a good quantity
RFC destination	Remote function call destination places an RFC call for communication between SAP ERP and a remote system
Routing	Sequence of operation/activites through which production takes place across the work centers
SAP UI5	HTML5-based UI with a collection of libraries that developers can use to build desktop and mobile applications that run in a browser

Term	Definition
SCADA	Supervisory control and data acquisition
Scrap	A finished good declared as waste
Setup time	Time to set up the line for handling different types or variants of production
Shift	Work schedule in which a group of workers rotates through a set of periods throughout the day, typically performing the same kind of work
SFA	Shop-floor automation; automation of production processes on plant floor
SLT replictaion	SAP system landscape transformation replication; Replication of data in real-time between different systems
Speed loss	Speed loss is time loss when a machine is running below the nominal speed. Calculated as: (Actual time taken to produce a product - Time required to produce the same product with nominal speed)
Standard rate	Nominal speed, or the rate at which a product can be ideally produced
Technical objects	ERP object that is linked with a hierarchy object
UoM	Unit of measurement
Utility	Element that aids in production process, such as electricity, water, etc.
View	UI5 component responsible for defining and rendering in UI
Workcenter capacity	Capacity is a logical unit used at a work center operation used for the production process, such as a machine or labor
WIP	Work in process
Worker UI	User interfaces for the production operator (sometimes used as operator dashboard also) that are configured to accomplish several tasks
WebAS	Web application server
XSLT	Extensible Stylesheet Language Transformations; a language for transforming an XML document into a desired format
Yield	Good quantity produced

Index

D. Saha et al., *Manufacturing Performance Management using SAP OEE*,
DOI 10.1007/978-1-4842-1150-2

E, F

G, H

I, J

K

L

M

N

O

P, Q

R

S

T

U, V

W, X, Y, Z